AMERICAN SECRET PROJECTS

2

AMERICAN SECRET PROJECTS

2

U S Airlifters 1941 to 1961

GEORGE COX AND CRAIG KASTON

Crécy

www.crecy.co.uk

Crécy Publishing Ltd

www.crecy.co.uk

American Secret Projects
U S Airlifters 1941 to 1961
George Cox and Craig Kaston

This book is dedicated to the design and industrial genius of the American aviation industry, which first conceived and then built an amazing panoply of aircraft to oppose the Axis Powers during the Second World War.

First published in 2019 by Crécy Publishing

A CIP record for this book is available from the British Library

Printed in Bulgaria by Multiprint

ISBN 9781910809167

Crécy Publishing Ltd
1a Ringway Trading Estate, Shadowmoss Rd
Manchester M22 5LH
Tel (0044) 161 499 0024
www.crecy.co.uk

FRONT COVER This specially commissioned artwork depicts the Fairchild M-99-07 heavy airlifter in service with the Military Air Transportation Service in the mid-1950s. In reality, the Douglas C-124 was placed in production and flew in these markings. *Artwork by Daniel Uhr*

TITLE PAGE A Douglas C-124 Globemaster II loads jeeps and armour in this early-1950s watercolour painting by configuration engineer and artist R. G. Smith. *Boeing*

REAR COVER

TOP: An artist's concept of the Boeing Model 731-16 in Boeing livery performing an air drop of supplies. *Boeing*

MIDDLE A model of Convair's proposed production version of the C-99 reveals the new nose loading doors and ramps, enlarged main cargo deck, and the raised cockpit under a B-36-styled canopy. Despite these and other changes, the revised design was not built. *NARA II via Dennis R Jenkins*

BOTTOM A model of the Fairchild M-258J (derived from the Fokker F-27) is posed to display the loading ramp and clamshell doors. *NASM*

FRONT FLAP A view of the Douglas XC-132 mock-up at the Santa Monica hangar where the XB-19 bomber had been built in 1937. *Boeing*

REAR FLAP

TOP Sir George Cox *Author*

BOTTOM Craig Kaston *Chad Slattery*

Contents

Introduction

The effectiveness of military strategy has always been dependent on the ability to move armies and their equipment rapidly and to support them thereafter. Over the centuries the horse, the wagon, the ship, the railway and the truck have all played their part in transforming the nature of military strategy. Experience during the Second World War made it clear that air transportation represented a similar advance.

Not only was the USA called upon simultaneously to fight battles in Europe, Africa, Asia and the Pacific, but it was also clear in the aftermath of the war that to enable it to project power and maintain global peace, America would have to maintain permanent bases in many parts of the world. It also needed to be able to deploy large forces at short notice.

This growing need for enhanced deployment/support capability led to a new requirement: an aircraft designed from the outset to transport fully equipped troops or to carry large, heavy and irregularly shaped cargo that could be easily loaded and unloaded. The aircraft also had to be robust enough to operate in near-battlefield conditions. It heralded the birth of the airlifter.

Over the following decades, aerospace technology would keep advancing and military requirements would keep changing. This would result in an endless stream of aircraft designs, surprisingly few of which would ever see the light of day. For every aircraft that made it into production and reached operational service, many others would only make it as far as an experimental prototype or a non-flying mock-up. But behind these, there were scores more: imaginative designs that would never be seen outside the aircraft manufacturers' advanced design offices. Even the successful designs were usually the outcome of earlier, unrevealed proposals that had been progressively refined.

Unlike proposals for new fighters or bombers, the military could not afford, or perhaps saw no reason, to order the construction of prototypes of several competing designs for airlifters. The choice therefore had often to be made off the drawing board. However, the decision as to which aircraft should be ordered was made not just made on the basis of estimated (or claimed) performance, but on issues such as confidence in meeting the specification, the perceived ability of the prime contractor to fulfil a large production order, cost, available funding and competition with other military programmes, as well as political considerations such as to where the work should be placed.

As a consequence, many of the failed designs described in this book were only 'failures' in the sense that the military was never persuaded to buy them. They inevitably include many proposals that would have turned into fine aircraft – and perhaps a few embarrassing failures.

Together all these designs chart the history of both aeronautical progress and military strategy over a fascinating seventy-year period.

Scope and structure

This book deals with developments from the emergence of the airlifter at the time of America's entry into the Second World War up until 1961. A companion second volume, *American Secret Projects 3*, continues the story from 1962 to the present day. Together they give a complete history of airlifter design, including those projects that led to successful aircraft and those proposals that never saw the light of day.

It covers strategic and tactical fixed-wing transports – the former concerned with moving troops and materiel around the globe, the latter with delivering them to the areas of conflict – but makes no attempt to cover all types of aircraft used for military transportation. Space alone forces the exclusion of the many unmodified civil airliners drafted into military service; small, special-task aircraft; flying boats; and rotary-winged aircraft. Any of these would justify a volume in their own right.

The projects and proposals are covered, as far as possible, in chronological order, looking at the historical context of each period and how this defined the capabilities that were sought. Events such as the Second World War, the Berlin Airlift, the Korean War, the Cold War, and the Vietnam War all had a big influence on military requirements. Some projects were the initiative of a particular aircraft manufacturing company, while others were prepared in response to an official invitation to tender.

Within each era, designs are grouped according to either their intended purpose or the official specification against which they were being submitted, enabling the reader to contrast the competing propositions. The individual projects are described and are illustrated exclusively with original factory drawings, company artwork and promotional models. All figures and dimensions are therefore given in their original form, with metric conversions provided in every case, and a Glossary is provided as an appendix.

To cater for the international nature and breadth of reader backgrounds, two 'primer' chapters are included in this first book. The first summarises the history of US military air transportation, setting it within the framework of its evolving command structure; the second examines the basic challenges of airlifter design.

In the second book, *American Secret Projects 3*, separate chapters are devoted to three specialised categories of airlifter, where developments span several decades. One of these covers the adaptation of large-scale airlifter airframes for special purposes; another looks at the specialised demands of delivering cargo and personnel to ships at sea; and a third looks at how airlifters were planned to be used to explore the potential for nuclear propulsion.

It should be stressed that neither book makes any pretence at being complete. Despite extensive research and unprecedented access to aircraft company records, there are undoubtedly many proposals for which no records have survived or, if they have, they have yet to be uncovered or declassified.

While the book confines itself to its specific subject – the design of the military airlifter in the United States – it must be remembered that this progression did not take place in isolation. The development of military airlifters has had a significant influence on the advance of aviation more generally. Not only is freight increasingly transported around the world by air, but the advances in military airframe design and engine technology have both influenced and benefitted from the parallel advances in commercial aviation.

The history of airlifter design is, therefore, a fascinating reflection of the advance of aviation more generally and of its influence on our lives and world events. This book and its companion second volume record for the first time the depth of creative thinking behind that history.

Sir George Cox, Buckinghamshire UK

Craig Kaston, Oxnard, California

Acknowledgements

This book has been made possible only by the generous and widespread support of many contributors, keen to see this hitherto under-explored subject accorded its proper place in aviation history. Special thanks must go to the Boeing Company for making available heritage materials for Boeing, Douglas and North American Aviation, and to Northrop Grumman Aerospace Systems Sector for the Northrop and Grumman archive information.

The authors are indebted to the following who so generously contributed their knowledge and insights:

Aerospace Projects Review and Scott Lowther

Air Force Historical Research Agency; Archie DiFante

Air Force Material Command (AFMC) History Office; Yancy Mails (Director, History & Museum Program) and Ray Ortensie (Historian)

American Aviation Historical Society (AAHS); Hayden Hamilton

The Boeing Company and Mike Lombardi, Tom Lubbesmeyer and Pat McGinnis, Corporate Historians

Grumman History Center; John Eagan

Glenn L. Martin Maryland Aviation Museum; Stan Piet (Archivist)

The Greater St Louis Air & Space Museum; Mark Nankivil (President)

Northrop Grumman Aerospace Systems Sector (for heritage Northrop and Grumman materials); Tony Chong, (Aerospace Systems Sector Historian)

San Diego Air and Space Museum; Katrina Pescador (Director of Volunteer Programs), Debbie Seracini (Archivist) and Pam Gay (Librarian)

The Secret Projects Forum and Paul Martell-Mead (together with the many dedicated contributors to the website across the world)

Wright State University Libraries, Special Collections; Bill Stolz (Archivist for Reference and Outreach)

Special thanks are due to John Aldaz, without whose encouragement the project would never had started, and without whose support it would never have been finished.

Also deserving special recognition for their assistance are Tom Culbert; Al Huber; Telka Kaston; Mike Machat; Paul Minert; Chad Slattery and Tommy H. Thomason.

Thanks are owed to: Mark Aldrich; Allen Arata; G. H. 'Gerry' Balzer; Bob Bradley; Tony Buttler; Dennis R. Jenkins; the late Harry Gann (for early inspiration); Chris Gibson; Tony Landis; Ray Leader (Flight Leader); Terry Panopalis; Mick Roth; Caroline Sheen; Bill Spidle; Jim Ueda; Tim White; and Chris Yasaki.

Thanks and appreciation are also due to Jeremy Pratt, Gill Richardson and Charlotte Stear and their production team at Crécy for all their patience and help.

Chapter One
Eighty Years of American Airlift

A brief overview

Before looking at the many design proposals for new airlifters, spanning several decades, it is useful to have a framework to enable these projects to be set in context.

They need to be seen against a background of the changing nature of conflict; changes in military requirements; advances in technology; inter-service rivalries; and an ever-changing political landscape and fiscal environment. Moreover, it has been a two-way process: the airlifter has not simply been shaped by these forces, but has, in turn, influenced them. Indeed, it would be no exaggeration to say that the development of the airlifter has transformed military strategy and significantly influenced US geopolitical policy.

ABOVE 1948: A line-up of Douglas C-54s prepares to take off from Rhein Main Air Base on a mission as part of the Berlin Airlift. *Boeing*

BELOW 2013: C-17s, KC-10s and C-5s fill a Travis AFB taxiway to fly missions in commemoration of the 11 September 2001 attacks.
US Air Force photo by Ken Wright

The birth of military air transportation

The origins of military air transportation can be traced back to the First World War when combat aircraft were used to evacuate wounded personnel from the battlefield. This was not the result of any planned strategy but rather a matter of expediency, employed by both the Allies and Axis Powers. The only available aircraft were two-seat combat aeroplanes, and lifting an injured soldier into the narrow rear seat of an open cockpit must have been a traumatic experience for all concerned. Nonetheless, the value of medical air evacuation was quickly established and by the war's end purpose-built air ambulances were being flown. These were converted Curtiss JN-4 Jennys, initially with the rear cockpit adapted to accommodate a semi-reclining individual but later modified to allow a flat stretcher.

In the post-war years medical evacuation was still seen as the main potential application for military air transportation. One early requirement was seen as an aircraft specially designed for crash rescue. However, the Chief Surgeon of the Air Corps Medical Section discovered from a careful study of statistics that 75% of accidents occurred on, or very near, aerodromes. Clearly a crash rescue aircraft was not a priority. The more pressing need was for a larger aeroplane for transportation of patients from outlying aerodromes and field hospitals to base hospitals.

It would not be true to say that no thought was given to other potential uses of air transport. In November 1917 the Committee of the General Staff formulated a plan for transporting troops to Mexico using adapted bomber aircraft. The scheme was remarkably ambitious, involving the conveyance of several divisions, including their field artillery and motor trucks. Indeed, it was way ahead of its time, and was killed off when the Air Service's Col 'Hap' Arnold and Col T.

Blane pointed out that the scheme would require more bomber aircraft than existed in the whole of the United States!

In the years following the war the Army still gave little thought to the wider application of air transportation. Indeed, in 1921 a paper entitled 'The System of Supply' made no mention of air conveyance – even though it was written by the Assistant Chief of the Supply Group, Air Service! This was perhaps surprising because by that time there were already around 125 commercial companies flying passengers and freight, and between them they were operating approximately 1,200 aeroplanes – though this has to be put in perspective by the fact that the average flight was just twenty-one minutes.

However, aeronautical engineering was advancing rapidly, resulting in huge strides in aircraft performance in terms of speed, range and payload. In early 1925 the Army Air Service (which would become the Army Air Corps the following year) ordered ten Douglas C-1 biplanes – the first aircraft to be classified under a cargo transport designation. These were all delivered by the end of the year and were followed by an order in 1926 for seventeen C-1Bs, which could carry six passengers or 2,500lb (1,140kg) cargo. These were shortly followed into service by the Fokker C-2, a high-wing, monoplane, tri-motor aircraft. It is a measure of the rapid advance in aviation that on 28 June 1927 a C-2 made the first non-stop flight from the West Coast to the Hawaiian Islands, a distance of 2,400 miles (3,860km), and on 7 January 1929 a C-2A flown by Major Carl Spaatz and Capt Ira Eaker set a world flight endurance record of 150 hours.

These aircraft were succeeded by orders for several other types, in every case an adaption of a commercial passenger aeroplane. However, although transport aircraft were becoming a well-established part of the Air Corps inventory, they were still not seen as forming a distinct or separate

capability. Numbering a few dozen in total, they were allocated as support aircraft to different airfields. Moreover, none had large cargo doors. There was no need; heavy freight went by train, and only urgent cargo went by air.

The first Army Air Corps transport squadron was not formed until 1935. Later that year the Corps procured a Douglas DC-2 for evaluation, under the designation XC-32. This was essentially a standard commercial airliner, but its evaluation led to an order for eighteen aircraft built to a military specification as the C-33. These had a strengthened floor and a large cargo door. By 1939 a further thirty-five Douglas C-39s – an aircraft also based on the DC-2 – had been added to the inventory, though given that hostilities were just about to break out in Europe this was still a miniscule fleet compared to the vast aerial transport capability that would shortly prove necessary.

The Second World War

The significance of the ability to move an assault force by air was quickly demonstrated by the German forces in the Second World War. This capability was based on the adaptation of an existing civil aircraft, the Junkers Ju-52. There were 552 Ju-52s in service at the start of the war, and a total of 2,804 would be delivered to the Luftwaffe between 1939 and 1944.

At the same time German aircraft companies were already starting to develop the first ever purpose-designed military assault transports. The Arado Ar-232, which was designed to replace the Ju-52, first flew in 1941. It had a 'pod and boom' fuselage, a high-mounted wing and a hydraulically operated rear loading door, features that would recur in several transport designs in later years. The aircraft also had a novel undercarriage arrangement, with the tricycle landing gear supplemented by eleven pairs of small wheels to support the fuselage during loading and unloading.

The Germans also arguably foreshadowed the giant airlifters of the

ABOVE The Messerschmitt Me-323 incorporated many future airlifter features including bow-loading and multiple engines on a high-mounted wing. *Wolfgang Muehlbauer Collection*

future with the Messerschmitt Me-323. With a wingspan of 181ft (55.2m) and a maximum permissible take-off weight of nearly 95,000lb (43,130kg), it was a veritable giant for its time. Originally conceived as a glider, it was developed into a six-engine transport. Nearly 200 were built but, being slow and vulnerable, it made little contribution to the war effort. However, in some ways it might be regarded as the forerunner of the modern airlifter.

Despite German thinking probably being ahead of that of any other nation at the time, the war also delivered a severe lesson in terms of the difficulty of supplying an army by air; or rather, it underlined just how massive a capability this required. In late 1942, with winter approaching, the German high command took the decision not to authorise a break-out by its army which was isolated in Stalingrad, but instead to attempt to resupply it by air. It was to prove catastrophic. The

270,000 men required around 700 tons (711 tonnes) of supplies every day, which would equate to around 350 Ju 52 delivery flights. It was a rate that was never achieved. The greatest amount supplied in any one day was just over 260 tons (264 tonnes) delivered in 154 flights, and the average was only around 85 tons (86 tonnes). Delivering so close to the front line overflying enemy-held territory, also resulted in huge losses of aircraft and personnel.

It demonstrated that the strategic use of air transportation to supply an army required far greater capability in terms of both numbers and size of aircraft, along with the availability of secure airfields and the ability to turn the aeroplanes around quickly.

With the war raging in Europe, in 1940 the US Army Air Corps ordered 545 Douglas C-47s (militarised DC-3s) – the first of more than 16,000 (including foreign-built) variants of the DC-3 to be produced. It also ordered its first four-

engine DC-4s. However, the immediate need was not so much for transportation of American forces, but rather to supply the hard-pressed British. To this end the Air Corps Ferrying Command (ACFC) was set up. With America's entry into the war, the emphasis switched to supplying materials to overseas American units, and in June 1942 the ACFC became the Air Transport Command (ATC), responsible for the War Department's strategic airlift missions. During the following three years it expanded enormously. By the time the war ended in September 1945, ATC had 3,386 aircraft and was operating around the globe.

Of the many notable wartime achievements of the ATC, the India-China airlift – 'flying the hump' as it became known – stands out, not just as a heroic campaign but as an early demonstration of just what air transport could achieve. The campaign was notable for two things. Firstly, it supported a

ABOVE An Army Air Corps C-39 (Douglas DC-2 with DC-3 tail) is loaded with cargo. *Boeing*

combat theatre that could not possibly have been sustained without air supply. Secondly, it was about as difficult an aerial supply route as one could possibly imagine. Starting in 1942, the ATC flew supplies from India to China, over Burma and over the Himalayas, to support both the Chinese war effort against the Japanese and the units of the USAAF based in China. This involved flying over some of the most inhospitable terrain on earth, crossing mountain ridges between 14,000ft (4,270m) and 16,000ft (4,880m) high, in unpredictable and frequently bad weather, without any radio navigation aids. Not surprisingly, it came at a huge cost, with 594 aircraft lost, missing or written off. It lasted for forty-two months, during which time the airlift delivered around 65,000 tons (59,000 tonnes) of supplies. Several different aircraft types were used but it was a campaign in which the Curtiss C-46 Commando really came into its own, due to its combination of range, lifting capacity and high-altitude performance.

The Navy too had established its own air transportation arm. Shortly after the Japanese declared war on the United States with the attack on Pearl Harbor, it created the Naval Air Transport Service (NATS). This began with the formation of squadrons with newly acquired Douglas R4Ds (C-47s) and R5Ds (C-54s) being formed alongside those utilising transport conversions of the Navy's big patrol bombers. At its peak during the Second World War, NATS operated worldwide and consisted of four wings of eighteen squadrons operating 540 aircraft with 26,000 assigned personnel.

BELOW The tenth C-54 built flies over Santa Monica in camouflage paint early in the war. The Olive Drab and Grey scheme was soon dropped for a bare metal finish. *Boeing*

Post-war developments

Although there was a massive, and undoubtedly welcome, reduction in military expenditure after the end of the war, it soon became clear that the world remained an unstable place and that the maintenance of peace and the projection of American influence would require substantial, continued investment in military capability. However, the environment had changed from that of wartime. Emphasis turned to economy and efficiency, and to getting value for money on behalf of the taxpayer. The starting point was the reorganisation of the government defence administration and the armed forces. In 1947 the Department of Defense (DoD) was formed, with the former Secretary of the Navy, James F. Forrestal, as its head. The relevant Act also established the United States Air Force (USAF) as an independent entity on 18 September 1947, separate from, and equal to, the Army and the Navy.

The newly formed USAF soon started to sort out its organisation. On 15 January 1948 a proposal was put forward to create a unified air transportation command operated by the USAF, to be formed by combining the Air Transport Command and Naval Air Transport Service. This action was directed by Secretary Forrestal, and the ATC and NATS were merged on 1 June 1948 to form the Military Air Transport Service (MATS), thus consolidating strategic airlift.

The Navy's long-range transport capability at this point consisted of only five squadrons, operating fifty-eight aeroplanes following the run-down at the end of the war. Although MATS was assigned to the Air Force, the Navy squadrons retained their identities and were primarily manned by Navy officers and enlisted men. The biggest change initially was that the aircraft no longer carried the marking 'Naval Air Transport Service'. The Navy retained responsibility for its short-range utility transportation, which subsequently included the specialised and increasingly important Carrier On-board Delivery (COD) requirement, together with USMC troop transportation.

When MATS became operational it had a total strength of 824 aircraft, including 239 C-47s and 234 C-54s, together with many other types inherited from both the Army and the Navy. For a world not engaged in large-scale armed conflict, this might have seemed an impressive capability. However, the next few years would prove that it would need to be expanded still further to meet the nation's demands. Indeed, its formation was very serendipitous; within just three weeks it would be called upon to face the biggest airlift challenge in history.

The Berlin Airlift

The strategic importance – and scale of potential – of air transport was dramatically demonstrated in 1948. At the end of the war the final front line in Europe had become the de facto demarcation line between the Soviet bloc and the Western Allies, partitioning Germany into two parts in the process. The capital, Berlin, lay within the Soviet bloc, but for political reasons had been split into four sectors, controlled by the Americans, the British, the Russians and the French. However, the relationship between the erstwhile allies became increasingly hostile and when the Americans and British combined their sectors in 1948 and introduced the new

BELOW Artist R. G. Smith captures the abysmal weather at Berlin's Templehof Airport in the autumn of 1948 at the height of the airlift. *Boeing*

Deutschmark as its currency, the Soviets reacted by blocking off all access by road, rail and canal. The only access to the West was by an earlier agreed air corridor; the Soviets stopped short of closing this as it would have meant shooting down aircraft and the start of a war with the nuclear-armed West. The blockade started on 24 June 1948, and within days the Americans and British had started an airlift.

The blockade lasted almost a year, eventually ending on 12 May 1949, with the airlift actually continuing until 30 September. During this time all food, fuel and essential materials had to be delivered by air, regardless of weather conditions – the sole means of support for a city of 4½ million people.

By the time the airlift was over, 2,323,738 tons (2,108,059 tonnes) had been delivered. It had involved 692 aircraft in total, utilising some nineteen different types, with everything available being pressed into service. The British, having a much more limited military airlift capability, had to rely mainly on chartered civilian airliners. The US fleet, using 330 aircraft in total, consisted largely of C-47s and C-54s. It was a massive logistics exercise. At its peak, one aircraft was arriving in Berlin every thirty seconds.

Not only did the Berlin Airlift demonstrate the huge potential of air transportation, but it also provided many lessons in terms of ground handling, and underlined the point that ease of access for loading and unloading was an important criterion for airlifter design.

The Korean War

In June 1950 MATS was thrown a further challenge when North Korea launched a full-scale invasion of South Korea. The following month MATS started its Pacific Airlift, involving some 250 aircraft.

By the time the Korean War had ended, MATS had airlifted more than 80,000 tons (72,600 tonnes) of cargo and 214,000 personnel across the Pacific. Its transports returning eastwards had carried home 43,000 casualties.

The Air Force's four cargo fleets

The demands of the Berlin Airlift had necessitated the commandeering of civilian aircraft and it was clear that, with the growing size of civilian air fleets, not only should the airlines handle the bulk of routine military movements but there should also be a more orderly way of meeting emergency needs.

This led to the creation of the Civilian Reserve Air Force (CRAF) – a virtual fleet that the military could call upon in times of crisis. To create it, the USAF entered into an arrangement with the airlines whereby the latter undertook to make aircraft and crews available in time of need. In return, the airlines involved were given the opportunity to fly military personnel and cargo in peacetime.

Meanwhile, a further major transportation fleet was being built-up, this time *within* the Air Force. The Strategic Air Command (SAC) had been formed in 1946 and was transferred to the Air Force in 1947. Its role had become truly 'strategic' in August 1948 when the Soviet Union detonated its first atomic bomb. From that point onwards, SAC was charged with providing the West's nuclear deterrent. Initially this took the form of a fleet of long-range Convair B-36 'Peacemaker' bombers. When these

were replaced by the highly advanced Boeing B-47 Stratojets in the early 1950s, SAC faced a problem: the latter were much faster than the B-36s but they had a much shorter range. Their effective deployment required the build-up of a global air-to-air refuelling capability. To this end SAC ordered the Boeing KC-97, the tanker version of the C-97 Stratofreighter. Over the following years it took delivery of no fewer than 816 KC-97s, all of them convertible for transport use. Given its independent nature, reflecting the style of its leadership, SAC became virtually an 'air force within an air force'.

Thus, by the early 1950s the USAF's transportation capability effectively consisted of four fleets:

- The Military Air Transport Service – MATS – for scheduled transport
- The Strategic Air Command – SAC – for SAC internal transport
- The Tactical Air Command – TAC – for combat (Army) cargo and carrying troops
- The Civil Reserve Air Fleet – CRAF – for wartime back-up support of MATS

The procurement policy for new aircraft was therefore a complex matter, influenced by the prevailing – and often conflicting – policies of the DoD, the Army, the Air Force, the individual commands and public (government) policy as expressed by Congress and influenced by the airline industry.

BELOW A very rare image of a Mk 6 nuclear weapon (in crate) being loaded in an SAC C-124A. Transport of weapons was a prime mission of SAC's four Strategic Support Squadrons in the early 1950s. *NARA II*

ABOVE While the troubled C-5 stole the headlines in the late 1960s, the C-141 labored quietly and reliably as the Air Force's first true jet-age airlifter. *NMUSAF*

The fight for the future of MATS

In 1958 and early 1959 MATS came under heavy fire. Increased demands had left its fleet in urgent need of modernisation but this was being impeded by political pressures to hand over the bulk of its role to the civil airlines. These campaigns were headed up by Representative Daniel Flood and Senator Mike Monroney, who argued that the airlines were better suited to handling the role, and that MATS should be restricted to carrying outsize cargo or to delivery to remote areas. This was vigorously opposed by the Air Force, led by MATS Commander Lt General William H. Tunner, who eventually won the day. Cleared of this obstacle, the Air Force issued a specification (SOR 182) for a new aircraft that was to lay the basis for its first purpose-designed jet airlifter, the Lockheed C-141.

The growing need for strategic reach

From 1960 onwards the US faced a steady decline in permanent overseas bases, strengthening the need for global deployment and support

capability. This led to the requirement for larger and longer-range aircraft, and to the concept of employing in-flight refuelling for transport operations, not just for combat aircraft.

However, when Robert McNamara took over as Secretary of Defense in 1961, he took a much tougher line on military expenditure, seeking greater efficiency and value for money on behalf of the taxpayer. This affected both procurement programmes and organisation structures. The former resulted in the cancellation of several high-profile advanced weapons programmes, while the latter led to the unification of various agencies and commands.

The commitment to build up the nation's airlift capability was retained, but the Air Force's Military Air Transport Service was obliged to become a more streamlined operation on 1 January 1966 under a new designation, the Military Airlift Command (MAC). Whereas MATS had been a unified Department of Defense agency, MAC was an entirely USAF command. As such, it was placed on an equal status with the USAF combat commands.

The unfulfilled quest for VTOL

Throughout the 1940s and '50s the development of military transportation had followed a fairly clear line of progression; the advances had been impressive but had largely followed an evolutionary rather than revolutionary line of development. Specialised aircraft had emerged that were bigger, faster and better suited to their role than their predecessors, but in the 1960s a more radical advance in capability was sought – and seen to be on the horizon.

The decade saw a great deal of effort devoted to the quest for a transport aircraft capable of taking off and landing vertically, thus able to operate from unprepared airstrips close to the front line. The advantages were clear but, despite a plethora of imaginative designs, these efforts eventually proved abortive. As will be seen in the subsequent volume, *American Secret Projects 3*, the technology of the time simply was not up to the task; the complexity involved and the deficiency in conventional flight performance outweighed any advantage over the use of helicopters.

Instead, attention eventually turned to the more attractive and more attainable advantages of short take-off and landing (STOL).

The Vietnam War

Despite all that had gone before, the importance and potential of US military airlift really came into prominence during the Vietnam War. It was a conflict that evolved through different phases, starting with years of counter-insurgency operations, before expanding into a full-scale offensive between 1965 and 1968.

The Navy became increasingly hard pressed from the standpoint of budget and pilot staffing to support its combat role in the war. As a result, it decided, without objection from the Office of the Secretary of Defense (OSD), to stop funding and staffing its relatively small contribution to MAC operations. All the Navy's squadrons that had been assigned to MATS were decommissioned in 1967. The Navy continued to operate a few transport squadrons that had not been assigned to MATS, including most notably those involved in Carrier On-board Delivery. Navy crews also flew C-130s for MAC until 1968, when all MAC C-130s were transferred to the Tactical Air Command.

The US involvement in the war finally ended in 1975. Over this period the supplies flown by Air Force transports far exceeded all the payloads airlifted in the Korean War, the Berlin Airlift and the China-Burma-India operation of the Second World War put together.

It was a conflict unlike the previous wars that the USA had fought, with an enemy employing tactics very different from the relatively static massed forces encountered during the Second World War or Korea. It provided many lessons with regard to the changing nature of warfare. To quote Richard H. Kohn, one-time Chief, Office of Air Force History:

'Few tactical airlift operations in Vietnam could be called routine; weather, terrain, enemy action and the usual snafus saw to that.

Tactical airlift forces lost 122 aircraft and 229 crewmembers in Vietnam, many while attempting to deliver cargo to friendly units surrounded or besieged by enemy forces.'

The lessons learned related to tactics, the effectiveness of different types of aircraft and the organisation of airlift capability. These lessons were systematically analysed, starting midway through the war with a review known as Project Corona Harvest. This exercise issued its final report in January 1973. A further review, looking back from the advantage of a slightly longer-term perspective, was written by Ray L. Bowers and published by the Office of Air Force History in 1983.

Never before had transport aircraft been required to operate routinely so close to front-line action. One clear lesson was the ineffectiveness in this type of war of parachute assaults, which required far greater flexibility and accuracy in the delivery of troops ready for action. This brought the helicopter into its own, even if the subsequent objective was to seize or prepare a fixed-wing advanced operating base. Another lesson learned was the flexibility of deployment that rapid airlift could allow. It enabled the short-notice concentration of offensive initiatives, or the rapid reinforcement of besieged forces. The latter was important as the North Vietnamese showed that they could easily cut off road access to threatened regions. Having a rapid airlift capability meant that defensive garrisons could be minimised.

The war also provided an opportunity to evaluate the effectiveness of the USAF's tactical transport aircraft, and its principal aircraft types – the C-130 Hercules, C-123 Provider and C-7 Caribou – came through with flying colours, proving effective, rugged and dependable. In particular, the C-130 proved exceptional. To quote Bowers's review:

BELOW A Lockheed C-130A delivers cargo without landing using the LAPES (Low Altitude Parachute Extraction System) at Khe San, Vietnam. *US Air Force*

ABOVE The introduction of the C-5 Galaxy brought capabilities that had been unimaginable a generation earlier. Here a C-130 fuselage is unloaded from a 105th Airlift Wing C-5A. *109 AW photo by MSGT Christine Wood*

'The Hercules could land at relatively primitive strips with 15-ton payloads, unload palletised cargo rapidly, and move on to the next task at healthy airspeeds. Moreover, a C-130 required only one or two refuellings in the course of a full mission day. Fewer than a hundred C-130s could thus do work equivalent to the capacities of fifteen hundred C-47s.'

In terms of future aircraft procurement, Corona Harvest envisaged the need for two types of advanced tactical transports, one to replace the C-130 and the other to replace the C-133s and C-7s. Experience in the war had further strengthened the argument to look once again at VTOL transport capability. To quote the Assistant Secretary of the Air Force in 1969:

'...we do know from our experience in Southeast Asia, specifically in such situations as developed around Khe San, a vertical or extremely short STOL logistics supply capability can be extremely important. In such situations, a V/STOL can provide a far greater operational flexibility than available through the use of helicopters or STOL aircraft.'

More controversial was the matter of control of the airlift capability in South East Asia and whether this should be kept separate from that of the strike aircraft force, as was the case in Vietnam. The Corona Harvest review concluded that this was in fact the correct course. An additional controversy was the long-standing division of the nation's tactical and strategic airlift resources under separate commands, with the inevitable duplication in control and support facilities. Following much debate, in the summer of 1974 the Secretary of Defense announced that all worldwide airlift resources and missions would henceforth be consolidated under the Military Airlift Command.

Middle East conflicts

While the Vietnam War was drawing to its conclusion, conflict in the Middle East – especially the 1973 Arab-Israeli war – underlined the need for the US to increase its strategic airlift capability. The repercussions included refitting C-5 Galaxies with new wing structures to restore capability, and converting C-141 Starlifters to accommodate a greater cargo volume and to be capable of in-flight refuelling. This is the point at which it could be argued that airlift had fulfilled its long-sought promise of giving American forces genuine global strategic mobility. This capability would prove invaluable in the following decades.

Air support for Special Operations

While massive effort had been put into resolving the Air Force's need for strategic airlift, the tussle with the Army over the operation of fixed-wing aircraft continued at the other end of the scale. The need to provide far more effective air support for Special Forces was thrown into the spotlight by the abortive Iranian rescue mission in April 1980. Operation 'Eagle Claw' not only failed to rescue the fifty-two American diplomats and citizens that had been taken hostage some six months earlier, but also resulted in the loss of life of eight US servicemen and an Iranian civilian, together with the destruction of two helicopters. The incident shook the nation and had wide-ranging repercussions.

One consequence was that Special Ops gained the right to operate its own combat airlift capability with small, off-the-shelf aircraft. It also brought about significant change within the Air Force. The task of supporting Special Forces operations had primarily been assigned to TAC, but at the end of 1982 this was handed over to MAC, and on 10 February 1983 a new command was formed: the Air Forces Special Operations Command (AFSOC). Its mission was (and remains): 'Provide our Nation's specialised airpower, capable across the spectrum of conflict… Any Place, Anytime, Anywhere.'

Iraq and Afghanistan

On 2 August 1990 Iraqi forces invaded neighbouring Kuwait, following which, with the United Nations' sanction, a coalition of forces led by the United States undertook a counter-invasion to free the country. Code-named Operation 'Desert Storm', it was launched on 16 January 1991 and was all over by 28 February. It involved moving nearly 700,000 military personnel and their equipment to the Gulf area and removing them thereafter – a logistics feat that would have been impossible in earlier times.

This global delivery/support capability would be further demonstrated with subsequent, and still ongoing, conflicts in the Middle East and Asia. Indeed, it would have proved impossible to sustain a substantial military presence in Afghanistan by any other means. The only land routes, one to northern Afghanistan (roughly 1,000 miles or 1,610km long), and the other to the south, went through Pakistan. They were highly vulnerable. At one stage Pakistan closed both roads for a period of seven months.

As a consequence, all personnel and all arms, ammunition and missiles could only be securely transported by air, with only fuel and non-critical supplies allowed to go by road, though to reduce costs the former goods were often shipped by sea to ports in the Persian Gulf, then flown into Afghanistan.

The ability of the USA to use airlift to project its power around the world had become an everyday fact of life.

The present day

At the present time the need for strategic and tactical airlift is well served by the fleet of C-5s, C-17s and C-130s, backed, if needed, by the Civil Reserve Air Fleet (CRAF). This is likely to remain the case for some time to come. However, in the meantime, a new airlift requirement has grown in significance.

The USA still has to face the long-standing threat of super-power confrontation and conventional warfare. At the same time, a new kind of conflict has emerged, one where the front line is neither well-defined nor static. This necessitates transport aircraft able to operate undetected in the conflict zone, inserting or extracting troops. This has brought about a resurgence of interest in V/STOL aircraft and also the need to look at the potential for applying low-observable, or 'stealth', technology to transport aircraft, a subject covered in *American Secret Projects 3*.

While the long-standing requirement for strategic tactical airlifters has been fulfilled, a new aspect of military airlift may well be opening up.

BELOW **Strategic airlift for the Gulf Wars was supplied by these three aircraft types, the C-141B, the KC-10A (which provided both cargo and refuelling services) and the C-5**. *Boeing*

LEFT Designing an airlifter to be filled efficiently is often a problem. Here, a unique solution to loading jeeps in a C-74 has been found. In this case, fuselage volume was used up before the airlifter's weight capacity. *Boeing*

BELOW In another loading case, the available floor space in this C-17 is filled with paratroopers while the overall volume and weight are not. *US Air Force photo by Tech. Sgt. Henry Hoegen*

Chapter Two
The Challenges of Airlifter Design

Conflicting demands and technological dilemmas

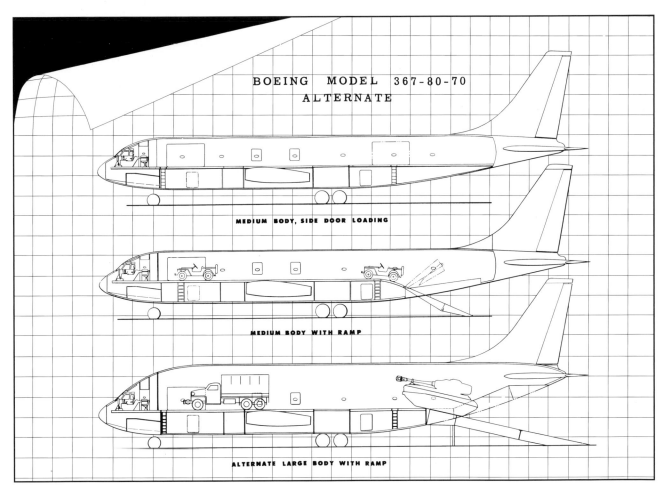

BOEING MODEL 367-80-70
ALTERNATE

MEDIUM BODY, SIDE DOOR LOADING

MEDIUM BODY WITH RAMP

ALTERNATE LARGE BODY WITH RAMP

Given that readers of this book will have various degrees of technical background, it is probably useful to set out the key challenges in designing an airlifter before presenting the various projects and proposals in the following chapters.

Designing for the future

One of the challenges of developing a new airlifter – as with any other large or complex aircraft – is that it is not being designed to meet today's needs.

Rather it is being designed against an assessment of what will be required in the future. Even where the latter has been clearly set out by the potential buyer, such as a specification by the Department of Defense (DoD) or the Air Force, the likelihood is that these requirements will be modified, perhaps repeatedly, before any decision is made to order the aircraft into production.

Moreover, it isn't just requirements that are subject to change. The normal development process for any new aircraft involves a series of stages starting with research and concept exploration, before

ABOVE Options considered by Boeing in the development of the original 'Dash-80' prototype. Large-body derivatives would be heavily studied in the late 1950s, but could not overcome the operational disadvantages of the high cargo deck. *Boeing*

moving on to outline proposal, detail design, mock-up construction, prototype building, flight testing, modification, acceptance trials and, finally, entry into service. Throughout this time, technology will have been moving forward on several fronts, particularly in areas such as avionics, materials and propulsion systems.

New proposals, therefore, have to be designed in *anticipation* of both future needs and relevant technological advances. This consideration has grown significantly over the years. The early aircraft described in this book went from concept to entering service in a period of around three years. Nowadays, it can take a decade or more.

Moreover, the entry into service is far from the end of the matter. Given the level of investment required to develop a wholly new aircraft, the most successful designs are those that prove capable of continuous development. They must be adaptable to new needs, capable of being modified to undertake new roles and take advantage of further advances in technologies such as engines and avionics. The most prominent example of this is undoubtedly the Lockheed C-130 Hercules. This aircraft was originally designed in response to an Air Force requirement for a new medium transport in 1951; it is still in production more than sixty years later, having been continuously and extensively developed in the interim.

The key requirements for a successful airlifter

Compared with other categories of military aircraft, the challenge of designing a successful airlifter might appear a somewhat simpler task. It does not require the speed, climb rate or manoeuvrability of a fighter, nor either the high- or low-level penetration capability of an attack aircraft. Conceptually it is little more than a truck on wings. At least that is the way it may appear at first sight. In practice, designing a successful airlifter has stretched the capability and imagination of some of the industry's leading engineers.

Quite aside from considerations of load-carrying capability and range, an airlifter needs the following attributes:

■ The ability to carry, and if necessary mix, cargoes of varying shape and size, from tanks and heavy artillery to personnel.

■ The ability to deliver its loads to short, semi-prepared or even unprepared airstrips.

■ At times, the capability to perform a very steep approach and climb-out, overflying hostile territory.

■ The ability to discharge its cargo rapidly with little or no local support facilities.

■ In many cases, the capability to air-drop loads without landing.

■ The reliability and robustness to carry out such missions repeatedly with a fast turnaround.

Providing access for loading/unloading

Many configurations have been tried for rapid loading and, more importantly, unloading of cargo. These include clamshell doors in either the nose or the tail, lifting noses, swinging noses, swinging tails and a whole variety of other ways of opening up the fuselage. To these means of access one must also add consideration of how the cargo can be loaded or unloaded, quickly and without any ground equipment. This can involve ramps or the whole aircraft 'kneeling'.

These features all come with their advantages and penalties. All such devices add weight and a degree of mechanical complexity, particularly if the aircraft is pressurised or the moving parts involve control runs. They also use up valuable space. Looking at an airframe from the outside, it is difficult to appreciate how much of the internal space is taken up by the means of loading/unloading the aircraft. Even on a highly successful airlifter like the C-130, only 45% (not counting cargo placed on the loading ramp) of the total fuselage length is usable carrying space.

Moreover, what determines the size of the largest item of payload that can be carried (such as a tank or vehicle) is not the internal dimensions of the cargo bay but the dimensions of the means of access. This particularly applies to the overhead clearance at the top of the loading ramp. This in turn is affected by its slope: the gentler the slope, the less door height is needed. However, the gentler the slope, the lower the aircraft has to be on the ground or the longer the ramp required.

BELOW Side doors can be problematic. Here, supplies are dispensed in flight from a C-47 over Burma during the Second World War. The officer on the left is performing a role known as the 'kicker'. *Author's collection*

ABOVE This makeshift ramp (attached to a cargo truck) allows a jeep to be driven into a C-74. Manoeuvring up a greasy, worn ramp in rain or snow would have been a challenge. *Boeing*

BELOW The structural design of the Douglas C-132 dictated a rather small aft loading aperture (shown in white) compared to the cargo hold. Although acceptable in 1953, it would have been marginal for Atlas missile loading in 1958. *Boeing*

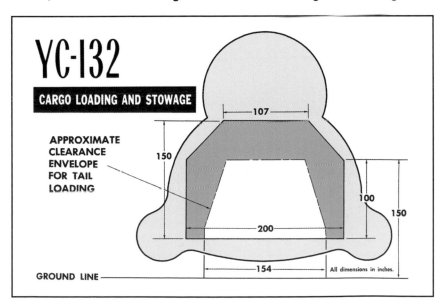

Providing an unobstructed cargo area

Clearly the cargo area needs to be unobstructed, both to make fullest use of the space and to provide ease of access throughout its full length. Ideally, it should be like an empty warehouse. The problem that this gives is where to position the wings. These need to be joined by an integral structure in the form of a carry-through box. If a low-wing configuration is used, as is the case with virtually every modern airliner, this requires the floor of the cargo area to be raised substantially to clear the wing box, thus reducing available space and creating a problem in terms of ease of access for loading and unloading.

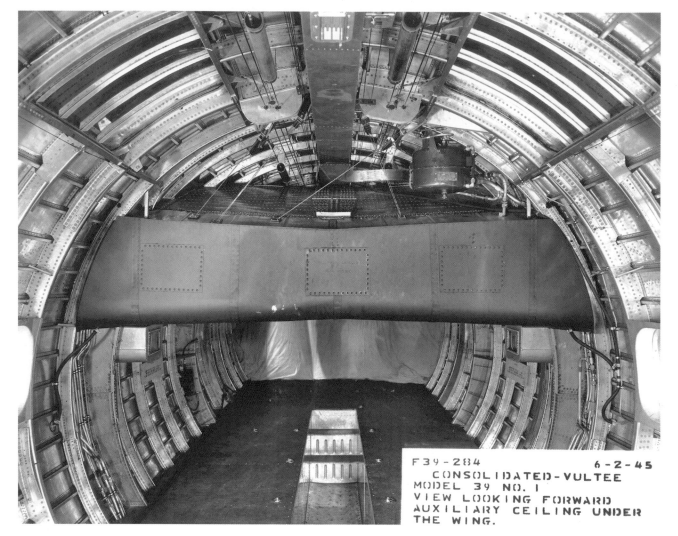

F39-284   6-2-45
CONSOLIDATED-VULTEE
MODEL 39 NO. 1
VIEW LOOKING FORWARD
AUXILIARY CEILING UNDER
THE WING.

ABOVE Convair's Model 39 prototype married a new circular fuselage to a B-24-type wing (painted black), which intruded into the cargo space. *San Diego Air and Space Museum*

BELOW This graphic presents why Douglas stayed with low-wing configurations through most of the process leading up to the C-141, despite the cargo deck loading issues. It also provides an interesting insight into what a high-wing cargo transport with a DC-8 fuselage might have looked like. *Boeing*

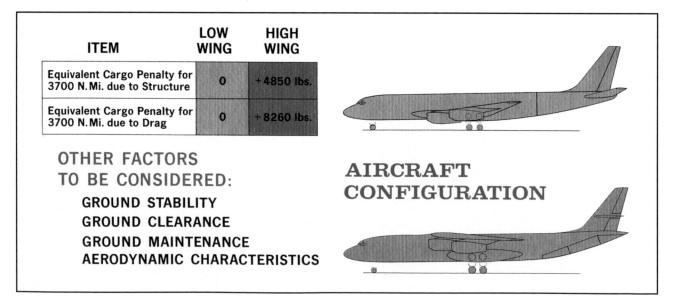

ITEM	LOW WING	HIGH WING
Equivalent Cargo Penalty for 3700 N.Mi. due to Structure	0	+4850 lbs.
Equivalent Cargo Penalty for 3700 N.Mi. due to Drag	0	+8260 lbs.

OTHER FACTORS
TO BE CONSIDERED:
   GROUND STABILITY
   GROUND CLEARANCE
   GROUND MAINTENANCE
   AERODYNAMIC CHARACTERISTICS

AIRCRAFT
CONFIGURATION

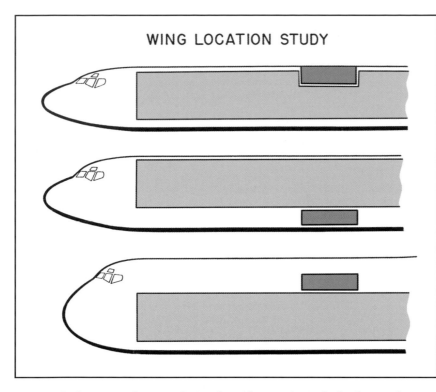

WING LOCATION STUDY

ABOVE The basic wing location choices faced by Douglas in the lead-up to the CX-4 competition. *Boeing*

A high-wing configuration solves both these problems, particularly if the wing is mounted above the fuselage. However, this introduces a new, three-fold set of considerations. Firstly, it requires a strengthening of the wing-bearing section of the fuselage. In flight, the latter is effectively hung from the wings; however, on the ground the same structure has to bear an opposite, compressive load, supporting the combined weight of the wings, the engines and the fuel tanks.

Secondly, whereas low wings allow for a short-stroke, easily retracted undercarriage with a well-spread structural load, this can only be achieved with a high-wing layout by having the main landing gear accommodated within the outer sides of the lower fuselage. This is necessary to keep the cargo bay clear and to give a wide enough track, but it is an arrangement that adds further to the structural strength required of the fuselage.

Thirdly, a high wing can cause airflow interference with the horizontal stabilisers if these are positioned at the same level.

BELOW Cargo handling during the Second World War: packages and small crates are unloaded by hand from a converted PBM-5. *Author's collection*

Cargo handling

Accompanying the evolution in airlifter technology has been a revolution in cargo handling, the significance of which is easily overlooked. In the 1930s, when air transportation started, cargo was limited to small packages. As airlifters increased in capability during the Second World War, both the individual size and the amount of cargo that could be carried increased. However, the loading arrangements changed very little, with manual or forklift handling and manual tie-down. Indeed, such systems continued to be used long after the war, even though the airlifters themselves had advanced much further in capability.

In an event whose significance is easily overlooked, the Douglas Aircraft Company was awarded a contract in 1959 to develop what was named Support System 463 – Logistics – the 'SS-463L Pallet Cargo Handling System'. This was designed to provide an efficient intermodal means of cargo transfer. With this system, air cargo could be loaded onto standard-size pallets that could be transported on

ABOVE Cargo handling in 1954: crates and boxes are loaded wall-to-wall during loading demonstrations in the XC-132 mock-up. Cargo nets are secured to the walls and deck. *Boeing*

BELOW Cargo handling in 2019: pre-packaged standard 463L cargo pallets are stowed in a C-5M. Space is provided around and between the pallets for crew access. Cargo is secured to the pallets and the pallets are latched to the floor. *US Air Force photo by 2nd Lt Steve Lewis*

roller-type conveyors within the terminal, transferred to ground vehicles, loaded onto the aircraft and moved along the cargo bay. Many of these roller systems were subsequently made capable of being stowed in the aircraft floor, enabling the deck to be changed to a flat surface to accommodate wheeled cargo.

The 463L pallet subsequently became the standard-size platform for military air cargo. As a consequence, since its inception airlifter cargo holds have been designed to fit the dimensions (or multiples) of the pallet. The system was also equipped for locking pallets into airlifter floor rails. These rails guided the pallets into the aircraft and were fitted with locks that provided lateral and vertical cargo restraint of up to 8Gs.

A single 463L pallet is 88in long by 108in wide by 2.25in thick (224cm by 274cm by 5.7cm) and includes tie-down rings to secure nets and cargo loads. An empty 463L pallet weighs 290lb (132kg), has a maximum load capacity of 10,000lb (4,540kg), and can be rolled into the airlifter and secured in minutes.

Effects of weight on operations and range

Throughout this book figures are given for the weights and ranges of the various aircraft and design proposals. However, it needs to be recognised that these are not simple, absolute numbers like, say, the physical dimensions of the aeroplane; rather they vary according to the operational circumstances.

The normally quoted Gross Take-off Weight (GTOW) is the designed maximum weight of the aircraft including crew, fuel and cargo. Clearly, the distance the aeroplane can fly is a balance between the last two elements. While this applies to any type of aircraft, it is far more significant in the case of an airlifter. For example, for a fighter or a bomber the quoted 'range' is normally the maximum distance or radius over which it is designed to carry out its role. For a military transport, every potential mission is a trade-off between payload and distance.

Designed to operate from remote airstrips, there is another limitation imposed on the maximum take-off weight by the available runway length. Moreover, aside from getting the aircraft off the ground, there is a further consideration in terms of the aerodynamic loads that are deemed acceptable. Under certain conditions there may be the opportunity to operate beyond the normal gross weight by accepting a higher wing loading. This limits manoeuvrability and reduces the structural safety margin, but could be justified by military needs.

The figures given in the following pages need to be understood against this background.

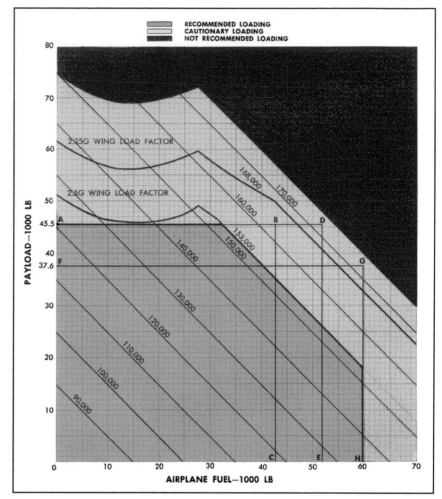

RIGHT Even high-floatation landing gear cannot compensate for poor soil conditions and surface durability. Taxiing across ruts from a previous test caused this C-5A to break through the soil surface, and it had to be dug out by hand shovels. *US Air Force*

Operating from semi-prepared airstrips

Most modern large aircraft require lengthy paved runways. While much of the time airlifters will operate from such bases, there is often a need to use less accommodating facilities, particularly during times of tension or conflict. Length of landing and take-off run therefore becomes a major consideration for an effective airlifter.

Moreover, the requirement is not only to be able to land at a semi-prepared airstrip, but also to land and take off from it repeatedly, without ploughing up the ground such that it becomes quickly unusable. This adds constraints in terms of footprint, wheel size and location, load per wheel and landing speed.

Engine choice

One of the basic dilemmas facing engineers in the decades covered by this book and its companion volume has been how best to power their proposed designs. As explained earlier, the design of a new aircraft has to make assumptions about the future availability of suitable powerplants. It is a two-way dependency, with the engine suppliers having to make assumptions about future aircraft developments.

All the early airlifters were powered by the piston engine. However, even though the technology was long-proven, it was at the extreme end of its development potential. It was also limited in both altitude and speed. The new jet engine opened up the possibility of raising these limits but, by comparison, was much less fuel-efficient. Moreover, the early turbojets developed relatively low thrust, requiring large aircraft like strategic bombers to be powered by six or eight engines (and even so requiring rocket-assistance for take-off at maximum weight).

The issue of how best to power new aircraft loomed large in many 1950s proposals – for bombers and attack aircraft as well as transports. On the one hand, piston-engine technology was reaching its limits in terms of scale and complexity, with even the well-proven bigger engines becoming very demanding in terms of maintenance. It was also a technology that was close to its performance limits. On the other hand, turbine technology was advancing fast and showing great potential. In theory, it was also much simpler.

Indeed, the first jet engines were little more than scaled-up superchargers, exhausting through a turbine. The early British (centrifugal compressor) jet engines proved so reliable that in 1946 six de Havilland Vampire single-engine fighters flew across the North Atlantic – without even the ability to relight an engine in flight! The only serious early technical limitation – the need for relatively sophisticated materials capable of operating at consistently high temperatures – had been largely overcome.

Early jet engines were, however, very fuel-thirsty and it was clear that greater efficiency could be achieved by using the hot exhaust gases to drive a propeller rather than just exiting the back of the engine in the form of pure thrust, effectively shifting a bigger air mass at a somewhat lower speed (a principle later to be exploited with high-bypass-ratio jet engines).

This would be a limitation for, say, interceptors, as at very high aircraft speeds the propeller tips would need to be travelling supersonically. However, it was ideally suited to transports, which had little to gain by travelling at near-sonic speeds. The answer was simply to stick a propeller on to the front of the existing jet engines. At least, that was the theory. The problem was that such a move necessitated adding the complexity of a gearbox and also introducing a more complex route for the airflow through the engine.

This complexity became even more of an issue when, to overcome the relatively low power of the early turbojets, two engines needed to be coupled together to drive dual propellers. For example, this was the case with the Allison T40 turboprop, which coupled two T38 turboprop power sections to a common gearbox. Basing a design around the assumed performance and reliability of such an engine resulted in problems for many new aircraft projects.

Indeed, the lack of a really big turboprop engine was to influence the design of American strategic bombers, which quickly switched to an all-turbojet philosophy, unlike the Russians, whose equivalent to the B-52 was the turboprop-powered Tupolev Tu-95 Bear.

BELOW A comparison between the first-generation C-130A/T56 engine and propeller and the current C-130J/AE-2100 (T56 derivative). The propeller has doubled the number of blades to cope with the added power from the AE-2100. *Author*

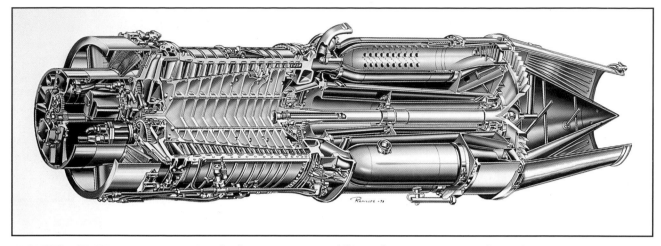

ABOVE The GE J47 was representative of a first generation axial flow turbojet. Air entering the intake is compressed and burned, driving the single stage turbine. *North American Aviation*

BELOW The GE TF34 engine is a high bypass turbofan with a bypass ration of 6.23 to 1 (bypass flow is shown in blue and core flow in red). Core flow is combusted and drives a four-stage low pressure turbine which drives the front fan. *General Electric*

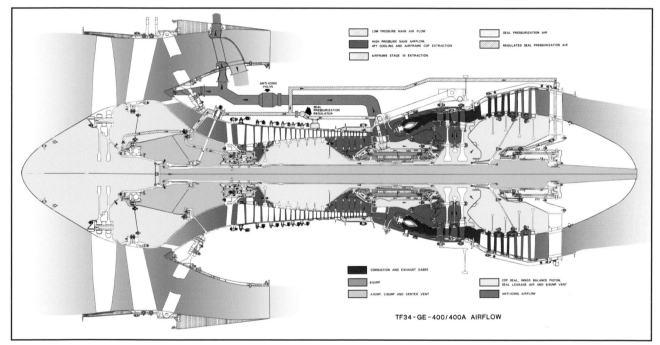

Perhaps the most significant engine development with regard to airlifter evolution was the advent of the high-bypass turbofan, which was introduced on the C-5 Galaxy.

Unlike the pure turbojet, only a small amount of air entering a turbofan engine goes through the core, where the air is compressed, heated and expanded through the turbine. Most of the airflow is accelerated by the large-diameter fan stages at the front of the engine. This air bypasses the core without combustion and fuel consumption. In essence, the turbofan trades the high exhaust velocity of the turbojet for the much greater mass of lower velocity of air moved by the fan. While thrust is proportional to the exhaust velocity, fuel consumption is related to the square of that velocity. The result, therefore, is a much more fuel-efficient engine, giving about twice as much thrust for the same fuel consumption as a turbojet of similar core size.

Jet Engine Progress

Date	Application	Engine	Static Thrust
1942	Bell XP-59 (first US jet aircraft)	GE J31	1,650lb (7.33kN)
1951	XC-123A (first US jet transport)	GE J47-GE-11	5,000lb (22.3kN)
1954	Boeing 376-80 (707/KC-135 prototype)	P&W JT3C (J57)	10,000lb (44.6kN)
1963	C-141A	P&W TF33-P-7 (JT3D)	21,000lb (93.4kN)
1968	C-5A	GE TF39-GE-1	41,000lb (182kN)
2006	C-5M	GE CF6-80C2	52,500lb (234kN)
2019	Largest jet engine currently available	GE GE9X	105,000lb (470kN)

The theory was understood from the early days of the jet engine, but could not be put into practice because of the unavailability of materials able to withstand the higher core operating temperatures required – an example of the interdependency of technological advances.

The subsequent advance of turbofans has led to a massive advance in scale, and hence thrust. This has given rise to a symbiotic relationship between the aircraft and aero-engine manufacturers, each designing products in anticipation of the other's needs.

When the Chase XC-123 – the first jet-powered US transport aircraft – took to the air, its four engines each produced a static thrust of just over 5,000lb (22.3kN); today's largest available turbofans produce more than 100,000lb (445kN).

Vertical/Short Take-Off and Landing

V/STOL was considered for some time to represent the future of military air transportation for its tactical elements. However, despite extensive experimentation involving many different technologies, it was to prove an elusive goal. Tilting engines, tilting rotors, lift-fans, separate lift-engines and thrust deflection were all explored.

VTOL problems related to three areas. One was controllability in the transition or hover; another (in the case of lift engines or deflected thrust systems) was the effect of downward engine exhaust both on the operating site and on hot gas re-ingestion; the third was the complexity and extra weight that the additional engine power brought with it, which restricted the payload and/or range. It was not that these

problems were insoluble, but rather that with the technology available at the time the cost of developing and operating the solutions was excessive.

Unlike aircraft designed purely for VTOL, STOL proved a far more fruitful path of development. STOL aircraft require less engine power, carry less surplus weight and are better attuned to normal cruise flight. As such, STOL gives much of the advantage of VTOL without its technological complexity and negative impact on conventional flight performance.

Slower landing and take-off speeds, and shorter ground runs, increase the ability to use forward-based, semi-prepared airstrips. Moreover, in a combat situation, particularly in an era of small, hand-held ground-to-air missiles, there is a clear advantage in having both a steep approach and a rapid climb-out.

BELOW The NC-130B STOL test bed lands at Moffett Field. The larger control surfaces can be seen; less visible is the 90° deflection of the flaps. BLC blowing over the flaps causes the unusual (and disconcerting) nose-down attitude. *NASA*

ABOVE A C-2A(R) at the moment of truth during a carrier landing. Already the throttles are being pushed to full power for a take-off in case the tailhook doesn't catch the arresting cable – there is less than 500 feet of deck remaining to the ocean.
US Navy photo by Mass Communication Specialist 3rd Class B. Siens

However, the short-field operating ability comes with challenges. Flight at slow speeds, such as immediately after take-off or prior to touch-down, greatly reduces the effectiveness of the aerodynamic control surfaces. This gives a particular problem with gusts and crosswinds, and with having sufficient elevator authority for round-out on landing. This can be countered by employing larger-than-normal tail surfaces. However, when these are coupled with wings optimised for maximum lift at very low speeds, they become the opposite of what is required for efficient, high-speed cruising flight.

Additionally, most approaches to achieving STOL (other than the expediency of using rocket-assisted take-off) rely on diverting the thrust of the engine, either directly by thrust vectoring or by using it to boost the effect of the flaps (flowing over either the upper or lower surface). This presents severe problems in the event of engine failure, resulting in direct loss of lift and potential asymmetric effects.

Carrier landings and take-offs

One specialised aspect of military air transport is Carrier On-Board Delivery, or COD. Added to all the other requirements described above, a COD aircraft needs to have the ability to land and take off from a very small, moving airstrip, using a trip-wire arrester system for landing and a catapult for take-off. Moreover, once on board the carrier the aircraft needs to be capable of being stowed efficiently, which requires the wings (and often the vertical fin) to be folded.

These requirements pose additional challenges for designers. Nonetheless, as will be seen in *American Secret Projects 3*, some remarkably large aircraft have been considered for adaptation to fulfil the COD mission.

Airlifter design in perspective

As shown in the following pages, the challenge of meeting the continuously evolving design requirements of airlifters has proved equally as taxing as any other type of military aircraft, and has resulted in a vast number of imaginative designs.

An airlifter may be many things, but a simple 'truck with wings' it isn't.

Chapter Three
Airlifter Development in the Second World War

1941 to 1945: An urgent response to a new type of warfare

CONSOLIDATED MODEL 36 TRANSPORT

CONSOLIDATED AIRCRAFT CORPORATION
SAN DIEGO, CALIF.

PH. 13624   36 Z 157
REF. 36 Z 022

ABOVE The Convair Model 36 transport version of the early B-36 bomber design.
San Diego Air and Space Museum

Converted airliner designs – the only viable immediate option

From a military airlift point of view, the Second World War was largely fought with whatever aircraft were most readily available at the outset, notably by converting airliners that were then either entering commercial service or at an advanced stage of development. Aircraft like the Douglas DC-3 and Curtiss CW-20 were progressive designs for their time, but were hardly ideal for the role into which they were conscripted. They were never intended for bulky cargo, easy loading of military hardware or air-dropping of supplies.

In the absence of either time or resources to develop custom-built military transports, the only other option would have been to convert bombers; indeed, this was tried but proved relatively unsuccessful. The British had made greater use of this approach, largely because they lacked available and suitable airliners, but similarly met with limited success. The adaptation had obvious appeal: bombers were the largest aircraft at

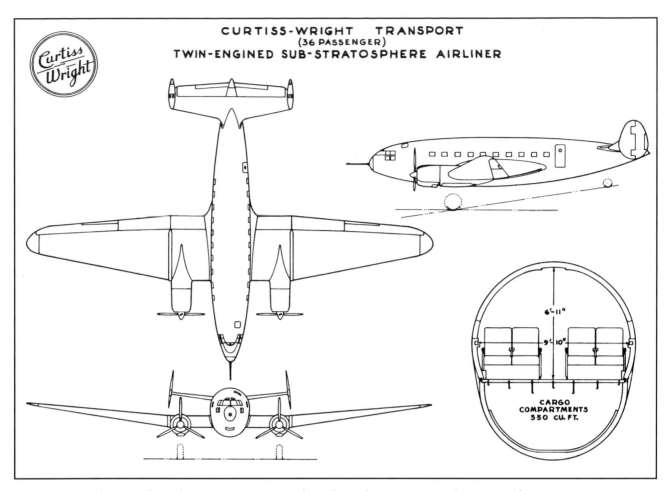

ABOVE Designed as an airliner, the Curtiss CW-20 was adapted into the C-46 Commando transport for wartime service.
G. H. Balzer collection

hand and were designed to carry heavy payloads over long distances. However, there were many problems: the lack of a through deck with the mid-fuselage blocked by the wing carry-through box; no large front or rear access doors; an aerodynamic fuselage designed for minimal frontal area, which was exactly the opposite to that needed by an airlifter; and a cargo deck that was either high above the ground or sloping.

Just about every bomber was tried. The B-17 became the C-108, the B-24 became the C-87, the PB4Y-2 became the RY-3, and the B 32 was proposed as the Convair Model 33, but none of them had a serious impact on airlift capability. As the war progressed the adapted airliners not only provided the necessary capability but were further developed for their new role, respectively being lengthened, strengthened and re-engined.

When the DC-3 first flew in December 1935 it was known as the DST, or 'Douglas Sleeper Transport', produced in response to an American Airlines requirement for a comfortable and spacious overnight transport. Nothing could be further from the future for which thousands of examples would be produced.

By late 1940 concerns about the war in Europe and Japan's expansionist policies in the Pacific had led to the Government placing substantial orders for new military aircraft, and in September an order was placed for 965 militarised DC 3s under the designation C-47. Deliveries commenced in October 1941 and, shortly after the declaration of war the following year, 213 DC-3s were impressed into service. During the war the AAF received a total of 7,772 C-47s.

The Curtiss CW-20 was a slightly later and larger aircraft than the DC-3,

although designed to compete in much the same market. When it first flew on 26 March 1940 it was actually the largest twin-engine aircraft in the world. As well as its load-carrying capacity, it also offered the advantage of having a pressurised cabin. The outbreak of war ended plans for a commercial future and production was switched to a militarised version, designated the C-46. Deliveries started in July 1942. After the first twenty five aircraft, production switched to the C-46A, which was unpressurised, as was the later C-46D version. During the war, 2,889 examples were delivered to the AAF.

The nearest to a purpose-built military transport was the four-engine Douglas C-54. This aircraft too had started its life as a commercial venture in 1936, sponsored by five leading airlines (American, Eastern, TWA, Pan American and United).

31

	Curtiss CW-20 (C-46A)	Douglas DC-3 (C-47B)
Powerplant	2 x P&W R-2800-51 piston radials @ 2,000hp (1,490kW)	2 x P&W R-1830-90B/C piston radials @ 1,200hp (895kW)
Empty weight	30,000lb (13,620kg)	18,135lb (8,233kg)
Loaded weight	49,600lb (22,518kg)	26,000lb (11,804kg)
Span	108ft 1in (32.97m)	95ft 6in (29.13m)
Length	76ft 4in (23.28m)	63ft 9in (19.44m)
Wing area	1,360sq ft (126.5m²)	987sq ft (91.8m²)
Payload	50 troops or 11,600lb (5,266kg) cargo	28 troops or 6,000lb (2,724kg) cargo
Max speed	270mph (456km/h)	224mph (360km/h)
Cruise speed	173mph (278km/h)	160mph (257km/h)

Douglas C-54D	
Powerplant	
Wingspan	117ft 6in (35.84m)
Length	93ft 10in (28.62m)
Height	26ft 7in (8.38m)
Wing area	1,460sq ft (136m²)
Max TOW	73,000lb (33,140kg)
Payload	15,600lb (7,080kg)
Max speed	275mph (442km/h)
Cruise speed	190mph (306km/h)
Range	3,100mi (4,988km)

However, flight testing, which started in 1938, revealed that the operating costs were higher than expected and Douglas set about substantially redesigning the aircraft, designating it the DC-4 and redesignating the previous prototype as the DC-4E. The process was well advanced when, in 1941, the US Government commandeered the whole project and ordered the aircraft into production as the C-54. The required changes included a strengthened floor, large rear cargo doors and an internal cargo hoist (necessitated by the fact that, having a nose-wheel landing gear, the whole fuselage was well above ground level). There was no experimental prototype and the first production model flew on 14 February 1942. The C-54, which was quickly to become known as the 'Skymaster', provided the basis of the Air Transport Command's (ATC) long-range capability throughout the war. In total 1,170 examples were delivered to the AAF.

Although a successful design and produced in numbers, the C-54 did not fulfil the vision that Douglas had laid out to the airlines in 1940, particularly in its lack of pressurisation. However, by 1944 the AAF was prepared to allow Douglas to begin engineering the improvements that the company had long planned. Moreover, since 1940 higher-powered engines had become available that now allowed an increased gross weight and thus greater capacity.

One of the first steps was to pressurise the C-54 and replace the 1,450hp (1081kW) Pratt & Whitney R-2000 engines with 2,100hp (1566kW) Pratt & Whitney R-2800s. The fuselage was lengthened by 41in (1.04m), and this became the first in a long series of powerplant upgrades and fuselage extensions to the basic design. Initially, this development was given the designation C-54B, but given the extent of the modifications it was subsequently redesignated XC-112, then XC-112A and YC-112A in turn.

The prototype was completed as the YC-112A and first flew on 15 February 1946, with its civil DC-6 version taking to the air just five months later, the first of more than 700 to be built. However, with the end of the war with Japan and a glut of practically new C-54s, the Army cancelled its development contract and Douglas focused its attention on the civil market.

Given the aeroplane's capability and solid heritage, it is hardly surprising that there was soon a resurgence of military interest once funding became available. The twenty-ninth example on the production line was customised as a personal transport for President Truman – the forerunner of 'Air Force

BELOW The versatility of the Douglas Model 450 (C-54A) is depicted with internal and external cargo carriage options. *Boeing*

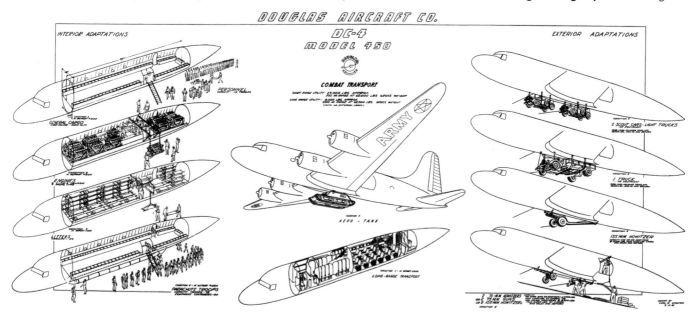

ABOVE An air-transportable T-9 light tank hangs from hardpoints under the centre wing section of a C-54 during early testing. Due to limited clearance, the turret had to be removed and was carried in the C-54 fuselage. *Boeing*

BELOW In late 1942 Douglas performed a quick study to investigate how to configure the C-54 as a bomber with a payload of eight 500lb (226.8kg) bombs. The two approaches were a belly gondola (top view) or internal accommodations (lower view). In both configurations a bombardier station was positioned aft of the nose gear and remote-controlled gun turrets (likely adapted from the system used on the A-26) were added. *Boeing*

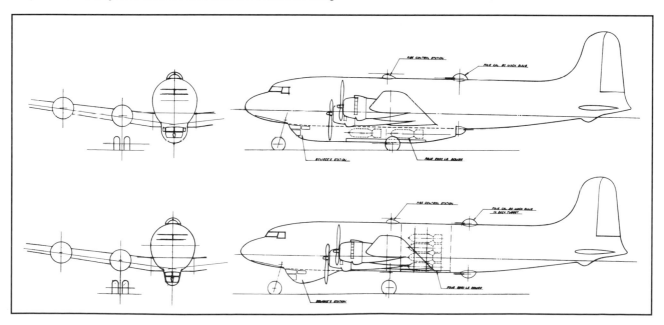

ABOVE The outdoor Douglas 'DC-6' mock-up has an R-2800 engine (left) and a V-1650 Merlin engine (right) on the wing, as seen at the Santa Monica plant on 13 August 1945. *Boeing*

One' – and in 1950 orders were placed by the USAF for 101 DC-6As under the designation C-118A, and sixty-five by the Navy as the R6D-1.

Douglas also explored variants with other engines, each given separate Army Air Force designations because of their military funding, but none of these got as far as flying. However, the Merlin-powered variant was licence-produced by Canadair Ltd as the Northstar for the RCAF and Trans Canada Air Lines.

Lockheed C-69 (Model L-049 Constellation)

During the war even new types that had been intended for the commercial market were diverted straight into military service. The Lockheed L-049 (which was to become the Constellation) was pressed directly into military use as the C-69, something that must surely have caused angst

Proposed DC-6 military developments

USAAF designation	Douglas specification	Engine type
XC-112	DS-478	P&W R-2800 piston radial
XC-114	DS-490	Allison V1710 piston inline
XC-115	TS-496	RR Merlin Series 90 (20SM) or Packard V-1650-131 piston inline
XC-116	DS-492	GE TG-100 turboprop

within TWA, which had sponsored the aircraft's development with its initial order in early 1940. The aircraft, which first flew on 9 January 1943 and was ferried the same day to Muroc Army Air Base for military trials, represented a major step forward in airliner technology. Fully pressurised, it was designed to carry forty or more passengers over 3,500 miles (5,600km). It also had a higher cruising speed – up to 327mph (526km/h) – than any other airliner. Of peripheral note is the Model 249 Constellation, which received a contract on 27 June 1941 for development as the XB-30 bomber in

competition with the Boeing B-29, Douglas XB-31, Consolidated (Convair) XB-32 and Martin XB-33 designs. Lockheed later withdrew from the competition.

By the time the Transport Airplane Requirements Board met in September 1942, the requirements of the Air Transport Command for Constellations had been radically altered. Although the Command stated that it could use C-69s to augment services performed by C-54s, it had no essential requirement for them provided an adequate number of the Douglas transports could be made available. Nor did Troop Carrier

ABOVE The Douglas YC-112A in flight over Santa Monica. *Boeing*
BELOW A profile view of the Douglas XC-116, which was to have been powered by four GE TG-100 turboprop engines. *Boeing*

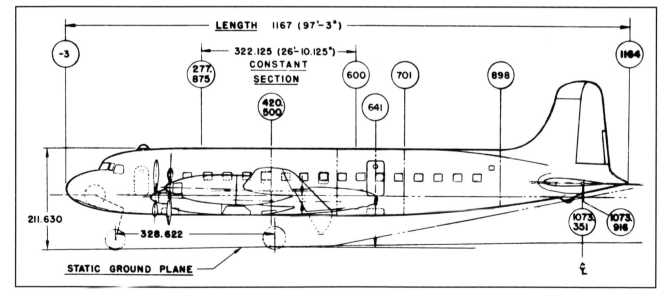

Command or Air Service Command require Constellations in either passenger or cargo-carrying form. The C-69 was a very advanced aircraft for its time, but perhaps better suited to luxury, high-speed air travel than military transportation.

Although not originally designed for military transportation, the three converted airliners – the Curtiss CW-20, Douglas DC-3 and Douglas DC-4 – provided extensive and invaluable service, making a huge contribution to the war effort. The scale of this contribution can be judged by the fact that by the time the war ended, some 12,000 of these aircraft types had been delivered to the AAF.

ABOVE The first Lockheed L-049 Constellation flies in its military colours under the C-69 designation. *Lockheed*

Second World War Constellation military developments

USAAF designation	Lockheed designation	No completed	Comments
C-69	049-46-10	14	Initial nine aircraft ordered by TWA, finished for USAAF
C-69A	049-43-11	0	Projected 100-person troop transport, cancelled
C-69B	349-43-11	0	Projected long-range troop carrier, cancelled on VJ Day
C-69C	049-46-19	1	VIP transport
C-69D	–	0	Gross weight increased to 100,000lb (45,360kg), cancelled
XC-69E	049-39-10	1*	C-69 prototype converted with 4 x R-2800 engines

* converted from first C-69, msn 049-1961

Douglas wartime transport proposals

While developing the DC-4, Douglas also explored a series of further medium-size transport proposals, capable of accommodating both troops and cargo. These designs were assigned various Model numbers including 400, 410, 415/415A, 425 and 458.

Type Specification 366 (TS-366), dated August 1940, described the Model 366 as a twin-engined low-wing aircraft (resembling a reduced-scale DC-4) tentatively dubbed the DC-6 for the commercial market. This was adapted into the 400 Series models listed above, where the fuselage cross section was retained and stretched, progressing to a high-wing configuration better suited to a cargo-carrying role. All the designs shared the same fuselage cross section but they varied in length. They all had a similar wing profile and empennage configuration, and all employed a tricycle landing gear. They also shared the unusual 'double bubble' arrangement that

Douglas favoured in the mid-1940s, with each pilot sitting beneath an individual fighter-type cockpit canopy. However, the big variation came in the form of engine arrangements, with two-, three- and four-engine proposals all being evaluated. This resulted in overall weights ranging from 32,000lb to 62,000lb (14,530kg to 28,150kg), capable of carrying twenty-eight to fifty-six passengers respectively.

Several of the high-wing aircraft featured a hinged rear fuselage, swinging open 90° to the starboard side to allow drive-on access via a ramp, while the

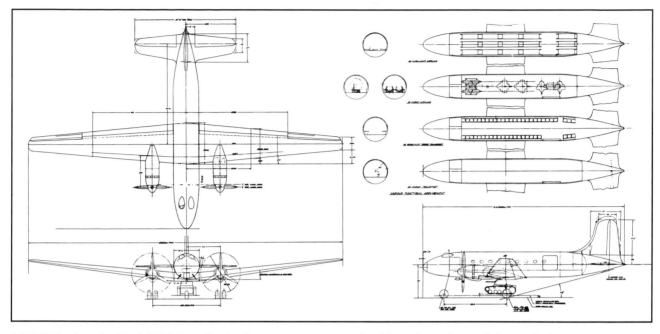

ABOVE The Douglas Model 400 'Douglas Combat Transport' was evolved from the earlier Model 366. The landing gear clearance was sufficient for external carriage of a light tank without removal of the turret. *Boeing*

Model 400 was planned with sufficient ground clearance to carry a light tank suspended beneath the fuselage.

The Douglas Model 410 of late December 1941 was a smaller twin-engine, low-wing design that shared design traits, such as the 'bug-eyed' cockpits and leading edge root extensions on the horizontal stabilisers, with the Model 415 and 425.

The Douglas Model 425 'Glider Tow, Cargo & Tank Carrier' of December 1941 carried forward the features of the Model 410 in an enlarged and heavier design with three engines. The wing planform was similarly increased in size from the 410, but retained a straight leading edge and a swept-forward trailing edge.

The fuselage was positioned high off the ground to enable the external carriage of a single T-9 tank (with turret removed) or a 75mm artillery piece, which was attached to hard points under the wing. Provision was also made for the carriage of six 'parachute equipment containers' in three rows under the fuselage. Two side-opening cargo doors were placed on the left side of the fuselage, and a ventral door and stairway were fitted to the aft under-fuselage. This could be alternately used as a paratroop door. Douglas also planned a commercial airline version (suitably modified) as the Model 426.

By 1943 the Models 410 and 425 had undergone a radical rethink. Both designs were now part of a 'modular' family of aircraft with a high wing, different fuselage lengths and the number of engines varying between two, three and four. The under-fuselage cargo capability was abandoned for an overall configuration that lowered the cargo deck for ease of loading and unloading.

The revised Model 425 had grown by a few feet in length and span while losing a few inches in height. Payload had increased by 2,000lb (907kg), but where the new model excelled was in cabin length, which grew from 38ft 7in (11.78m) to 50ft 10in (15.51m).

Douglas Model 400

Powerplant	2 x P&W R-2000 piston radials @ 1,350hp (1,007kW)
Wingspan	100ft 4in (30.58m)
Length	69ft 3in (21.11m)
Height	29ft 5.25in (8.97m)
Wing area	1,026sq ft (95.31m²)
Empty weight	20,021lb (9,081.3kg)
Normal gross weight	30,000lb (13,607.8kg)
Useful load	9,979lb (4,526.4kg)

Douglas Model 410

Powerplant	2 x P&W R-2000 piston radials @ 1,350hp (1007kW)
Wingspan	100ft 4in (30.58m)
Length	69ft 3in (21.11m)
Height	27ft 6in (8.38m)
Wing area	1,026sq ft (95.31m²)
Empty weight	20,021lb (9,081kg)
Normal gross weight	30,000lb (13,607kg)
Useful load	9,979lb (4,082kg)

Douglas Model 425/458

	December 1941 (low wing)	November 1943 (high wing)
Powerplant	3 x P&W R-2000 piston radials @ 1,350hp (1007kW)	3 x P&W R-2000 piston radials @ 1,350hp (1007kW)
Wingspan	105ft (32.00m)	110ft (33.50m)
Length	80ft 3in (24.50m)	81ft 4in (24.80m)
Height	27ft 3in (8.30m)	26ft 8in (8.13)
Wing area	1,100sq ft (103.2m²)	1,129sq ft (104.9m²)
Empty weight	27,000lb (12,247kg)	28,500lb (12,927kg)
Normal gross weight	41,000lb (18,598kg)	45,000lb (20,412kg)
Payload	14,000lb (6,350kg)	16,500lb (7,484kg)

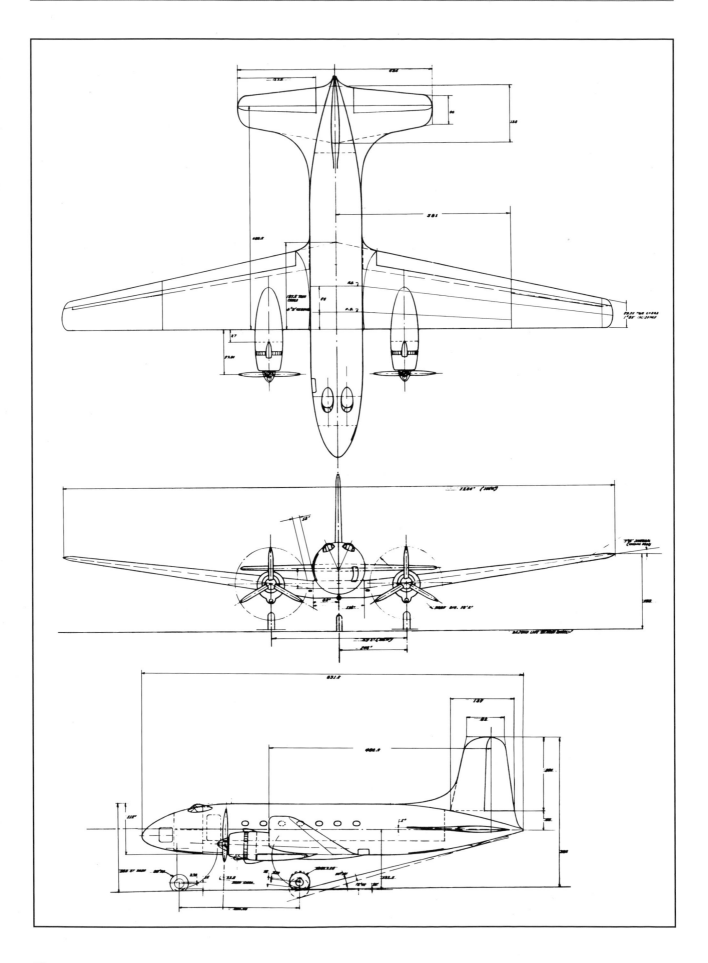

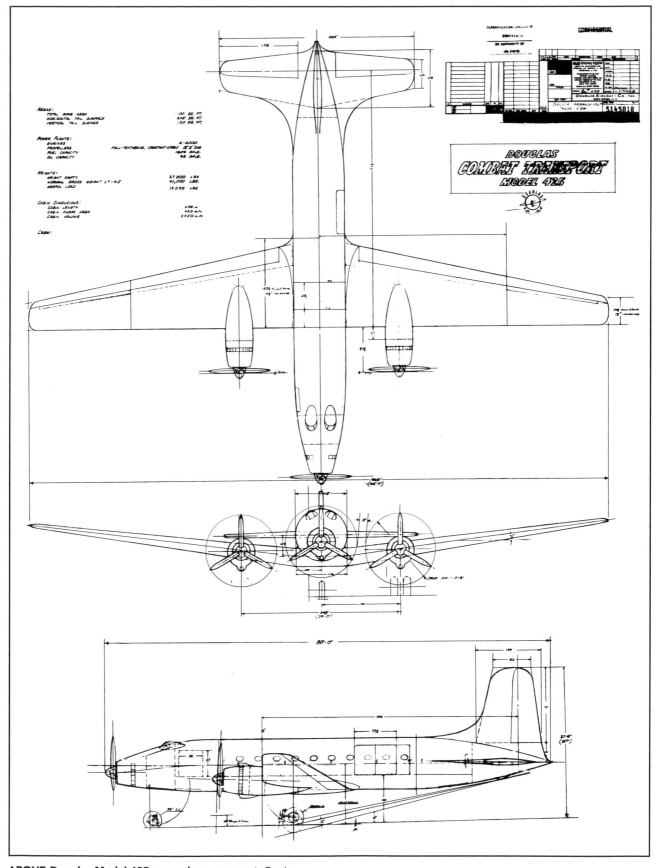

ABOVE Douglas Model 425 general arrangement. *Boeing*
OPPOSITE Douglas Model 410 general arrangement. *Boeing*

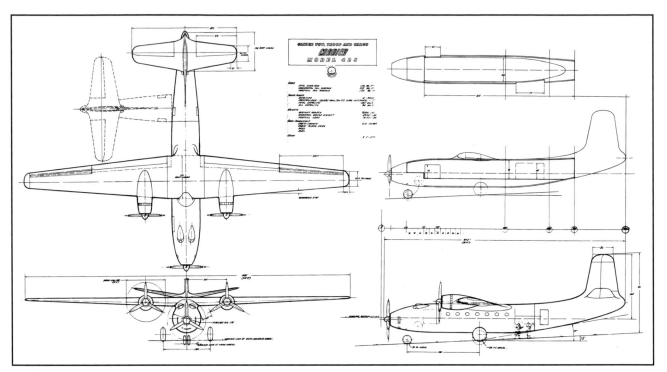

ABOVE The revised Douglas Model 425 (later redesignated as Model 458A) 'Cargo and Troop Carrier'. *Boeing*

BELOW Variations on a high-wing theme: applications of the Douglas Models 425 (three upper) and 410 (two lower) with different fuselage lengths and engine options, sketched on 2 November 1942. *Boeing*

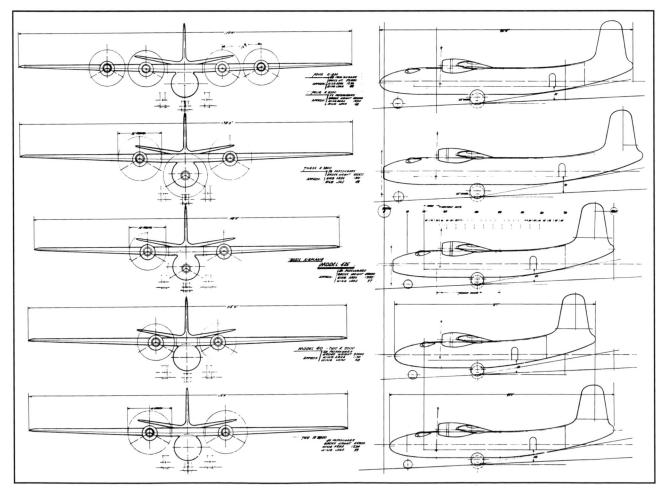

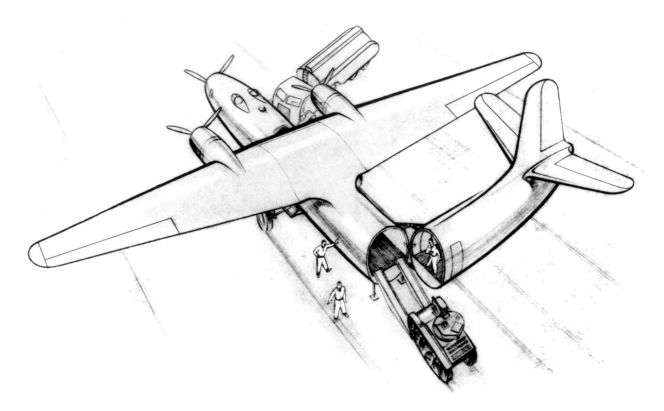

ABOVE The Douglas Model 458A with swing tail. *Boeing*

The cargo door arrangement remained the same with a large set of doors in the aft left fuselage, and a smaller upward-opening door on the forward right side. Later, the cargo doors were deleted when a swing tail/aft fuselage was devised. This version was later given the Model 458A designation, somewhat surprisingly placing it in a large family of pusher-propeller designs similar to – and evolving from – the XB-42 experimental bomber.

Other than the 'bug-eyed' cockpit arrangement, the overall appearance of the high wing aircraft was remarkably modern-looking, with many features that would become standard in latter-day transports. In particular, this was the first incidence of Douglas designing an aircraft with provisions to stretch it later in life. This would subsequently prove to be a key to the success of the company's airliners.

However, despite offering advantages over the adapted airliners that were being rapidly pressed into service, none of these proposals proceeded further. This was presumably because the marginal advantages that they offered did not warrant distracting the company from the more urgent task of mass-producing C-47s and C-54s (together with combat aircraft such as A-20s, A-26s and SBDs, plus licence-produced B-17s and B-24s).

The first purpose-designed US military transports

With the challenge of providing immediate airlift capability largely resolved, military thinking turned to a better long-term solution to the problem. In part, this was intended to overcome the limitations of using aircraft originally designed for other purposes, and was probably spurred by the thought of what might happen if the US lost Hawaii or if the UK was to fall. This was arguably the birth point of modern airlifter design.

However, during the first months of the war there was another consideration. With production of aircraft cranking up to unprecedented levels, there was concern about the supply of critical materials, especially light metal alloys. As a consequence, when in 1941 the War Department issued a requirement for a twin-engine transport aircraft, capable of carrying an 8,000lb payload and of being end-loaded from a truck, it also specified that it should be constructed from wood. Four manufacturers responded, including Curtiss and Fairchild. A further company came forward with another solution to the problem: namely, to build the aeroplane out of stainless steel.

Budd RB-1 Conestoga (C-93A)

Responding to the same projected aluminium shortage as Curtiss and Fairchild with their all-wood aircraft proposals, the Edward G Budd Manufacturing Company of Philadelphia came forward with a proposal to the Navy for a similar aircraft constructed of stainless steel. Although Budd had no record of aircraft construction, it was a well-established manufacturer of steel-clad railroad stock, and its proposed design appeared to show considerable merit.

As a consequence, the Bureau of Aeronautics (BuAer) placed a contract in August 1942 for 200 aircraft under the designation RB-1, and this was followed by an order from the AAF for a further 600 aircraft under the designation C-93A.

The first flight of the RB-1, dubbed the Conestoga, took place on 31 October 1943. The aircraft had many advanced features that included a high wing, a flight deck perched above the cargo area, and an integral electrically operated rear ramp that allowed drive-on access. However, its modern airframe design was not matched by a correspondingly high level of performance. It proved to have poor flying characteristics and its weight, which was 3,000lb (1,360kg) heavier than the C-47 (which had the same engines), had a marked effect on performance, particularly on range. In the meantime, the feared shortage of aluminium did not materialise. As a consequence, the Navy order was cut back to twenty-five aircraft and the Army Air Force order was cancelled. Seventeen RB-1s were eventually delivered to the Navy, but none ever saw service.

Curtiss CW-27 (YC-76)

The Curtiss Model CW-27 proposal was a conventionally configured, high-wing aircraft, powered by two Pratt &

Budd RB-1 (C-93)	
Powerplant	2 x P&W R-1830-92 piston radials @ 1,200hp (895kW)
Wingspan	100ft (30.50m)
Length	68ft (20.75m)
Height	31ft 9in (9.68m)
Wing area	1,400sq ft (130.2m²)
Empty weight	20,156lb (9,151kg)
Max TOW	33,860lb (15,370kg)
Payload	9,600lb (4,358kg) or 24 troops
Max speed	197mph (317km/h)
Cruise speed	165mph (265km/h)
Range	650mi (1,046km) at maximum gross weight

Whitney R-1830 radial engines. It had a tricycle landing gear, with the main wheels retracting into bays at the rear of the engine nacelles. The whole of the nose – including the landing wheel – was hinged on the right-hand side and could be swung open to allow loading at truck-bed height. The only unusual feature about the aircraft's appearance was the flight deck, which was raised above the rest of the fuselage to allow an unobstructed cargo bay.

The Army Air Force was sufficiently impressed to place a production order for the aircraft, starting with eleven test examples under the designation YC-76. The prototype, by now called the 'Caravan' within the company, flew on

ABOVE A profile view of the Budd RB-1 Conestoga. *US National Archives (NARA) via Dennis R. Jenkins*

1 January 1943, arguably making it the first-ever purpose-designed US military transport to fly. Tests, however, revealed numerous problems. Moreover, because laminated mahogany had been used for the construction, the aircraft was no lighter than either the C-46 or the C-47. Although all eleven YC-76s were completed, together with the first five C-76s, the War Department cancelled the contract on 3 August 1943, and no C-76 saw active service.

Curtiss YC-76	
Powerplant	2 x P&W R-1830-92 piston radials @ 1,200hp (895kW)
Wingspan	108.2ft (33.00m)
Length	70.8ft (21.60m)
Height	27.3ft (8.32m)
Wing area	1,560sq ft (145m²)
Empty weight	18,262lb (8,291kg)
Loaded weight	28,000lb (12,712kg)
Payload	9,700lb (4,404kg) or 23 troops
Max speed	192mph (309km/h)
Cruise speed	160mph (257km/h)
Range	750mi (1,207km)

OPPOSITE Navy RB-1 Conestoga general arrangement. *NARA via Dennis R. Jenkins*

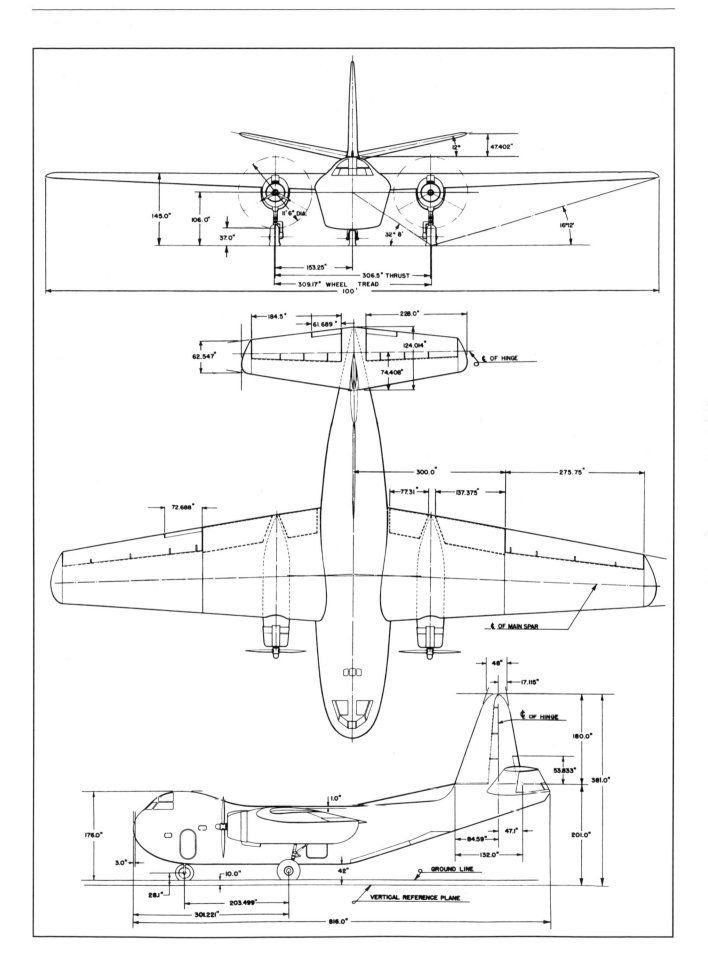

ABOVE A YC-76 is seen at Curtiss Wright's new St Louis factory with a C-46A in the background. After the war McDonnell would take over the factory complex, where it would build thousands of fighter aircraft. *San Diego Air and Space Museum*

Fairchild M-78 (C-82)

The Fairchild proposal enjoyed a much more successful future. The company opted for an unusual twin-boom configuration, and submitted its proposal, designated the Model 78, in November 1941. Early the following year it completed a mock-up, which was inspected by members of the AAF's Materiel Command, who were apparently impressed by the configuration's easily accessed rear-loading facility. However, by this time concerns about a potential alloy shortage had diminished and Fairchild was asked to redevelop the design as a metal aircraft, powered by more powerful Pratt & Whitney R-2800 engines, capable of lifting a payload of 23,600lb or 10,714kg (equivalent to that of the C-46).

BELOW A sketch layout of the wooden Fairchild C-82. *NASA*

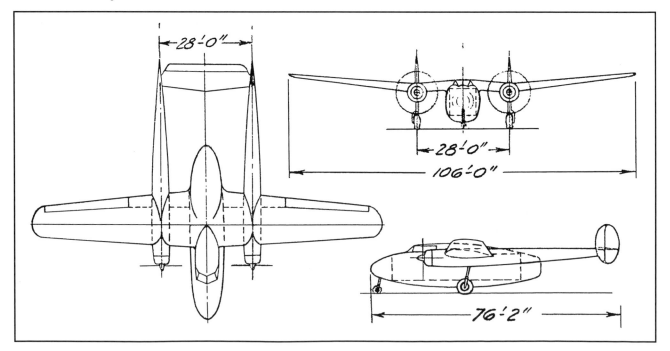

ABOVE This wind tunnel model of the early Fairchild C-82 design was tested at the NACA Langley Memorial Aeronautical Laboratory (LMAL). *NASA*

An order was placed for a prototype designated XC-82, which flew on 10 September 1944. Initial testing proved so successful that a second prototype was cancelled and an order placed for 100 aircraft, under the designation C-82A. It thus became the first aircraft specifically designed to carry troops and military cargo to enter volume production. Officially named the 'Packet', but more popularly known as the 'Flying Boxcar', the XC-82 flew with both names painted on its nose. The C-82A entered service shortly after the war had ended; however, far from having missed the boat, it was to play a significant future role in military transportation.

Fairchild C-82	M-78 (wood, 1942)	M-78 (metal, 1945)
Powerplant	2 x P&W R-2800-43 piston radials @ 2,000hp (1,491kW)	2 x P&W R-2800-85 piston radials @ 2,100hp (1,566kW)
Wingspan	106ft (32.31m)	106ft 6in (32.48m)
Length	76ft 2in (23.22m)	77ft 1in (23.51m)
Height	n/a	26ft 5in (3.50m)
Wing area	1,400sq ft (130.2m²)	1,400sq ft (130.2m²)
Max TOW.	40,000lb (18,1446kg)	54,000lb (24,516kg)
Payload	9,800lb (4,445kg)	42 troops or 18,000lb (8,172kg)
Max speed	217mph (349km/h)	250mph (402km/h)
Cruise speed	170mph (274km/h)	218mph (351km/h)
Range	3,140mi (5,053km)	2,140mi (3,443km)

RIGHT Paratroops jump from a Fairchild C-82A. Poor cockpit visibility in this nose-high attitude caused immediate safety complaints, and formation flights were restricted when dropping parachutists. This would result in the revised C-119 cockpit design. *US Air Force*

The quest for large, long-range airlift

With the growing need to supply and support forces fighting on different continents, attention inevitably turned to purpose-built, large-scale, long-range military transport aircraft. Boeing and Convair both responded by taking the wings, tail surfaces and powerplants of large bombers and marrying these to new fuselages. Douglas, with a strong base of existing transport aircraft, chose to build on its well-established transport designs, reworking them to larger sizes.

Boeing Models 367 (C-97) and 377

In 1942 Boeing started to develop a transport aircraft based on its B-29 bomber, which at that time was just about to fly. Known as the Model 367, the design took the wings, engines and tail surfaces

of the bomber and married them to a 'double-bubble' fuselage, with the lower fuselage taken from the B-29. Early the following year the Army ordered three prototypes as the XC-97, the first of which flew on 4 November 1944. During 1943, modified variants (primarily involving engine changes) were designated Models 367A to F. Boeing then adopted a revised designation system whereby the basic model number was followed by two sets of digits indicating engine selection and airframe configuration. Thus, the former Model 367B retroactively became the Model 367-3-3 with the installation of the R-4360 in place of the R-3350 engine.

The aircraft was too late to see service in the war, but in July 1945 the AAF ordered ten for service trials: six YC-97A cargo carriers, three YC-97B troop transporters, and a single YC-97C passenger aircraft. Meantime, Boeing had further developed the B-29 into the B-50, and a number of the improvements, including more powerful engines, were

incorporated in the transport aircraft. With these modifications, the C-97A was ordered into production by the newly formed USAF, entering service with MATS in early 1949.

Apart from serving in small numbers as a long-range strategic transport for the next thirteen years, the C-97 was to find its greatest success in forming the basis for Strategic Air Command's initial air-refuelling capability in the 1950s. Designated the KC-97 'Stratotanker', it would continue in this role until the 1960s.

Boeing XC-97A (Model 367-1-1)

Powerplant	4 x P&W R-4360-59B @ 3,500hp (2,610kW)
Wingspan	141ft 2.76in (43.08m)
Length	110ft 4in (33.65m)
Height	33ft 2.8in (11.66m)
Wing area	1,734sq ft (161m²)
Max TOW	175,000lb (79,450kg)
Payload	134 troops or 52,800lb (23,971kg)
Max speed	375mph (603km/h)
Cruise speed	300mph (483km/h)
Range	4,300mi (6,920km)

BELOW Boeing's C-97 concept depicted in service in the south-west Pacific. *Boeing*

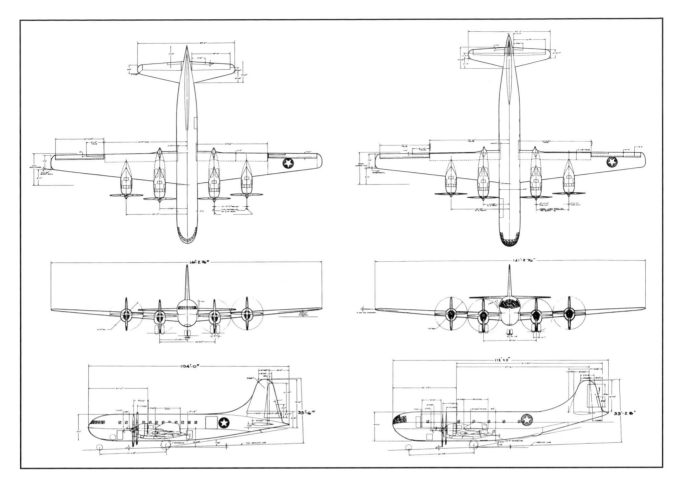

ABOVE The Boeing 367-2 (left) was intended as a passenger transport and did not have the raised aft fuselage and cargo loading ramp as did the 367-3 model, which also retained the B-29-style cockpit transparencies. *Boeing*

BELOW The third Boeing XC-97 is seen in flight, powered by Wright R-3350 engines as used on the B-29. The engine type was changed to the R-4360 with the first YC-97A. *G. H. Balzer collection*

ABOVE This image of an Army truck gingerly backing its way into the first Boeing XC-97 points out a shortcoming of the design – the awkward and difficult ramp angle is forced by the low door frame height, which in turn is due to structural considerations.
G. H. Balzer collection

The commercial adaptation of the Model 367 was offered to the airlines as the Boeing Model 377 'Stratocruiser'. The aircraft was structurally similar to the YC-97 (indeed, it was the eleventh aircraft diverted from the YC-97 production line), but had a completely redesigned interior. Fifty-five of these aeroplanes were sold to Pan Am, BOAC and Scandinavian Airlines. As such, it became the first US transport designed for military use to find a successful place in the commercial market – a reversal of the earlier norm.

Douglas Model 415/415A (C-74 Globemaster)

With the Douglas C-54 having been pressed into service to give the Army a long-range high-speed transportation

capability, it is hardly surprising that the War Department would be receptive to a scaled-up version of the aircraft that could carry a much heavier payload.

The earliest known Douglas Model 415 drawings date from mid-January 1942, scarcely six weeks after the Japanese attack on Pearl Harbor. The design appears to be an amalgam of features from the Model 400/410/425 family of transports including the tail design, and the Model 423 very heavy bomber design (from late October 1941), with which it shared a common wing planform and size as well as the proposed Pratt & Whitney 'X-Wasp' 3,000hp (2,240kW) engine.

Douglas's January 1942 proposal met with resistance from the Army Air

Corps. While the cargo capability was impressive (two T9E1 tanks, or two 105mm Howitzers, or two angle dozers, or three disassembled P-40 Warhawks), the projected cost was correspondingly very high: $5 million for one aircraft or $1 million each for a production quantity of 150, less government furnished equipment (GFE), such as engines. It was quickly made clear that even in wartime the Army Air Force was not prepared to pay this cost. The reasons for such a high price estimate are unknown; perhaps it was related to the expense of building a new facility large enough to manufacture the aircraft with its wingspan of 207ft (63.14m), which would need to be amortised against the production run.

ABOVE The first Douglas C-74 sits on the tarmac at Clover Field, Santa Monica. *Boeing*

Douglas returned to Washington in February 1942 to brief a revised proposal, the Model 415A. While the fuselage was generally the same as earlier, the wing with its smaller span of 173ft (52.84m) had about 85% of the area of the previous one, and the projected gross weight was reduced by 33%. Wright R-3350 Duplex Cyclones were introduced in place of the previously proposed Pratt & Whitney 'X-Wasps'. The R-3350, already in advanced high-priority development for the Boeing B-29, offered earlier availability. An alternative layout was also offered with six unspecified engines (possibly the Pratt & Whitney R-2800, six of which would have yielded the same aggregate power as the four R-3350s). Unit cost was projected to be $500,000 each for a production run of 300, or $900,000 each for a quantity of fifty (in each case, less GFE).

This revision met with approval and Douglas was issued a letter of intent in March 1942, which enabled the company to start detailed work. The airframe design process was generally complete when the Pratt & Whitney 'X-Wasp', now under procurement for the AAF and designated the R-4360, replaced the Wright R-3350 in April 1943 (the Allison V-3420 was also studied as an option but not adopted). This engine change caused disruption as it required the redesign of the nacelle, wing and ancillary structures. The nearly complete engineering for the project was transferred from the Douglas Santa Monica facility to the new Long Beach factory in early March 1944 to start manufacture. Delayed by higher engineering priorities (XB-42 and XB-43) and manufacturing demands (A-26), the first flight did not take place until 5 September 1945 and, with the war's end, the contract was curtailed; only fourteen aircraft were completed. In retrospect that decision might have proved unfortunate because the eleven aircraft that went into service with the Army Air Force

(soon to be become the USAF, and transferred to MATS on its creation) were to prove highly valuable in both the Berlin Airlift and Korean War.

Potential airline application had figured large in Douglas's thinking from the outset, although work had been sidelined by the war effort. Indeed, potential airline interests had also been recognised in Douglas's Detail Specification DS-448 issued 11 May 1942. Later, the airline specification of the Model 415 was updated, both to incorporate the R-4360 engine and to accommodate Pan Am's particular wishes. These changes were embodied in DS-471, which was issued on 4 May 1944 specifying the Douglas Model 'DC-7-471'. It outlined a pressurised, 108-passenger 'day plane' version of the C-74. However, with the economies of scale eliminated when C-74 production was subsequently curtailed in the post-war era, the costs rose beyond what Pan Am was prepared to pay and the design was quietly dropped.

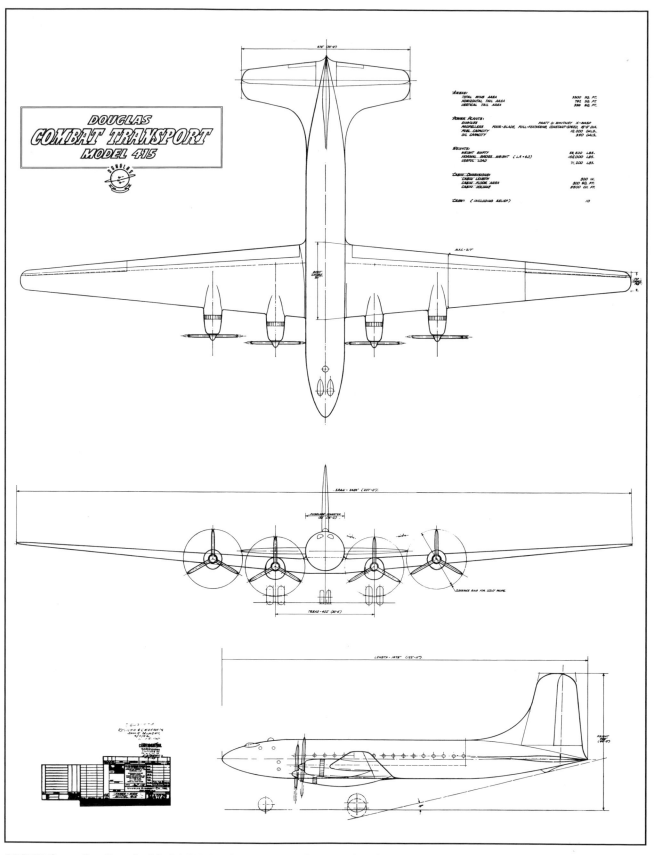

ABOVE The earliest Douglas Model 415 Combat Transport drawing, dated 19 January 1942. The wingspan was set at 207ft (63.14m). *Boeing*

OPPOSITE A Douglas draft drawing for a Model 415 with six engines (believed to be R-2800s). *Boeing*

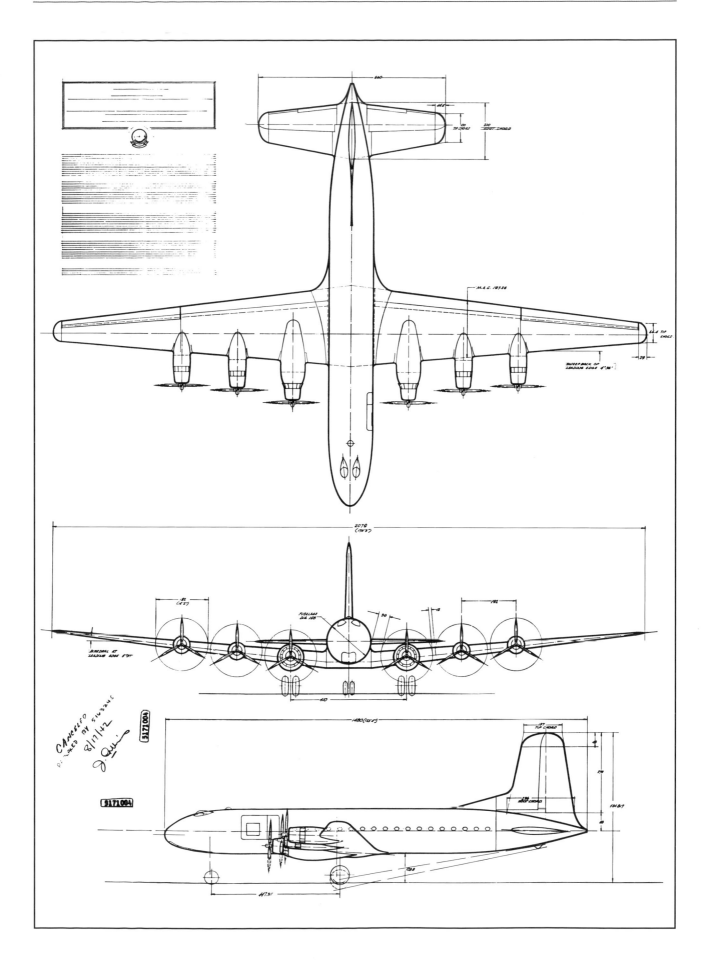

Douglas C-74 development	Model 415 (Jan 1942)	Model 415A (Feb 1942)	Model 415A (1945)
Powerplant	4 x P&W 'X-Wasp'* radials @ 3,000hp (2,240kW)	4 x Wright R-3350-31 radials @ 2,200hp (1,641kw)	4 x P&W R-4360-27 radials @ 3,000hp (2,240kW)
Wingspan	207ft (63.14m)	173ft 3in (52.84m)	173ft 3in (52.84m)
Length	122ft 11in (37.47m)	120ft 10in (36.83m)	124ft 2in (37.87m)
Height	46ft 3 in (14.10m)	39ft 10in (12.14m)	43ft 8.8in (13.30m)
Wing area	3,300sq ft (306.6m²)	2,500sq ft (232.3 m²)	2,510sq ft (233m²)
Max TOW	165,000lb (74,900kg)	125,000lb (56,699kg)	165,000lb (74,900kg)
Max payload	54,200lb (24,585kg)	52,082lb (23,624kg)	125 troops or 48,150lb (21,860kg)
Max speed	278mph (447km/h)		312mph (502km/h)
Cruise speed	235mph (378km/h)		260mph (418km/h)
Max range	6500mi (10,461km)		7,200mi (11,580km)

* Known temporarily as the 'X-Wasp', the R-4360 did not receive its military designation until 1 March 1942.

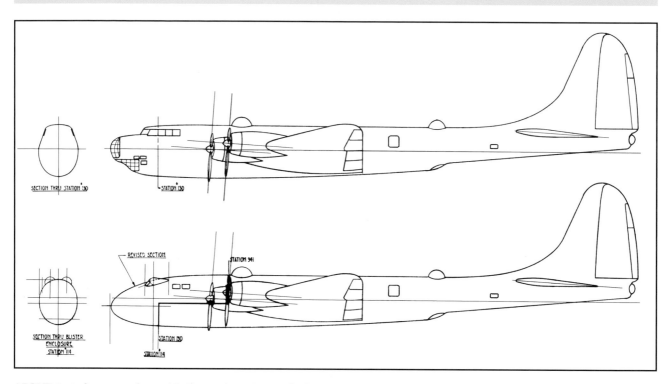

ABOVE A study was performed in September 1942 to fit the proposed Douglas C-74 'bug-eyed' cockpit and nose section to the Douglas XB-19 as a flying test bed. Instead, the XB-19 was diverted to flight test the Allison V-3420 engine as an alternative to the R-3350, which was experiencing major difficulties on the B-29. *Boeing*

LEFT The 'bug-eyed' canopies were a distinctive feature of the Douglas C-74 but proved to be impractical. *Boeing*

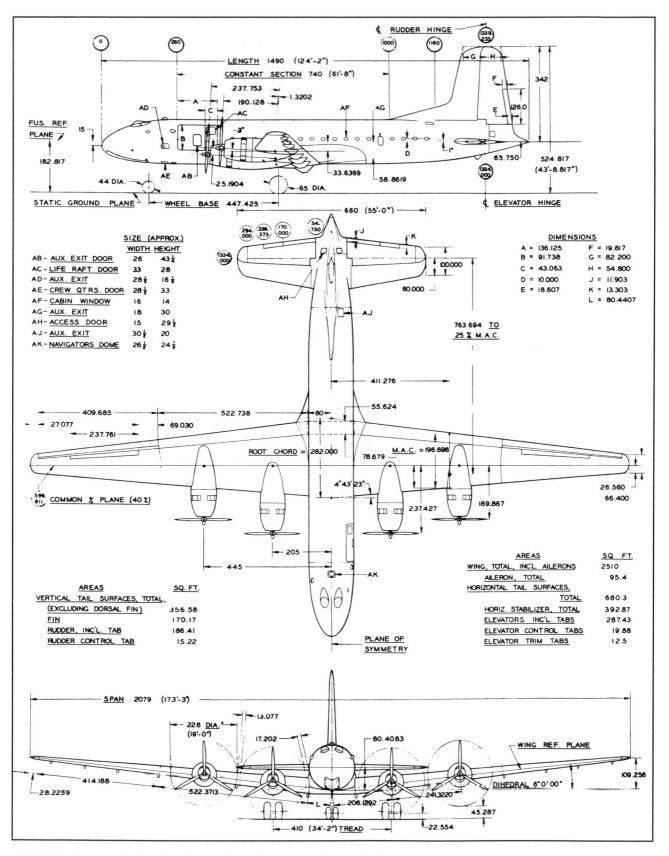

ABOVE The Douglas Model 415A (C-74A Globemaster) as built in 1945. *Boeing*

Ultra-large airlifters

While the Army moved quickly to obtain what was a scaled-up development of the C-54, its requirement for a new large transport aircraft also resulted in proposals from numerous other aircraft manufacturers. This undoubtedly suited the military, for it wanted to preserve a broad-based manufacturing capability and promote competition. In an era before the introduction of more formalised definitions of requirements and requests for proposals, the outcome was a plethora of ad hoc submissions. Not surprisingly, some of these concentrated on scaling up earlier designs or on exploiting technology that had been developed for bombers. For example, why not take the wings, engines and tail surfaces from the most advanced bomber under development at the time, the massive B-36, and marry them to a fuselage specifically designed for military transportation?

Convair XC-99

In 1942 the Consolidated Vultee Aircraft Corporation (subsequently Convair) was engaged in the design of the XB-36 'Intercontinental Bomber', an aircraft of a size, payload and range way beyond that of any existing bomber. Given its load-carrying potential, the Army Air Force (AAF) placed an order with the company to develop a transport variant using the same wings, engines and tail surfaces, assigning it the XC-99 military designation.

Initially the Model 36, as it was known within the company, had a slender double-deck fuselage with twin vertical stabilisers. However, by October 1942 changes were made in parallel with improvements in the design of the XB-36, including a new single tail. This was sufficiently different to merit a new Convair designation, the Model 37.

Although work continued throughout the war, going through detailed design into prototype construction, other priorities meant that the aircraft did not fly until 23 November 1947. The XC-99 was capable of carrying 400 troops or 100,000lb (45,359kg) of cargo. However, by the time it flew the Air Force's

Convair XC-99	
Powerplant	(6 x) P&W R-4360-41 piston radials @ 3,500hp (2,610kW)
Wingspan	230ft (70.15m)
Length	182ft 6in (55.66m)
Height	57ft 9in (17.60m)
Wing area	4,772sq ft (444m²)
Max TOW	220,000lb (99,790kg)
Payload	100,000lb (45,359kg) or 400 troops
Max speed	307mph (494km/h)
Cruise speed	240mph (386km/h)
Max range	8,100mi (13,033km)

BELOW The revised Convair Model 37 transport design based on the B-36 bomber.
San Diego Air and Space Museum

MODEL
37
CONSOLIDATED AIRCRAFT CORPORATION
SAN DIEGO, CALIFORNIA
PHOTO NO. 13744   DRG. NO. 37 Z 010

10-8-42

ABOVE The sole Convair XC-99 is seen at the mid-point of its service, assigned to the San Antonio Air Materiel Area. Open belly hatches can be seen at the bottom of the fuselage. *Terry Panopalis Collection*

requirements were either already being served or likely to be met by other aircraft, at lower cost and requiring less operational support and smaller airfields. Nonetheless, the sole example was accepted by the Air Force on 26 May 1949, entering service with the Strategic Air Command. It was transferred to the Air Materiel Command on 20 September 1950 and served until being retired in 1957, as the B-36 was also being phased out of service.

Kaiser Cargo flying wing

One of the few, wholly new designs to be put forward during the war was submitted by Kaiser Cargo, which proposed a massive, highly innovative flying wing transport. Its impressive set of (claimed) performance criteria included extreme long range and a remarkably low stalling speed when fully loaded of just 78mph (125km/h). The only obvious drawback to the configuration was the very restricted view from the flight deck, which was sandwiched between the two inner engines. Less obvious but quite open to question was the suitability of the unproven flying wing design without any sweepback to give longitudinal stability.

Kaiser Cargo flying wing	
Powerplant	4 x P&W R-2800-2SC13-6 piston radials @ 2,100hp (1,566kW)
Wingspan	290ft (88.45m)
Length	58ft (17.68m)
Height	25ft (7.62m)
Wing area	7,920sq ft (735.8m²)
Gross weight	175,000lb (79,450kg)
Max speed	219 mph (352km/h) at sea level or 228mph (367km/h) at 16,000ft (4,992m)
Payload	75,600lb (34,292kg) with 1,000mi (1,609km) range
Ferry range	8,400mi (13,516km)

BELOW An early low-fidelity free-flight spin test model of the Kaiser Cargo flying wing shows the original tip-fin configuration. *NASA*

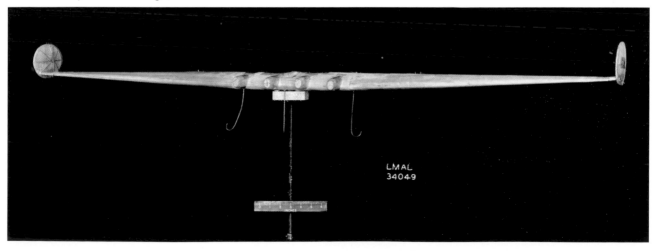

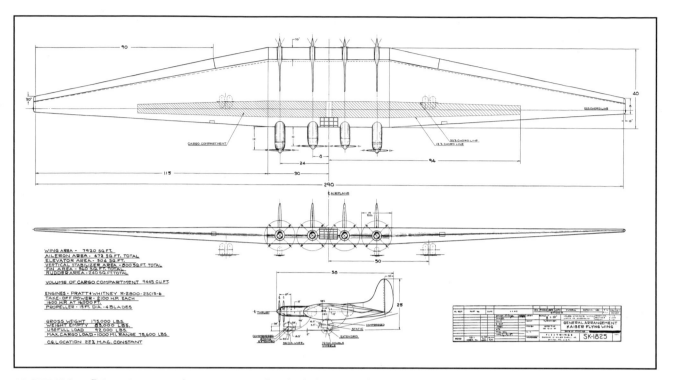

ABOVE Kaiser flying wing general arrangement. The shaded area on the drawing indicates the span-wise cargo compartment. *NARA II*

BELOW A sketch of cargo loading in the Kaiser flying wing. One difficulty was that the cargo (including trucks and artillery) had to turn 90° from entry to the span-wise cargo compartment. *NARA II*

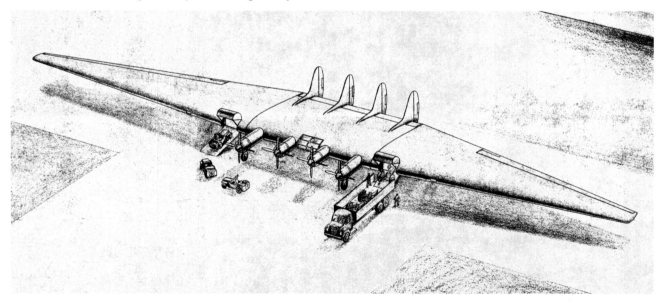

Extensive wind tunnel tests were carried out at NACA's facilities at Langley Memorial Aeronautical Laboratory. The initial configuration, with vertical fins mounted at the wingtips, was discarded and replaced by several different vertical tail sizes attached to the trailing edge of the wing. Eventually, a departure from a pure flying wing configuration was trialled using twin booms to support the twin vertical fins and a horizontal stabiliser. It was a bold proposition but nothing came of it beyond laboratory experiments.

OPPOSITE TOP A large scale model of the Kaiser Cargo flying wing was tested for several years in the NACA wind tunnel complex at the Langley Memorial Aeronautical Laboratory. *NASA*

OPPOSITE BOTTOM Although full-scale development of the Kaiser Cargo Flying Wing was never undertaken, the wind tunnel testing continued for several years, providing useful data. Most of the variation was in the placement of the vertical stabilisers from the wingtip to the wing trailing edge, and ultimately on tailbooms. *NASA*

FILE CARD

NACA
LMAL 42806

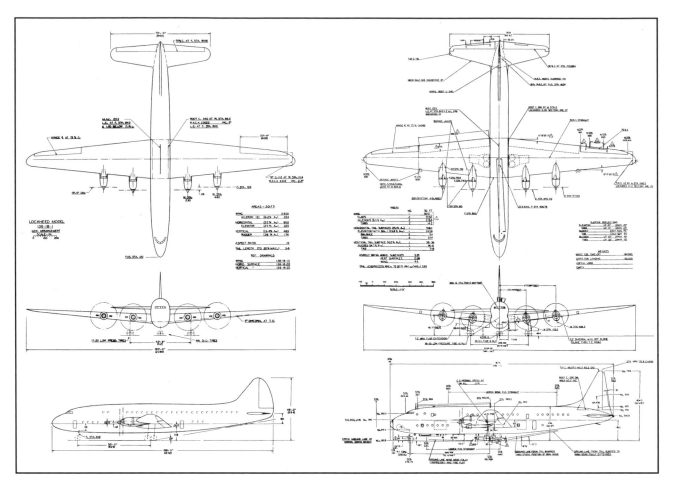

Lockheed Model 89 (XR6O-1/XR6V-1)

Lockheed used its airliner design experience to produce a huge conventional commercial/military aircraft with a double-deck fuselage. This had started out as a joint Navy/Lockheed/Pan Am study in 1942, initially under the designation L-089. Two examples flew successfully as the XR6O-1 Constitution (later redesignated XR6V-1 when the Navy code letter for Lockheed was changed from 'O' to 'V').

The wings retained the overall planform of the smaller C-69 Constellation, but the double-decked fuselage lacked the latter's graceful lines (which, incidentally were designed not for their aesthetic appeal but for aerodynamic considerations and had a triple tail simply to reduce fin height and enable the aircraft to fit existing hangars). Nonetheless, it was an impressive and good-looking aeroplane, and flew on 9 November 1946.

ABOVE The initial L-089 Constitution design on the left, and the aircraft as built on the right. *Lockheed*

BELOW This Lockheed comparison of fuselage cross sections explained how the 'double bubble' fuselage made for an efficient airliner. Conversely, it also showed why the enormous Constitution (like the XC-99) made a poor outsized cargo carrier as it lacked the absolute cross section needed for this mission. *Lockheed*

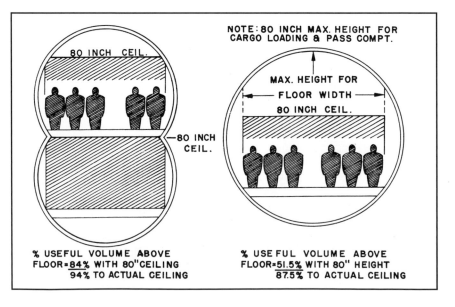

ABOVE The first XR6V-1 is posed near the Lockheed facility at Burbank Airport.
Lockheed

Lockheed Model 89 (XR6O-1, later XR6V-1) Constitution	
Powerplant	4 x P&W 4360-22W piston radials @ 3,500hp (2,610kW)
Wingspan	189ft 1in (57.67m)
Length	156ft 8in (47.78m)
Height	50ft 4.5 in (15.4m)
Wing area	3,610sq ft (3335m²)
Max TOW	184,000lb (83,536kg)
Payload	69,425lb (31,519kg) or 204 troops
Max cruise speed	269mph (433km/h)
Range	5,390mi (8,673km)

However, the Constitution was short on power for its size. It was reported to have been designed to accept engines up to 5,000hp (3,728kw), but unfortunately none were to become available until after the aircraft was already obsolete. It was further hobbled by a nacelle design that caused poor engine cooling; flying with the cowling flaps fully open to reduce engine temperatures increased drag and reduced range. No production contract ever followed the construction of the two prototypes.

1945 heavy troop carrier and heavy cargo aircraft

In 1945 the War Department solicited a number of aircraft manufacturers to start work on two new types of aeroplanes for the Troop Carrier Command; between them they were to provide the capability of moving an entire army division, including its mechanised equipment. The bulk of the work would be done by the smaller of the two aircraft, which would consequently be produced in larger numbers, with the other aircraft being looked upon to transport heavier items of equipment.

The smaller of the two aircraft would be required to carry a load of 50,000lb (22,700kg) over a radius of 1,000 miles (1,609km), the larger to carry up to twice that weight. Particular

attention was paid to the required load handling facilities, with a cargo floor just 41in (104cm) from the ground reached by a self-contained ramp so that motorised vehicles could be loaded under their own power. The aircraft was also required to have good low-speed handling characteristics and to be equipped to carry paratroopers, airborne troops and casualties. It was further required to carry armour protection for the crew and to have self-sealing fuel tanks, the first time that such capabilities had ever been specified for a cargo aircraft.

The heavier of the two new aeroplanes was required to have a capacity of 70,000lb to 100,000lb (31,780kg to 45,359kg). This would enable it to carry equipment, such as a medium tank, that was too heavy for the lighter aircraft. This necessitated an aircraft with a design gross weight of between 240,000lb and 270,000lb

(108,960kg and 122,580kg). Size and weight aside, the requirements were substantially the same for both aircraft.

Boeing and Douglas were solicited for designs for the larger aircraft, though no details could be found of the Boeing proposal, other than the fact that it was assigned the Model Number 456 on 4 December 1945.

Fairchild and Martin were approached for the smaller aircraft. Fairchild detailed four M-99 variants, the M-99-01 to 04. Updated versions – respectively designated the M-99-05 to 08 – were proposed in 1946 and are covered in Chapter Four.

Douglas (Long Beach) Model 1008 heavy transport

Drawings dated 30 August 1945 reveal the Douglas Model 1008 to be a most unusual aircraft. The wing and empennage configuration was completely conventional. Indeed, the wings and large elements of the fuselage were taken from the C-74. What was anything but conventional was the arrangement of the engines. To allow both a low-set wing (with the wing carry-though box beneath the cargo floor) and minimum ground clearance for the fuselage, the four R4360 engines were removed from the wings.

They were replaced by four Allison V-3420 engines, two of which were accommodated in the lower front fuselage in an 'engine room' and two mounted in another compartment in the upper aft fuselage. The V-3420 was a high-power 24-cylinder engine essentially formed by mating two V-1710 engines to a common crankshaft. It was intended to power various proposed aircraft including experimental fighters and bombers. Since none of these proposals ever went beyond the prototype stage, the engine was never produced in numbers. Each pair of V-3420s was to drive a set of counter-rotating propellers in the nose and tail respectively.

The rear arrangement was reminiscent of the dual pusher-prop

Douglas Model 1008	
Powerplant	4 x Allison V-3420 pistons @ 2,600hp (1,940kW)
Wingspan	173ft 4in (52.87m)
Length	137ft 2in (41.83m)
Height	48ft 8in (14.83m)

configuration of the Douglas XB-42 bomber, which had flown on 6 May the previous year and was an example of the company's willingness to try innovative approaches to aircraft design.

Fairchild heavy transport

Little is known of Fairchild's very large airlifter design other than views in the 'Ornamental Design' patent filed by Armand Thieblot of Fairchild on 8 November 1946. Based on the evidence that was submitted, the aircraft was perhaps designed for the very heavy payload mission, using the general C-82 layout. The counter-rotating propeller installation suggests the use of Pratt & Whitney R-4360 engines (other users of

BELOW The Douglas Model 1008, a reconfigured C-74. *Boeing*

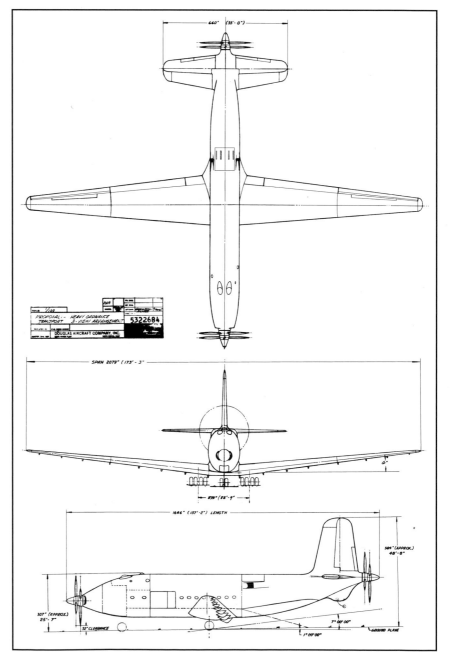

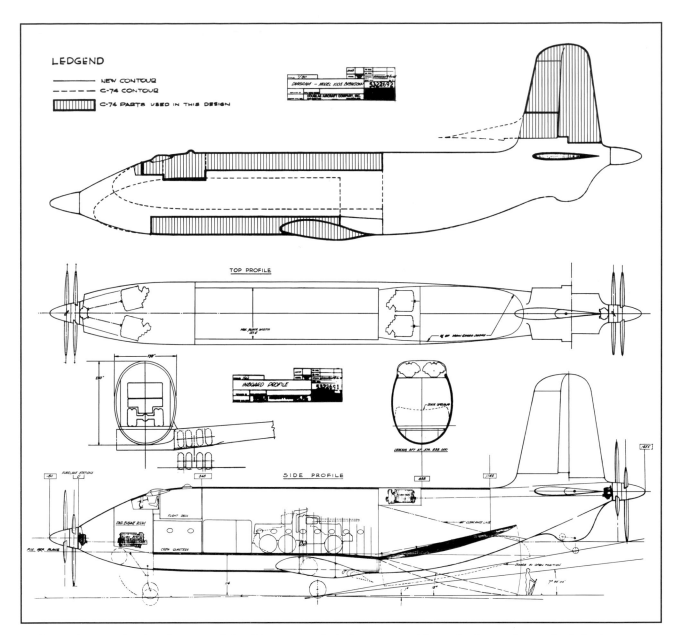

ABOVE A diagram showing the reuse of the C-74 structure including upper and lower fuselage, wings and tail. *Boeing*

the engine/propeller combination being the Boeing XF8B-1, Douglas XTB2D-1 Skypirate, Hughes XF-11 and Northrop XB-35), although the intended use of the Wright XR-3350-16 cannot be completely discounted. The power supplied by six engines in this class would be sufficient for an airframe grossing approximately 250,000 to 280,000lb (113,500 to 127,100kg).

RIGHT Drawings from the 'Ornamental Design' patent assigned to Fairchild's Chief Engineer, Armand Thieblot, in 1946. *USPTO*

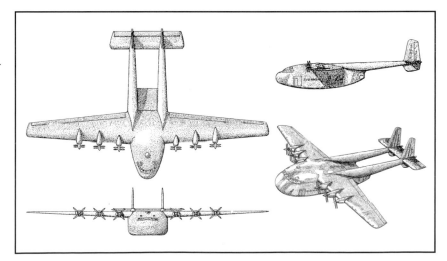

Martin Model 229 heavy transport

When it first flew in July 1942, the Martin Model 170 had been the world's largest flying boat, and the following year it became the largest flying boat ever to enter service with the US Navy. Originally designed as a patrol bomber, it was subsequently decided to convert it into a transport aircraft and, its capability in this role having been demonstrated, a production order was placed under the designation JRM-1 Mars. The end of the war came after only five aircraft had been delivered. However, when the Army Air Force issued Specification R-1800-E on 13 March 1945 calling for a multi-engine, medium-range, heavy cargo and troop carrier, it was inevitable that the Glenn L. Martin Co should put forward what was essentially a land-based version of the Mars.

To be powered by four Wright R-3350-C18C5 radial engines, the Model 229 was of a similar conventional configuration to the earlier flying boat, marrying the wings and tail surfaces to a new fuselage with large swinging-nose cargo access at the front.

Given the already proven performance of the Mars, it must have made an appealing offering, but no

production order was forthcoming. In retrospect this might have been a missed opportunity: the capability and the quality of the Mars airframe was demonstrated by the fact that one of the original aircraft was still flying and performing outstanding service as a water-bomber some seventy years later.

Although Boeing, Douglas, Fairchild, Lockheed and Martin had all responded with proposals that, at least on paper, met the stipulated requirements, the Army chose not to pursue any of the designs for a radical new cargo aircraft. The end of the war had reduced both the pressure and the money to fund such an aircraft and, while the existing transport fleet had its drawbacks, there was a surfeit in terms of numbers. Recognising that problem, Gen 'Hap' Arnold directed on 27 August 1945 that the AAF should reduce transport procurement to the absolute minimum for development purposes.

Martin Model 299

Martin Model 299	
Powerplant	4 x Wright R-3350-C18C5 piston radials @ 2,700hp (2,014kW)
Wingspan	200ft (61m)
Length	119.6ft (36.50m)
Height	46.5ft (14.20m)
Wing area	3,686sq ft (331.8m²)
Max TOW	150,000lb (68,100kg)
Payload	40,000lb (18,160kg)
Max speed	237mph (381km/h) at 6,200ft (1,891m)
Cruise speed	156 mph (251km/h) at 5,000ft (1,525m)
Range	3,038mi (4,888km)

BELOW A sketch of the Martin Model 229. *NARA II*

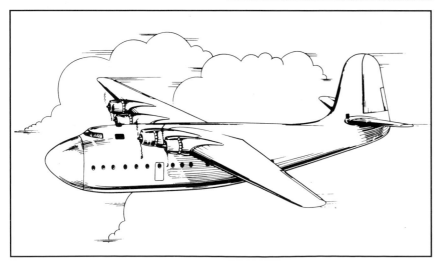

Second World War developments in perspective

The Second World War had emphasised the importance of military airlift, both to support assault forces and to maintain and supply armies fighting thousands of miles from home. At the outset the US Army's airlift capability was very limited, but this was transformed over little more than three years. What made this possible was the advanced state of American civil aviation in the period immediately preceding hostilities, together with the huge industrial infrastructure of the US.

The militarised versions of the Douglas DC-3 (C-47), DC-4 (C-54) and Curtiss CW-20 (C-46) were produced in vast numbers and played a major part in the war effort. However, they also showed that aircraft designed for passenger transport had limitations when it came to many aspects of military use. Their cargo holds were not designed for bulky loads; they were not intended for operation from semi-prepared airstrips; little thought had been given to facilities for rapid loading and unloading; and they were simply not big enough.

The war stimulated much effort into bespoke designs that would overcome these deficiencies, but hostilities ended before any of these projects reached fruition, at least as far as big, strategic transports were concerned. A handful reached the prototype stage in the early post-war years. A single Convair XC-99, two Lockheed R6Vs and fourteen Douglas C-74s were completed, and all flew, seeing (limited) military service. These 'supersized' transports were built with military funds but were developed and marketed with an eye to the post-war civil market; none of them adapted to the military mission particularly well. The Army Air Force also had large fleets of medium size transports (C-46s, C-47s and C-54s) that simply could not be scrapped to make way for new aircraft.

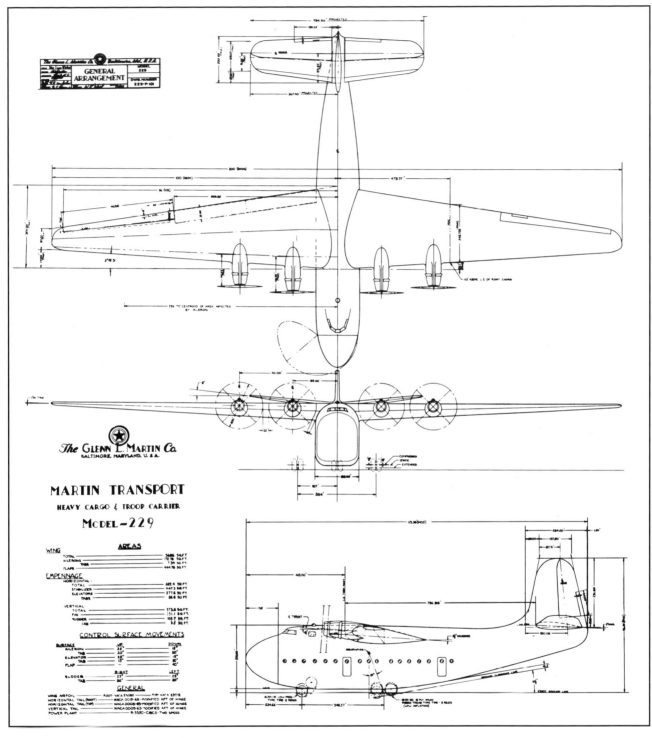

ABOVE Martin Model 229 general arrangement. *NARA II*

The same was not true at the tactical end of the scale, as the war saw the emergence of the Fairchild C-82, which achieved the distinction of being the first mass-produced transport designed from the outset for military purposes.

Apart from the inevitable accelerated advances in technology, the war had two outcomes that would have an important bearing on the future of military air transportation. First, it increased immeasurably the Army's understanding of the power and nature of airlift; second, thanks to the wartime production of bombers as well as transports, it created an industry well-versed in the manufacture of large aeroplanes.

What could not be seen with the ending of the war, with all its hopes for a more peaceful world, was that these attributes would soon assume major importance.

Chapter Four
Learning the Lessons of War

1945 to 1950:
Overcoming the limitations of converted airliners

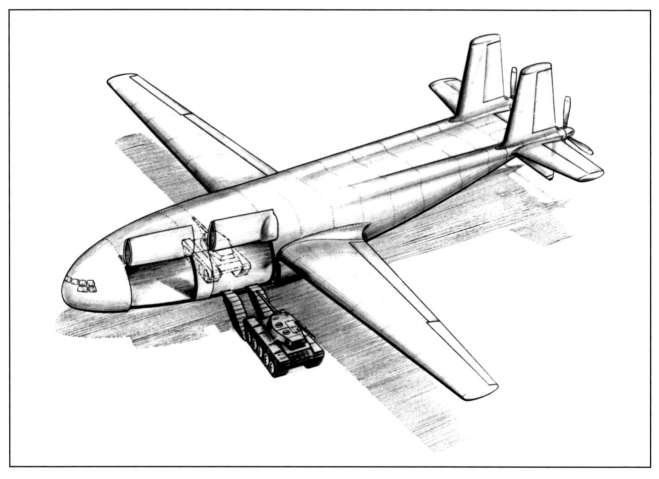

ABOVE The Douglas Model 1105A-T side-loading heavy airlifter design of June 1947, with four buried piston engines driving twin propellers through long extension shafts. *Boeing*

While none of the wartime design efforts resulted in a new transport aircraft that would see service before the war ended, that is not to say that these efforts were wasted. The lessons learned would form the basis for the future development of military airlift.

An informative and fascinating insight into the USAAF's early post-war thinking and plans for the future of air transportation appeared in a lecture given in June 1946 by its New Development Division. Titled 'ND54 –

New Special Aircraft', it covered transport, gliders and liaison aeroplanes, describing several types currently under development, together with the rationale behind the requirements that they were intended to fulfil.

In some aspects, such as describing the features of aircraft like the Chase XC-122 and the Convair XC-99, the lecture was highly detailed and specific. In others, such as designs for aircraft to operate out of short, hastily prepared airstrips, it was remarkably candid in

admitting that the Army did not yet have the answers. Overall, there was recognition that, although the future may not be clear, projection of military power was going to require a much more advanced capability than had been available during the Second World War:

ABOVE XCG-17 (the glider conversion of the Douglas C-47) glides in for landing in February 1945. The engines and propellers have been replaced by aerodynamic fairings. *Boeing*

'It is apparent when looking back to the recent war that, although airplanes such as the C-46 and C-47 performed outstanding service in all theatres and that the C-82 and C-97 airplanes can continue this service, the use of such airplanes does not allow air power to be used to the extent of its capabilities when advanced designs are considered. In advanced designs it will be necessary to consider as yet unthought-of features to enable airplanes to be used to the utmost of their capabilities and to increasing the flexibility of their use.'

In the aftermath of the war aircraft manufacturers were able to turn their attention to a new generation of transportation aircraft, freed from the need to keep improving and producing existing aeroplanes under pressure. It meant that the Army could reflect on its needs, and that the companies could contemplate new designs free of concerns about whether the proposals could be rushed into production.

The five years following the end of the war saw a mixture of formal and informal competitions to select and acquire new military transport aircraft, together with numerous unsolicited submissions from manufacturers. Looking at the many design proposals of the time, it is not always easy to see where they fitted into the process. However, while the path of progress took many twists, and went up the occasional cul-de-sac, it nevertheless moved forward significantly. In all, it was an important period in aviation history, representing a major transition in both military thinking and aircraft design philosophy.

Cargo gliders

From today's standpoint, it is easy to overlook the part that gliders played in the mind of military planners in the aftermath of the war.

The use of gliders had proved effective in rapid assault situations; it was a role for which they had been employed by both German and Allied forces. Their main advantage was the capacity to deliver troops and equipment within a concentrated area, ready for action rather than being spread out, which was the inevitable result of mass parachute dropping, particularly in high winds. It is reported that in the air invasion of Sicily the troops were so scattered that it took a week for some of them to reach the designated assembly point.

As the war progressed, the Army Air Force also explored further possible uses for gliders, taking advantage of the increased towing power available from the Douglas C-54. In mid-1944 it converted a C-47 transport into a glider by removing the engines and stripping out all related equipment. The nacelles themselves were retained to accommodate the retractable landing gear, but their cowlings were replaced with streamlined fairings. Ballast weights were added to compensate for the removed powerplants and to keep the centre of gravity within flight limits.

The XCG-17, as it became known, first flew on 14 June 1944. The tests involved various towing arrangements, including using dual C-47s with one releasing the tow after take-off. The latter must have proved quite a demanding procedure, and the eventual preferred solution was to use a single C-54.

Part of the objective was to produce a glider that could not only be used as an assault aircraft but could also increase the available capacity to carry supplies 'over the hump' to China. To this end the XCG-17 could carry a much higher payload than any of the conventional gliders. Also, being more aerodynamically efficient, it could be towed at far higher speeds.

Tests went well. However, despite having a low approach speed and a shallow glide angle, the XCG-17 proved unsuitable for landing in unprepared fields, which ruled out its use as an assault glider. Moreover, while it was undergoing trials, the need for additional capacity to supply forces in China had diminished. The project was therefore terminated; the test aircraft had its engines reinstalled and was returned to its original role.

Douglas XCG-17 cargo glider	
Wingspan	95ft 6in (29.11m)
Length	63ft 9in (19.43m)
Height	17ft (5.20m)
Wing area	987sq ft (91.70m²)
Max TOW	26,000lb (11,790kg)
Payload	15,000lb (6,800kg)
Max tow speed	290mph (467k/h)

Glider requirements in the post-war era

As the war came to a conclusion and planners turned to future military capability, gliders still figured prominently in the Army's thinking. Indeed, their future use was seen as much more ambitious than their earlier deployment. Since the new gliders were not being produced for any specific conflict or combat theatre, they would have to be capable of being stored and maintained. This would require the wood-and-fabric construction used earlier to be replaced by either a metal monocoque airframe or welded tubing with a metal covering.

The Army also wanted its future gliders designed for longer flights. In this context it should be remembered that when a glider is on tow, the linking cable supplies the necessary forward

	Desired	Acceptable
Maximum tow speed	190mph (306km/h)	180mph (290km/h)
Stalling speed, with flaps	55mph (89km/h)	65mph (105km/h)
Maximum sink rate at 70-90mph (113 to 145km/h)	1,750ft/min (534m/min)	1,500ft/min (458m/min)
Landing roll on a hard surface	250ft (76m)	500ft (153m)

speed, but it does not provide any directional stability; the glider has to be actively flown in close formation with its tug aircraft for the flight's entire duration, demanding continuous concentration by the pilot. The Army, therefore, stipulated that:

'The new gliders … will have adequate and comfortable arrangements which will offer relief from pilot fatigue during long missions. All flight controls will be duplicated for the co-pilot and be within comfortable reach for both pilot and co-pilot.'

The new gliders were also to be designed to be towed at 200mph (322km/h), a much higher speed than their predecessors, necessitating among other things full cantilever wings and a retractable undercarriage. In other words, the new gliders were required to be built like conventional aircraft, rather than the very basic machines they succeeded.

The competition for two new assault gliders

On 31 January 1946 Air Service Technical Command wrote to several leading aircraft manufacturers announcing a competition to build two new assault gliders, a 'light glider' capable of carrying an 8,000lb (3,632kg) payload, and a 'heavy glider' capable of carrying 16,000lb (7,264kg).

In both cases the fuselage was to be of steel tube and monocoque construction, with no use of fabric, and it had to be possible to load the aircraft from the rear through an opening the size of the cross section of the cargo compartment. Other aspects of the specification included the following performance at design gross weight:

The internal space requirements – which had been formulated in consultation with both the Airborne Infantry and the Army Engineering Corps – called for the aircraft to have an unobstructed cargo space 35ft long, 8ft 8in wide and 7ft 11in high (10.67 by 2.64 by 2.41m). Floor strength and tie-down parameters were stipulated, thereby making full use of the overall load-carrying capability of the aircraft. Other more detailed requirements specified things like removable armour plate for the pilots; individual removable folding seats for troop-carrying purposes; the provision of static lines and jump lights for paratrooper drops; and 'adequate ventilating and sanitary systems'.

It was intended that both the heavy and light gliders would be towed by the Fairchild C-82, but preliminary studies indicated that the performance would be marginal when towing the heavier glider. Further studies were therefore commissioned, looking at the possibility of equipping the C-82 with more powerful engines.

As was its custom at the time, the Air Technical Service Command of the Army Air Force created a 'reference design' to give Air Force engineers a baseline to explore the problems that would face the bidders.

It was stated that the proposals would be judged on:

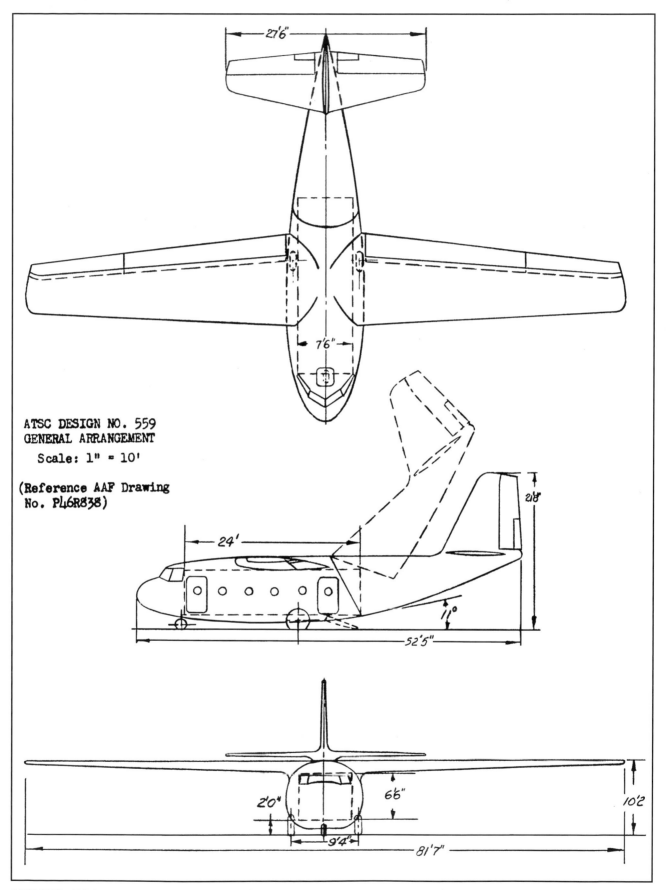

ATSC DESIGN NO. 559
GENERAL ARRANGEMENT

Scale: 1" = 10'

(Reference AAF Drawing
No. P46R838)

ABOVE The US Army Air Force 'light glider' reference design. *NARA II*

- The entire configuration of the design and its compliance with the requirements as outlined in the representative model
- The cost
- The delivery dates
- The past performance of the contractor

The timescale appeared to reflect a degree of urgency attached to the programme. Notification of willingness to participate was required by 18 February 1946 – within just two weeks – with proposals for the light glider required by 15 April and the heavy glider by 1 June. It was hoped that a contract for prototypes of the former could be placed within the current fiscal year, but regardless it was stated that

contracts for all gliders would be issued by the start of the 1947 fiscal year.

Although the requirement was issued to numerous companies, most declined to pursue it. It appears that only Bell, Chase, Douglas and Hughes responded with proposals. North American worked on a design for the heavy glider, which was given the project number RD-1413, but withdrew without submitting a proposal.

Bell Model D-44 and Bell D-45

Bell was the only company not to offer a conventional configuration for its proposals. Both its light and heavy

gliders, known as the Model D-44 and Model D-45 respectively, adopted a twin-boom/cargo-pod layout. The high-mounted wings were swept back slightly to keep the centre of lift behind the centre of gravity. The planform resembled the earlier Bell XP-52 and XP-59 pursuit aircraft, albeit with longer, higher-aspect-ratio wings.

The pods had clamshell doors at the rear, allowing loading or unloading with the pod attached to the glider. Alternatively the pods, which had a faired, non-retractable landing gear, could be detached and towed away, while the aircraft remained supported on retractable struts.

BELOW Bell Model D-44 (left) and Model D-45 (right) general arrangement. *NARA II*

Bell cargo gliders	Model D-44	Model D-45
Wingspan	91ft 10in (28.01m)	113ft 1in (34.49m)
Length	59ft 5in (18.12m)	84ft 3in (28.75m)
Height	21ft 4in (6.51m)	26ft (7.93m)
Payload	8,000lb (3,632kg)	16,000lb (7,264kg)

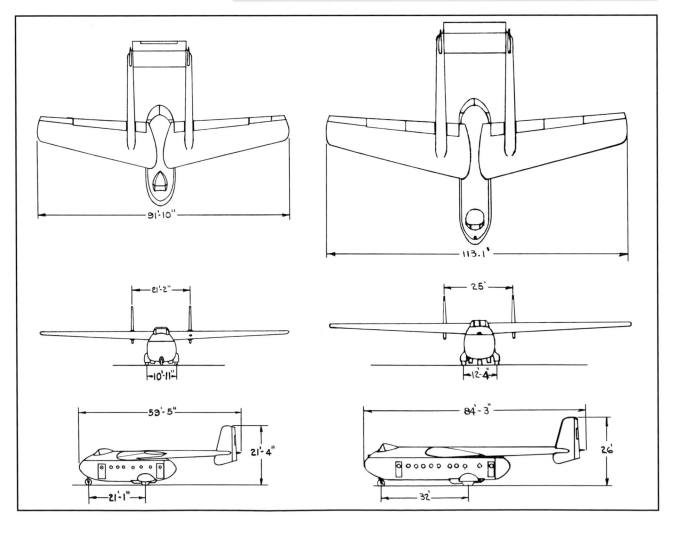

ABOVE A cargo pod being removed from the Bell Model D-44, which remains supported on retractable struts. *NARA II*

Chase MS-3 and MS-7 gliders

The Chase Aircraft Company, which had been formed specifically to develop assault gliders, was already working on a range of designs and had no problem adapting these to meet both sets of requirements.

Initially proposed before the competition, the MS-1B was a successor to the XCG-14A already being developed under contract to the Army Air Force. With the release of the military characteristics for the light glider, Chase revised its specification to match, and changed the company designation to MS-7. The Army Air Force then awarded

Chase a 'letter contract' on 24 January 1946 for what was now designated the XCG-18, presumably removing it from the light glider competition. Interestingly, Chase retained the metal tube structure for the XC-18 fuselage rather than the aluminium monocoque construction that was apparently specified for the competition; the tube design may have been regarded as simpler and more rugged.

Chase's proposal for the heavy glider was the MS-3 (which received the military designation of XCG-20 on contract award). With its retractable landing gear and smooth fuselage lines, it was a remarkably elegant-looking aircraft. Indeed, to modern eyes it

looks more like an airliner awaiting the attachment of engines than an assault glider. A major revision to the wing and tail during the development phase resulted in the aeroplane being redesignated as the MS-3A.

Both aircraft had an integral ramp built into the underside of the aft fuselage.

Douglas (Long Beach) Model 1028 (XCG-19) and Model 1029 cargo gliders

The Douglas entries in the competition were its Models 1028 and 1029. They were similar in appearance with a conventional configuration, a high wing and an upswept rear fuselage with a rectangular cross section. For loading, the Model 1028's rear fuselage was hinged to swing sideways, thus fulfilling the stipulated access requirement. In contrast, the larger Model 1029 had clamshell doors, each with an additional triangular folding panel for ground clearance together with an integral ramp.

Chase assault gliders	MS-7 (XCG-18)	MS-3A (XCG-20)
Span	86ft 4in (26.33m)	110ft (33.55m)*
Length	53ft 5in (16.29m)	77ft (23.49m)
Height	20ft (6.10m)	29ft 1in (8.81m)
Wing area	880sq ft (81.84m²)	n/a
Design gross weight	29,000lb (13,166kg)	n/a
Payload	8,000lb (3,632kg)	16,000lb (7,264kg) or 66 soldiers
Stalling speed	56.5mph (90.9km/h)	n/a
Design max tow speed	200mph (322km/h)	n/a
* MS-3 was 102ft 2in (31.16m)		

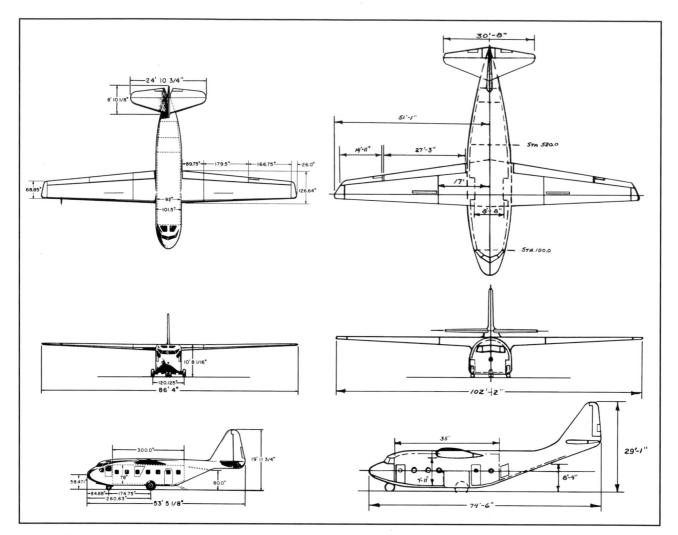

ABOVE Chase MS-7 (left) and MS-3 (right) general arrangement. *NARA II*

BELOW The prototype Chase MS-7/XCG-18 glider. *US Air Force*

ABOVE A ground view of the second of the two Chase MS-3A/XCG-20 glider prototypes. *Chase*
BELOW The second prototype Chase MS-3A/XCG-20 glider under tow. *US Air Force*

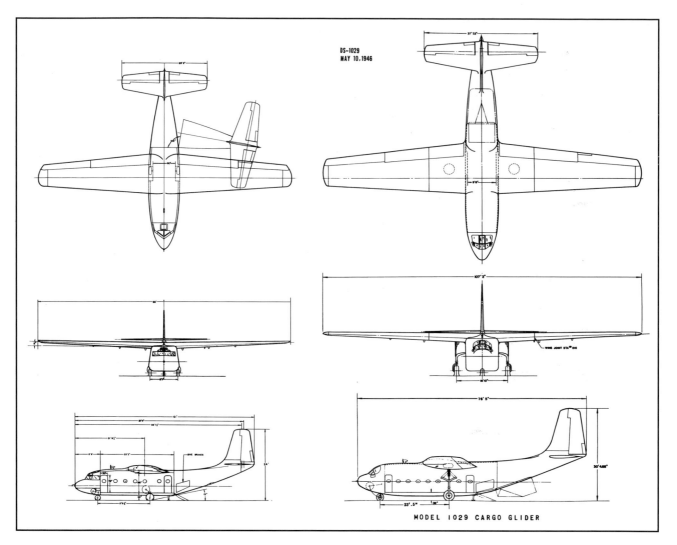

ABOVE General arrangement of the Douglas Model 1028 Light Assault Glider (left) and the Model 1029 Heavy Cargo Glider (right). *Boeing*

Douglas assault gliders	Model 1028 (XCG-19)	Model 1029
Wingspan	85ft (25.92m)	107ft 3in (32.71m)
Length	61ft (18.60m)	76ft 5in (23.30m)
Height	24ft (7.32m)	25ft 8in (7.83m)
Design gross weight	14,200lb (6,441kg)	28,500lb (12,927kg)
Payload	8,000lb (3,632kg)	16,000lb (7,264kg)
Max tow speed	200mph (322km/h)	190mph (306km/h)
Stalling speed	55mph (88.5km/h)	61mph (98km/h)

Hughes assault gliders	Model 31	Model 32
Wingspan	73ft 6in (22.42m)	90ft (27.45m)
Length	72ft 5in (22.09m)	87ft 3in (26.61m)
Height	26ft 6in (8.08m)	33ft 1in (10.09m)
Height (tail raised)	40ft 2in (12.25m)	n/a
Wing area	900sq ft (834m²)	1,360sq ft (149m²)
Gross weight	15,500lb (7,037kg)	28,190lb (12,798kg)
Payload	8,000lb (3,632kg)	16,000lb (7,264kg)
Stalling speed	53mph (85km/h)	60mph (97km/h)
Max tow speed	200mph (322km/h)	190mph (306km/h)

Hughes Models 31 and Model 32

The two Hughes proposals, its Models 31 and 32, were similar in configuration, both having an elegant streamlined appearance. The difference, apart from scale, was that the lighter glider had a hinged, upward-swinging rear fuselage to facilitate access to the cargo bay, whereas its heavier companion had a full-width loading ramp that formed the lower surface of the upswept rear fuselage.

Both gliders were to be similar in construction and divided into three modules: forward including the cockpit, the centre section including the cargo section, and the aft fuselage. The forward section was to be made of phenolic-infused glass fibre panels; the light glider featured a clear-view nose

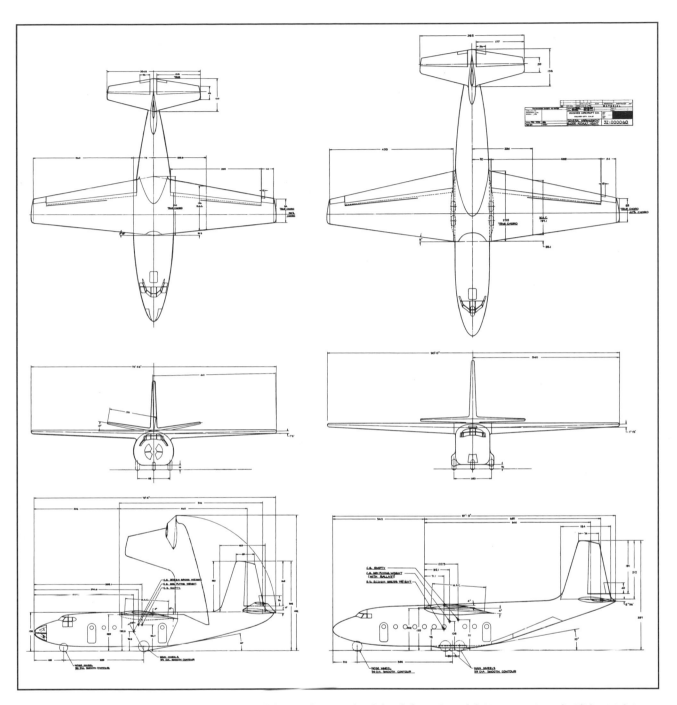

ABOVE General arrangement of the Hughes Model 31 Light Assault Glider (left) and Model 32 Heavy Assault Glider (right). *NARA II*

with Plexiglas panels. The centre and aft fuselage sections were to be of aluminium monocoque construction.

North American project RD-1413 heavy glider

There was a fifth, virtually unknown, submission prepared for the heavy glider competition: North American Aviation's RD-1413. This internal

designation/charge number appears to have been the only glider studied in NAA's history.

While no surviving illustration or drawing could be located, its unusual preliminary design was described as follows. The glider fuselage was 4ft (1.21m) in diameter, carrying the pilot and co-pilot in tandem. The wings, empennage and retractable short field

skids were attached to the glider 'boom'. The cargo/passenger compartment was a detachable fuselage 'egg' hanging from a rack under the glider. Concepts explored for the 'egg' were to make it expendable, or to include a motor drive, making it mobile before take-off and after landing. Also explored was the possibility of using the 'egg' as a form of landing barge, able to be dropped offshore.

The nascent effort was cancelled by NAA Chief Engineer Raymond Rice on 5 May 1946 in a short internal memo. This was followed by a brief letter, dated 14 May to the Commanding General, Air Materiel Command, stating that 'the contractor feels that it should not enter the glider proposal program at this time. It is felt that the resources of the contractor should be directed towards powered aircraft inasmuch as previous experience is in this field.'

The outcome of the glider competitions

In assessing the heavy glider proposals, the Army Air Force awarded points under three categories:

General Suitability
(airframe, landing gear, cockpit design, internal power, flight characteristics, cargo and troop carrying capability)
550 points

Performance
(glide angle, sink rate, landing requirements, towing demands)
350 points

Manufacturer's status
(background, experience, financial health, workload)
100 points

Total   1,000 points

The evaluation was completed in late 1946, with Chase rated best on suitability and Hughes on performance. Chase and Douglas shared the highest ratings on company status. Overall, the four heavy glider competitors were scored as follows:

Chase Model MS-3	843.7 points
Douglas Model 1029	827.4 points
Hughes Model 32	783.9 points
Bell Model D-45	749.5 points

Having lost the heavy glider competition to Chase, Douglas was declared the winner of the light glider contest and was awarded a contract to construct a prototype of the Model 1028 as the XCG-19 – while the AAF

continued to fund the development of the Chase XCG-18. In contrast to the latter, the Douglas glider utilised a full-monocoque, stressed-skin design. Matters came to a head in early 1947 with major reductions in the Research and Development Budget. Forced to choose, the AAF cancelled the Douglas contact in March 1947. with the mock-up approximately 60% complete.

At the same time, the Army's interest in gliders was waning. Given that the new generation of gliders were no longer the inexpensively constructed, disposable airframes of the Second World War, but aerodynamically sophisticated metal aircraft with the ability to use short-length unprepared airfields, why not put engines on them? Attention therefore turned to opportunities afforded by light assault aircraft.

This was really the death knell for the concept of the assault glider, although it took some time to become official policy. In September 1950 both the Army and Air Force agreed that gliders were no longer part of their plans, then in April 1952 the Joint Airborne Troop Board at Fort Bragg issued a memo stating that 'Gliders, as an airborne capability, are obsolete, and should no longer be included in airborne techniques, concepts, and doctrine, or in reference thereto.' None of the post-war proposals ever resulted in an operational glider aircraft. However, they helped lay the foundation for the Air Force's future assault transport capability.

Putting engines onto gliders

The concept of 'powered gliders' (aeroplanes built as gliders but with engines subsequently added) had been investigated during the Second World War, when the Waco CG-4 was modified to take two engines. Given the designations XPG-1 and XPG-2, a range of different engines was tried. After the war ended a production run of ten aircraft powered by two Ranger 200hp (149kW) L-440-7 engines was undertaken under the designation

PG-2A. The CG-4 was, however, a very basic, low-speed airframe, with a maximum payload of 4,197lb (1,904kg). Although hugely successful as an assault glider (nearly 14,000 were built), it was not well suited to adaptation as a powered transport.

With the advanced post-war glider designs, the prospect of an effective conversion was much more realistic. These metal gliders had the aerodynamic characteristics and structural strength that allowed them to be towed at speeds that matched the latest transport aircraft, while retaining the ability to deliver troops and equipment into short, unprepared fields. This made them obvious candidates for adaptation as powered assault aircraft.

Elements of the Army Air Force argued against the powered glider concept – including the term itself. Lt Gen Ira C. Eaker wrote: 'The Air Force is opposed to a powered glider. As a matter of fact it is a misnomer. There is no such thing as a powered glider, it then becomes an airplane.' It was inevitable that the manufacturers that had produced modern glider designs all offered powered versions as alternatives. This was very timely in terms of the change in Army and Air Force thinking.

Douglas (Long Beach) Models 1044 and 1072 light assault transports

Douglas designed powered versions of both its light and heavy assault gliders, designating them Models 1028A and 1029A respectively. Both were to be powered by Fairchild Ranger XV-770-10 engines.

After the cancellation of the original Model 1028 glider, Douglas continued to work on its powered derivative under the designation Model 1044. A number of versions were investigated with different engine options, and were split between the assault transport and civil feeder airliner variants.

The final design, from January 1947, was the Model 1044G, which was then redesignated as the Model 1072. This

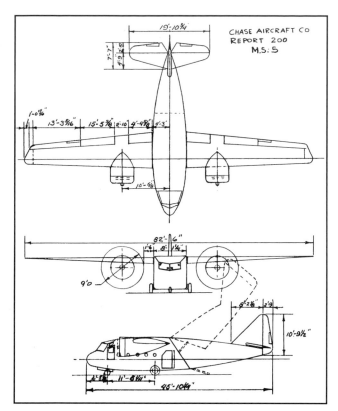

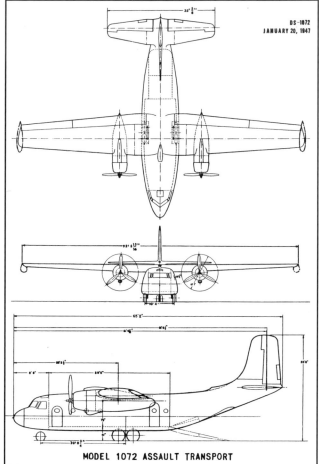

ABOVE Chase proposed modifying the XCG-14 design to the MS-5 'powered glider' in 1945. *US Air Force*

RIGHT Douglas Model 1072 assault transport general arrangement, in a drawing extracted from report Design Specification DS-1072. *Boeing*

version differed from the earlier Model 1044 by being slightly heavier and having an extended wing. It was no more successful than its predecessors and was the end of this line of development.

BELOW The Douglas XCG-18 'powered glider' with removable Ranger engines. *Boeing*

Douglas (Santa Monica) Model 1105B/1107 assault transport

Douglas's other line of assault transport development in April 1947 took a far more radical approach. Originally labelled the Model 1105B, this design was one of a group of low-wing pusher aircraft that built on the design experience gained with the pusher XB-42 bomber. Other similar designs in the Model 1105 family included a heavy transport, a jet bomber and a three-jet airliner with the engines buried in the belly, aft of the wing.

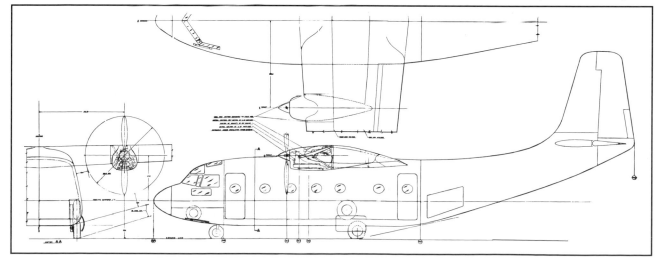

Douglas post-war assault transports	Model 1044	Model 1072
Powerplant	2 x P&W R-2000 piston radials @ 1,450hp (1,081kW)	2 x Wright R-1820 piston radials @ 1,425hp (1,063kW)
Wingspan	85ft (25.93m)	92ft 5.81in (29.13m)
Length	64ft (19.52m)	65ft 2in (19.88m)
Height	25ft 8in (7.82m)	25ft 8in (7.83m)
Wing area	885sq ft (82.3m²)	992sq ft (92.2m²)
Gross weight	31,000lb (14,070kg)	32,000lb (14,515kg)
Payload	8,000lb (3,628kg)	n/a
High Speed	286mph (463km/h)	n/a
Cruise speed	220mph (354km/h)	n/a
Endurance	7 hours	n/a
Range	n/a	1,005mi (1,617km)

Douglas Model 1107 assault transport	
Powerplant	2 x Wright R-1820 piston radials (Cyclone 9CAD) @ 1,425hp (1,063kW)
Wingspan	92ft 2in (28.09m)
Length	71ft 0in (21.64m)
Height	26ft 6in (8.08m)

A 30in (76.2cm) stretch to the forward fuselage and a vertical fin 30in (76.2 cm) taller led to the medium assault transport being redesignated as Model 1107. It was a low-wing aircraft with the two engines buried in the mid fuselage, driving a single pusher propeller in the tail. This resulted in a very futuristic-looking design, with a clean wing allowing for full-span flaps. Adding to the uniqueness of the design was the flattened oval cross section of the fuselage. Very large, upward-folding doors – extending almost the whole length of the port-side fuselage ahead of the wing – allowed exceptional access, with loading by either forklift truck or external ramps.

Promotional artwork also shows cargo being air-dropped through centreline doors under the fuselage, but the practicality of ejecting large loads is questionable, considering the impact on the shift in CG by emptying a cargo bay housed entirely in the front of the aircraft. Douglas continued to work on these developments, but none progressed beyond the concept stage. However, as discussed later, the more radical configuration would later re-emerge in the form of a heavy assault transport from the same family.

Chase MS-7/C-122 assault transport

While various other contractors came forward with proposals to put engines on their glider proposals, Chase had the advantage of having already flown its all-metal XCG-18A thirty-two-place glider in late 1947 and had received a contract for five YCG-18As for service testing. Given the change in philosophy, the Air Materiel Command asked Chase to complete the last aircraft with Pratt & Whitney R-2000-83 1,100hp (820kW) engines. This flew on 18 November 1948, having been given the designation YC-122.

This was seen as a very significant step for the company. On 29 November *Aviation Week* reported: 'The successful first flight of the versatile, new YC-122 Air Force assault transport

BELOW The Douglas Model 1107 assault transport was scarcely larger than the conventional Model 1072, but presented a much sleeker profile. *Boeing*

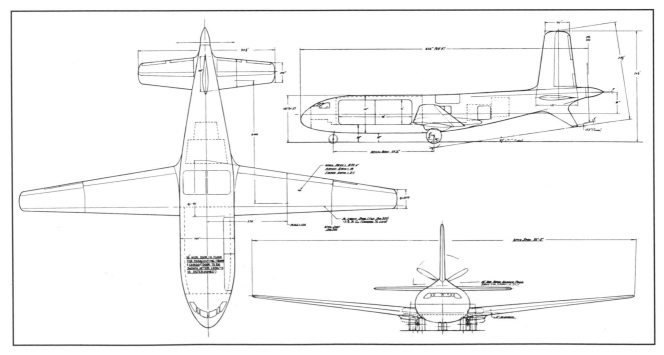

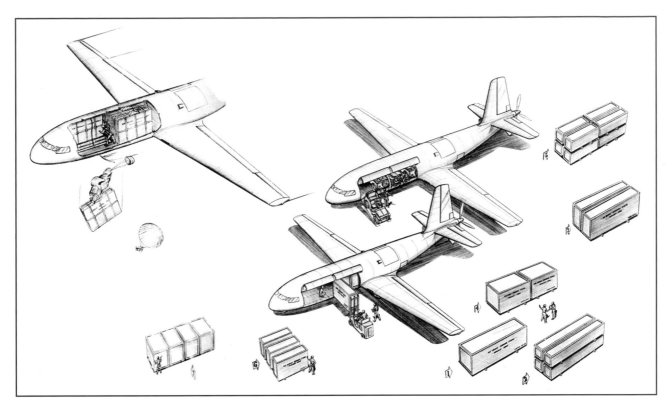

ABOVE The Model 1107 is seen here with different packaged cargo options. The inset art highlights cargo air-drop through the centreline belly door. *Boeing*

BELOW The Chase YC-122A (left) and YC-122C (right) with extended fuselage and enlarged tail. *US Air Force*

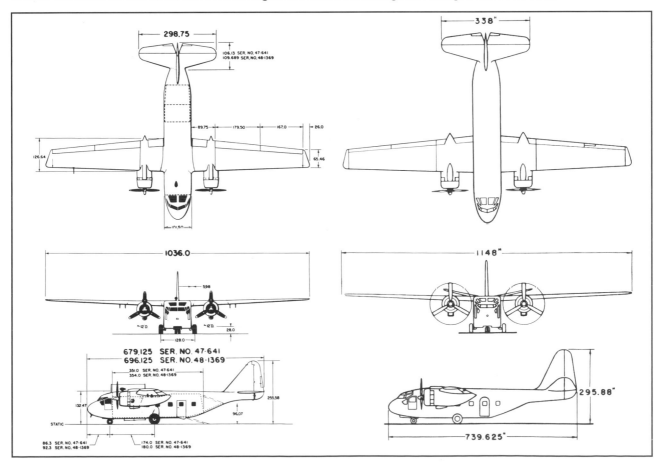

ABOVE This flightline scene at the Chase factory shows (from left to right) a YC-122C, the YC-122A and the YC-122B. *Author's collection*

BELOW Chase YC-122C aircraft stand at Fort Bragg during the 'Southern Pine' joint Army and Air Force field exercises on 30 July 1951. *US Army*

Chase MS-7 'Avitrucs'	MS-7/YC-122	MS-7A/YC-122A	MS-7B/YC-122B	MS-7C/YC-122C
Powerplant	2 x P&W R-2000-11 @ 1,300hp (969kW)	2 x P&W R-2000-11 @ 1,300hp (969kW)	2 x Wright R-1820-101 @ 1,450hp (1,081kW)	2 x Wright R-1820-101 @ 1,450hp (1,081kW)
Wingspan	86ft 4in (26.33m)	86ft 4in (26.33m)	95ft 8in (29.18m)	95ft 8in (29.18m)
Length	56ft 7in (17.28m)	58ft (17.69m)	61ft 7in (18.48m)	61ft 7in (18.48m)
Height	21ft 3.6in (6.49m)	21ft 3.6in (6.49m)	24ft 7in (7.49m)	24ft 7in (7.49m)
Wing area	706sq ft (65.7m²)	706sq ft (65.7m²)	c.1,050sq ft (97.7m²)	c.1,050sq ft (97.7m²)
Design gross weight	n/a	n/a	32,000lb (14,530kg)	32,750lb (14,530kg)
Max gross weight	n/a	n/a	36,000lb (16,340kg)	36,000lb (16,340kg)
Payload	n/a	n/a	n/a	7,500lb (3,405kg) or 30 troops
Cruise speed	n/a	n/a	n/a	175mph (282km/h)
Max speed	n/a	n/a	n/a	220mph (322k/h)
Range	n/a	n/a	n/a	2,900mi (4,666km)
Range (max load)	n/a	n/a	n/a	875mi (1,408km)

could catapult comparatively small Chase Aircraft into a leading position as a manufacturer of cargo planes.'

The prototype was followed by a second example with the more powerful 1,300hp (970kW) R-2000-3 engines and a slightly stretched fuselage, which was given the YC-122A designation. Even more powerful engines in the form of 1,450hp (1,080kW) Wright R-1820-101s were fitted in the enlarged YC-122B and YC-122C aircraft, which featured a lengthened fuselage, a greater wingspan and a redesigned empennage. The Air Force ordered one YC-122B and nine YC-122Cs for service testing. However, while these participated in operational field exercises over the next five years and helped build up experience of operating small troop and cargo-carrying aircraft under difficult conditions, they did not result in any production order for the aircraft.

Chase MS-8/XC-123 airlifter

Before it had made its initial flight, the first XCG-20 prototype was repurposed and modified to take two 2,100hp (1,566kW) Pratt & Whitney R-2800 engines. This effort was given a higher priority than the XCG-20 glider, and the XC-123 flew as a powered aircraft (on 14 October 1949) before the second XCG-20 flew as a glider the following year.

Following six months of initial flight testing, the XC-123 was sent to Eglin AFB for extensive field testing. The evaluation confirmed that the Air Force had found a tactical transport of high potential, and Chase was awarded a contract for 300 aircraft under the designation C-123B.

In the words of E. R. Johnson, in his book *American Military Transport Aircraft since 1925*: 'Perhaps more than any other aircraft design, the C-123 "Provider" established the pattern for modern military transports.' However, although the C-123 was to prove a very

significant step forward in military transports, the story was not to end so happily for Chase. As described in the following chapter, the transition from prototype-builder to major supplier was to prove a step too far for the company.

Chase XC-123 'Avitruc'	
Powerplant	2 x P&W R-2800-83 piston radials @ 2,100hp (1,566kW)
Wingspan	110ft (33.55m)
Length	77ft 1in (23.51m)
Design gross weight	44,550lb (20,230kg)
Payload	21,130lb (9,593kg) or 60 troops

Chase MS-14/XC-123A jet airlifter

On 26 September 1950 the Air Force asked Chase to submit a price to install Allison T38 turboprops in the second XCG-20, which was still configured as a glider. Contract negotiations became protracted, particularly when Chase re-evaluated its projected costs and presented a '700 per cent' cost increase to the Air Force. The Air Force ultimately changed its mind and redirected the effort to installing turbojets rather than turboprops. This resulted in the installation of four J47-GE-11s in two

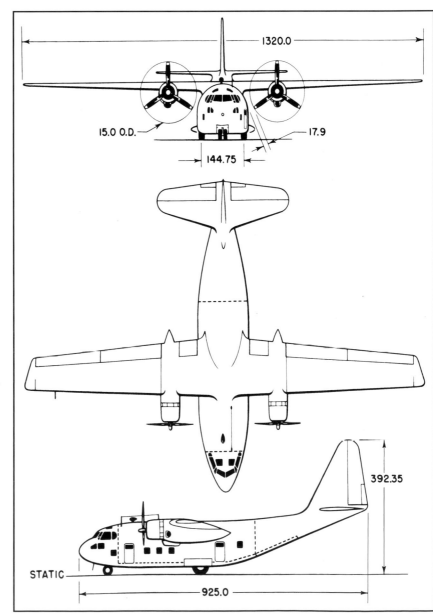

RIGHT The Chase XC-123 conversion of the first XCG-20 glider. *Chase*

ABOVE The roll-out of the Chase XC-123 piston-engine conversion of the XCG-20 glider. *Chase*
BELOW The Chase XC-123A during initial flight testing. *Chase*

twin-engine pods mounted on pylons beneath the wings. Both the pods and the pylons were adapted from those used on the Convair B-36D bomber, which in turn had been developed for the Boeing B-47.

This conversion was given the designation XC-123A, and the aircraft flew in this form on 21 April 1951, thereby becoming the United States' first-ever pure jet transport. It was equivalent in power to the much heavier North American B-45 bomber, but without the latter's high-speed design features or pressurisation. The 25-hour flight test programme was 95% complete when it was terminated following the crash of its sister aircraft, the piston-powered XC-123. Consideration was given to converting it to piston engines

BELOW The Chase XC-123A on the ground, showing the dual J47-GE-11 engine nacelles. *Chase*

to support the upcoming C-123B production contract, but this was opposed by Chase, which proposed building two YC-123Bs instead.

Ultimately, the XC-123A airframe was converted to the XC-123D test aircraft by Chase's successor company, Stroukoff, and flew as a piston-powered aircraft. Having had previous stints as a glider and jet-powered aeroplane, it is probably the only airframe ever to have flown in all three of these configurations.

Chase XC-123A

Powerplant	4 x GE J47-GE-11 turbojets @ 5,200lb (23.1kN)
Wingspan	104ft 11in (32m)
Length	77ft 1in (23.51m)
Wing area	1,136sq ft (105.7m²)
Design gross weight	67,000lb (30,420kg)
Payload	33,200lb (15,070kg)
Max speed	500mph (805km/h)
Cruise speed	400mph (644km/h)

The competition to provide a new assault transport

Although the C-123 was eventually to emerge as a highly successful transport aircraft, it had competition. While the process of putting engines onto gliders, described above, was taking place, the Army was reconsidering its tactical support requirements and asked the USAF to carry out a systematic assessment of various contenders for an assault transport.

The evaluation took place in the summer of 1950 when the competing aircraft were assessed by the Air Force's Air Proving Ground Command at Eglin AFB. It involved the Chase YC-122C and XC-123, as well as the Chase gliders on which they were based, the YCG-18A and XCG-20; a modified Fairchild C-82; and the Northrop YC-125.

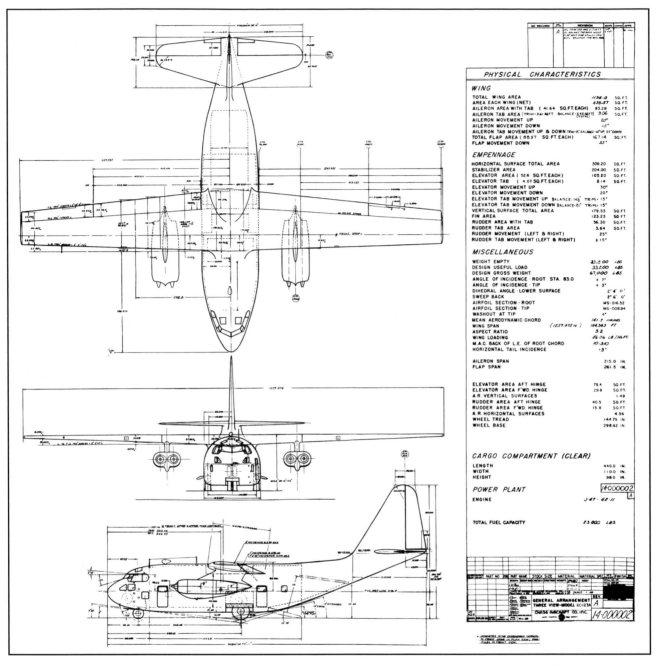

ABOVE Chase XC-123A general arrangement. *NARA II*

All but the last contender have been described earlier. Northrop's YC-125 originated as the N-23 Pioneer, an optimistic project aimed at the anticipated post-war market for commercial aircraft. At that time virtually every manufacturer had either private light aircraft or commercial passenger/transport aircraft under development. Under the sponsorship of Northrop's Board Chairman and General Manager, La Motte Cohu, the company designed a rugged tri-motor cargo and passenger transport intended for the South American market, and the N-23 first flew on 21 December 1946. By 1947, however, the market for new aircraft was flooded with the release of hundreds of virtually new C-47s and C-54s from surplus government stocks at low cost. As a consequence, most of the proposed generation of post-war transports never made it past the design stage.

Northrop then turned to marketing the design to the Air Force, resulting in a contract award on 8 March 1948 for thirteen YC-125A aircraft for Assault Transport evaluation and ten YC-125B aircraft for the Arctic Rescue (later Escape & Evasion) mission. The fixed-price contract was for what was initially understood to be an 'off-the-shelf' aircraft.

Necessary design changes for the military mission turned what was to become known as the N-32 Raider into an aircraft that shared only its wing

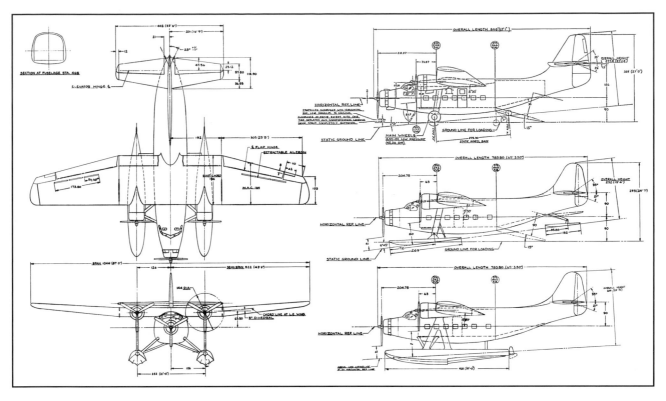

ABOVE The early Northrop YC-125 float configuration, with skis (middle right), and the YC-125 as built with a larger tail and rudder (top right). *Courtesy of Northrop Grumman Corporation*

planform with the baseline N-23. The latter's gross weight of 25,000lb (11,350kg) had increased to the YC-125's 40,900lb (18,569kg). Engines were uprated, from 800hp (597kW) to 1,200hp (895kW). As work was ongoing, Northrop suffered the loss of a thirty-plane follow-on contract for C-125s as well as the final cancellation of the RB-49 flying wings; in one step, 55% of Northrop's business base was gone. This forced the remaining programmes to pay for a larger share of Northrop's fixed costs. The company was forced in 1949 to declare a loss of $4.4 million on the $5.9 million dollar Raider programme, together with the write-off of the entire

$751,791 cost of the N-23 Pioneer programme, which had no commercial prospects after the crash of the prototype on 19 February 1948.

Northrop's woes did not end there. During the first flight of the first YC-125B on 1 August 1949, the test pilot experienced 'extreme longitudinal instability, right wing heaviness, and general poor handling characteristics'.

Successive flights were devoted to proving the performance and correcting the noted problems. The aircraft was then sent for evaluation as an Assault Transport at the Air Proving Ground at Eglin AFB in the summer of 1950. The eventual conclusion was that the YC-125 was not well suited to either of the two roles for which it was being considered, Arctic Rescue and short field assault.

BELOW The Northrop N-23 Pioneer with its circular fuselage cross section.
Courtesy of Northrop Grumman Corporation

Northrop YC-125B Raider	
Powerplant	3 x Wright R-1820-99 piston radials @ 1,200hp (895kW)
Wingspan	86ft 6in (26.38m)
Length	67ft 1in (20.33m)
Height	23 ft 1 in (7.04 m)
Max take-off weight	41,900lb (19,020kg)
Payload	10,000lb (4,540kg) or 36 troops
Max speed	207mph (333km/h)
Cruise speed	171mph (275km/h)
Range	1,856mi (2,986km)

ABOVE The Northrop YC-125B on skis at Wright Field. *US Air Force*

BELOW A Northrop YC-125A loading test at Northrop's Plant 1, Hawthorne, California. *Courtesy of Northrop Grumman Corporation*

section III • *GENERAL MAINTENANCE* • **dual wheels** ·· **pontoons**

To reduce foot print pressures for soft ground operation, an additional standard wheel-axle assembly may be installed on each main landing gear. This is easily accomplished by jacking, or taxiing the airplane up an inclined ramp. The airplane structure is designed to accommodate floats, and it is hoped that future procurement may include them.

PAGE 28

ABOVE Alternative Northrop C-125 landing gear configurations. *Courtesy of Northrop Grumman Corporation*

The Air Force's competitive trials for the new assault aircraft, conducted from May to September 1950, were extremely rigorous and demanding.

The specified requirements included the ability to operate from rough terrain; the ability to clear a 50ft (15.25m) obstacle within a 2,000ft (610m) take-off run (or snatched pick-up in the case of a glider); the ability to land over a 50ft (15.25m) obstacle within 1,500ft (457.5m); a minimum cruise speed of 150kt (278km/h); a minimum speed with full controllability of 78kt (144km/h); and a minimum range with maximum cargo of 650nmi (1,203km). There were two categories of cargo-carrying capacity specified, light and medium, totalling 8,000lb (3,632kg) and 16,000lb (7,264kg) of bulk cargo respectively.

The rough landing and take-offs took place from an area described as 'a large sand and weed patch, rutted, and marred from previous equipment and explosive tests'. Perhaps unsurprisingly, all the aircraft suffered damage. The Chase YCG-18 glider landed with its nose-wheel up and suffered considerable skin damage; the Chase XCG-20 glider was damaged when a tow-rope broke and tore into its fuselage.

Of the powered contestants, the Fairchild C-82 hit the 50ft (15.25m) landing obstacle, landed tail first and snapped off the left boom and horizontal stabiliser; the Chase XC-123 taxied into a sand-filled bomb crater and twisted its undercarriage; and one of the Northrop YC-125As bent a propeller and broke its landing gear on successive short-field landing attempts,

while a second airframe was damaged beyond economical repair in an extremely hard landing in very gusty winds. Not for the first – or last – time, the ability to operate from short, unprepared airstrips was an easier requirement to specify than to satisfy.

The outcome of the evaluation, which was set out in a report issued by the Air Materiel Command on 15 October 1950, placed the Chase XC-123 in first place followed by the C-122, C-82 and YC-125, in that order.

Some of the board recommendations were:

■ The C-123 be … procured to fill both the Light and Medium category requirements

■ The modified C-82 not be procured as an assault transport

- The C-125 airplane be dropped from any further consideration as an Air Force airplane
- The use of gliders be discontinued and that assault transports be used.

The debate over powered versus unpowered gliders had been finally settled.

Upgrading the C-47: the Super DC-3

Given the success and massive production output of the DC-3, it is hardly surprising that in the post-war era Douglas looked at ways of further improving the basic design, particularly to extend the life and usefulness of the large numbers of civil and ex-military aircraft now in commercial service. Additionally, the DC-3 was facing the twin challenges of increasingly stringent

Civil Aeronautics Agency (CAA) performance and safety regulations and competitive challenges from the Convair 240 and Martin 2-0-2 airliners (both of which would have pressurised derivatives).

Accordingly, Douglas offered operators a major rebuild and modification programme. This involved extending and strengthening the fuselage, squaring off the wingtips, adding 4° of sweep to the trailing edges of the wing (to compensate for CG shift), and uprating the engines. Termed the Super DC-3, the aircraft showed a marked improvement in performance over the basic model, able to carry thirty-eight passengers (as opposed to thirty) and to cruise around 20% faster. Despite this improvement, the aeroplane failed to find a commercial market, with only three examples sold.

Douglas sold the prototype to the Air Force, which stripped out the plush interior and evaluated it as the YC-129 for a new 'Escape & Evasion' mission requirement. As such, it was fitted to take sixteen Aerojet 14AS-1000 Jet Assist Take-Off (JATO) 'bottles' to shorten take-off, a drag chute in the tailcone to shorten landing, and up to eight fuel tanks in the passenger cabin to extend range. It was later redesignated the YC-47F. However, no order was forthcoming from the Air Force for the 'special operations' mission, and the requirement appears to have faded away or been allocated to other unspecified aircraft.

Meanwhile, Douglas saw an opportunity to exploit further the concept of a much improved C-47 by giving it a more accessible fuselage for military cargo. The company examined

BELOW The initial Douglas Super C-47/DC-3 featured tip extensions to the vertical and horizontal stabilisers and control surfaces. This was later deemed insufficient and was replaced by a new angular design with more surface area. *Boeing*

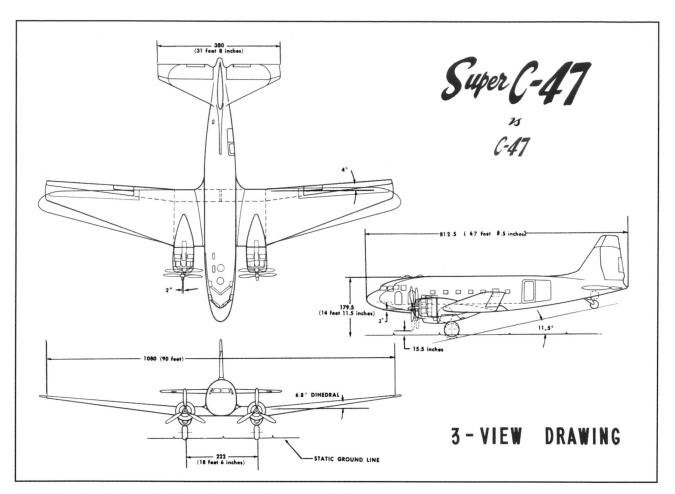

ABOVE The Douglas Super C-47 (in red) compared to the standard C-47 (in green). *Boeing*

BELOW The Douglas YC-129 stands on the Edwards AFB flightline for 'Escape & Evasion' testing on 23 November 1950. Modifications included mountings for two rows of RATO bottles, cabin fuel tanks for extended range, a drag chute, and dual-wheel main landing gear. *Boeing*

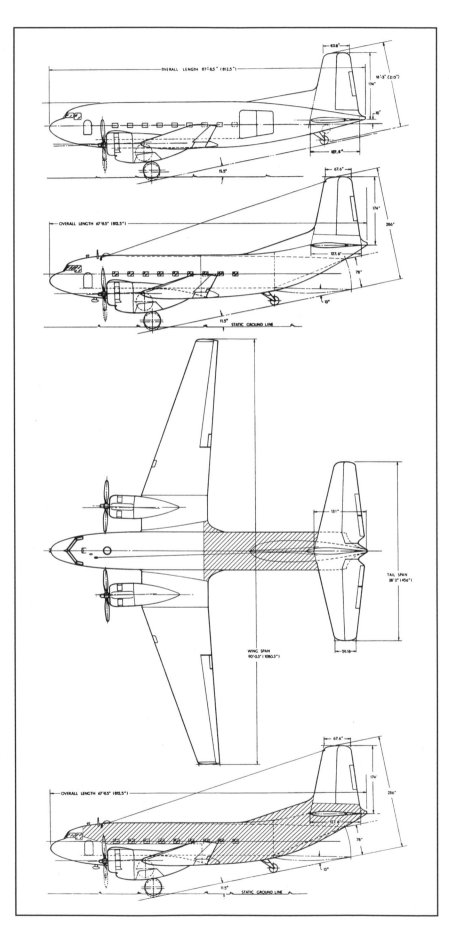

various options for both squaring off the upper aft fuselage cross section and introducing a tail ramp. However, it then went a step further with its Model 1213A/B Super C-47, which featured an upward-hinging aft fuselage.

Unfortunately, none of these proposed adaptations appeared sufficiently attractive to the Air Force, although Douglas was able to obtain a contract for the conversion of 100 aircraft to the R4D-8 (later C-117D) for the Navy and Marine Corps. Nevertheless, this was the end of the line for the venerable design; not even an improved DC-3 could replace a DC-3.

Douglas 'floating wing' proposals

Of all the ideas to extend the capability of existing aircraft, surely none was more bizarre than the 'floating wing' concept proposed by Douglas. Initially developed by German engineer and designer Dr Richard Vogt, the concept was tested by the USAF as a means of range extension for fighters. The first tests were performed successfully when a Culver PQ-14 linked up with a C-47 on 7 October 1949. Further testing led to straight-wing EF-84D Thunderjets linking up with an ETB-29A in Project 'Tip-Tow', then with a swept-wing RF-84F linking with a JRB-36 in Project 'Tom-Tom'.

Douglas's aim was to extend the range and/or payload of types like the C-47 and C-54 by carrying the extra fuel or cargo in pods beneath lengthy outer-wing extensions. The unusual feature of this arrangement was that these extensions would be permanently connected by chord-wise hinges to the inner wing rather than rigidly fixed. They would

LEFT Douglas DC-3S tail ramp options: the baseline version (with side cargo door) is top left, with the partial fuselage replacement (from wing trailing edge aft) illustrated in the middle and top views. The more extensive fuselage replacement with a squared crown section extending to the cockpit is bottom left. *Boeing*

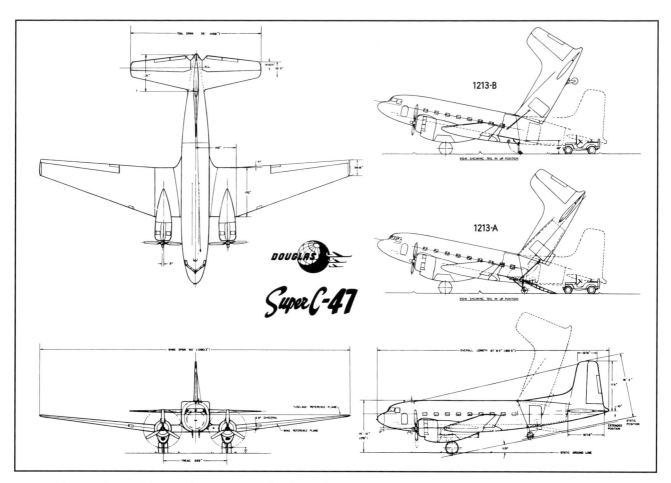

ABOVE The Douglas Model 1213A/B Super C-47 lift-tail assault transport. The Models 1213A and B featured differing tail wheel positions. *Boeing*

thus be free to 'float' up and down at the tip, with the same angle of attack as the wing but with a varying degree of anhedral/dihedral. The extensions would have trim tabs but no ailerons.

The centre of lift of the extended wing would be designed to be as close as possible to the CG of the extension including its pod, to avoid any twisting moment on the main wing. After initial flight testing it was also proposed to add flaps to the extensions, which would be geared to the main wing flaps.

On the ground each pod would be supported by its own retractable landing gear, with the outer wing designed to become airborne before the rest of the aeroplane and to touch down slightly later. The only foreseen drawback was the 146ft (44.53m) width of the landing gear. This meant that narrow runways could only be used 'when reasonably smooth turf was available to each side'.

The estimated gains in performance were quite substantial:

	C-54G	'Floating wing' C-54	Increase
Max payload (2,100 miles)	16,500lb (7,491kg)	26,500lb (12,031kg)	60%
Payload at max range	10,200lb (4,631kg)	20,200lb (9,171kg)	98%

In both cases, the penalty in take-off distance was just 6%.

Douglas foresaw other applications for the system, particularly as the aircraft could be flown without the pods, with just a landing strut attached beneath the wing extensions. This allowed the pods to be detached after landing. As a result, specially designed pods could be used as:

■ troop carriers for fifty fully equipped troops

■ portable barracks for Arctic or tropical conditions

■ ready-made radar stations

■ temporary advanced/HQ depots

■ photographic facilities complete with operatives

■ ambulance facilities (pressurised, unlike the C-54, by its own Auxiliary Power Unit)

Plans were drawn up for both the C-47 and the C-54 to use the 'floating wing' arrangement, and on 24 April 1950 a proposal was made by Douglas Santa Monica to flight test the concept using an adapted C-54G. To minimise costs and reduce the proof-of-concept timescale, the initial pods were to take the form of B-50 jettisonable fuel tanks carrying water ballast, supported on

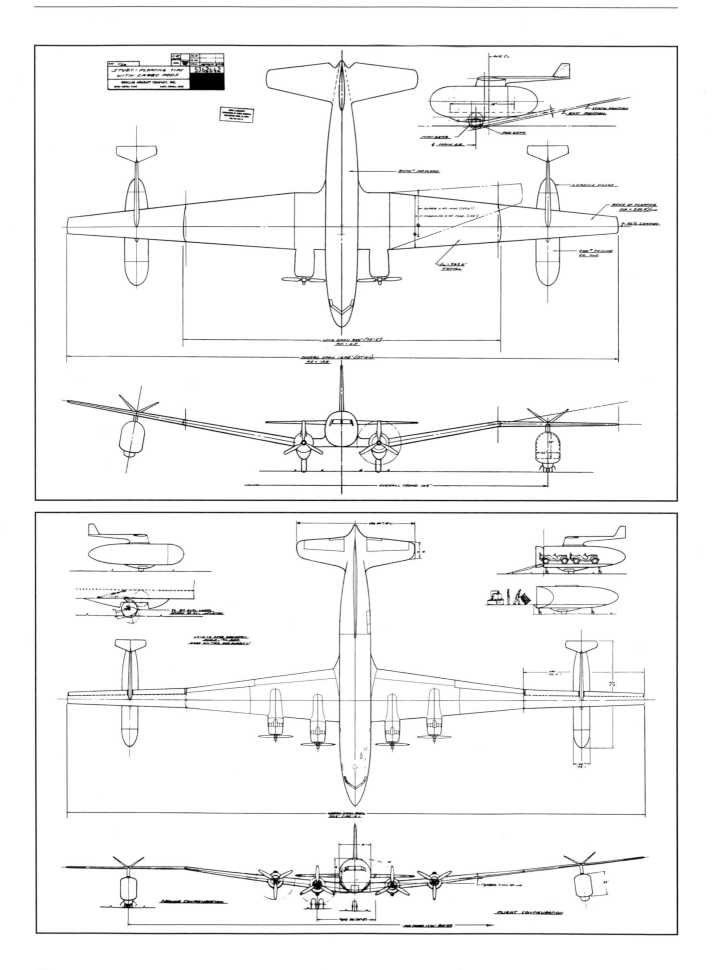

the ground by a non-retractable landing gear. The tanks were fitted with a dump valve to enable them to be emptied in flight, and a facility was provided to jettison both wingtips simultaneously in the event of difficulties.

Despite the predicted, highly impressive increase in performance over the existing fleet of C-47s and C-54s, the Air Force declined the proposal. Perhaps it seemed just too radical.

The C-119A: growing a medium transport

Pleased with the C-82, the Army Air Force had Fairchild continue production after the end of the Second World War (although second-source production by North American Aviation was cancelled after three had been built).

Nonetheless, there was room for improvement in several areas. For example, visibility from the cockpit

was poor and, as with most aircraft, more power would improve performance. By September 1946 Fairchild proposed a 55% increase in power by replacing the Pratt & Whitney 2,100hp (1,566kw) R-2800 engines with the 3,250hp (2,424kw) R-4360.

Other changes included a stretched forward fuselage with revised cockpit design, general airframe strengthening, and extension of the tail booms to retain stability and control. Although Fairchild requested wind tunnel testing of the latter feature, the Air Force turned it down, reasoning that static analysis of the 4ft (1.22m) extension would be sufficient (which turned out not to be the case).

The modification an of existing aeroplane was recognised by Major General Lawrence Craigie (of the AMC Engineering Division) as being more expeditious and cheaper by

several million dollars than opening a competition for a wholly new design.

The 137th C-82 was diverted from the production line and modified as the Fairchild Model M-105 (Air Force designation XC-82B, later XC-119A, and still later C-119A), making its first flight on 17 December 1947. However, a decision by the USAF Aircraft & Weapons Board in August, requiring the cargo compartment to be widened to 96in (2.44m), was made too late to be implemented. As a result this was the only C-119A built. The required cargo compartment change was duly incorporated in the next aircraft, now designated C-119B; the aircraft also benefitted from a revised landing gear. The first C-119B was delivered in December 1948, which (fortuitously) meant that it was in production when the Korean War broke out.

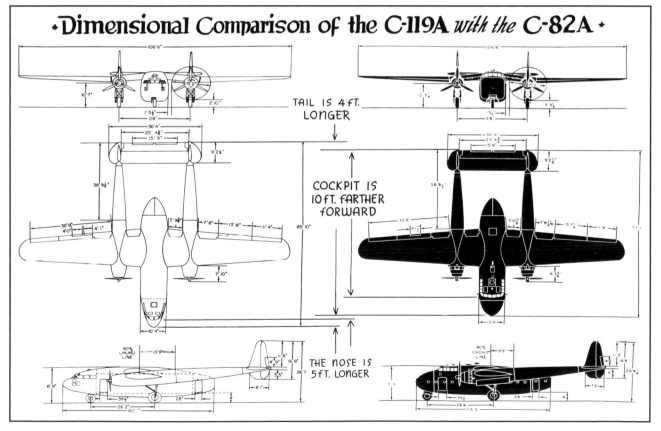

ABOVE A comparison of the new Fairchild C-119A and the C-82A. *NARA II*

OPPOSITE TOP The Douglas DC-3S 'floating wing' concept from May 1950. The extensions required completely new outer wing panels. *Boeing*

OPPOSITE BOTTOM Douglas C-54 'floating wing' extensions – a longer-term proposal. *Boeing*

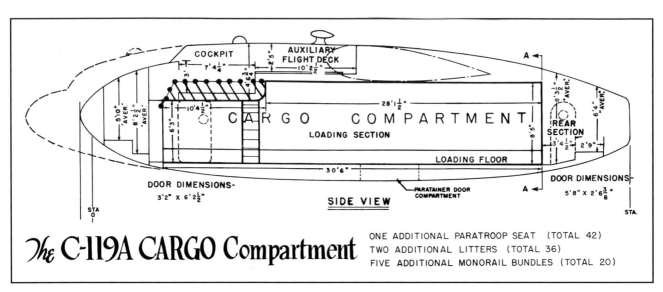

ABOVE A comparison of the Fairchild C-119A and C-82 fuselages and cargo compartments. Moving the C-119A cockpit forward enabled the cargo compartment height to be extended for its entire length. *NARA II*

BELOW The sole Fairchild C-119A is seen in flight. Dorsal and ventral surfaces would later be added to the booms in an attempt to cure directional stability issues, particularly during single-engine operation. *San Diego Air and Space Museum*

The renewed search for a heavy cargo aircraft

While the efforts to satisfy the requirement for a new assault transport were taking place, the post-war years also saw the Army, and later the Air Force, endeavouring to fulfil the need for a new heavy cargo aircraft. As with the requirement for a tactical support aircraft, the path to an eventual solution was far from straightforward.

The Army initially set out a specification of its requirements in May 1945. This resulted in some imaginative proposals, but none got as far as a flying prototype, a consequence of the Army Air Force's lack of funding in the immediate post-war cutbacks. The newly formed Air Force tried again with a further set of requirements on 13 February 1948, entitled 'Military Characteristics – Heavy Cargo'. Meantime, the aircraft manufacturing companies were largely intent on adapting and promoting

their existing offerings. The eventual outcome of all these initiatives was to give the Air Force its first long-range aircraft capable of carrying bulky items like trucks and artillery pieces.

Boeing Model 367 studies

With Boeing working on a greatly improved development of the B-50 Superfortress, designated B-54 (formerly YB-50C), and with its YC-97 (Model 367) under test, it was a logical move for the company to utilise this work in developing a new cargo transport. In

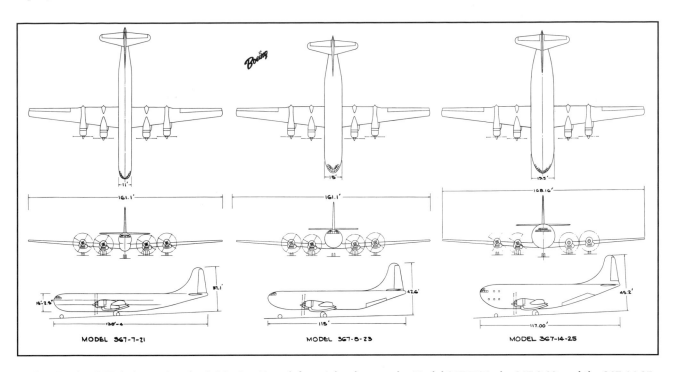

ABOVE Boeing 367 designs using the B-54 wing. From left to right, they are the Model 367-7-21, the 367-8-23, and the 367-14-25. *Boeing*

mid-1948 Boeing undertook studies to enlarge the Model 367 utilising the wing and powerplants of the B-54. It was to have a 161ft (18.60m) wingspan, and four Pratt & Whitney R-4360 engines with GE superchargers and Variable Discharge Turbines (VDT). Unlike the 'in-line' design proposed for the B-36C, the turbo-supercharger and exhaust units were mounted in the lower left quadrant of the engine nacelle. Also in common with the B-54C, an additional set of dual-wheel outrigger landing gear was stowed in the outer engine nacelles.

These studies eventually focused on three options; each used a generally common wing, but explored a different fuselage configuration. The 367-7-21 retained the 11ft (3.36m) upper lobe of the production 367 and 377 aircraft while increasing the overall length to 130ft 4in (39.75m), essentially a 'long, thin' option. The 367-8-23 explored a 115ft (35.05m) fuselage length with a circular cross section of 15ft (4.78m) diameter. The 367-14-25 embodied an even larger 19.5ft (5.95m)-diameter fuselage (with two decks) and a slightly increased wingspan. The two wide-body options had the benefit of slightly raising the new fuselage above the wing

compared to the 367-7-21, which retained the original fuselage structure with the lower lobe dating back to the B-29 design.

However, on 18 April 1949 the concurrent B-54 project was cancelled. This caused this family of transport designs to lose the benefit of a wing design that was to be funded by the

bomber's development. At the same time Boeing had to address the issue that the cargo deck was perceived to be too high off the ground. These considerations terminated this line of development, but it was certainly not the end of Boeing's interest in producing a new heavy cargo carrier within the Model 367 family.

BELOW This Boeing engineering sketch compares the enlarged 367-13-23 with its assessment of the enlarged Douglas C-74. *Boeing*

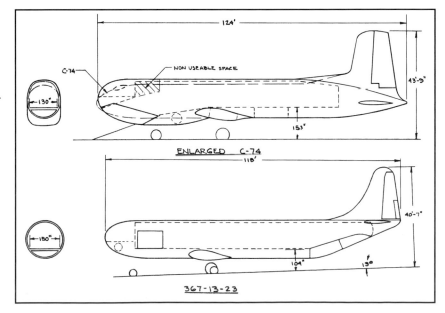

Boeing Model 470

The Boeing Model 470 was a new design intended to meet the Air Force's combined heavy cargo-troop carrier requirement. It had the distinctive cockpit glazing of the C-97 but, that aside, bore little resemblance to any other Boeing aeroplane. It was a high-wing aircraft to maximise the cargo volume, but had the inner sections of the wing canted down to reduce the length of the main landing-gear struts. The landing gear itself was unusual in that it comprised sixteen main wheels, mounted in four sets of four, dropping down from the rear of the engine nacelles. The two tail wheels were attached to the bottom of the twin vertical fins carried on the horizontal stabilisers. All the tyres on the aeroplane were the same diameter. Loading access was via two clamshell doors beneath the flight deck.

With specifications dating from 15 July 1948, the aircraft was to be powered by four Pratt & Whitney R-4360 engines and had a crew of six. The design gross weight was approximately 230,000lb (104,400kg), with a maximum payload of about 75-80,000lb (34-36,300kg), which compared favourably with the Convair XC-99.

What appears to have been an alternative version, the Boeing Model 467, appears on Boeing project listings as a 'Four Turboprop Heavy Transport'. It was presumably powered by the Wright T35, the only turboprop engine sufficiently far advanced in development to be considered at the time. However, neither the Model 470 nor the Model 467 found favour with the Air Force.

Boeing Model 470	
Powerplant	4 x P&W R-4360 VDT piston radials @ 3,150bhp (2,350kW) normal or 4,300bhp (3,208kW) take-off
Wingspan	229ft (69.84m)
Length	128ft (39.04m)
Wing area	3,500sq ft (315m²)
Design gross weight	230,000lb (104,420kg)
Payload	53,000lb (24,060kg)

BELOW Boeing Model 470 general arrangement. *Boeing*

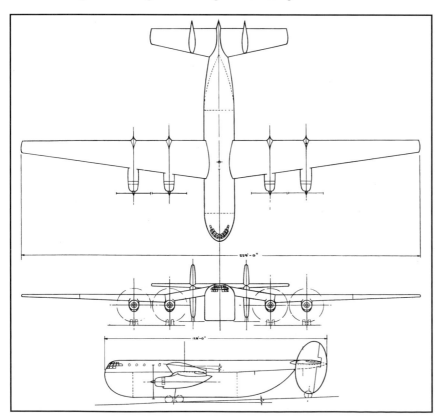

Convair Advanced C-99

The origins of the Convair XC-99 were described in Chapter Three, together with its capabilities and inherent limitations. Nonetheless, the Army concluded that it could do better. It summarised:

'The XC-99 will meet some of the requirements set forth in "Military Characteristics – Heavy Cargo" dated 17 February 1948, such as performance, range and cargo load that can be carried; however, it does not meet some of the fundamental requirements of a heavy cargo airplane, in that the interior dimensions are too small, the floor line is too high above the ground line, straight away loading is restricted, and tie-down fittings are not of sufficient strength.'

However, when it came to the 1948 requirement for a new heavy transport, the XC-99 had the advantages of being a flying aircraft with its development costs already largely written off. Convair made a significant effort to revise the XC-99 into what it called the 'Advanced C-99'. The fuselage was completely redesigned, with new upper and lower fuselage cross sections enabling the carriage of larger cargo. In addition, loading provisions were revised, with clamshell doors provided at both the nose and the tail for the lower deck. However, the placement of the wing was unchanged and it effectively partitioned the cargo deck into two sections.

Convair even went as far as to propose mating the swept wings and tail surfaces from the YB-60 (its competitor to the B-52) to the Advanced C-99 fuselage, terming this the Model 6 in a new corporate project numbering system.

Douglas (Santa Monica) Model 1036 and Douglas (Long Beach) Model 1040

The Douglas Models 1036 and 1040 were both early post-war attempts to utilise features of the C-74 within an airframe

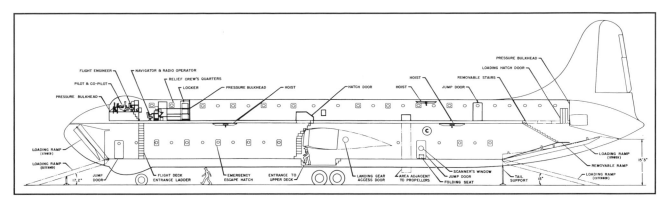

ABOVE The inboard profile of the Convair Advanced C-99 shows the revised fuselage with deeper main cargo deck. *NARA II via Dennis R. Jenkins*

RIGHT A fuselage cross section comparison between the XC-99 (left) and C-99 (right) shows how Convair attempted to improve the C-99's cargo capacity. While the maximum widths of both the cargo compartments were reduced, the usable floor widths were greatly increased. Only the upper deck of the C-99 was to be pressurised. *NARA II via Dennis R. Jenkins*

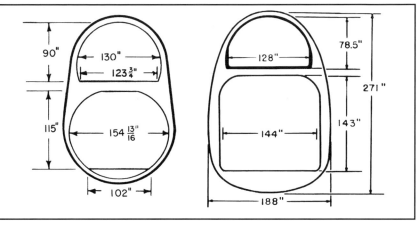

better suited to transporting heavy cargo. Both were high-wing designs with deep, rectangular-sided fuselages, and rear-opening clamshell doors beneath an extended upper fuselage that carried the empennage. Neither proceeded beyond the drawing board, eventually being succeeded by a more evolutionary development of the C-74.

RIGHT The Convair Model 6 (in the company's new numbering series) combined the fuselage of the Advanced C-99 with the wing, empennage and engines of the YB-60, but it was no more successful than its predecessor. *NARA II*

BELOW A cutaway model of the revised Convair C-99 (note the B-36 cockpit arrangement). *NARA II via Dennis R. Jenkins*

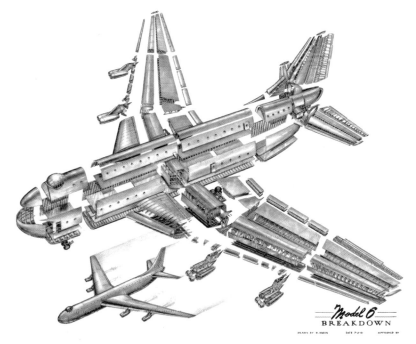

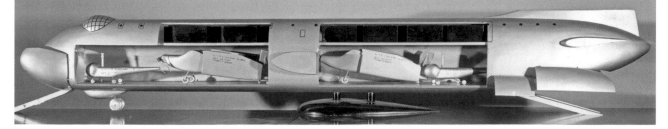

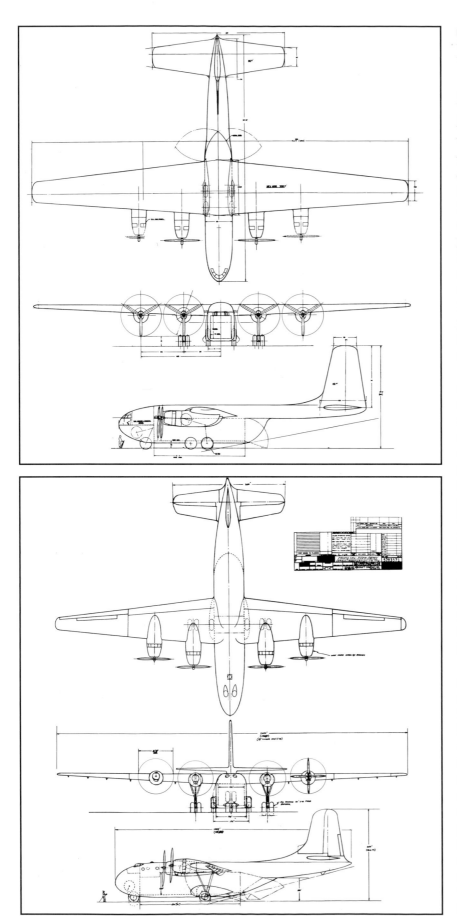

LEFT Douglas (Santa Monica) Model
1036 general arrangement from June
1946. *Boeing*

Douglas (Santa Monica) Model 1105

While other manufacturers (together with Douglas) were looking at ways of extending their earlier designs, Douglas (Santa Monica) carried out studies in 1947 for an entirely new transport capable of carrying a 40,000lb (18,160kg) payload, under the designation Model 1105. At least two different configurations were considered, as represented by the Models 1105A-C and 1105A-T. Little is known about these proposals, but surviving drawings show an interesting contrast in design approaches.

The Model 1105A-C was a relatively conventional design. Indeed, it displayed many features that would become commonplace in later generations of military transports. Powered by four engines, it featured a high wing and large clamshell doors located at the rear of the fuselage. The twelve-wheel main landing gear retracted into large fuselage fairings beneath the wing. Together with two pairs of nose wheels, this arrangement hints that the aircraft was intended for rough-field operations. The large size of the vertical stabiliser shows that controllability at low speeds was an important consideration. Together these features indicate that the aircraft was intended as a heavy assault transport.

The Model 1105A-T was quite different. Other than being of similar size and powered by four engines, it had almost nothing in common with its stablemate. The four R-4360 engines were buried in pairs in the upper-mid fuselage, with each pair coupled to a shaft driving a pusher propeller at the rear of the aircraft. The aft fuselage swept upwards, but this was to provide propeller blade clearance during rotation, rather than to accommodate a loading ramp. The cargo bay, entirely positioned ahead of the mid-mounted wing, was accessed via large doors on the port side of the front fuselage.

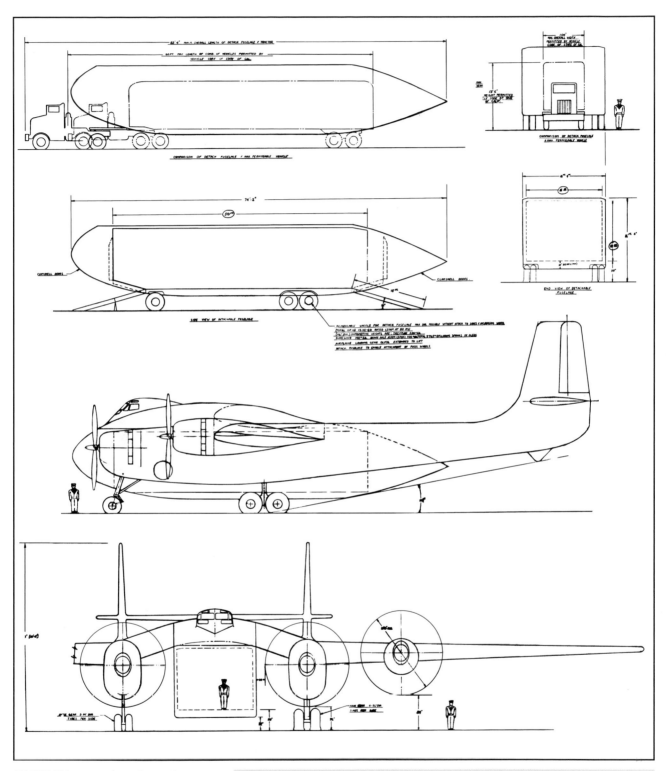

ABOVE This unnumbered Douglas (Long Beach) twin-boom pod-carrier study concept from May 1947 used C-74 wings and engines, but little else. *Boeing*

OPPOSITE The Douglas (Long Beach) Model 1040 from June 1946 reflects its C-74 heritage. *Boeing*

Douglas heavy transports of June 1946	Model 1036	Model 1040
Powerplant	4 x P&W R-4360 piston radials @ 3,000hp (2,240kW)	4 x P&W R-4360 piston radials @ 3,000hp (2,240kW)
Wingspan	172ft 3in (62.50m)	208ft 9in (63.63m)
Length	113ft 10in (34.70m)	117ft 0in (35.66m)
Height	47ft 7in (14.50m)	46ft 7in (14.20m)
Wing area	3,000 sq ft (279m²)	n/a
Gross weight	n/a	162,000lb (73,442kg)

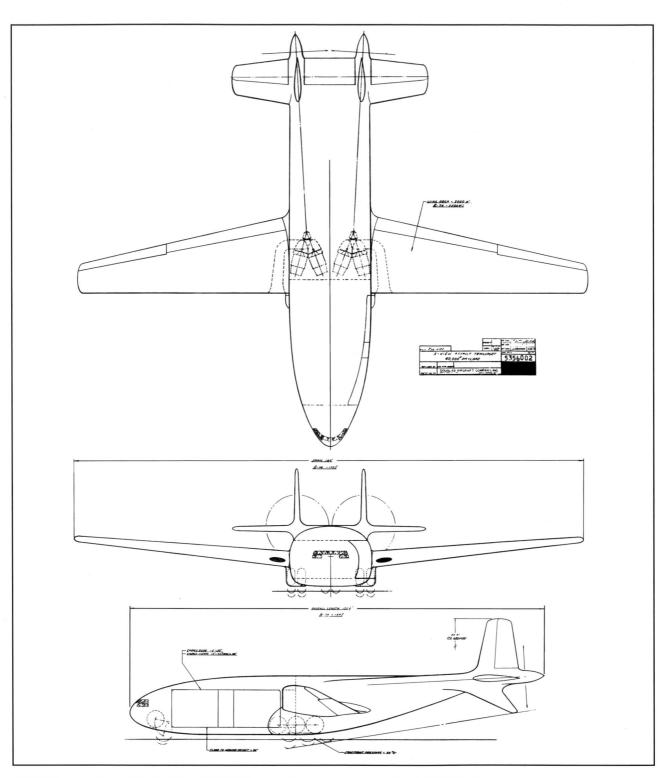

ABOVE Douglas (Santa Monica) Model 1105A-T general arrangement from March 1947. *Boeing*

The unusual appearance of the aircraft was heightened by the tail surfaces. The two vertical stabilisers were mounted on either side of the fuselage with a control surface positioned between them (augmenting the horizontal stabilisers), and there were two ventral fins beneath the tail to protect the propeller tips in the event of over-rotation of the aircraft during take-off or landing. The wing area was 20% greater than that of the C-74. As described earlier, Douglas also developed a smaller version of this design, as an assault transport with a single pusher propeller, under the designation Model 1107.

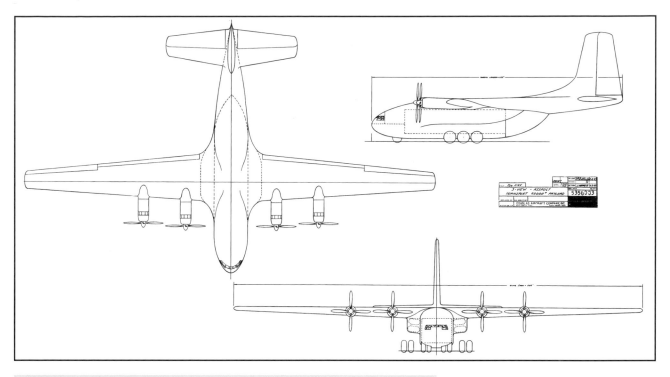

Douglas (Santa Monica) 1947 heavy		
assault transports	Model 1105A-C	Model 1105A-T
Powerplant	4 x P&W R-4360 piston radials @ 3,500hp (2610kW)	4 x P&W R-4360 piston radials @ 3,500hp (2610kW)
Wingspan	209ft 0in (63.70m)	164ft 0in (50.0m)
Length	155ft 0in (47.24m)	132ft 6in (40.39m)
Height	n/a	38ft 9in (11.81m)
Wing area	n/a	3,000sq ft (278.7m²)
Payload	40,000lb (18,140kg)	40,000lb (18,140kg)

ABOVE The Douglas (Santa Monica) Model 1105A-C, a 40,000lb assault transport from April 1947. *Boeing*

Fairchild Model M-99

Fairchild studied a number of options under the generic designation of Model 99, before producing two proposals. These designs were worked on in parallel, with both submissions issued in March 1946. The Models 99-05/06 and 07/08 were aimed at the same mission, namely 'The transportation of troops, casualties, and heavy military ordnance and vehicular equipment and to tow gliders.' However, they took completely different approaches to meeting the requirement.

The two aircraft were designed to have a similar gross weight of around 160,000lb (72,570kg) and both provided for easy-loading, drive-on access through the aft end of the fuselage. They also shared a similar landing gear arrangement – or 'alighting gear' as Fairchild described it – consisting of a tricycle undercarriage

with tracked treads rather than wheels. However, the overall configurations were wildly different.

The Models 99-05 and 06 were high-wing, twin-boom aircraft, very similar to the company's highly successful C-82, but they had more than twice the gross weight and were powered by four rather than two engines.

The cargo bay was 12ft wide and 60ft in length (3.66m by 18.30m), of which 40ft (12.20m) was unobstructed, with a height clearance of 12ft (3.66m). Access was provided by full-width side-opening doors at the rear of fuselage, with an integral ramp. A further, unique, feature was a droppable centre section, 12ft by 20ft (3.66m by 6.10m), allowing sizeable loads to be air-dropped without needing to be manoeuvred around the fuselage.

The Model 99-07 was a canard-configured layout, a design intended to maximise the greatest possible use of the fuselage length. The cargo bay was 77ft (23.49m) long and 12ft (3.66m) wide, with a 13ft 8in (4.17m) height at the entrance, 12ft 6in (3.81m) over the wing and 12ft (3.66m) at the far end. Unlike the Models 99-05 and 06, it was only

Fairchild Models 99-05 and 06	99-05	99-06
Powerplant	4 x P&W R-4360-C12 piston radials @ 2,800hp (2,089kW) (normal), 3,800hp (2,835kW) (military power/water injection)	4 x Wright T35-1 turboprops @ 5,500hp (4,103kW)
Wingspan	118ft 4in (36.09m)	118ft 4in (36.09m)
Length	115ft (35.07m)	115ft (35.07m)
Height	38ft (11.59m)	38ft (11.59m)
Wing area	3,500sq ft (315m²)	3,500sq ft (315m²)
Max TOW	163,000lb (73,936kg)	170,000lb (77,110kg)
Payload	40,000lb (18,160kg)	40,000lb (18,160kg)

DWG. NO. 99-060
MODEL M-99-05
DRAWN- A.E.H.- 3-15-46
FAIRCHILD AIRCRAFT

ABOVE Brochure artwork for the Fairchild M-99-05. *NARA II*

BELOW Brochure artwork showing the Fairchild M-99-05 droppable centre floor section. *NARA II*

DWG. NO. 99-061
MODEL M- 99-05
DRAWN R.L.G. 3-15-46
FAIRCHILD AIRCRAFT

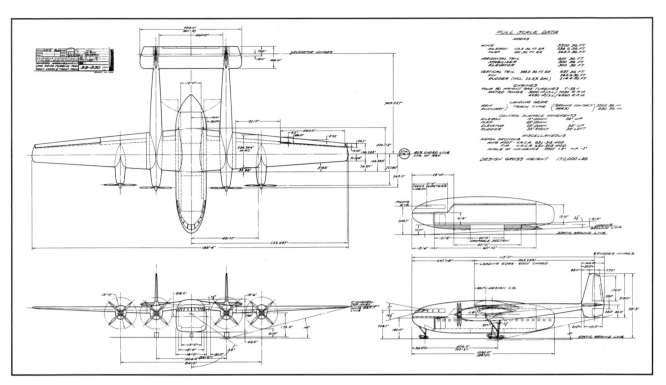

ABOVE Fairchild M-99-05 general arrangement. *NARA II*

BELOW A depiction of the Fairchild M-99-07 with tracked landing gear. Despite the numerous fuselage windows, this design was configured as a cargo transport. *NARA II*

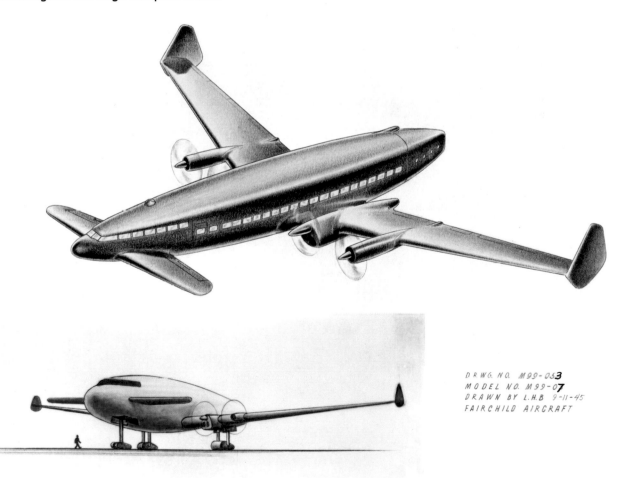

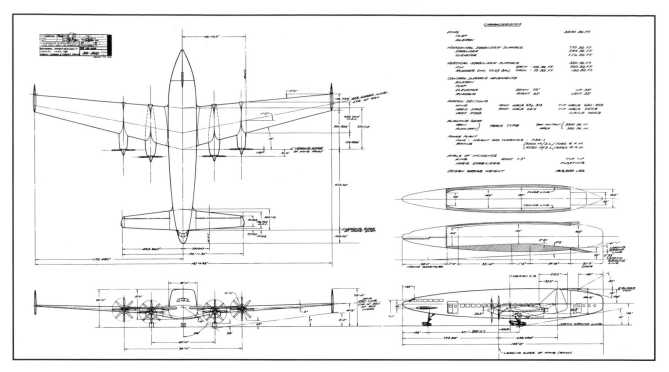

ABOVE Fairchild M-99-07 general arrangement with tracked landing gear. *NARA II*

Fairchild Model 99-07	
Powerplant	4 x Wright T35-1 turboprops @ 5,500hp (4,103kW)
Wingspan	187ft 1in (57.07m)
Length	125ft (38.13m)
Height	23ft 6in (7.17m)
Wing area	3,500sq ft (315m²)
Max TOW	165,000lb (74,910kg)
Payload	40,000lb (18,160kg)

offered with Wright T35-1 turboprop engines. Brief mention was made of a high-wing canard variant (presumably the M-99-08, formerly the M-99-04) with a flat cargo floor that did not 'hump' over the wing carry-through structure. No go-ahead was given for a prototype of either basic design.

Lockheed L-168 Constitution derivative

Lockheed responded to the heavy lift requirement with four different design options under the L-168 designation. The lead offering was the L-168-1, a modified Constitution design featuring an enlarged bottom deck with fore and aft loading doors. Utility was somewhat

BELOW General arrangement of the Lockheed L-168-1, derived from the R6V Constitution, drawn with four Pratt & Whitney R-4360 piston engines. *Lockheed*

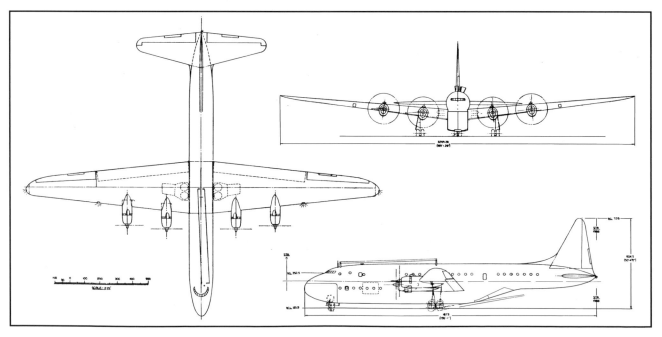

limited as the ceiling was significantly lower under the wing carry-through structure.

Lockheed did not specify the final engine selection, leaving that decision to the Army Air Force. The crux of the dilemma was that the R3350 offered better range with lower performance, but the T35 offered higher power and speed at the cost of much higher fuel consumption.

Lockheed Model L-168-1	
Powerplant	4 x P&W R-4360 radial pistons @ 3,500hp (2,610kW) or 4 x Wright T35-1 turboprops @ 5,500hp (4,103kW)
Wingspan	189ft 1in (57.63m)
Length	156ft 8in (47.75m)
Height	50ft 5 in (15.36m)
Max TOW	210,000lb (95,254kg)
Payload	50,000lb (22,680kg)

The answer: evolution from the C-74

Despite the many imaginative designs described above, the eventual solution to the Air Force's requirement for a heavy cargo transport emerged from the progressive development of a wartime-designed transport.

Douglas's truncated production of the C-74 Globemaster ended with the fourteenth example. With no other military production on the immediate post-war horizon, Douglas's Long Beach Division turned to design studies to improve the C-74. (In fact, excess factory space was leased to

Douglas Globemaster and Globemaster II	Model 415A (C-74)	Model 1196 (C-124A production)
Powerplant	4 x P&W R-4360-49 piston radials @ 3,250hp (2,324kW)	4 x P&W R-4360-20W or 20WA piston radials @ 3,500hp (2,610kW)
Wingspan	173ft 3in (52.84m)	173ft 3in (52.84m)
Length	124ft 2in (37.87m)	127ft 1in (37.71m)
Height	43ft 8.8in (13.30m)	48ft 3.6in (14.72m)
Wing area	2,510sq ft (233m²)	2,510sq ft (233m²)
Empty weight	87,297lb (39,597kg)	94,840lb (43,019kg)
Design gross weight	145,000lb (65,771kg)*	175,000lb (79,379kg)**
Max TOW	208,000lb (94,347kg)***	210,000lb (95,254kg)***
Max payload	65,000lb (39,484kg)	75,500lb (34,019kg)
Max speed	312mph (502km/h)	58kt (478km/h)
Cruise speed	260mph (418km/h)	175kt (324km/h)
Max range	7,200mi (11,580km)	5,460nmi (10,112km)

* 3.0g load factor. ** 2.5g load factor. *** overload, at 2.0g load factor

North American Aviation to produce B-45 jet bombers.)

These studies took three approaches:

- Improve the weight/payload capability of the basic C-74
- Improve the C-74 powerplants
- Improve the volumetric capacity and loading capability of the C-74

As the design authority for the C-74, studies took place at the Douglas Long Beach Division, competing against the 'clean sheet' designs from Santa Monica. The final two derivatives combined the increased gross weight and increased volume options but stayed with Pratt & Whitney R-4360s (slightly uprated). These were the Model 1128 with single deck and a raised ceiling, and the Model 1129, which (1) raised the top of the fuselage further and (2) added a fold-away second deck together with a deepening of the forward fuselage to permit installation of clamshell doors.

Payload for the two designs was set at 50,000lb (22,700kg). Wingtip tanks (of 1,500lb/680.4kg fuel capacity) were initially added as a load relief to the outer wing panels until static testing of the C-74 outer wing panel revealed that this was unnecessary. Combustion heaters (for de-icing hot air) in wingtip pods were added during the C-124 production run.

The actual date of the Air Force's decision to go with Douglas remains unclear, but it appears to have been made in November 1947. The 'C-124' designation first appears in a Douglas report on the Models 1128 and 1129 dated 2 December 1947. The Douglas Model 1129 Design Specification (DS-1129) was issued on 20 January 1948 and the formal contract with the Air Force was signed on 5 April 1948.

As detailed design progressed the Design Specification was revised to DS-1129A. The prototype was given the designation YC-124 and the name 'Globemaster II'. It made its first flight

Douglas C-74 design derivatives leading to the C-124			
Douglas model	Gross weight	Engine type	Notable features
'XC-74X'	180,000lb (81,700kg)	T35-1	Santa Monica proposal
1040	162,000lb (73,550kg)	R-4360	C-74 wings and empennage
1040A	172,000lb (78,090kg)	R-4360	rear ramp, swing-tail
1041	162,000lb (73,550kg)	T35-1	rear ramp
1041A	172,000lb (78,090kg)	R-4360-C16	rear ramp, extra main gear
1106 & 1106A/C/D	145,000lb (65,830kg)	R-4360s (alternatives)	enlarged fuselage
1110 & 1110A/C/D	145,000lb (65,830kg)	R-4360s (alternatives)	
1113 & 1113A/C/D	165,000lb (74,900kg)	R-4360s (alternatives)	enlarged fuselage
1114 & 1114A/C/D	165,000lb (74,900kg)	R-4360s (alternatives)	
1119	165,000lb (74,900kg)	R-4360-20W	decreased wingspan
1122	167,000lb (75,820kg)	R-4360-20W	75ST aluminium outer wing panels
1128	178,000lb (80,810kg)	R-4360-20W	revised fuselage, tip-tanks
1129	178,000lb (74,900kg)	R-4360-20W	deeper fuselage, bow doors

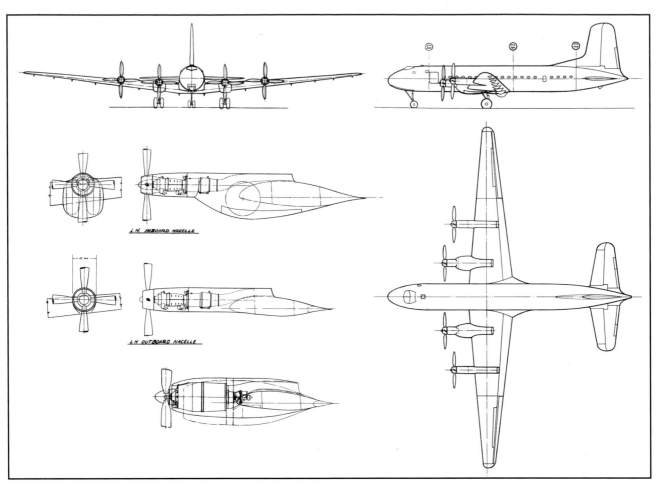

ABOVE The Douglas 'XC-74X' design from August 1947 explored the adaptation of the airframe to the first-generation turboprop engines. The Pratt & Whitney PT-2C (later designated the T34) was an axial-flow turboprop engine that presented a much slimmer profile than the Wright T35 (bottom, at the same scale) and utilised three centrifugal compressors in series. In either case, the inboard nacelles could not be reduced in size for drag reduction because of the space needed for main landing gear stowage. *Boeing*

BELOW A single-deck, raised-ceiling adaptation of the Douglas C-74 with a swing-tail. *Boeing*

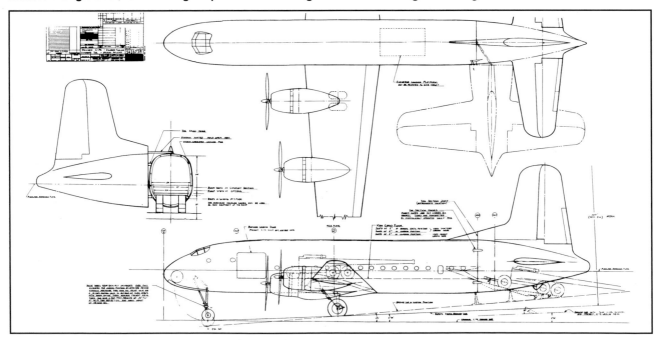

on 27 November 1949 using wings removed from the fifth C-74 and married to a new fuselage. (As such, it retained that C-74's serial number of 42-65406. Due to some confusion at Douglas, the allocated Buzz Number of CA-406 was painted on the tail, rather than the serial number.)

The first C-124A was accepted by the Air Force on 23 April 1950 as the Douglas Model 1196. The Model 1197 was to have been built as the C-124B with revised Pratt & Whitney R-4360 engines, but went no further. C-124Cs were produced per DS-1317 as the Douglas Model 1317 with R-4360-63 engines, new propellers and other minor changes. In all, 448 C-124s were built and the type served until 1974, playing a significant role in both the Korean and Vietnam wars.

The post-war years in perspective

As described in the previous chapter, the Second World War had left no doubt about the future importance of military air transportation. It had also underlined the need for a variety of aircraft to meet different missions, ranging from front-line tactical support to global strategic supply. Moreover, experience had shown that military transport aircraft required special characteristics, in many ways quite different from those of commercial airliners.

Both a need and an opportunity existed to capitalise on the wartime experience and introduce a new range of transport aircraft, specifically

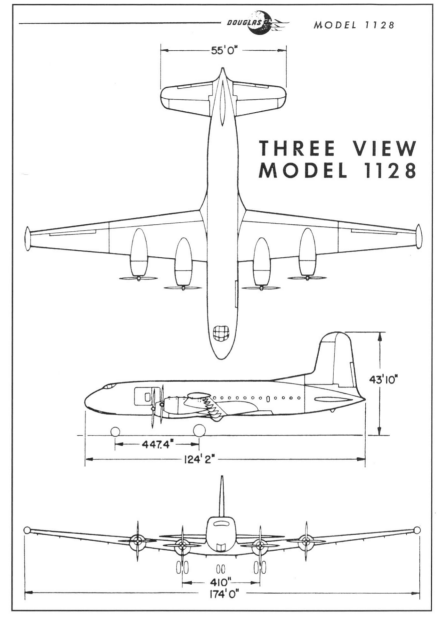

THREE VIEW
MODEL 1128

ABOVE The Douglas Model 1128, with a single deck and slightly squared fuselage cross section. *Boeing*

BELOW A double-deck version of the Douglas C-74 with a side cargo door and rear ramp. *Boeing*

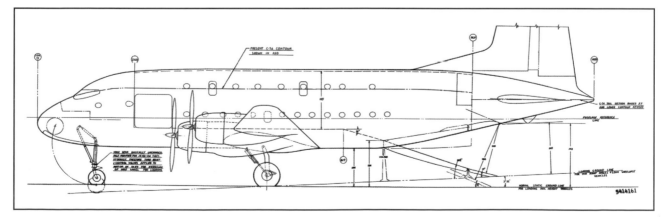

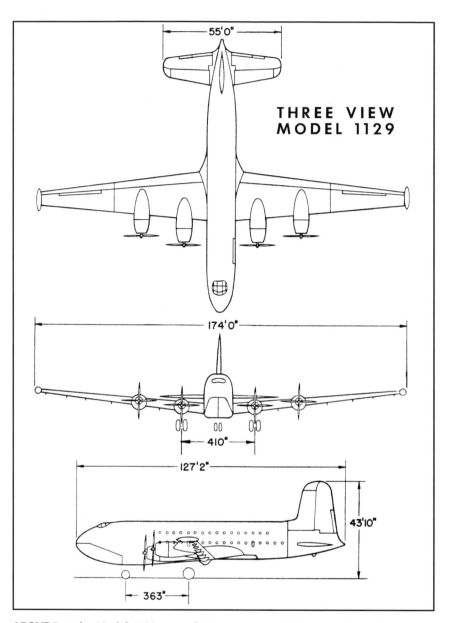

**THREE VIEW
MODEL 1129**

55'0"

174'0"

410"

127'2"

43'10"

363"

ABOVE Douglas Model 1129 general arrangement in 1948. It was later designated the C-124. Initially, fuel was to also be carried in wingtip tanks, but these were deleted from the production aircraft design. *Boeing*

designed for different missions. However, this was not a priority for the armed forces, particularly at a time when funding was being reduced to peacetime levels. 1947 was a particularly bad year, with the Research & Development budget reduced by 75%. The Air Force had a much more pressing need to upgrade its bomber and fighter squadrons, where the rapid advance of the jet engine was rendering wartime front-line aircraft obsolete.

The immediate post-war transport fleet may not have been ideal for its

role, but it was large in number and it did the job. There was no wholesale move to modernise it, at least not at a strategic level. Indeed, some examples (such as the C-47 and, to a lesser extent, the C-46) would continue in service for the next twenty-five years.

None of the three large aircraft that had emerged from wartime design work – the Convair XC-99, Lockheed XR60-1 Constitution and Douglas C-74 – was ordered into large-scale production. The first two flew only as prototypes (albeit being put to some

use by the Air Force and Navy respectively) and the C-74 would require substantial redesign before emerging as the successful C-124A airlifter. Although limited urgency appears to have been given to the development of a heavy cargo aircraft, certainly compared with other types of military aircraft, the timing was fortuitous. The first C-124A was delivered in May 1950; the Korean War started on 25 June.

Progress was also made in extending airlift capability at the tactical end of the range, with aircraft designed to support the Army by operating from short, semi-prepared airstrips close to the front line. The Fairchild C-82 entered service as the war ended, earning it the distinction of being the first mass-produced transport airplane designed from the outset for military use. The other significant aircraft in this category was the Fairchild C-123, which had emerged from a competition originally seeking a new assault glider. As a powered aircraft, the C-123 was poised to set the pattern for modern tactical transports for decades to follow.

The rise of the assault transport, able to operate from rough, forward airstrips, also marked the demise of the glider. Gliders had been used successfully by the Germans in the early stages of the war, and by the Allies to support the D-Day landings and other operations, and as such they still played a part in post-war military thinking. In retrospect it is clear to see that assault gliders had seen their day. They were an aspect of military strategy which, like the static trench warfare of the First World War, had featured in just one conflict.

Many lessons had been learned from the Second World War. Unfortunately, such wartime lessons are not always applicable to the next conflict. By the end of the 1940s the newly formed MATS had a capability unimagined a decade earlier. This was just as well, as it would face major demands on its services in the coming years.

ABOVE This cutaway model of the Douglas C-124 shows the cargo space. The inclined ramp limited the flat floor space, and the folding ramp was unusable for cargo stowage. The cargo cart on the ground marks the location of the elevator, retained from the C-74. *Boeing*

RIGHT Typical mixed troop and cargo carriage in the C-124. The upper deck panels in the upper left and right foreground have been folded up in the configuration used to accommodate outsized cargo. *Author's collection*

BELOW Douglas also developed an airdrop system for the C-124. Cargo-bearing pallets were mounted on rails leading to a retractable segment in the elevator bay. *Boeing*

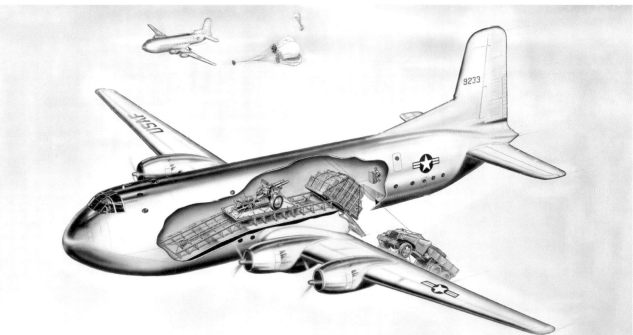

Chapter Five
Stretching Yesterday's Technologies

1950 to 1955:
The search for a new medium airlift aircraft capability

ABOVE Fairchild's operational concept for the pack-plane, with cargo, communications, headquarters and hospital pods delivered to the field site. *Fairchild*

If the 1940s had demonstrated the importance of military air transportation, the next decade was to see its transformation. Not only had the Second World War shown the strategic value – and indeed necessity – of being able to move and support troops quickly, but the Berlin Airlift had additionally demonstrated the enormous potential of air supply. Moreover, far from living in the more peaceful world that everyone hoped

would emerge from the defeat of the Axis powers, America and its allies were soon engaged in a further conflict in Asia and were having to gear up for a long-term, high-readiness, armed stand-off in Europe.

After a brief interlude of scaling down investment in military research and new equipment, expenditure was ramped up to new levels with considerable urgency attached to the outcome. The result was a plethora of new aircraft designs of all

kinds: interceptors, attack aircraft, strategic bombers and transports. And it was out of this era that the modern airlifter was born.

One concept that received intense attention in the first three years of the decade was that of the cargo pod carrier.

ABOVE A notional turbojet multi-purpose pod-carrier concept provides a contrast to the XC-120 as it air-drops a cargo pod for parachute descent. Remote-controlled defensive armament is installed in tail and wingtip positions.
US Air Force

RIGHT The pod concept in action: rapidly transported workshops perform repair work in an austere location. This reflected the lessons learned during the 'Island-hopping' campaign in the Pacific Theatre during the Second World War.
US Air Force

This was by no means a new concept, having been proposed during the Second World War and pursued in the immediate post-war years. The cargo pod was forcefully supported by Lt Gen Joseph Gavin in his 1947 book *Airborne Warfare*, in which he proposed air-deliverable 'KIWI' pods to carry supplies, soldiers and weapons directly to the battlefield. It is unknown if this was a major stimulus, but the pod concept was to be tested within two years and was to play a role in two 1951 formal design competitions known as XC-

Medium and XC-Heavy. Indeed, it would form the focus of the latter competition, as discussed in Chapter Six.

However, the direction of travel was far from clear. The 1950s proved to be a decade of changing, and at times conflicting, military requirements, with aircraft companies responding with attempts to exploit new advances in technology and aeronautical engineering.

At the same time these contractors wanted to sell whatever products they had on hand, particularly if a basic airframe could serve both military and civilian markets. As a consequence, developments did not always follow a clear-cut or obvious path.

How these designs evolved, and how others fell by the wayside, is the subject of this and the following chapter. They were the outcome of two processes. One was the evolutionary development of existing aircraft, progressively improving their capability and taking advantage of parallel advances in technology; the other was in response to formal competitions to meet new military requirements.

Evolutionary developments of existing aircraft

Not surprisingly, the starting point for the development of more advanced airlifters was the further improvement of existing aircraft. Boeing, Douglas and Fairchild all had successful transports in production and each sought ways of either extending the life of these aircraft or using them as platforms for new designs. The C-54, C-97 and C-74 would all give rise to further generations of proposed airlifters.

Fairchild C-119

As described in the previous chapter, the Fairchild C-119 was developed from the successful C-82. The first production version, the C-119B, had entered service in 1949, with an improved version, the

C-119C, following in 1950. Despite its pedigree, numerous problems were encountered with the aircraft, resulting in a stream of modifications.

The invasion of South Korea in 1950 by North Korea (later aided by China) against the backdrop of the Cold War opened the US budget purse strings to an extent unimaginable in 1947. To enable the envisaged '95 Wing Air Force', industrial production had to be raised to near-Second World War rates. In late 1950 it was predicted that some 1,800 C-119s were needed for the USAF and allied air arms.

Against this backdrop, Henry Kaiser was awarded a production contract within a week of his visit to the Pentagon in December 1950. His Kaiser-Frazer Company was to serve as a second-source supplier for the C-119 at the Willow Run Facility, an enormous factory that had been completed during the war by Ford for B-24 production.

The process of helping Kaiser (a potential competitor) to construct an aircraft factory from a near-empty building was a difficult and distracting process for Fairchild, even though the effort was paid for by the Air Force. In addition to its own engineering requirements for C-119 production and

future development, Fairchild was required to assist Kaiser with tooling and also deliver a production baseline for the C-119F, even while that aircraft was under development and subject to continuous modification.

Meantime, Fairchild was also working to improve a flawed aeroplane amidst quickly changing production requirements. To this end, effort progressed along three fronts:

- Production improvements to the C-119 (such as the change from the Pratt & Whitney R4460 to the Wright R3350 engine, which had better fuel consumption)

- Pack-plane development, extending from the experimental XC-120 to the proposed production C-128

- Correction of the C-119's faults, with remedies embodied in the new C-119H

However, within twenty-five months of the announcement of the need for 1,800 aeroplanes, Fairchild was informed that the Air Staff had decided that 'there were no further requirements for C-119 aircraft'. Such was the constantly changing environment in which the aircraft companies were operating.

BELOW The Fairchild XC-120, with cargo pod attached. *Fairchild*

ABOVE The Fairchild XC-120 without the cargo pod. *Terry Panopalis collection*

Pack-planes: the XC-120 and YC-128 (YC-119D/E)

Encouraged by the Air Force, the Fairchild C-119 design was particularly suited for testing the pack-plane concept. The derivative, which was known internally as the M-107, received the XC-120 designation.

The lower part of the C-119's fuselage was removed, leaving a minimal upper section containing the flight deck. The residual fuselage had a flat lower surface to which a specially designed pod was mated. Pods could be fitted out for various roles, such as freight carrying, medical treatment/evacuation, or transportable workshop facilities, then simply towed into place beneath the carrier aircraft. The problem of the removal of the C-119's nose-wheel was resolved by having twin sets of wheels swinging forward from the nacelles behind the engines that housed the main landing gear. The first flight was made without the pack on 11 August 1950, and with it on 29 August.

The XC-120 itself was never considered for production by the Air Force, which regarded it as a proof-of-concept test bed, stating that the 'purpose of the project was to create a laboratory aircraft by the cheapest and

Fairchild XC-120 (Model M-107)	
Powerplant	2 x P&W R4360-20 radial pistons @ 2,650hp (1,976.1kW) normal rating or 3,250hp (2,423.5kW) military rating
Wingspan	109ft 3in (33.30m)
Length	83ft 0in (25.30m)
Height	24ft 7in (7.49m)
Pack length	55ft 11in (17.05m)
Pack width	11ft 6in (3.50m)
Pack height	10ft 2in (3.10m)
Wing area	1,447.24sq ft (134.5m²)
Design gross weight	64,000lb (29,030kg)

most expeditious means'. However, Fairchild pursued the pack-plane concept further, and set about correcting the deficiencies in the XC-120 revealed by testing.

This resulted in a further improved pod-carrying variant of the C-119, the M-142. Rather than have a detachable lower fuselage, the M-142 retained the overall aerodynamic profile of the C-119, but with the mid-aft section of the fuselage forming the detachable pod. This configuration had the advantage of retaining the tricycle landing gear and much of the fuselage of the standard C-119. The concept was further developed with the Model M-144, a similar design powered by two Allison XT40-A-6 turboprops.

The addition of cargo pod features added an empty weight increase of 1,706lb (775kg), which had to be subtracted from the payload. The forward fuselage between the nose and wing leading edge was shortened by 22in (56cm) and the top of the fuselage over the equipment deck aft of the cockpit was raised 9in (23cm) for better avionics and equipment access.

On 5 December 1949 Fairchild submitted a proposal to modify a standard C-119C into the M-142, at a total price increase of $1,539,862. Although initially authorised under the Air Force C-128 designation, a Procurement Directive was issued on 18 September 1950 covering construction of two aircraft, redesignated within the C-119 model number series. The Fairchild M-142 (powered by Pratt & Whitney R-4360-20W engines) was now to be prototyped as the YC-119D and the M-156 (powered by Wright R-3350-30Ws) was to be the YC-119E.

On 26 June 1951 the YC-119D was cancelled and a stop-work order was issued for the YC-119E pending flight test and evaluation of the YC-119H. On 7 November 1952 Headquarters AMC recommended that the YC-119E be cancelled and that the aeroplane be converted into a C-119F. However, as will be seen later in this chapter, this was not the end of pod-carrying proposals.

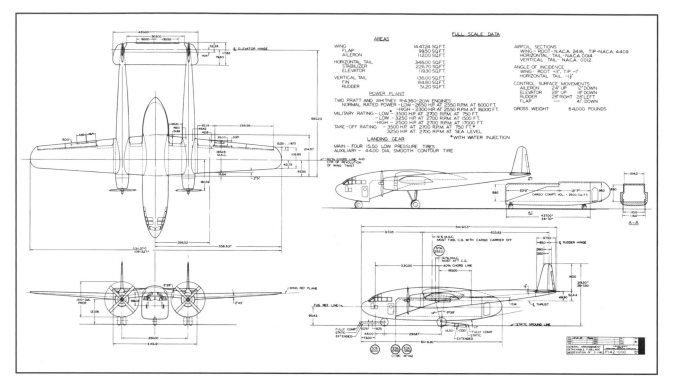

ABOVE Fairchild's piston-engined M-142 pod carrier. *National Air & Space Museum (NASM)*

BELOW Fairchild's M-144 design, powered by Allison XT40-A-6 engines. *NASM*

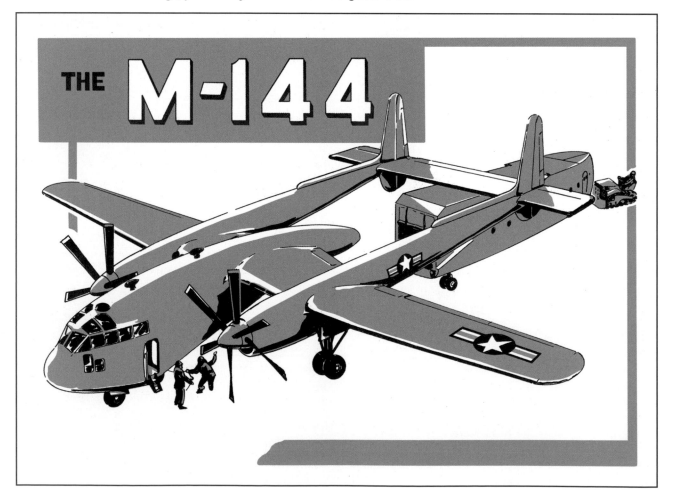

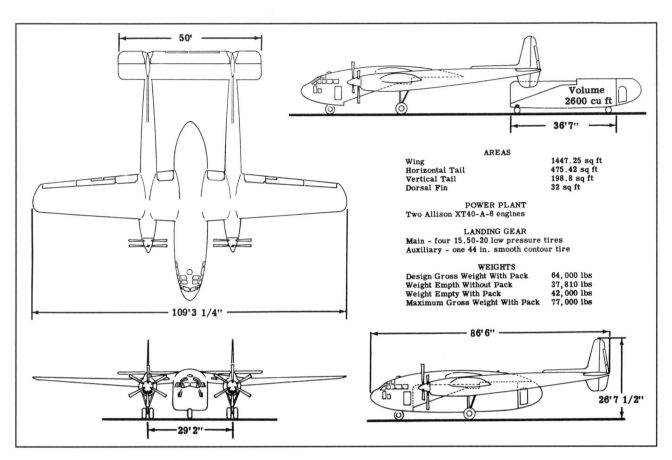

AREAS

Wing	1447.25 sq ft
Horizontal Tail	475.42 sq ft
Vertical Tail	198.8 sq ft
Dorsal Fin	32 sq ft

POWER PLANT
Two Allison XT40-A-6 engines

LANDING GEAR
Main - four 15.50-20 low pressure tires
Auxiliary - one 44 in. smooth contour tire

WEIGHTS

Design Gross Weight With Pack	64,000 lbs
Weight Empth Without Pack	37,810 lbs
Weight Empty With Pack	42,000 lbs
Maximum Gross Weight With Pack	77,000 lbs

ABOVE The turboprop-powered Fairchild M-144 required increases in the size of the vertical and horizontal stabilisers and the addition of dorsal fin surfaces. *NASM*

BELOW The Allison XT40-A-6 engine was cleanly faired into the existing C-119 nacelle structure. *NASM*

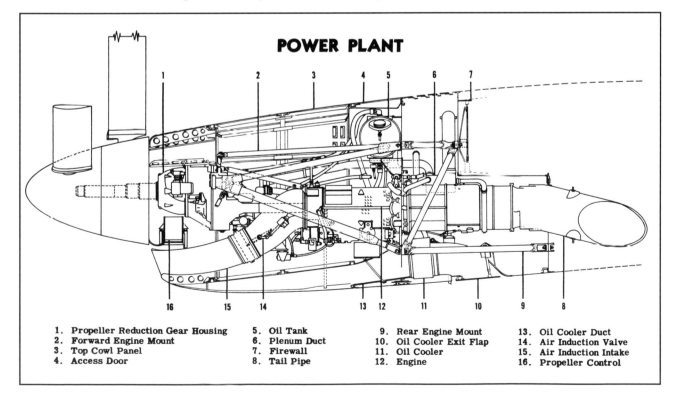

POWER PLANT

1. Propeller Reduction Gear Housing
2. Forward Engine Mount
3. Top Cowl Panel
4. Access Door
5. Oil Tank
6. Plenum Duct
7. Firewall
8. Tail Pipe
9. Rear Engine Mount
10. Oil Cooler Exit Flap
11. Oil Cooler
12. Engine
13. Oil Cooler Duct
14. Air Induction Valve
15. Air Induction Intake
16. Propeller Control

Fairchild advanced cargo pod carriers	Fairchild M-142	Fairchild M-144
Powerplant	2 x P&W R-4360-20W piston radials @ 3,500hp (2,610kW)	2 x Allison XT40-A-6 turboprops @ 5,850eshp (4,362.3kW)
Wingspan	109ft 3.3in (33.30m)	109ft 3.3in (33.30m)
Length	84ft 9.5in (25.83m)	84ft 9.5in (25.83m)
Height	26ft 7.5in (8.10m)	26ft 7.5in (8.10m)
Pack width	11ft 6in (3.51m)	11ft 6in (3.51m)
Pack length	45ft 5.8in (13.85m)	45ft 5.8in (13.85m)
Pack height	9ft 4in (2.84m)	9ft 4in (2.84m)
Wing area	1,447.24sq ft (134.5m²)	1,447.25sq ft (134.5m²)
Design gross weight	64,000lb (29,030kg)	64,000lb (29,030kg)
Pack off	56,843lb (25,784kg)	n/a
Pack weight (empty)	4,390lb (1,991kg)	4,390lb (1,991kg)
Limit dive speed	272kt (503.7km/h)	n/a
Cruise speed	217kt (401.9km/h)	n/a

BELOW General arrangement of the M-194, showing a number of small modifications including squared stabilisers and wingtips, spoilers for roll control, 'beavertail' aft fuselage fairing, and redesigned main landing gear as used on the YC-119H. *NASM*

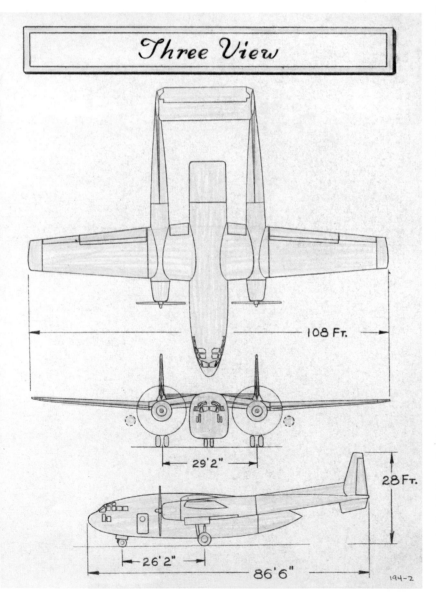

The M-194 C-119 'Advance Base'

Seeking a further opportunity to widen the potential missions for the C-119, Fairchild proposed the M-194 'Advance Base' variant. This had the highly innovative feature of a detachable – and air-droppable – fuselage floor. This enabled the base of the fuselage to be treated as if it were a giant pallet that could be loaded, wheeled into place and air-dropped. It was also claimed that using the system permitted greater accuracy of delivery while avoiding the problems of CG shift normally associated with transferring and ejecting cargo in flight.

A further unusual feature was the installation of two Fairchild J44 engines, which retracted into the upper aft fuselage. These would be used during take-off, landing and emergencies. Since the take-off weight of a twin-engine aircraft is determined by its single-engine climb capability (which was minimal in the C-119), these engines permitted a further 6,000lb (2,724kg) to be added to the maximum take-off weight.

Further adding to the utility of the aircraft, Fairchild proposed a quick-conversion kit to add an air-refuelling capability, with tanks installed in the cargo bay and a single operator extending a drogue hose out of the rear cargo door.

C-119H Skyvan: the ultimate packet

The production C-119 had so many unsatisfactory performance and stability problems that Headquarters, Air Materiel Command (AMC) and Fairchild spent more than a year investigating possible modifications to correct them. The company finally submitted a proposal designed to remedy stability defects, reduce wing loading to permit safe operation at slow speeds, improve take-off and climb characteristics, and increase the structural strength of the airframe. Particular attention was paid to simplifying the structural design to

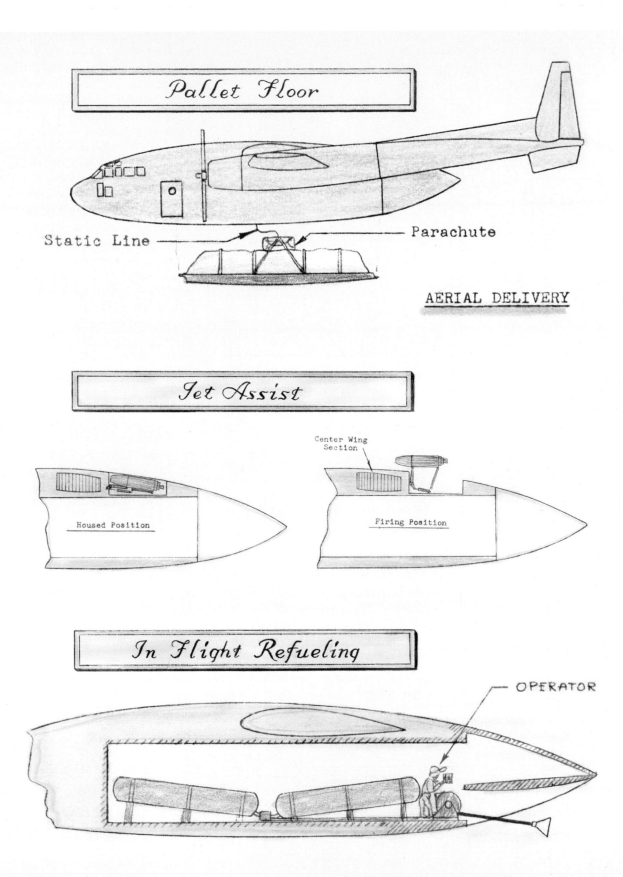

Pallet Floor

Static Line — Parachute

AERIAL DELIVERY

Jet Assist

Housed Position

Center Wing Section

Firing Position

In Flight Refueling

OPERATOR

ABOVE Several of the proposed Fairchild M-194 'Advance Base' enhancements to the C-119. The droppable pallet consisted of the cargo deck, which would be released in flight. *NASM*

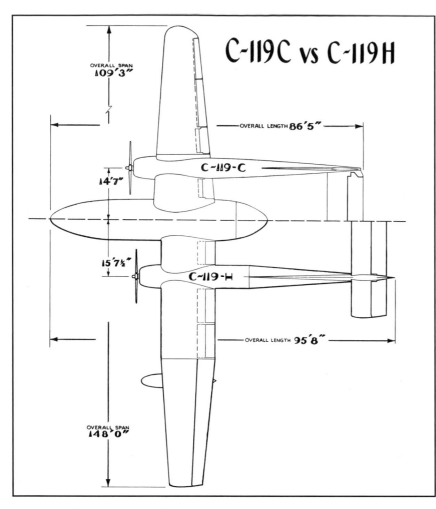

ABOVE Outline comparison of the Fairchild C-119C and C-119H. *NASM*

1,000mi (1,609km)-radius resupply mission, with all its performance exceeding that of the production C-119, except cruising speed, which was expected to suffer about a 12% loss.

On 7 March 1951 Headquarters USAF issued Procurement Directive 51-137 for a long-wing C-119. The directive established $1,750,000 for the project and authorised a delay of three months in the C-119 detachable pod programme. On 23 July 1951 a supplemental agreement to the C-119 production contract was issued to cover construction and testing of the YC-119H. After reviewing engineering data and model test results, Headquarters AMC and Wright Air Development Center (WADC) decided to initiate production of the aeroplane even before the prototype was built and flown.

On 1 December 1951 General Bradley recommended to Headquarters USAF that initial production of 195 C-119Hs be authorised. However, on 2 January 1952 Headquarters USAF was informed that AMC had reviewed the C-119H programme, and that full production implementation of the aircraft was being withheld until the prototype had completed its test programme.

On 9 January 1952 Headquarters AMC sent a planned production schedule to Fairchild that included a production rate for 151 C-119Hs. This was several months before the prototype made its first flight on 27 May 1952. In comparison with the C-119C, the YC-119H showed marked improvement in ease and effectiveness of control, and some improvement in take-off and landing distance. Although the aeroplane was about 20kt (27km/h) slower at cruising speed than the C-119C, it had very good single-engine performance at 80,000lb (36,287kg) gross weight.

improve ease of manufacture, increase life, reduce maintenance and simplify repairs. While the fuselage remained generally the same as the C-119C, every other part of the aeroplane was revised. The wingspan was substantially increased, from 119ft 3in (36.37m) to 148ft (45.14m), with a straight centre section and outer panels featuring a straight-line taper. More effective slotted, extending wing flaps were used and the ailerons were given hydraulic boost.

Of particular significance, all the fuel was now carried in external underwing tanks. This simplified and lightened the (now dry) wing.

The vertical stabilisers were greatly increased in size for improved single-engine controllability and were attached directly to the horizontal stabiliser, which significantly reduced torque loads on the boom structure; this latter factor had made it almost

impossible to increase the stabiliser size in the original C-82 design. The nacelles were constant in section and interchangeable left and right.

A redesigned rough field landing gear was installed with a trailing beam and much simpler support strut arrangement. Provisions were also made to convert to a dual-tandem gear arrangement for soft-surfaced runways. The aeroplane was designed to carry 16,000lb (7,264kg) of payload on a

Fairchild medium cargo aircraft growth

Year	Aircraft	Gross weight
1944	C-82	Designed for 42,000lb (19,051kg)
1945	C-82	Grew to 54,000lb (24,494kg)
1947	C-119	Designed for 64,000lb (29,030kg)
1951	C-119C	Operated at 73,150lb (33,180kg)
1951	C-119H	Designed for 80,870lb (36,682kg)
1951	M-160A	Designed for 124,180lb (56,327kg)
1951	XC-Medium (C-130)	USAF requirement approximately 120,000lb (54,431kg)

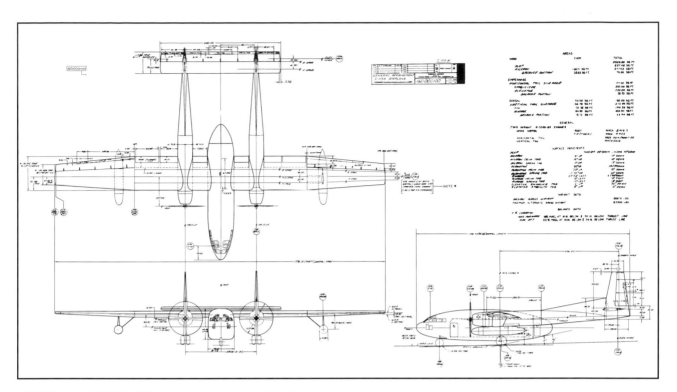

ABOVE Fairchild YC-119H general arrangement. *Fairchild*
BELOW The Fairchild YC-119H in flight. *Fairchild*

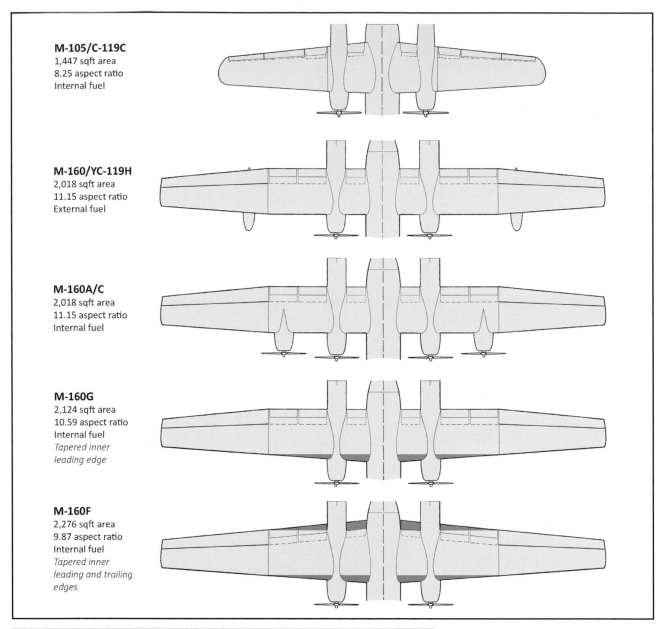

M-105/C-119C
1,447 sqft area
8.25 aspect ratio
Internal fuel

M-160/YC-119H
2,018 sqft area
11.15 aspect ratio
External fuel

M-160A/C
2,018 sqft area
11.15 aspect ratio
Internal fuel

M-160G
2,124 sqft area
10.59 aspect ratio
Internal fuel
Tapered inner leading edge

M-160F
2,276 sqft area
9.87 aspect ratio
Internal fuel
Tapered inner leading and trailing edges

ABOVE Fairchild C-119 wing and engine development. Later versions were to use T40 turboprop engines and were equipped with M-142 detachable fuselage pods. *Authors, based on Fairchild descriptions*

LEFT A display model of the Fairchild M-161, a four-engine variant of the C-119H. *NASM*

However, the aeroplane had other problems. The C-119H weighed about 51,000lb (23,133kg) empty, or almost 5,000lb (2,268kg) more than estimated. This was partly the result of an aluminium shortage that had forced Fairchild to substitute steel in various parts of the structure, making it tail-heavy. Counteracting this required about 1,000lb (454kg) of lead to be added to the nose section before test flying. Additionally, the Air Force felt that the structure had been overbuilt, with the potential for gross weights of more than 100,000lb (45,359kg), which may have been true as Fairchild's derivative M-160A was to gross at 124,180lb (56,327kg).

Fairchild had initiated the C-119H project originally to correct deficiencies in production C-119s. However, the Air Force felt that the work had been built up into a major modification programme, with many of the changes being introduced without first obtaining Government approval. When the company submitted its charges for the C-119H programme, Headquarters Air Materiel Command disallowed most of the profit on the unauthorised work.

On 11 January 1953 AMC was advised that the Air Staff had decided that there were no further requirements for C-119 aircraft. At the time Fairchild was already looking into subcontract work; it had realised that if the C-119H project was not successful, production at Hagerstown would end when the C-119F and G contracts were completed. Production of the C-119s continued into 1955 and concluded with 1,114 delivered by Fairchild and seventy-one by Kaiser-Frazer. As it turned out, the facility was saved when Fairchild successfully bid to produce another aircraft involved in the Kaiser debacle, as described below.

ABOVE Fairchild's YC-119H prototype at rest. The greatly enlarged dorsal and vertical fins were apparently sized for a four-engine configuration. *Fairchild*

Fairchild C-123 developments

To trace the convoluted design history of the C-123, it is first necessary to understand the complex events of 1950-53. It had seemed that the Chase Aircraft Company was poised on the brink of success when, on 12 March 1951, it was awarded a letter as a preliminary contract for 398 C-123Bs.

In reality, the company's situation was dire for three reasons. First, Chase occupied leased Navy production facilities at the airport at Trenton, New Jersey, which, with the advent of the Korean War, were due to revert to the Navy. Furthermore, these facilities were

sufficient to build only one aircraft every five months. Second, the company was much better suited to research and development than it was to volume production. Indeed, it had never built more than nine aircraft of any one type. Third, Chase's cost overruns on the prototype contracts for the XCG-20 glider types and XC-123 and its conversions had caused the Air Force to so lose confidence that it informed the company on 20 December 1950 that no further contracts would be issued.

The Air Force was in the undesirable position of having sponsored an aircraft design that had won two competitions and that it was under pressure from the Army to procure, while at the same time having no confidence in its builder. On 7 March 1951 Michael Stroukoff, Chase's founder and Chief Engineer, briefed the Air Force that Chase had concluded a lease on a Birmingham, Alabama, facility for production, and that it planned to revamp its senior management by two major hires: the soon-to-retire Major General Elwood 'Pete' Quesada as President, and General George C. Kenney as Chairman of the Board. However, these moves failed to impress the Air Force; rather, they raised ethical questions about approaching military personnel when they were still serving.

The Air Force held internal discussions in late April 1951 to

Fairchild 'Big Wing' C-119 developments

M-160	[C-119H] Medium Cargo versions [M-160A to Q]
M-161	[C-119H] Medium Cargo – four R-2800 engines
M-163	C-119 assault transport
M-164	Partial external fuel, large centre section (four R-2800)
M-167	XC-120-type detachable pack with 'Big Wing'
M-168	C-119H with detachable pack
M-169	T40-A-6 turboprop version of C-119H
M-170	T40-A-6 turboprop detachable fuselage (M-142) version of C-119H
M-173	Four-engine (R-3350) version C-119H-type cargo carrier
M-179	Four Wright Turbo Cyclone R-1820-82 engines (version of C-119H)
M-180	Four P&W R-2800-12 'Twin Wasp' engines
M-182	Commercial Cargo (C-119H)
M-190	Four-engine freighter version of C-119H
M-191	Land-based ASW (C-119H four-engine model)
M-210	SAC, TAC, and MATS versions of C-119H

ABOVE The first Stroukoff-built C-123B with the revised (but not final) vertical stabiliser. *Author's Collection*

BELOW A Fairchild-built C-123B, with the large dorsal fin added on the production aircraft, releases the starboard nacelle fuel tank in a test. This capability was touted as a safety feature and was added after the XC-123 centre wing fuel tanks exploded and the aircraft was destroyed by fire after a crash-landing on 27 June 1951, killing the pilot and injuring the other crew members. *Fairchild*

On 24 June 1953, in the midst of Congressional hearings into what had by then become a scandal, the Air Force terminated the Kaiser C-123 and C-119 contracts. After massive cost overruns and schedule slips (primarily on the C-119), just two C-123B aircraft had been built at Trenton. In September 1953 Kaiser's Willys Motors subsidiary paradoxically bought the remaining 51% of Chase Aircraft from Stroukoff and his associates, announcing that it would not bid for full production of the C-123. This was because the week before it had leased the entire Willow Run facility to General Motors, which had suffered a devastating factory fire at another facility and needed the production space. With the proceeds from the sale of the company, Michael Stroukoff incorporated the Stroukoff Aircraft Corporation and purchased back the Trenton assets of the former Chase Aircraft Company from Willys.

The Air Force then put the C-123 'build to print' contract out to the industry, with bids due in September 1953. Companies invited to bid were Convair, Martin, Lockheed and North American Aviation. Fairchild placed an unsolicited bid and was notified that it had won the production contract on 12 October 1953 after committing to a price that was 10% lower than its closest competitor. The fixed-price 'build to print' contract had the interesting side-effect that the aircraft was produced using Chase drawings and part numbers. This resulted in every C-123 built by Fairchild having a manufacturer's data plate stamped with the Chase 'MS-8B' designation, not a Fairchild model number.

Winning this contract was a must for Fairchild because the C-119 had lost favour with the Air Force, and plans for combined production to support a 95-wing Air Force had been repeatedly scaled back. Moreover, Fairchild had bet on the C-119H design and did not bid in the XC-Medium competition – with the result of watching from the sidelines as the Lockheed C-130 (whose development is discussed later) replaced the C-119.

determine which aircraft company would be best suited to take over the production contract. AVCO, Beech, Douglas, Fairchild and Goodyear were all short-listed. Most of the contractors were eliminated due to either not having sufficient capacity to absorb the additional engineering or production load (Douglas, Fairchild), or not having sufficient engineering staff (AVCO, Goodyear). Interestingly, Beech was assessed as offering the best prospects for a successful production run, taking over

the Chicago plant where Douglas had produced the C-54 during the Second World War. However, the company was not awarded the contract because Henry Kaiser informed the Air Force on 4 May 1951 that he had purchased 49% of Chase and planned to move C-123 final assembly to the Willow Run production facility with some sub-assemblies being built at the Trenton plant. The Air Force was initially placated and allowed the plan to proceed. However, its earlier fears proved well-founded.

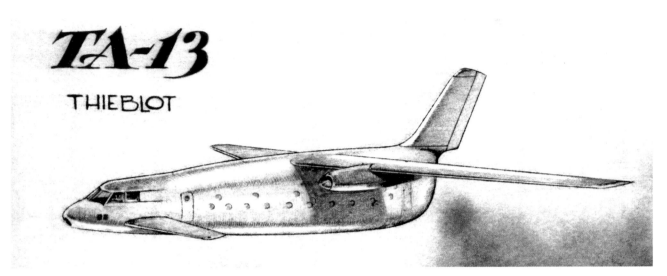

Thieblot TA-13

Even as the C-123 production saga was being settled, another competitor appeared – the A. J. Thieblot Aircraft Engineering Company – with its TA-13. Based in West Virginia, Thieblot had been founded by Armond J. Thieblot, former Chief Engineer at Fairchild. The unconventional canard layout was in fact based on previous work headed up by Thieblot on Fairchild's M-99 heavy airlifter, the M-121 long-range bomber and the M-128 naval attack aircraft.

Adding further to the unusual design was its trimotor configuration. In addition to the wing-mounted Allison T38 turboprop engines, a small unspecified turbofan engine was installed in the nose to provide boundary layer control pressurised air to the 'eleflaps' mounted on the all-moving canard. There is no record of interest by the Air Force. However, Thieblot later patented the design when he returned to Fairchild in 1959, after selling his company to Vitro Corporation.

BELOW The Thieblot Aircraft Company's TA-13 was actually a trimotor design with a turbofan engine buried in the nose, its exhaust feeding blown flaps in the canard for take-off and landing. *NARA II*

ABOVE Thieblot TA-13 general arrangement. *NARA II*

Thieblot Model TA-13 assault transport	
Powerplant	2 x Allison YT38 turboprops @ 3,475shp (2,591.3kW)
	1 x Turbomeca Aspin II geared turbofan @ 800lbst (3.56kN) for BLC
Wingspan	105ft 4in (32.10m)
Length	83ft 0in (25.30m)
Height	29ft 5in (9.00m)
Wing area	1,214sq ft (112.8m²)
Max TOW	48,000lb (21,170kg)
Payload	24,000lb (10,890kg) or 60 troops or 40 litters
Cruise speed	200kt (370km/h)
Combat speed	301kt (558km/h)
Combat radius	758nmi (1,450km)

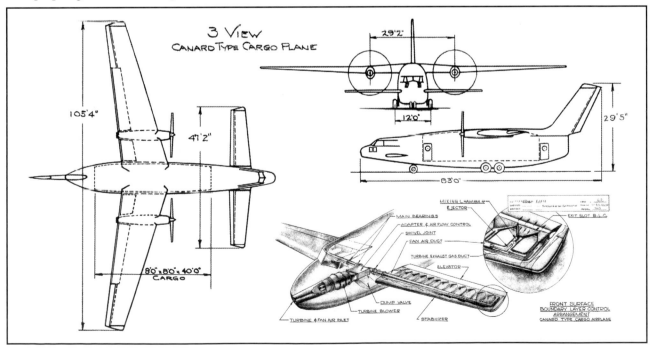

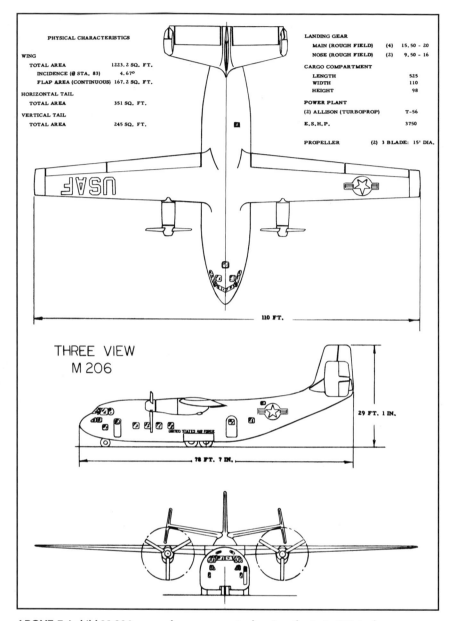

PHYSICAL CHARACTERISTICS

WING

TOTAL AREA   1223.2 SQ. FT.

  INCIDENCE (@ STA. 83)   4.67°

  FLAP AREA (CONTINUOUS)   167.2 SQ. FT.

HORIZONTAL TAIL

  TOTAL AREA   351 SQ. FT.

VERTICAL TAIL

  TOTAL AREA   245 SQ. FT.

LANDING GEAR

  MAIN (ROUGH FIELD)   (4)   15.50 - 20

  NOSE (ROUGH FIELD)   (2)   9.50 - 16

CARGO COMPARTMENT

  LENGTH   525

  WIDTH   110

  HEIGHT   98

POWER PLANT

(2) ALLISON (TURBOPROP)   T-56

E.S.H.P.   3750

PROPELLER   (2) 3 BLADE: 15' DIA.

110 FT.

THREE VIEW M 206

29 FT. 1 IN.

78 FT. 7 IN.

ABOVE Fairchild M-206 general arrangement, showing the twin T56 turboprops, revised main landing gear and triple tail. *NASM*

BELOW The Fairchild M-206 had this unusual T56 engine installation, which ducted intake air through the spinner. *NASM*

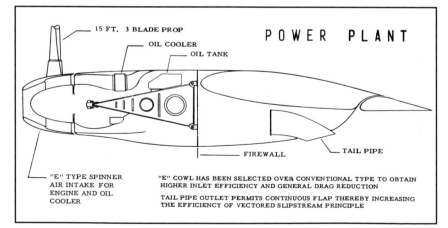

15 FT. 3 BLADE PROP

OIL COOLER

OIL TANK

POWER PLANT

FIREWALL

TAIL PIPE

"E" TYPE SPINNER AIR INTAKE FOR ENGINE AND OIL COOLER

"E" COWL HAS BEEN SELECTED OVER CONVENTIONAL TYPE TO OBTAIN HIGHER INLET EFFICIENCY AND GENERAL DRAG REDUCTION

TAIL PIPE OUTLET PERMITS CONTINUOUS FLAP THEREBY INCREASING THE EFFICIENCY OF VECTORED SLIPSTREAM PRINCIPLE

Fairchild Model M-206 assault transport	
Powerplant	2 x Allison T56 turboprops @ 3,750eshp (2,796.4kW)
Wingspan	110ft 0in (33.53m)
Length	78ft 7in (23.95m)
Height	29ft 1in (8.86m)
Wing area	1,223.2sq ft (113.6m²)
Max TOW	80,000lb (36,290kg)
Payload	14,323lb (6,497kg)
Max speed	299kt (554km/h)
Cruise speed	243kt (450km/h)
Range	1,825nmi (3,380km)

Fairchild M-205 and M-206

In August 1954, after an initial assessment of the Chase C-123B, Fairchild proposed two improved versions: the M-205 with the Wright R-3350 piston engine, and the M-206 with the Allison T56 turboprop. These were attempts to address the shortcomings of the C-123B – namely, being underpowered, having poor directional stability at high angles of attack, and having a landing gear that limited the aircraft's gross landing weight.

These shortcomings have to be seen in the context of the aircraft's otherwise admirable qualities, and were not black marks on Michael Stroukoff's record as a designer. Indeed, it was a tribute to his original design that the CG-20 glider was rugged enough to withstand the addition of engines and extra fuel while still retaining its basic utility and cargo load.

Fairchild addressed the directional stability issue by reducing the size of the vertical stabiliser and adding two endplate surfaces with rudders. The main landing gear was modified with a set of long-stroke, levered tandem main wheels. It is unclear whether these improvements were originated by Fairchild or Stroukoff, since the tail assembly is similar to the Chase XC-Medium proposal design. The tandem main landing gear arrangement would be incorporated in the Stroukoff YC-134. This does not imply any impropriety; Fairchild and Stroukoff apparently had a close business relationship, bound by the aircraft's design.

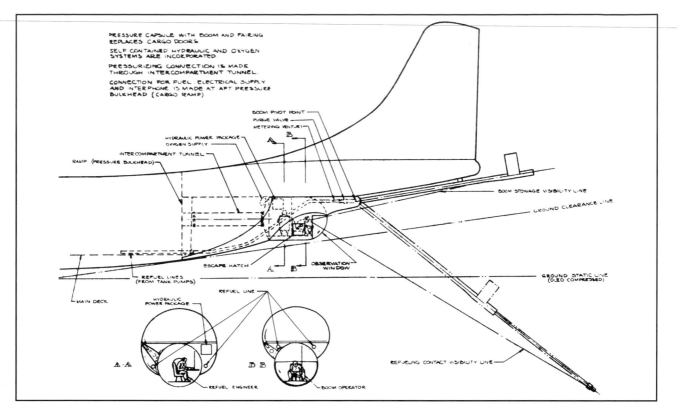

PRESSURE CAPSULE WITH BOOM AND FAIRING
REPLACES CARGO DOORS

SELF CONTAINED HYDRAULIC AND OXYGEN
SYSTEMS ARE INCORPORATED

PRESSURIZING CONNECTION IS MADE
THROUGH INTERCOMPARTMENT TUNNEL.

CONNECTION FOR FUEL, ELECTRICAL SUPPLY
AND INTERPHONE IS MADE AT AFT PRESSURE
BULKHEAD (CARGO RAMP)

BOOM PIVOT POINT

PURGE VALVE

METERING VENTURI

HYDRAULIC POWER PACKAGE

OXYGEN SUPPLY

INTERCOMPARTMENT TUNNEL

RAMP (PRESSURE BULKHEAD)

BOOM STOWAGE VISIBILITY LINE

GROUND CLEARANCE LINE

ESCAPE HATCH

OBSERVATION WINDOW

REFUEL LINES
(FROM TANK PUMPS)

MAIN DECK

GROUND STATIC LINE
(OLEO COMPRESSED)

HYDRAULIC
POWER PACKAGE

REFUEL LINE

REFUEL LINE

REFUELING CONTACT VISIBILITY LINE

A A

B B

REFUEL ENGINEER

BOOM OPERATOR

ABOVE The Boeing Model 495 also had provision for a 'flying boom' refuelling system with a pressurised compartment for the engineer and boom operator. *Boeing*

BELOW The Boeing Model 495 featured an inverted gull wing to shorten the length of the main gear struts and reduce weight. *John Aldaz photo*

Chase/Stroukoff XC-Medium

The one existing record of a Chase submission for the XC-Medium competition is a conceptual painting. It shows an aircraft powered by four XT40-A-6s with counter-rotating propellers, a mid-wing configuration and a double-deck, circular-section fuselage with an upswept rear fuselage supporting the horizontal stabiliser and triple vertical fins. If not for the engines, it would in fact look more like a concept from the previous decade than a major step forward in airlifter design. Equally mystifying is the selection of a mid-positioned wing, which forced the main cargo deck far above the truckbed height that the Air Force and Army desired. This was one of three reported Chase submissions to the competition.

Douglas (Long Beach) Models 1309 and 1316 XC-Medium

At the time of the XC-Medium and XC-Heavy competitions, the three Douglas plants at El Segundo, Santa Monica and Long Beach were operating as semi-autonomous units, reflecting the company's decentralised structure and history. Douglas consequently submitted three different designs, two conventional from Long Beach and one from Santa Monica that was radically different.

Douglas's Long Beach Division proposed a low-wing conventional configuration for the XC-Medium requirement. It was offered in two versions: the Model 1309, powered by Allison Model 501-D2 (T38) turboprops, and the Model 1316, equipped with Wright R-3350 piston radial engines. The latter, of course, was

ABOVE Artwork depicting one of three reported Chase/Stroukoff XC-Medium proposals. *American Aviation Historical Society*

at variance with the Air Force's specified requirements. However, it appears that there was a faction within the USAF's technical facility at Wright Field that had some reservations about the yet-to-be-fully-proven turboprop technology and suggested that a back-up proposal with piston engines would not be a bad idea. There is a record of a similar hint being given to Boeing.

The aircraft had an upswept rear fuselage with an integral drop-down ramp. Unlike Lockheed's design, the ramp could not support cargo when it was stowed for flight, limiting its utility. The aircraft featured a four-wheeled main landing gear with a very short strut that gave it a tail-down 'sit' for loading efficiency.

Douglas Models 1309 and 1316 (XC-Medium)	Model 1309	Model 1316
Powerplant	4 x Allison 501-D2 (T38) turboprops @ 3,478shp (2593.4kW)	4 x Wright R3350 piston radials @ 3,700hp (2,759kW)
Wingspan	134ft 2in (40.89m)	134ft 2in (40.89m)
Length	112ft 1in (34.16m)	112ft 1in (34.16m)
Height	39ft 1.5in (11.92m)	39ft 1.5in (11.92m)
Wing area	2,000sq ft (185.8m²)	2,000sq ft (185.8m²)
Design gross weight	125,000lb (56,700kg)	136,000lb (61,690kg)
Payload	58,650lb (26,600kg)	59,000lb (26,760kg)
Max speed	337kt (624km/h)	283kt (524km/h)
Cruise speed	300kt (556km/h)	262kt (485km/h)
Combat range	1,725nmi (3,195km)	1,670nmi (3,093km)

Douglas Model 1252 (XC-Medium)	
Powerplant	4 x Allison T38 turboprops @ 3,750eshp (2,796.4kW)
Wingspan	159ft 8in (48.67m)
Length	118ft 3in (36m)
Height	34ft 10in (10.64m)
Wing area	2,400sq ft (223.0m²)
Design gross weight	142,000lb (64,410kg)
Payload	36,000lb (16,330kg)
Max speed	331kt (613km/h)
Cruise speed	299kt (554km/h)
Range*	2,780nmi (5,149km)

* range with fuel in pod up to maximum weight, 4,075nmi (7,543km)

Douglas (Santa Monica) Model 1252 (XC-Medium)

The Douglas Santa Monica Division took a more radical approach to meeting the XC-Medium requirement, adopting a scaled-down version of its Model 1240 entry to the XC-Heavy competition (described in the next chapter). The Model 1252 was a straight-wing, four-engine aircraft with an asymmetric configuration. Its port boom housed the flight deck and the four-person crew.

Unlike the Fairchild XC-120 pod-carrier described previously, the Model 1252 was designed to be highly flexible in the cargo it could transport. The payload slung beneath the centre section of the wing had to be aerodynamically compatible with the rest of the aeroplane, but did not form an integral part of the fuselage profile. One desk model, for example, displays the aircraft transporting a single Navaho missile. A cargo of two or three 'Transit Vans' (a concept described later) could also be carried with the use of a faired set of adapter beams mating to the wing centre section.

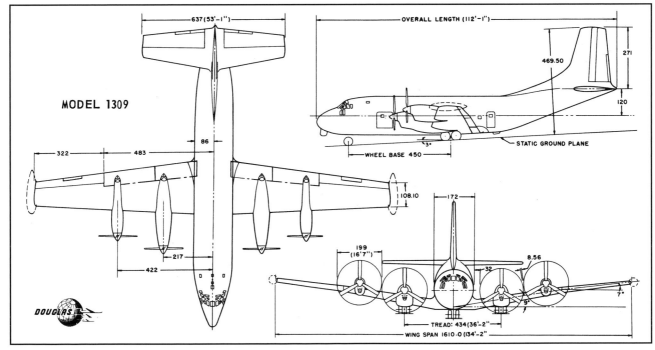

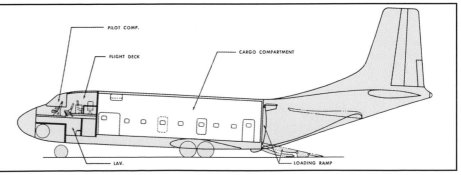

ABOVE Douglas Model 1309 general arrangement. It was powered by four Allison T38 turboshaft engines. *Boeing*

RIGHT The inboard profile for the Models 1309 and 1316. The loading ramp performed double duty, folding up to become the aft pressure bulkhead. *Boeing*

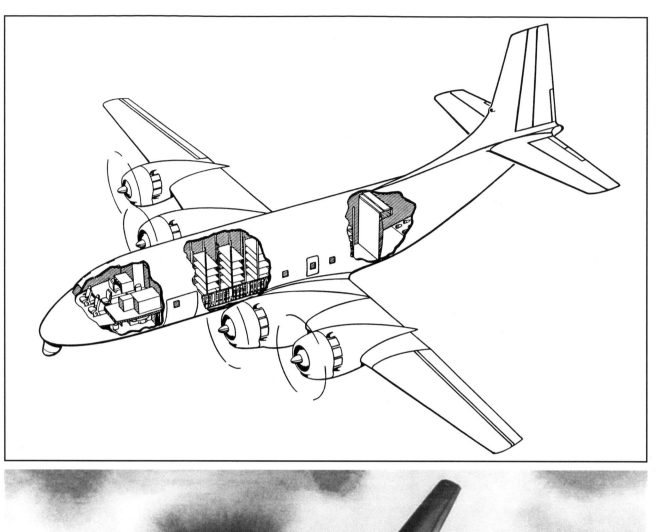

Since the aircraft was intended to fly into and land in combat zones, removable dural armour plating could be installed to protect the pilot, co-pilot and engines. Self-sealing fuel tanks were also standard.

Lockheed California L-206 XC-Medium

Lockheed worked up three different designs before finalising its XC-Medium submission. The first two, bearing the Lockheed Temporary Design Numbers (TDN) L-206-1 and L-206-2, were very similar aircraft, sharing a conventional high-wing configuration and differing only in wing size. The third, the L-206-3, was a far less conventional design, using a pod-carrier solution to meet the requirement. All three were to be powered by four T38 turboprops.

The L-206-2 was smaller and some 10,000lb (4,540kg) lighter than the

L-206-1. It could cruise slightly faster but carried less payload and had a shorter range.

Unusual for a pod-carrying aircraft, the L-206-3 did not use a twin-boom configuration, relying instead on a conventional layout with a single, very slim fuselage. The landing gear consisted of main wheels that retracted into the aft section of the inboard engine nacelles, and small wheels (in lieu of the normal nose-wheel) that retracted into the front part of the nacelles.

The cargo pod was designed to fit the underside of the fuselage, with full-width clamshell doors at both fore and aft ends. It incorporated a ramp for air-dropping and featured small extendable wheels for ground handling. While the L-206-3 offered the advantage of a quicker turnaround on the ground, it was 10,500lb (4,540kg) heavier than the -1. It was also slower, with less range and less payload. After evaluating the trade-offs offered by each version,

Lockheed selected the L-206-1 as the basis for the company's XC-Medium submission.

On 2 July 1951 Lockheed was announced as the winner of the competition, narrowly beating the equivalent Douglas designs, and a letter contract was issued on 11 July. The aircraft was to be powered by the Allison YT38-A-8 engine (subsequently redesignated YT56-A-1). It was assigned the Lockheed Model Number 082-44-01 and the Air Force designation XC-130. By March 1952 Lockheed had built a mock-up at its Burbank plant and on 19 September the Air Force issued an order to produce two prototype aircraft.

The only significant external change made as the design progressed after the mock-up review was to reposition the

OPPOSITE TOP The Douglas Model 1316 was powered by four Wright R3350s, and is shown here with transverse-mounted aeromedical evacuation litters. *Boeing*

OPPOSITE BOTTOM The Douglas Model 1252 with external cargo/troop pod. *Boeing*

BELOW Douglas Model 1252 general arrangement. *Boeing*

Lockheed L-206-3 (XC-Medium)	
Powerplant	4 x Allison T38 turboprops @ 3,750hp (2,796.4kW)
Wingspan	132ft 8in (40.44m)
Length	87ft 6in (26.67m)
Height	43ft 3in (13.18m)
Wing area	1,344.6sq ft (124.91m²)
Max TOW	130,000lb (58,970kg)

Lockheed L-206-1 (XC-Medium) later, XC-130	
Powerplant	4 x Allison YT38-A-8 turboprops @ 3,750hp (2,796.4kW)
Wingspan	132ft 7in (40.41m)
Length	95ft 0in (28.96m)
Height	38ft 4in (11.68m)
Wing area	1,744.6sq ft (162.08m²)
Max TOW	113,000lb (51,260kg)
Payload	23,700lb (10,750kg)
Combat speed	346kt (640km/h)
Combat range	1,942nmi (3,597km)

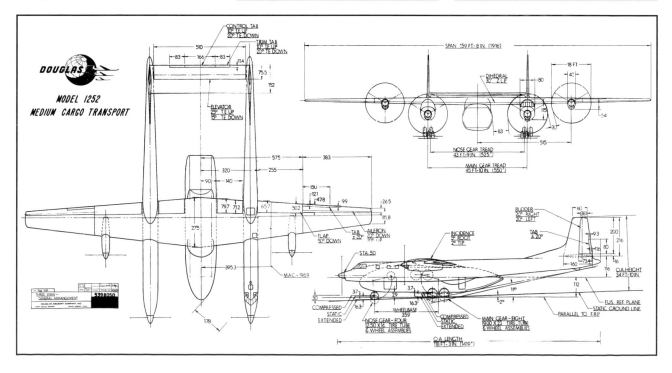

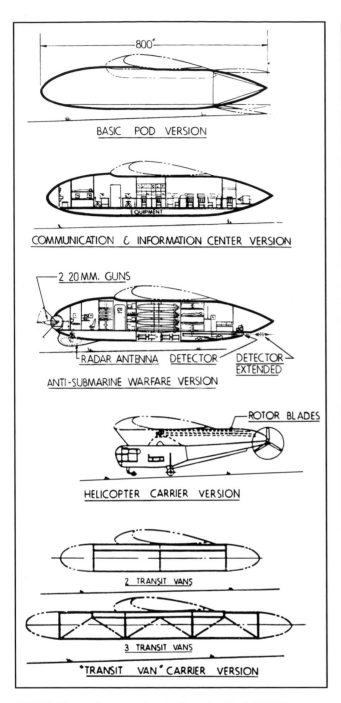

BASIC POD VERSION

COMMUNICATION & INFORMATION CENTER VERSION

2 20 MM. GUNS

RADAR ANTENNA   DETECTOR   DETECTOR EXTENDED

ANTI-SUBMARINE WARFARE VERSION

ROTOR BLADES

HELICOPTER CARRIER VERSION

2 TRANSIT VANS

3 TRANSIT VANS

'TRANSIT VAN' CARRIER VERSION

ABOVE Alternative pods for the Douglas Model 1252 included an anti-submarine version with a torpedo bay and 20mm cannon turret in the nose. A helicopter (Sikorsky H-5) could be ferried to a remote location for a rescue mission, and Transit Vans could also be carried. *Boeing*

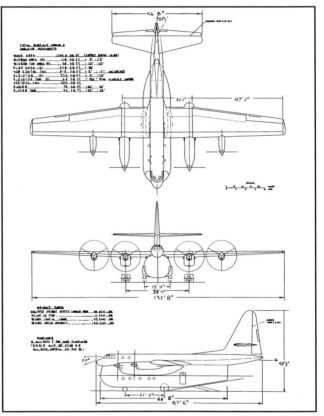

ABOVE A display model of the Douglas Model 1252, shown carrying a Navaho missile. *John Aldaz photo*

ABOVE Lockheed CL-206-3 external pod-carrier general arrangement. *Lockheed*

horizontal stabiliser from part way up the vertical fin to the top of the rear fuselage. Redesignated the YC-130, it first flew on 23 August 1954. Although designed and built in Burbank, the two YC-130s were the only examples constructed there. Production was transferred to the Lockheed Georgia company at Marietta, and all C-130s have since been built there. The Lockheed C-130 has arguably become the most successful military transport in aviation history, rivalled only by the DC-3/C-47.

OPPOSITE TOP Details of the Lockheed L-206-3 detachable cargo pod. Only the forward fuselage would be pressurised. *Lockheed*

OPPOSITE BOTTOM The Lockheed L-206-1 (XC-130) with conventional cockpit glazing, under-fuselage radar and cruciform tail. All three features changed before the YC-130's first flight. *US Air Force*

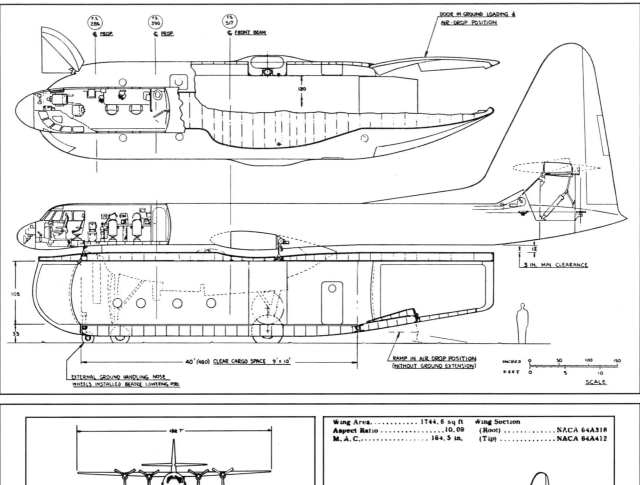

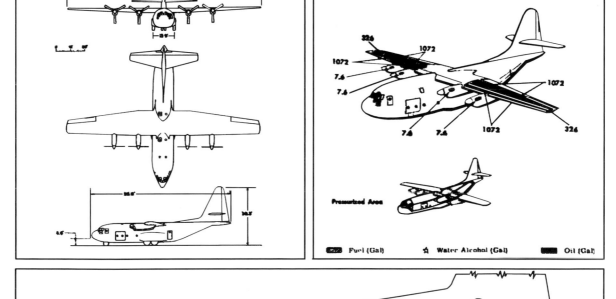

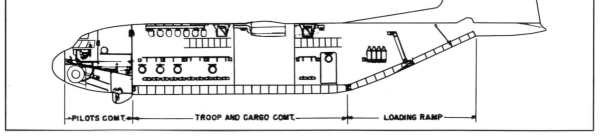

ABOVE The Lockheed L-206-1/Model 82/YC-130 mock-up review at the Lockheed plant at Burbank Airport. The horizontal stabiliser was still to be mounted on the tail (represented by the painted ellipse). *San Diego Air and Space Museum*

BELOW The first YC-130 prototype is parked on Lockheed's ramp at Burbank airport. With the exception of the short nose, it is almost indistinguishable from the standard body length Hercules that is still in production in 2019. *Lockheed*

Early 1950s medium airlifters in perspective

By the mid-1950s the Air Force finally had its long-sought medium airlifter. The path to its acquisition had certainly been far from straightforward; the manufacturers initially squeezed the full development potential out of their earlier successful aircraft, while the Air Force explored the promise of new configurations such as canard layouts,

pod-carriers and 'Pi-Tail' aircraft.

In the end, the chosen aircraft, the C-130, mirrored the C-123, with the elements of airlifter design characteristics that are now well accepted and have become the norm in configuration. These elements included the aft cargo ramp with upswept fuselage, the high wing and

the fuselage-mounted main landing gear, all integrated into an well-executed design. Nevertheless, when the C-130 first flew in August 1954 Lockheed anticipated a production run of just 300 units. Even the best pundit could not have imagined that, sixty years and 3,000 aircraft later, Lockheed would still be producing it.

Chapter Six
Development of Heavy Airlift Capability

1950 to 1957: The struggle to match a new level of military requirement

ABOVE The XC-132 mock-up is seen after relocation to the Douglas plant at Tulsa, Oklahoma, in January 1956. *Boeing*

While the development of a tactical transport was taking place, as described in the preceding chapter, military attention was also focusing on a parallel requirement: the need for a heavy strategic airlifter. This prompted two lines of response from the major aircraft manufacturers. One was to extend the development of their existing, proven designs, arguably to the limit; the other to was to approach the problem afresh, coming up with a wholly new aircraft, in some cases employing a revolutionary new configuration. These differing approaches would pose an interesting dilemma for the Air Force.

Further evolution of the C-97: the Boeing Model 367 Series

While the C-97A entered service during the second half of 1949, Boeing was already looking at ways of further exploiting the aircraft's potential. In 1950 the company flight tested an airborne tanker version, trailing a 'flying boom' aerial refuelling system it had devised. Involving three modified C-97A aircraft, under the designation KC-97A, these trials proved highly successful. They led to a production order for what was to become the world's first dedicated flying tanker, with 816 aircraft eventually delivered to the Air Force. All of these were also convertible for transport use if needed.

Beyond this, Boeing looked for other ways of either enhancing the C-97's capabilities or offering a successor. These possibilities were explored within an extensive series of designs under the same generic designation as the original C-97, the Model 367. The 367 Series progressed through multiple different iterations, some considered in more depth than others.

Turboprop-powered C-97 developments

An early step in enhancing the C-97's performance was to explore the possibility of replacing the piston radial engines with turboprops. Examples of this were the 367-22-1 and 367-41, using the Pratt & Whitney T34 and Allison T40-A-8 engines respectively. Apparently the Air Force showed little interest in such possibilities, though later, and somewhat ironically, two KC-97Gs were modified in 1955 at the Air Force's request to serve as flying test beds for the Pratt & Whitney YT34-P-5 engine. These were initially given the designation YC-97H, but when the H suffix was assigned to another C-97 variant they were redesignated YC-97J. For a time it was proposed that the aircraft be given a completely new designation, YC-137, but this did not occur. Boeing assigned it the Model Number 367-86.

Flight testing confirmed the anticipated substantial improvement in performance from the lighter and more powerful engines in terms of cruising speed and climb rate, albeit with a reduction in range.

Boeing 367-31-43 wide-body

Despite all the progressive improvements proposed for the C-97 and the fact that the aircraft was embarking on a successful service career, no proposal to develop it managed to win a production contract. The major obstacle was probably the fact that the lower fuselage (inherited from the B-29 and dating back to 1942) was too narrow and hampered by the low-wing configuration, making it unsuited as an effective logistics transport.

One early attempt to overcome this limitation was the Model 367-31-43, which incorporated a much-modified fuselage. It also introduced 'gull wings' with the inner sections canted upwards to allow clearance for the larger propellers necessitated by greater engine power.

BELOW T34 turboprop installation for the Boeing Model 367-41A. *Boeing*

Boeing C-97 developments	Boeing KC-97G	Boeing YC-97J
Powerplant	4 x P&W R-4360-59B piston radials @3,500hp (2,610kW)	4 x P&W YT34-P-5 turboprops @5,700hp (4,250kW)
Empty weight	82,500lb (37,455kg)	72,188lb (32,773kg)
Gross weight	175,000lb (79,450kg)	175,000lb (79,450kg)
Max speed	375mph (694km/h)	417mph (671km/h)
Climb to 20,000ft (6,100m)	50min	14.4min
Range	4,300mi (6,919km)	2,300mi (3,700km)

ABOVE Artwork showing the stretched Boeing Model 367-22-1 with Allison XT40 turboprops. *Boeing*

BELOW An Army 6-ton 6x6 truck is fit-tested in a mock-up of the Boeing 367-31-43 fuselage section. The XB-52 nose mock-up section is under construction in the background. *Boeing*

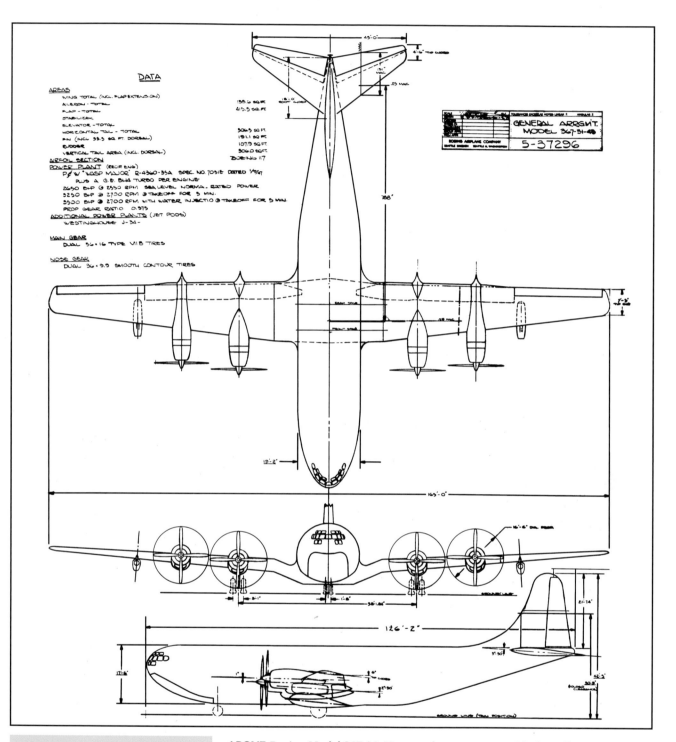

ABOVE Boeing Model 367-31-43 general arrangement with the gull wing, R4360 piston engines and two J34 podded jet engines. *Boeing*

Boeing Model 367-31-43	
Powerplant	4 x P&W R-4360-35A radial pistons @ 3,500hp (2,610kW)
	2 x Westinghouse J34-WE-38 turbojet engines @ 3,800lbf (16.9kN)
Wingspan	165ft 0in (50.3m)
Length	126ft 2in (38.46m)
Height	42ft 5in (12.93m)
Max TOW	190,000lb (86,180kg)
Useful load	60,000lb (27,220kg)
Max speed	322kt (596km/h)

Boeing swept-wing Model 367s

The most promising step in developing the Model 367 was the introduction of swept-back wings, enabling the aircraft to cruise at higher Mach numbers. This was a logical progression as Boeing was at the time the world's leading company in applying swept-wing technology to large aircraft. The remarkably advanced B-47 had first flown in 1947 and the B-52 prototype would fly in 1952. Initially the sweepback was only applied to the wings, with the vertical and horizontal stabilisers retained from the C-97A (which themselves had been adapted from the B-50). An example of this stage in the design progression was the Model 367-60, described by Boeing as the 'Improved C-97'.

18° swept-wing 367 aircraft

The first step in the 1950 effort to advance the C-97 began with the engineering of a large, slightly-swept wing with an area of 2,460sq ft (228.5m²). This compared to the production C-97C with a wing area of 1,769sq ft (164.4m²). The new wing had the benefits of enabling a higher speed, a greater fuel load and supporting a greater gross weight without increasing either wing loading or stall speeds to an unacceptable degree.

Boeing Model 367-31-43	
Powerplant	4 x P&W R-4360-35A radial pistons @ 3,500hp (2,610kW)
	2 x Westinghouse J34-WE-38 turbojet engines @ 3,800lbf (16.9kN)
Wingspan	165ft 0in (50.3m)
Length	126ft 2in (38.46m)
Height	42ft 5in (12.93m)
Max TOW	190,000lb (86,180kg)
Useful load	60,000lb (27,220kg)
Max speed	322kt (596km/h)

The 367-60 was followed by the 367-62, which was billed as the 'Advanced C-97'. The gull-wing design was replaced by a 'flat' wing (but with dihedral) while retaining the 18° sweep. A new swept empennage replaced the rounded tail design dating back to the B-29. However, the Model 367 did not follow a straightforward, sequential path. The 367-62 and -63 variants, for example, used the swept wing, but reverted to piston engines.

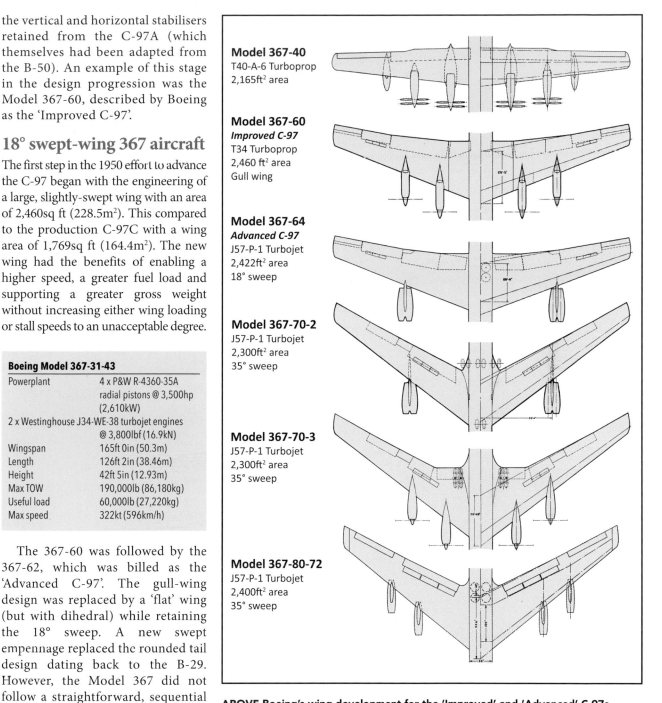

Model 367-40
T40-A-6 Turboprop
2,165ft² area

Model 367-60
Improved C-97
T34 Turboprop
2,460 ft² area
Gull wing

Model 367-64
Advanced C-97
J57-P-1 Turbojet
2,422ft² area
18° sweep

Model 367-70-2
J57-P-1 Turbojet
2,300ft² area
35° sweep

Model 367-70-3
J57-P-1 Turbojet
2,300ft² area
35° sweep

Model 367-80-72
J57-P-1 Turbojet
2,400ft² area
35° sweep

ABOVE Boeing's wing development for the 'Improved' and 'Advanced' C-97s, starting with the 367-40 at the top and ending with the 367-80-72 at the bottom, a form recognisable as an immediate ancestor to the KC-135 and 707-120.
Boeing, modified by authors

Boeing Model 367-60 Series, propeller-driven	Model 367-62	Model 367-63	Model 367-65
Powerplant	4 x P&W R-4360 CB-11 piston radials @ 3,800hp (2,834kW)	4 x Wright R-3350 piston radials @ 3,500hp (2,610kW)	4 x P&W T34 turboprops @ 5,750eshp (4,288kW)
Wingspan	140ft 0in (42.67m)	140ft 0in (42.67m)	140ft 0in (42.67m)
Length	123ft 4in (37.57m)	123ft 4in (37.57m)	123ft 4in (37.57m)
Height	40ft 8in (12.40m)	40ft 8in (12.40m)	40ft 8in (12.40m)
Wing area	2,460sq ft (228.5m²)	2,460sq ft (228.5m²)	2,460sq ft (228.5m²)
Design gross weight	n/a	n/a	151,000lb (68,492.4kg)

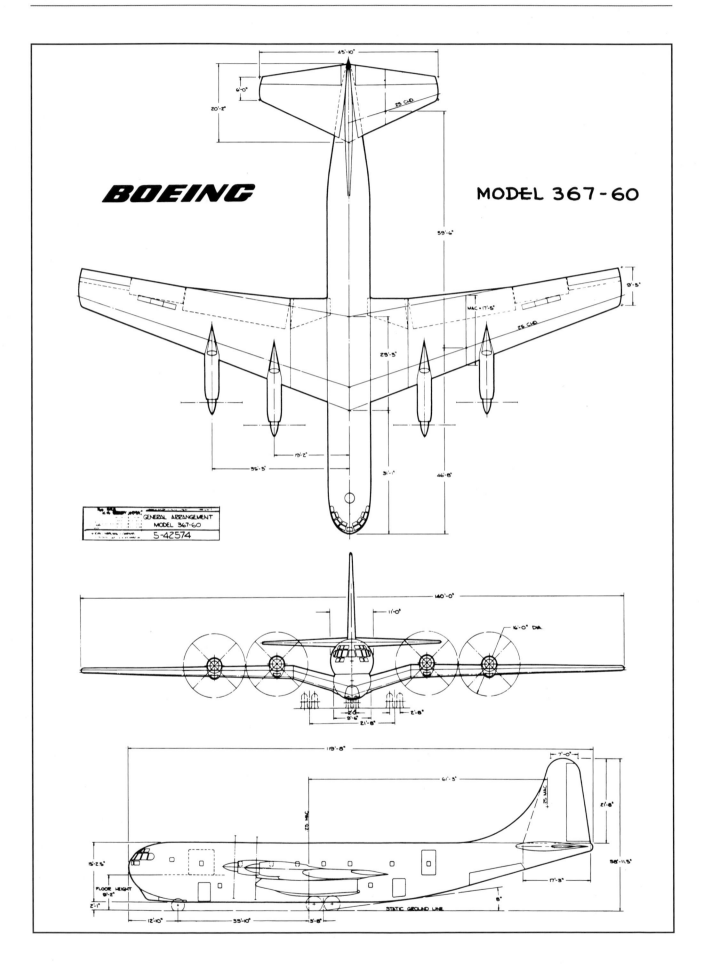

BOEING

MODEL 367-60

GENERAL ARRANGEMENT
MODEL 367-60
5-42574

ABOVE A display model of the Boeing Model 367-60 'Improved C-97' with the gull wing that incorporated the upswept centre wing section and T34 turboprop engines. *Author's collection*

ABOVE The Boeing Models 367-62 and -63 reverted to piston engines but retained the 18° swept wing and the new swept tail surfaces. *Boeing*

BELOW Boeing Model 367-60-64 general arrangement, with four Pratt & Whitney XJ57-P-1 engines and the 25° swept wing. Successive derivatives incorporated a wing with increased sweep. *Boeing*

25° swept-wing 367 aircraft

The Model 367-64 retained the 18° wing and was to be fitted with four XJ57 (JT-3B) turbojets rated at 9,250lb (41.15kN) thrust. However, this design evolved into a family of higher-performance special mission aircraft with a wing that had a yet higher sweep angle of 25° and an area of 2,516sq ft (233.7m^2). Variants included:

- **Model 367-64-1** Four Wright J67 turbojets. Maximum speed was estimated at 513kt (950.1km/h) and gross weight at 210,000lb (95,254kg), almost double the 120,000lb (54,431kg) of the original XC-97.

- **Model 367-64-3** Heavy jet reconnaissance aircraft with a crew of twelve. Design initiated on 13 July 1951.

- **Model 367-64-60** US Navy land-based minelayer with four Westinghouse J40-WE-8 turbojet engines. Performance was estimated as a maximum speed of 510kt (945km/h) and a 2,400nmi (4,440km) range. Gross weight was set at 180,000lb (81,650kg) with a 16,000lb (7,260kg) payload of mines.

OPPOSITE Boeing Model 367-60 'Improved C-97' general arrangement. *Boeing*

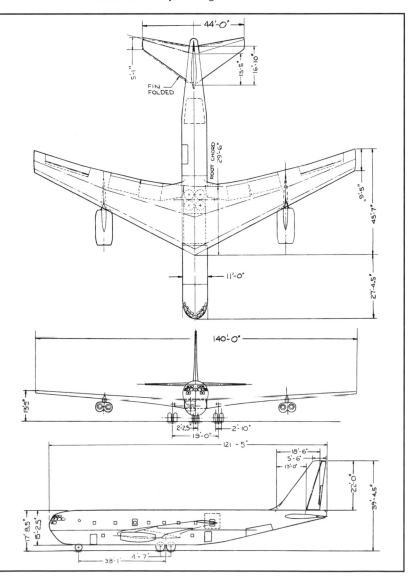

ABOVE The Boeing Model 367-64-1 went to a 25° swept wing for higher performance. *Boeing*

35° swept-wing 367 aircraft

Developed almost in parallel with the 18° sweep 367 was the 367-70 Series. This was a more ambitious line of development, incorporating a wing swept to 35°. This high degree of sweep had been pioneered on the B-47, but many challenges had to be faced in adapting it to the transport role.

One drawback of the B-47 wing was that it was optimised for high speed and low drag; all of the fuel was therefore carried in the fuselage or in large drop tanks. Fortunately, the

Boeing Model 367-71-5	
Powerplant	4 x P&W J57-P-1 turbojets @ 9,250lb (41.15kN)
Wingspan	140ft 0in (42.67m)
Length	118ft 0in (35.97m)
Height	40ft 8in (12.40m)
Max TOW	160,000lb (72,570kg)
Payload	47,500lb (21,550kg)

technique of thickening the wing root and inboard wing without aerodynamic penalty had been pioneered on the B-52, and this thickening provided the extra volume needed for fuel carriage in the wing. Even with this problem overcome, the 367 still faced challenges. For example, the Model 367-70-2 had issues with landing gear placement and weight and balance, forcing the nose landing gear to be placed in an aft position and creating an abnormally short wheelbase. For correct placement, the main landing gear had to retract into the fuselage aft of the wing, resulting in a narrow wheel track, which could result in tricky ground handling in crosswinds.

This problem was rectified in the 367-70-3 and later models with a revised inner wing to which the main landing gear was attached. Known

examples of this group of designs are the 367-70-2 with Olympus engines, the -3 with Pratt & Whitney T34 turboprops, and the -5 with XJ57-P-1 engines.

The 367-70 series marked the high point of advanced design for an aircraft scarcely seven years old. With the wing and engine design now in hand, revisions to improve the fuselage would lead to the 367-80/81/82 series of aircraft, described in the next chapter. All of this exploratory design work was leading to one of the most influential aircraft in the history of aviation: the Model 367-80 – better known by its derivatives, the Boeing 707 airliner and KC-135 jet tanker.

KC-97 tanker aircraft

The rapid, iterative development of the Model 367 from piston engines to jets, and from a 1941-technology straight

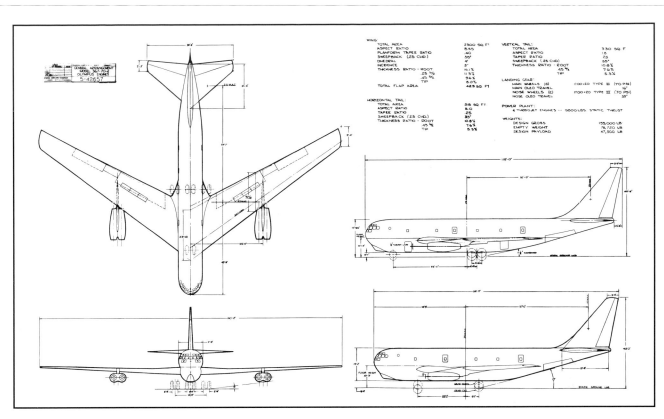

ABOVE Boeing Model 367-70-2 general arrangement. It has the final 35° wing sweep and four Wright J67 Olympus engines. The three two-wheel main landing gear bogies were attached to, and retracted into, the fuselage. The longer 367-70-5 with Pratt & Whitney J57 engines and improved landing gear arrangement is shown for comparison (upper right). *Boeing*

BELOW This artwork depicting the Boeing Model 367-71-5 shows the broad chord centre wing, which allowed a wider main landing gear track for improved ground handling. The gear struts were now attached to the rear wing spar and retracted inboard into the fuselage. *Boeing*

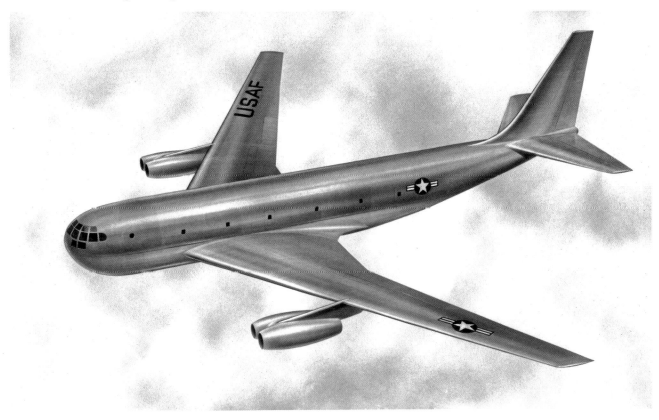

wing to a state-of-the-art swept wing, left the Air Force with one problem – it still did not have a tanker force (other than KB-29s) for the B-47s that were being delivered.

Boeing presented several possible solutions in the Model 367-75 to -78 series. These were:

- Model 367-75: extended wing and turboprop engines

- Model 367-76: improved version of KC-97A test bed aircraft

- Model 367-77: stretched fuselage and swept version of the baseline wing, with turboprops

- Model 367-78: stretched fuselage and extended straight wing, with turboprops

In the end the Air Force decided to purchase a large number of minimally modified C-97 aircraft. These were designated the KC-97F (159 built) and the KC-97G (592 built), with external fuel tanks. Both types were produced under the Boeing Model Number 367-76-29.

Sometime after the many turboprop versions of the Model 367 were passed over by the Air Force, Boeing was awarded a contract to convert two KC-97Gs currently on the production line to serve as flying test beds for the T34 engine (in addition to the YC-124B and four converted C-121 Constellations). Initially the aircraft were to be designated YC-97H, but this was changed to YC-137 for a short while

before being changed to YC-97J (the C-97H designation having been allocated to another model in the meantime).

No matter what they were called, the two aircraft served initially with the Military Air Transport Service Test Squadron (Turboprop) of the 1700th Air Transport Group at Kelly AFB, San Antonio, Texas. After the squadron was disbanded, the aircraft were flown by the San Bernardino Air Material Area at Norton AFB in California until they were retired in 1964. The second aircraft was soon removed from storage and formed the basis of the Aero Spacelines Super Guppy. The first aircraft was later salvaged to provide parts for further Guppy conversions.

BELOW Some of the last efforts to improve on the C-97 were the Boeing Models 367-75 and -78, which replaced the piston engines with T34 turboprops and successively stretched the wing, then the fuselage. *Boeing*

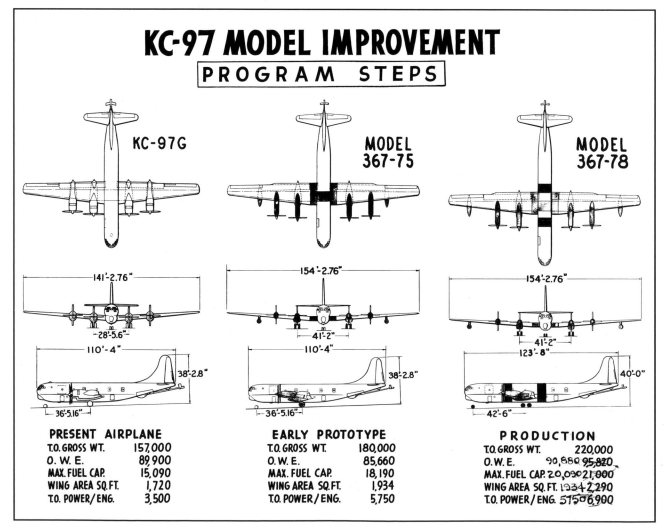

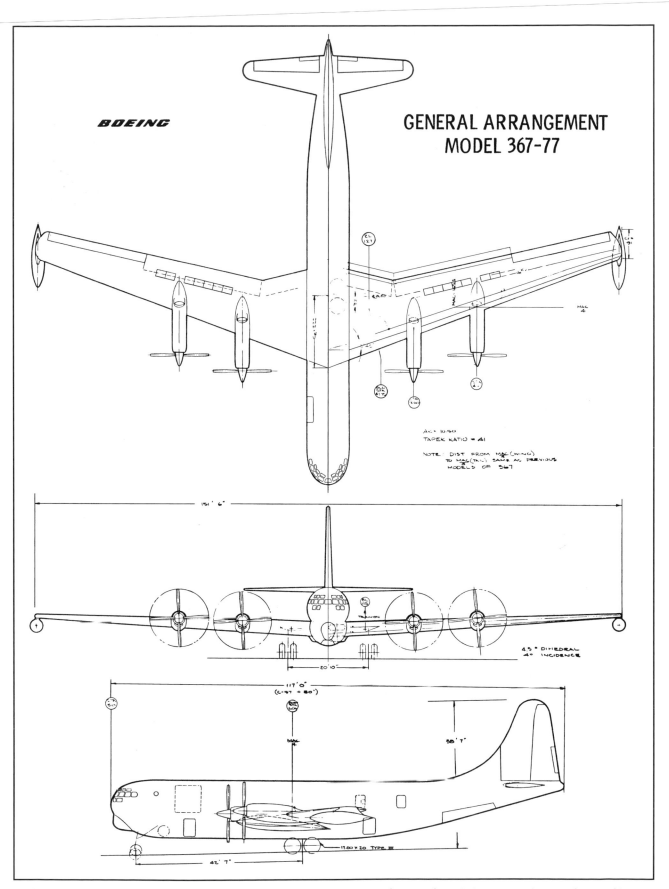

GENERAL ARRANGEMENT MODEL 367-77

ABOVE The Model 367-77 had the fuselage stretched by 80in (203cm), and swept the existing outer wing panels, attaching them to a new wing centre section. A new four-wheel main landing gear was required to support the extra weight. *Boeing*

ABOVE The second of two Boeing YC-79Js (Model 367-86-66) was test flown with YT34-P-5 engines in 1955. The pictured aeroplane was later used as the basis for the Aero Spacelines 377-SG Super Guppy. *Boeing*

Boeing Model 493 heavy airlifter

Recognising the constraints imposed by the C-97 fuselage, Boeing developed a heavy transport, the Model 493, with a much larger fuselage with a circular cross section. This appears to have been spun off from the Model 367

series of designs and developed in parallel. The initial versions of the Model 493, dating from April 1950, retained the basic C-97 wing and tail surfaces.

In essence, Boeing was pursuing two paths: on the one hand, it was exploring a series of designs marrying new wings to the C-97 fuselage, while

on the other it was working on proposals that married the C-97 wings to a redesigned fuselage.

The point of departure for the Model 493 appears to have been the Model 367-34-44 with its single-lobe, wide-body fuselage 200in (5.08m) in diameter. The similar-looking Model 493-3-2 incorporated a number of changes. These included increasing the fuselage diameter to 214in (5.44m) to accommodate a second deck (like the C-124); moving to T34 turboprop engines; deleting the nose cargo doors; and, most importantly, introducing a revised wing centre section that lowered the fuselage for easier loading. However, the limitations of using what were basically the C-97 wings and tail surfaces soon resulted in the development of the Model 493 with all-swept surfaces.

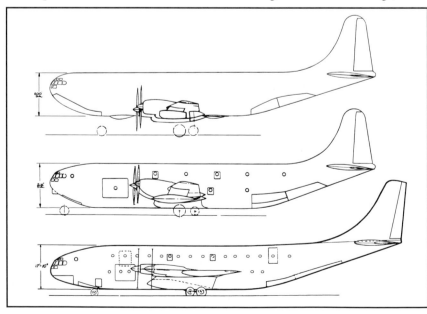

LEFT A comparison of the piston-engined Boeing Model 367-34-44 with nose and tail ramps, the turboprop Model 493-3-2 with gull wing, lowered fuselage, side loading door and tail ramp, and the Model 493-8. *Boeing*

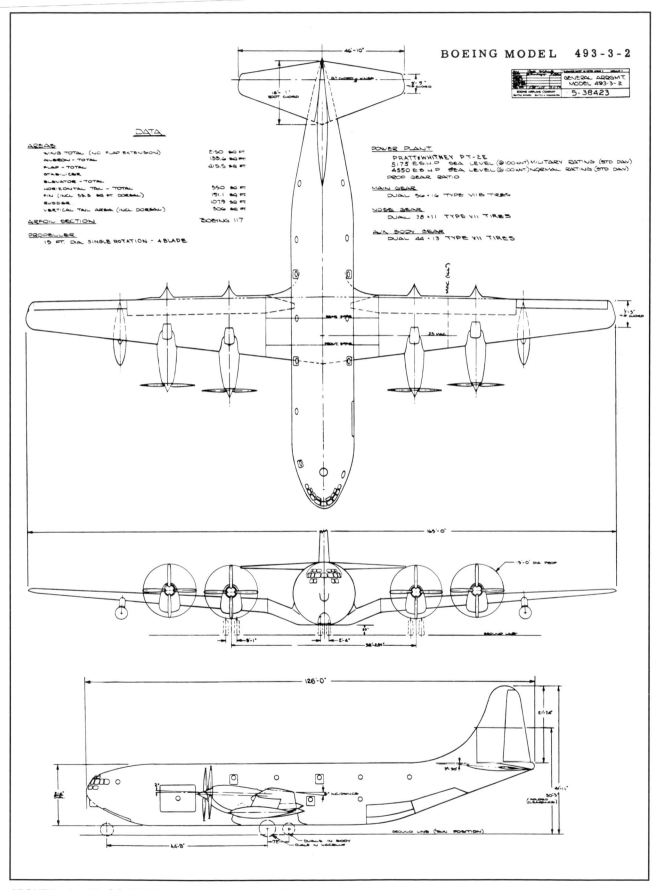

ABOVE Boeing Model 493-3-2 general arrangement. *Boeing*

By December 1950 the design iteration process had reached the Model 493-8, an even larger aircraft with an 18° swept gull wing. This was related to the 18° wing developed for the 'Advanced C-97', but the span was widened from 165ft (50.33m) to 182ft 8in (55.71m), which increased the aspect ratio and improved aerodynamic efficiency. To support the increased gross weight, a triple main landing gear was introduced, with two dual-tandem four-wheel bogies retracting inboard into the wing roots and a four-wheel

coaxial unit retracting into the lower centre fuselage. Nonetheless, the design still reflected its C-97 lineage. It has been suggested that the Model 493 was given the designation C-127, but this is not borne out by Air Force records, which indicate that the Douglas turboprop C-124 had briefly received this designation before 'YKC-124B' and 'YC-124B' were assigned.

It appears that this line of development – which was poised to lead to a heavy turboprop airlifter with which Boeing could challenge the

BELOW General arrangement of the Boeing Model 493-8. *Boeing*

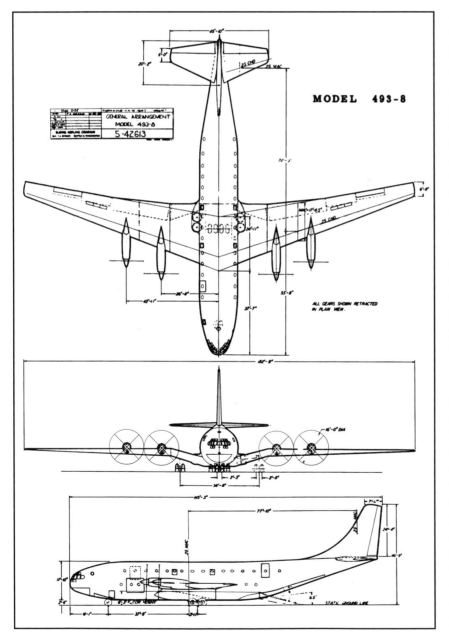

Boeing Model 493-8 heavy airlifter	
Powerplant	4 x P&W Advanced T34 turboprops @ 8,300eshp (6,189.3kW)
Wingspan	182ft 8in (55.68m)
Length	145ft 3in (44.27m)
Height	40ft 9in (12.42m)
Wing area	3,050sq ft (283.4m²)
Max TOW	220,000lb (99,790kg)
Payload	85,000lb (38,560kg)

Douglas C-124X – was cut short by the announcement of the Air Force's XC-Heavy competition based on the concept of a pod-carrying plane, as discussed later in this chapter.

Douglas's path from the C-124 to the C-133

With the C-124 Globemaster II starting to roll off the production line in 1950, Douglas was already exploring ways of carrying the design forward. Specifically, it was looking at using components of the C-124 such as the wings and tail surfaces and marrying them to the advanced new turboprop engines being offered by Allison, Pratt & Whitney and Wright.

All of these proposed designs had a similar fuselage of circular cross section, which unlike the C-124 enabled the whole aeroplane to be pressurised. This was important to permit cruising at the higher altitudes, which the new turboprop engines required for efficient operation.

Although none of these proposals resulted in hardware or even a mock-up, the C-124 story was far from over. Indeed, the Douglas design team was to carry it forward through a number of successive steps, eventually leading to a far more ambitious and capable aircraft: the C-133. Compared with the Douglas Santa Monica XC-132 (discussed later), this was a more conventional design, based upon – though extensively developed from – the C-124, which was already providing the backbone of the Air Force's heavy-lift capability.

ABOVE A Robert McCall painting commissioned by Douglas featuring the YC-124B, R6D, F4D and D-558-2. *Boeing*

Douglas C-124 improvements

While looking at more advanced developments based on the C-124, Douglas also looked at immediate opportunities to exploit the aeroplane's potential.

The first step in the evolution of the C-124 was to fit more powerful engines. This began with the issuance of a Detail Specification for the Model 1197, dated 15 June 1949. Designated the C-124B, the primary difference was the new 'C-series' Pratt & Whitney R-4360 to specification 7078 replacing the lower-powered R-4360-20W used on the C-124A. Due to a gearing change in the engine, slower-turning Curtiss 18ft 1in (5.51m) propellers

RIGHT The C-124A and C-124C tanker conversions were developed at the same time as the KC-97, but Douglas was unable to unseat Boeing as a tanker provider. *Boeing*

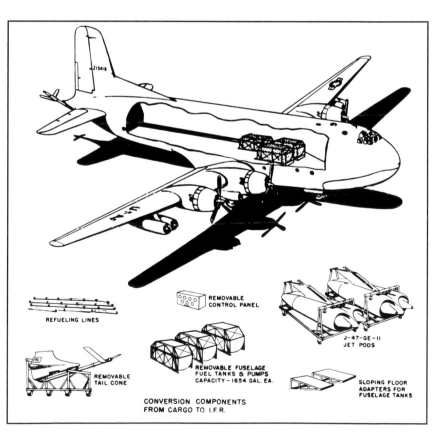

REFUELING LINES

REMOVABLE
CONTROL PANEL

J-47-GE-11
JET PODS

REMOVABLE
TAIL CONE

REMOVABLE FUSELAGE
FUEL TANKS & PUMPS
CAPACITY - 1654 GAL. EA.

SLOPING FLOOR
ADAPTERS FOR
FUSELAGE TANKS

CONVERSION COMPONENTS
FROM CARGO TO I.F.R.

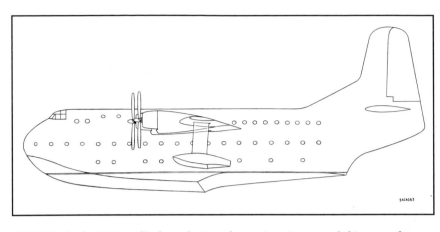

ABOVE A single 1951 profile from the Douglas engineering records hints at a future not pursued: a seaplane version of the Globemaster II. No other data could be found. *Boeing*

Turboprop-powered C-124 developments

By 1949 the first generation of high-powered turboprop engines by US engine-makers had become sufficiently mature to be considered for installation in operational aircraft. The relevant development efforts were (per an inter-service agreement) managed by the Navy and resulted in two engines in the 5,000hp (3,730kW) class: the Pratt & Whitney PT-2 (designated the T34) and the Allison Model 500 (T40). Both Boeing and Douglas explored integrating them into existing airframes.

Douglas created two C-124 design variants with a basically common airframe to utilise either engine. The Model 1183 employed the Allison XT40-A-6 turboprop and was proposed in several variants, including the following:

■ **Model 1183B** Refueller (hose and drogue)

■ **Model 1183D** Cargo transport

■ **Model 1183E** Refueller (flying boom)

However, confidence in the T40 evaporated in the early 1950s due to its disappointing (and sometimes catastrophic) performance on the Douglas A2D Skyshark; in one case, the complete engine and its counter-rotating propellers separated from the aircraft in flight. The Navy persevered with this engine on its RY-1 and R3Y-1 and 2 Tradewind seaplanes, but the gearbox issues were never fully resolved.

were to replace the smaller units installed in the C-124A. With the higher-powered engines and structural strengthening, the maximum gross take-off weight was increased from 175,000lb (79,450kg) to 183,000lb (83,082kg). This engine did not reach production and consequently neither did the C-124B. This designation was later confusingly reapplied to the Model 1182 turboprop development.

The subsequent re-engined Douglas Model 1317 development did reach production. Designated C-124C, it used the R-4360-63 or 63A engine rated at 3,800hp (2,834kW), allowing the gross weight to be increased to 194,500lb (88,224kg). Entering service in 1952, 243 examples of the C-124C were built by the time deliveries were completed in 1955.

Douglas was not about to be caught flat-footed as Boeing developed tanker versions of the C-97. On 21 April 1950 the company proposed a conversion of the C-124A, which would offer refuelling through the installation of a tailcone and flying boom, with a pressurised compartment for the boom operator. Other components included extra fuel tanks in the cargo area, with their required plumbing and controls. Four J47-GE-11 jet engines (for the C-124A) or two podded J35-A-23 engines (for the C-124C) would be installed to boost climb rates and increase speeds at higher altitudes. At a mission radius of 1,000nmi (1,850km), the aircraft, with J47 augmentation, could offload 6,770 gallons (25,627 litres) of fuel, while the aircraft with the J35 installation could offload 7,700 gallons (29,148 litres).

BELOW A model of the Allison T40-A-6 nacelle installation on the Douglas Model 1183. *Boeing*

BELOW Since each T40 engine had two turbine (power) sections, the exhaust was substantially different and larger than that for the Pratt & Whitney T34. *Boeing*

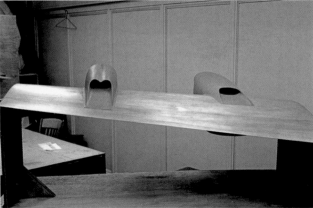

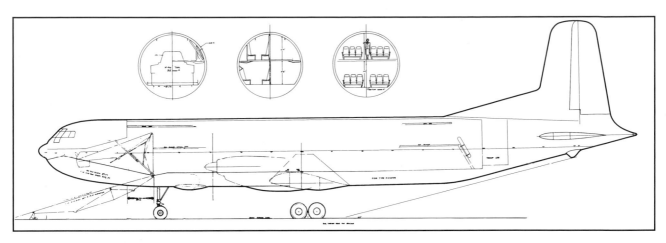

All the variants were based on the same new circular-section fuselage, with the Models 1324A and 1324C making the most use of YKC-124B/YC-124B elements. These two models utilised the latter's wing except for the centre section through the fuselage, and took the wing flaps and the horizontal tail from the YC-124B. Those variants listed with the extended leading edge had a 7% broader chord with a sharper leading edge profile, replacing that of the slower C-74, which dated from 1942.

BELOW Long-bodied Douglas Model 1324F general arrangement, with T40 engines, and the short Model 1324A (right middle) with T34 engines. *Boeing*

ABOVE The initial Douglas Model 1324 layout sketch retained the C-124 nose ramp and general tail shape. However, the folding nose ramp took up cabin space that could have been used for cargo. The fuselage cross section shows (from left to right) an M-48 tank, troop seating and airline-style seating. *Boeing*

Douglas Model 1324 ('C-124X')	Model 1324A	Model 1324F
Powerplant	4 x P&W T34-P-6 turboprops @ 5,700eshp (4,250.5kW)	4 x Allison T40-A-8 turboprops @ 7,500eshp (5,592.7kW)
Wingspan	180ft 10.5in (55.11m)	180ft 10.5in (55.11m)
Length	142ft 5in (43.41m)	159ft 1in (48.49m)
Height	54ft 11in (16.74m)	54ft 11in (16.74m)
Wing area	2,670sq ft (248.1m²)	2,883sq ft (267.8m²)
Design gross weight	210,000lb (95,250kg)	315,000lb (142,880kg)
Payload	81,000lb (36,740kg)	129,000lb (58,510kg)
Max speed	315kt (583km/h)	332kt (615km/h)
Cruise speed	273kt (506km/h)	310kt (574km/h)
Combat range	1,800nmi (3,330km)	1,680nmi (3,110km)

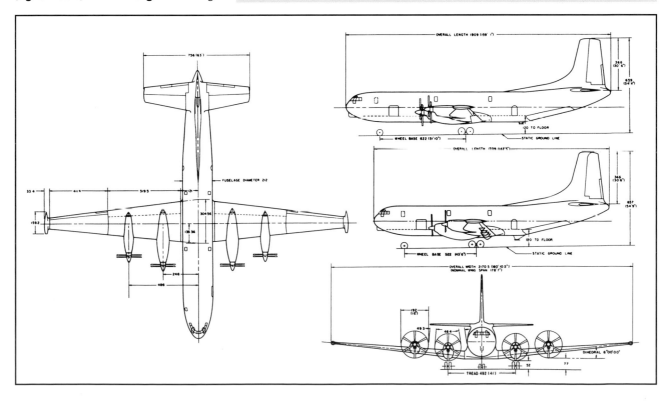

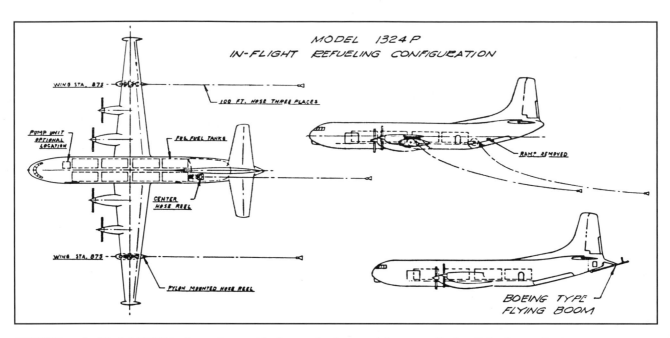

ABOVE Douglas Model 1324P tanker variants with three-point hose and drogue or Boeing flying boom. *Boeing*

Despite the improvement in wing and fuselage geometry, the Model 1324 cargo deck was still 10ft (3.05m) above ground level, an improvement from the C-124's 13ft (3.97m) but far from truckbed height. The logical next step was to keep the pressurised fuselage, but move the wing to the top. This allowed the fuselage to be lowered relative to the ground, with the deck height now reduced to 40in (1.01m). The C-124 wing was abandoned and a new wing introduced, which incorporated a revised airfoil section, thickness, twist, and leading and trailing edge sweep angles.

BELOW The auxiliary second deck in the Douglas Model 1333 was deleted for the pure 'logistic' mission. *Boeing*

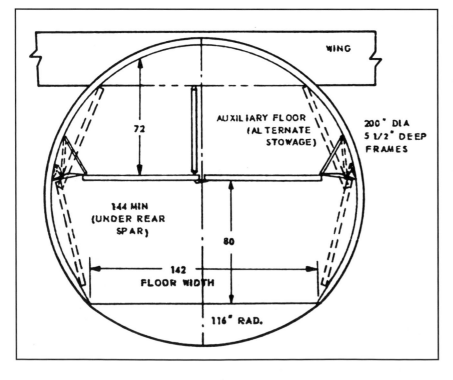

Douglas Model 1333 (USAF C-133)

The high-wing design became the Model 1333 (Douglas still referred to it as the C-124X), which appealed sufficiently to the USAF for it to approve detailed development on 24 March 1953 (while issuing a 'stop work' order on the Model 1324). Initially, the new aircraft still had the fold-down upper-deck floor of the C-124, but almost immediately the Air Force requested weight reduction studies to evaluate the elimination of this secondary deck together with all passenger provisions and even pressurisation.

On 10 August 1953 Douglas was notified that the Model 1333 had been allocated the Air Force designation C-133, and on 10 September direction was formally given to delete provisions for passenger carriage. The Model 1333 had thus become a pure 'logistic' transport, with the combat troop-carrying role left to the C-130 and long-distance troop carriage contracted out to the civil airlines.

With no other aircraft offering the immediate prospect of similar performance or capabilities, the C-133 was ordered into production without going through a formal competitive

process and without requiring dedicated prototypes. Fifty aircraft were ordered off the drawing board, all intended for active service. It is interesting to note that the C-133 shared no design commonality with the other major Douglas transport project of the time, the YC-132. Both proposals were developed independently, in parallel, by the Douglas Long Beach and Santa Monica Divisions respectively.

The first aircraft flew on 23 April 1956 and the C-133A entered service just sixteen months later. With its tapered high-aspect-ratio wings, the resulting design was an elegant-looking aircraft. Although its design ancestry was the most continuous of any airlifter and could be traced back to the early years of the Second World War, the C-133 looked a thoroughly modern, new-generation aircraft, certainly by comparison with its immediate predecessor. It also brought a whole new capability to USAF's Military Air Transport Service (MATS).

ABOVE The initial Douglas Model 1333/C-133 configuration is depicted with the double row of fuselage windows, indicating that the secondary deck was part of the design at this point in 1953. *Boeing*

BELOW The first C-133A is posed in the southern end of Building 13 at the Douglas Long Beach facility for the CTC (Contractor's Technical Compliance) inspection for the Air Force in November 1955. The rollout would be five months later. Scarcely ten years before, C-74s had been assembled in this building, and in six years the giant D-902 CX-HLS mock-up would occupy this space. *Boeing*

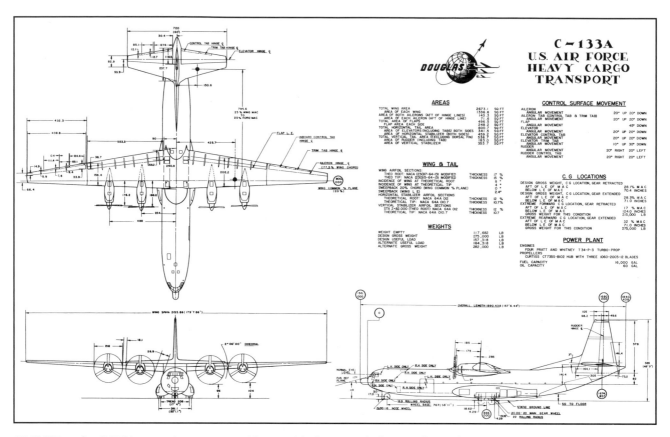

ABOVE Douglas C-133A general arrangement (drawn with the revised aft cargo doors also used on the C-133B). *Boeing*

C-133A production was followed by the C-133B, which replaced the upper rear cargo door with a side-opening clamshell arrangement. This extended the usable area of the cargo hold by 3ft (0.91m), permitting Titan missiles to be carried. The last three C-133As on the production line were also completed with this arrangement, but without other C-133B features.

The ability to carry outsize cargo, particularly ballistic missiles, brought a capability to MATS (later MAC) that could not be provided by any other aeroplane. However, the aircraft was not without its problems. Perhaps inevitably, performance was affected by the fact that the engines did not deliver

either the power or the reliability that was expected; additionally, the aircraft's weight crept up as the design progressed. The C-133 also suffered from several unforeseen aerodynamic problems involving excessive drag, partially caused by vortices flowing along the aft fuselage.

Douglas Model 1333 (C-133A) Cargomaster	
Powerplant	4 x P&W T34-P-3 turboprops @ 5,500shp (4,101.3kW)
Wingspan	179ft 7.9in (54.76m)
Length	157ft 6.4in (48.02m)
Height	48ft 9in (14.86m)
Wing area	2,673.1sq ft (248.3m²)
Design gross weight	275,000lb (124,7380kg)
Payload	109,500lb (49,440kg)
Max speed	304kt (563km/h)
Cruise speed	295kt (546km/h)
Combat range	1,637mi (3,032km)

RIGHT A cutaway view of the Douglas C-133B. *Boeing*

Douglas-Air Force C-133B

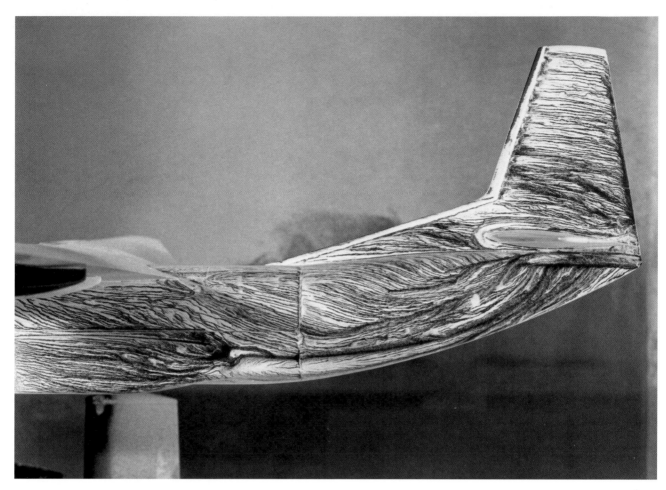

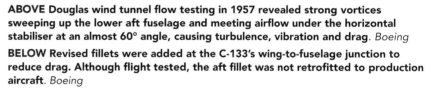

ABOVE Douglas wind tunnel flow testing in 1957 revealed strong vortices sweeping up the lower aft fuselage and meeting airflow under the horizontal stabiliser at an almost 60° angle, causing turbulence, vibration and drag. *Boeing*

BELOW Revised fillets were added at the C-133's wing-to-fuselage junction to reduce drag. Although flight tested, the aft fillet was not retrofitted to production aircraft. *Boeing*

ABOVE A 'scab' fairing was retrofitted to the tailcone of all C-133s to smooth airflow and was fitted over the existing structure. *Boeing*

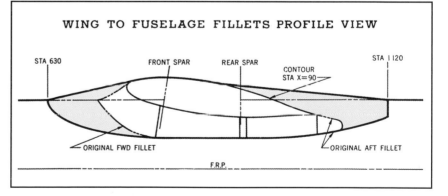

WING TO FUSELAGE FILLETS PROFILE VIEW

STA 630   FRONT SPAR   REAR SPAR   CONTOUR STA X = 90   STA 1 120

ORIGINAL FWD FILLET   ORIGINAL AFT FILLET

F.R.P.

Throughout its life the C-133 suffered from vibration that proved impossible to rectify. Problematic wing characteristics near the stall required vortex generators to be added to both upper and lower wing surfaces; steps had to be taken to strengthen the fuselage; and the vortices produced by the undercarriage housings remained an unresolved problem.

The aircraft was designed for a relatively short life of 10,000 flight hours. Even the early C-130A – designed primarily for assault landings – was only intended to reach 15,000 flight hours. However, through a continuing series of modifications and life-extension programmes, some C-133s actually reached 19,000 hours. Over its fifteen-year service life, nine aircraft out of the fifty built were lost in accidents.

Douglas C-133 model summary

Douglas Model	Description
Model 1324	Transitional design between Model 1283 (YKC-124B) and Model 1333
Model 1333	C-133A (35 built)
Model 1371 Logistic	C-133A 'Optimum Change Configurations with Allison T54 Engines'
Model 1371A Tactical	C-133A 'Optimum Change Configurations with Allison T54 Engines'
Model 1374 Logistic	C-133A 'Minimum Change Configurations with Allison T54 Engines'
Model 1374B Tactical	C-133A 'Minimum Change Configurations with Allison T54 Engines'
Model 1379 Logistic	Wide-chord [turbine] T34-P-6 (PT2G-4) engine configurations
Model 1380 Tactical	Wide-chord [turbine] T34-P-6 (PT2G-4) engine configurations
Model 1382	Airborne Early Warning (AEW) test bed
Model 1430	C-133B (15 built)
Model 1444	Flight Demonstration Vehicle for a nuclear-powered turboprop engine
Model 1476	Design with 6,000eshp Allison T61 engines and revised fuselage aerodynamics
Model 1493	Follow-on production of C-133A configuration with T61 engines (proposed but not built)
Model 1494	Rework of C-133A Nos 1-33 to install T61 engines
Model 1495	Rework of C-133B to install T61 plus build of three additional aircraft (proposed but not built)

OPPOSITE TOP The Douglas Model 1382 was proposed with two different antenna configurations as an Airborne Early Warning test bed. The first enclosed a large parabolic antenna housed in a huge teardrop-shaped radome. *Boeing*

OPPOSITE BOTTOM The second Model 1382 configuration was to test an end-fired antenna array in a 'saucer' rotodome. A larger vertical tail and endplates were needed for both antenna options. *Boeing*

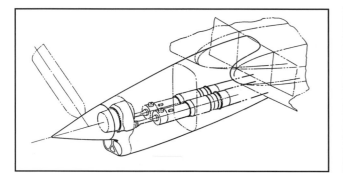

ABOVE Allison T54 engine installation as planned for Douglas Models 1371 and 1374. The T54 engine was to have twin T56 power sections with their power combined in a gearbox driving a single-rotation propeller. *Boeing*

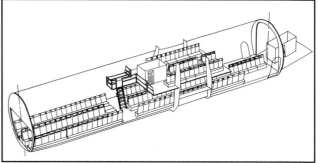

ABOVE For added troop carrier capacity, the Douglas Model 1380 was to have a 'mezzanine deck' added to the centre fuselage. The additional flooring at this level, fore and aft, would have raised the seating capacity to 288 troops. *Boeing*

The ultimate C-133: the Douglas Model 1476

In May 1959 Douglas offered a development of the C-133B, with improved cargo capacity, resulting from more efficient and powerful engines together with a redesign of the rear fuselage. The aircraft was given the company designation of Model 1476. The Pratt & Whitney T34-P-9W engines would be replaced by Allison T61s (Model 550-D4), similar in power rating but much more fuel efficient.

To improve performance still further, the upswept rear fuselage of the C-133B was replaced by a more aerodynamically efficient, symmetrically tapered profile, similar to that of the DC-7. Douglas also added a fairing at the rear of wing/fuselage intersection, which eliminated a problem with airflow separation in this area, further reducing drag. However, this extensive redesign of the aft fuselage raised the issue of how to preserve the full cargo bay access allowed by the upswept design of the C-133B. Douglas resolved this by having the rear section of the Model 1476's fuselage swing upwards. The inclusion of an inward-folding retractable door in the bottom of the fuselage meant that full access could be provided with the tail swinging up by 35°. This was important as a 90° swing would have required greater structural strengthening and the complexity of breaking the control runs.

The maximum take-off weight and maximum range would be the same as for the C-133B. However, over a 3,500nmi (6,482km) range, the Model 1476 could carry a payload of 76,000lb (34,504kg) as opposed to the C-133B's 52,000lb (23,608kg). Overall, Douglas estimated that simply changing the engines would result in a 43% improvement in cargo-carrying capability and productivity, in return for a 17% change in the aircraft's design. Combining the engine swap with the proposed redesign of the rear fuselage would yield a 46% load improvement for a 30% modification of the C-133B.

However, despite the apparent advantages of extracting far higher performance from the development of an established design, the C-133's time had passed. The Cargomaster, as it became known, would represent the high-water-mark for US turboprop development; never again would the US

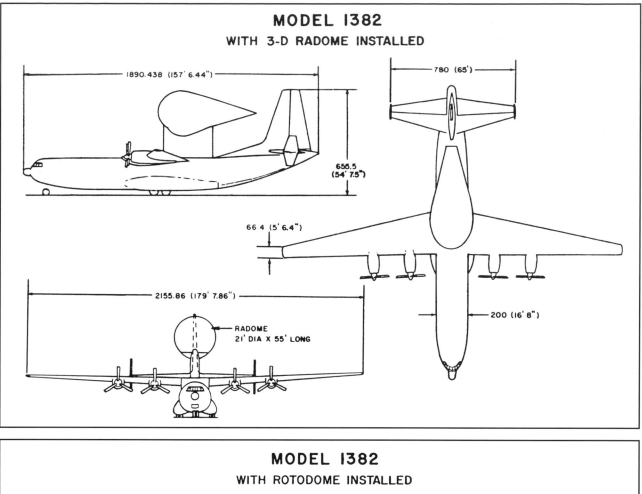

MODEL 1382
WITH 3-D RADOME INSTALLED

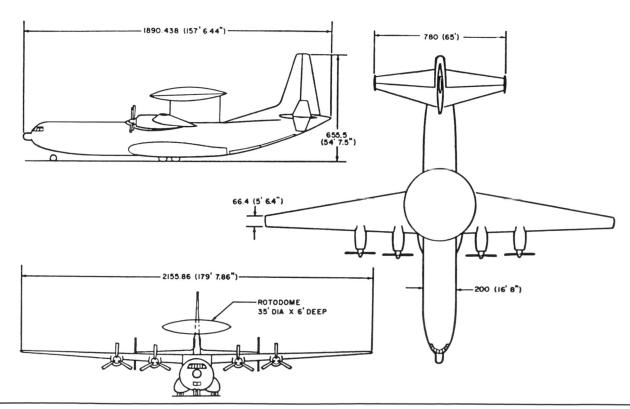

MODEL 1382
WITH ROTODOME INSTALLED

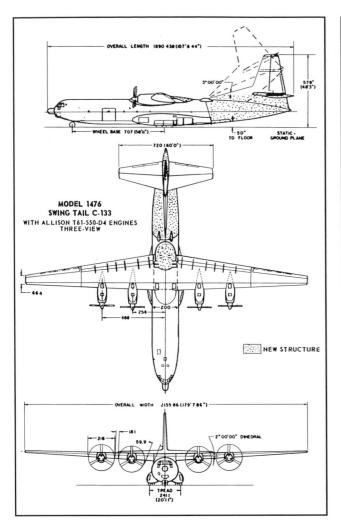

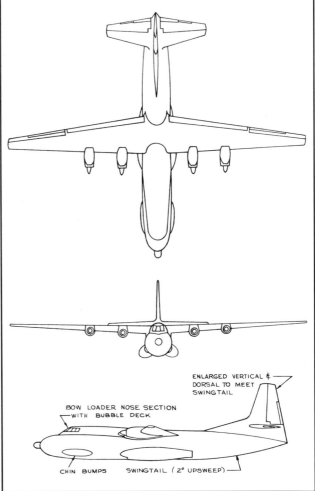

ABOVE Douglas Model 1476 general arrangement (lift-tail C-133). *Boeing*

ABOVE The Douglas Model 1476 'bowloader' version of the C-133. *Boeing*

build an aircraft of this size with turboprop engines. By 1959 the USAF was almost ready to develop new heavy

airlifters, but with the first of the turbofan engines. However, in the meantime (as described below) another

large – ultimately abortive – turboprop-powered airlifter development was under way.

Big pod-carrying designs

BELOW A wind tunnel model of the Douglas Model 1476 'bowloader' configuration. The 'chin bumps' would likely have housed the pair of relocated nose landing gear wheels. *Boeing*

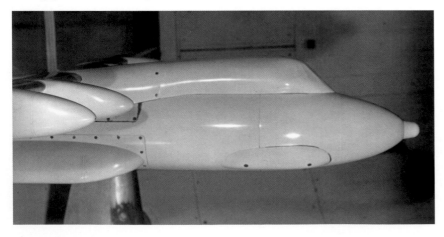

In the eighteen months prior to the XC-Heavy competition, Douglas and Northrop had made early investigations into the conventional (relatively speaking) pod-carrying aircraft, and an alternative concept called the 'Transit Van'. Proposed in 1949 by Transit Van Corporation of Redwood City, California, the Transit Van was a precursor of what would today be called a multimodal shipping container, but tailored for truck and aircraft use.

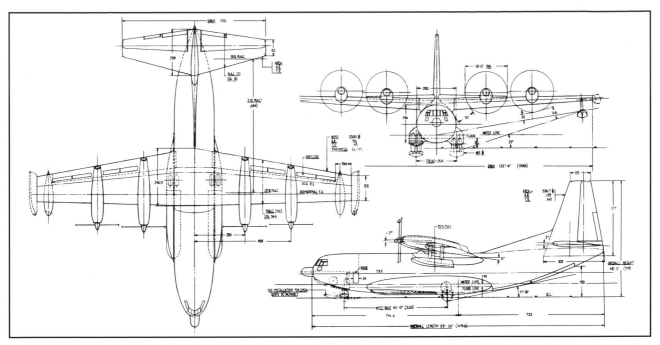

ABOVE A shortened C-133A was used as a basis for a Douglas 1957 heavyweight 'Pantabase' study, with skis, floats and conventional landing gear. The study did not progress to having a Model Number assigned. *Boeing*

BELOW This untitled Douglas preliminary sketch from the spring of 1949 laid out a design using the DC-6 as a basis for carrying two detachable and roadable cargo pods under the wings. *Boeing*

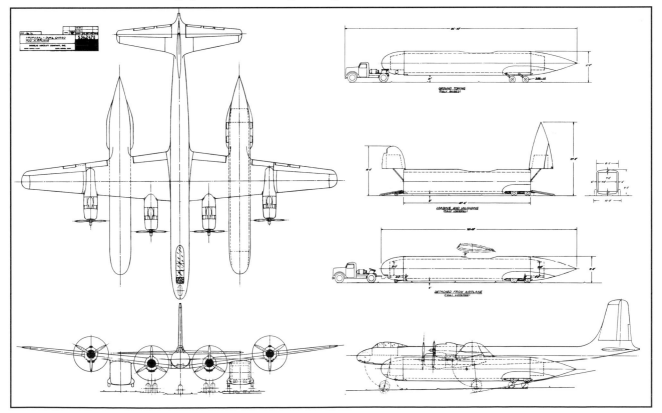

Northrop Model N-9-derived cargo pod carrier

Northrop had first conceived of a cargo version of the basic N-9 flying wing bomber in the early 1940s, with a design that may have been designated the N-10. It was not, however, pursued at the time because of the work necessary to bring the XB-35 to fruition.

In 1949 attention returned to cargo versions of the original N-9 series of flying wings, now coupled with the new powerful turboprop engines that were being proposed and developed.

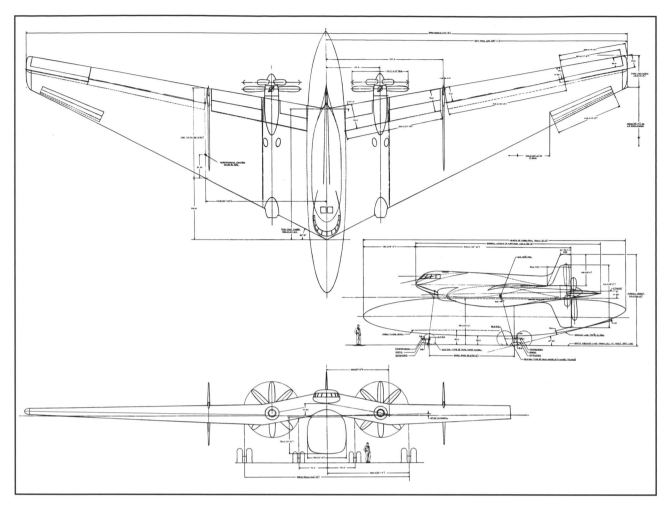

ABOVE Northrop cargo pod carrier general arrangement, based on the company's XB-35 and XB-49 bomber designs.
Courtesy of Northrop Grumman Corporation

These included the XT37 Turbodyne (which had originated with Northrop in 1941) and Allison's XT40, developed under Navy sponsorship. The initial studies dating from April 1949 retained the outer wing panels of the XB-35/YB-49 family. New wing centre sections had to be engineered since the original structure had 'bridge truss' ribs, which were spaced too closely to allow an unobstructed area for large cargo or passenger seating. A preliminary design layout from 27 April 1949 featured a raised centre section accommodating an external 75ft-long cargo/passenger pack capable of seating eighty-four combat troops. This could be exchanged with a 'bomber' pod. An alternative version of the wing retained the 'flat' wing profile and carried cargo pods outboard of each of the two engines.

By July 1949 the 26°-sweep XB-35 planform had been superseded by one with a 37° sweep and a thinner airfoil, permitting higher speeds. This basic wing layout had been developed in 1948 for the N-31 bomber proposed in response to the Medium Bomber Competition conducted under Project MX-948.

Northrop Centreline cargo pod flying wing – twin engine	
Powerplant	2 x Allison Model 500 C-1 turboprops @ 7,500shp (5,592.7kW)
Wingspan	172ft 0in (52.43m)
Length	53ft 0in (16.20m)
Height	26ft 0in (7.90m)
Cargo pack length	75ft 0in (22.90m)

Northrop advanced cargo flying wings	Allison engines	Turbodyne engines
Powerplant	4 x Allison 500 C-1 turboprops 7,500shp (5,592.7kW)	2 x 'Improved' Northrop XT37-NA-3 @ turboprops @ 12,000shp (8,948.4kW)
Wingspan	184ft 2in (56.11m)	172ft 0in (52.43m)
Length	102ft 9in (31.32m)	80ft 2in (24.43m)
Height	34ft 0in (10.36m)	33ft 0in (10.06m)
Cargo pack width	8ft (2.44m)	8ft (2.44m)
Cargo pack length	20ft (6.10m)	20ft (6.10m)
Cargo pack height	8ft (2.44m)	7ft (2.13m)
Wing area	5,018sq ft (466.68m²)	4,444.4sq ft (466.19m²)
Design gross weight	283,000lb (128,366.6kg)	206,000lb (94,440kg)
Payload	70,000lb (31,751.5kg)	66,000lb (29,940kg)
Cruise speed	380-400mph (612-644km/h)	380-400mph (612-644km/h)
Range	3,500mi (6,482km)	3,500mi (6,482km)

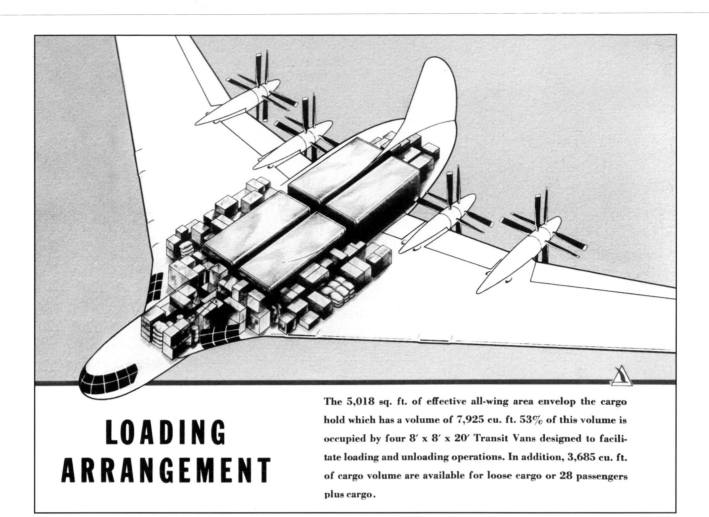

LOADING ARRANGEMENT

The 5,018 sq. ft. of effective all-wing area envelop the cargo hold which has a volume of 7,925 cu. ft. 53% of this volume is occupied by four 8' x 8' x 20' Transit Vans designed to facilitate loading and unloading operations. In addition, 3,685 cu. ft. of cargo volume are available for loose cargo or 28 passengers plus cargo.

ABOVE Northrop's ultimate cargo flying wings were developed in concert with the N-31 medium bomber and were to be powered by Turbodyne XT37 or Allison XT40 turboprops. *Courtesy of Northrop Grumman Corporation*

BELOW General arrangements of the Northrop advanced flying wing Transit Van carriers using the Allison T40 turboprops **(left)** and the **Northrop XT37 turboprops (right)**. *Courtesy of Northrop Grumman Corporation*

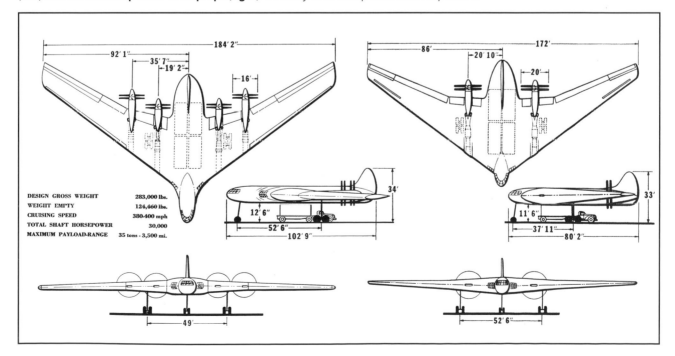

DESIGN GROSS WEIGHT	283,000 lbs.
WEIGHT EMPTY	124,460 lbs.
CRUISING SPEED	380-400 mph
TOTAL SHAFT HORSEPOWER	30,000
MAXIMUM PAYLOAD-RANGE	35 tons - 3,500 mi.

For the cargo development, external pod carriage was eliminated in favour of internal carriage of Transit Vans; various loads of two, three and four were studied. For greater efficiency and range, the wing aspect ratio was increased, resulting in a graceful layout. Although the advanced cargo wing was primarily intended for commercial air freight service, sales brochures were circulated touting commercial and military applications; the last was issued in May 1950.

Development of large flying wings (both the cargo and bomber variant) ended in early-to-mid-1950 due to little customer interest. Northrop retrenched following the RB-49 and C-125 cancellations, and focused on bringing the high-priority F-89 interceptor through development and into service.

The XC-Heavy competition

The XC-Heavy competition began in 1951 with the USAF wanting to exploit the versatility of the pod plane. In particular it wanted payloads that could include detachable bomber pods

(complete with a bombardier), cargo pods, and parasite attack or reconnaissance aircraft, long-range missiles such as the Snark or Navaho, or other types of payload attached to the underside of the aircraft. Only two manufacturers responded formally to the XC-Heavy competition, Boeing and Douglas, though Lockheed also carried out some preliminary studies. Between them they produced some truly remarkable designs.

Boeing Model 497 XC-Heavy

With the release of the XC-Heavy RFP, Boeing's focus switched to a new design series, the Model 497. The company's work concluded that the highest potential was offered by a single, slim fuselage configuration with high-aspect-ratio wings, capable of carrying a variety of external payloads.

Boeing Model 497 (XC-Heavy)	
Powerplant	6 x P&W T34-P-10 turboprops @ 8,300eshp (6,189.3kW)
Wingspan	213ft 0in (63.92m)
Length	148ft 5in (45.24m)
Height	61ft 6in (18.75m)
Wing area	3,600sq ft (334.5m²)
Max TOW	360,000lb (163,290kg)
Payload	100,000lb (45,360kg)

The Model 497 was a massive aircraft with a span of 213ft (64.97m), powered by six Pratt & Whitney T34-P-10 turboprops. The inner section of the wings had a marked anhedral, which gave the fuselage a ground clearance of 18ft (5.49m), enabling the aircraft to carry a wide variety of external loads. This included a cargo pod, a dual horizontal lobe personnel pod, a refuelling pod, either three Rascal or three Navaho missiles, or a parasite attack/reconnaissance aircraft.

USAF XC-Heavy requirements	
Bulk cargo capability	100,000lb (45,359kg) of cargo over 3,500nmi (6,479km)
Fuel (cargo) capability	140,500lb (63,787kg) over 2,200nmi (4,072km) or 72,000lb (32,688kg) over 4,500nmi (8,330km)
Refuelling capability	110,000lb (49,940kg) of fuel within a radius of 2,500nmi (4,628km)

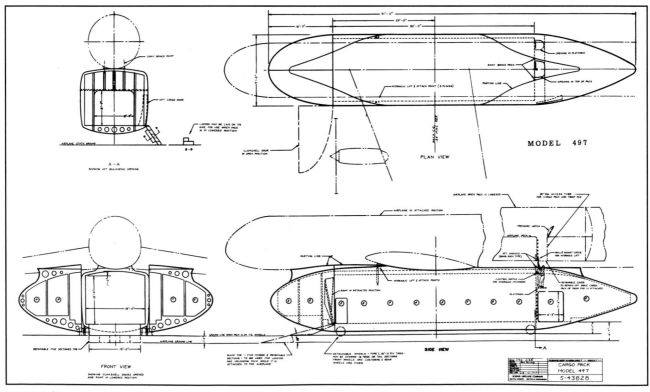

ABOVE The cargo pod for the Boeing Model 497. *Boeing*

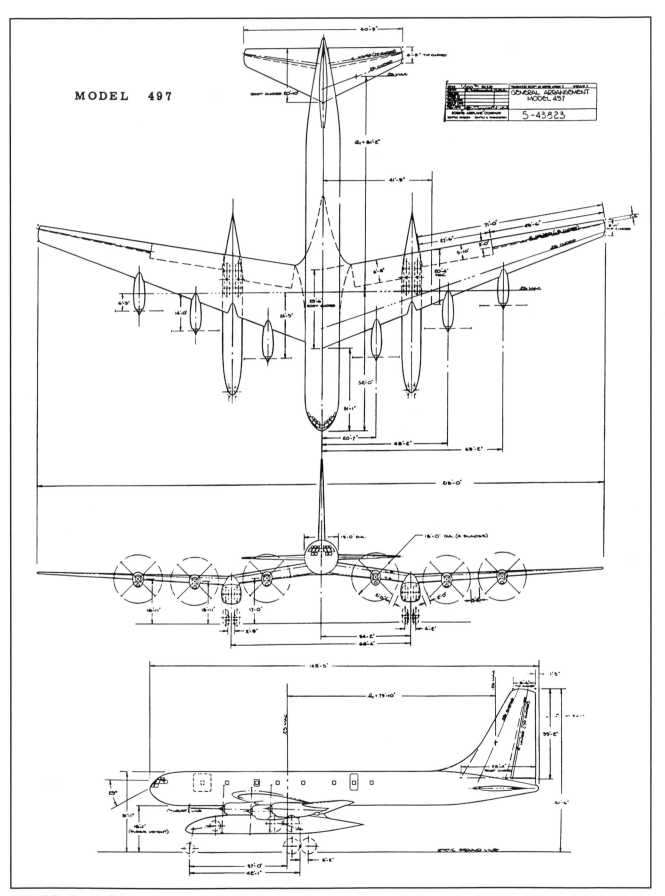

ABOVE Boeing Model 497 general arrangement. *Boeing*

LEFT A display model showing the Model 497 in the clean configuration. *Boeing*

project. Some seem to believe that Boeing now has all it can handle with its present and projected work load.' From the customer's point of view, this was likely a valid concern. Boeing was managing the rapid ramp-up of B-47 production (arguably the most advanced bomber of the time) and was deep into detailed engineering for its successors, the XB-56 medium bomber and the B-52 heavy bomber (which was to fly within a year). At the same time production was surging on the KC-97 tankers for these bombers. All three projects were receiving the top priority necessary to meet General Curtis LeMay's demands for his Strategic Air Command. Whether this concern had any bearing on Boeing's failure to win the XC-Heavy contract is unknown. As will be seen, the Douglas Model 1240 did not win the competition either.

Boeing presented briefings on the Model 497 to the Air Force on 28 March 1951 and felt that the proposal had been well received. One bit of unwelcome news was that '…one disturbing subject kept cropping up in every branch we visited – the ability of Boeing to handle another major

BELOW Cargo-carrying options for the Boeing Model 497: from top left they are parasite bomber aircraft, cargo pod, passenger pod, missile carriage, tanker pod, and Navaho missile and reconnaissance aircraft. *Boeing*

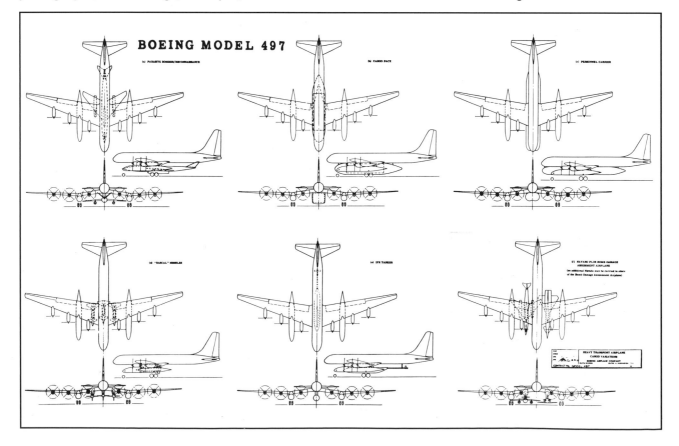

ABOVE The initial Douglas Model 1240 concept (seen with cargo pod) had cockpits in both booms. Jet engines were housed in the aft ends of the outboard engine nacelles. *Boeing*

Douglas Model 1240 XC-Heavy

The highly unconventional Douglas Model 1240 reflected the company's continuing work on a long-range bomber with the load spread across a very high-aspect-ratio swept wing, designated the Model 1211J. Unlike Boeing, Douglas used a twin-boom design as a basis for the proposed Model 1240.

In a 3 November 1950 report the Model 1240 was described variously as the 'All-Purpose Airplane' or 'Universal Airplane'. The design started off with an integral fixed pod with a cockpit in the front. However, this later changed to a detachable-pod configuration with two cockpits, one placed in either boom. This left the space between the booms free for pod attachment and gave much greater flexibility of use.

RIGHT The Model 1240 as drawn in August 1950. *Boeing*

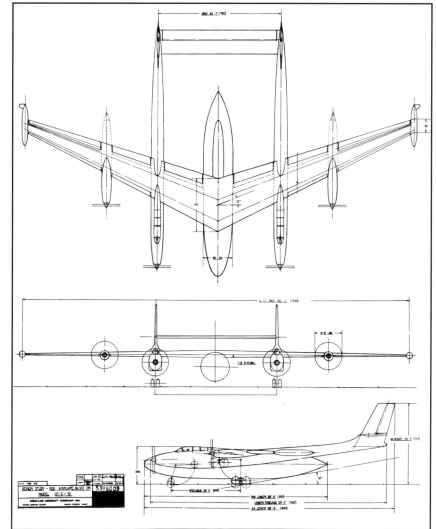

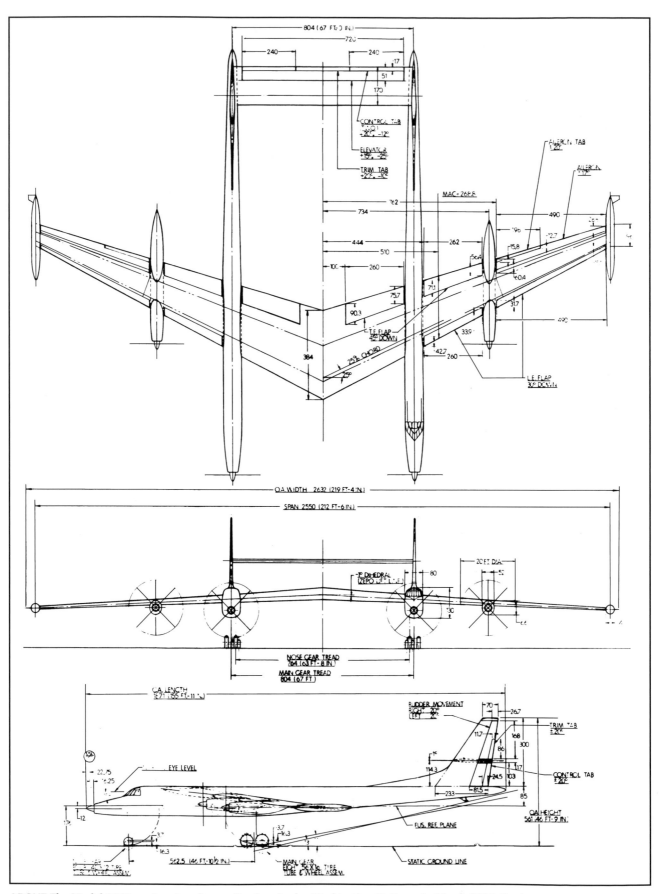

ABOVE The Model 1240 carrier aircraft as refined and submitted to the Air Force in March 1951. *Boeing*

Douglas introduced the Model 1240 by announcing:

'During the past year the Douglas Company has conducted an extensive study program to determine optimum configuration for [a] high speed, long range Strategic Bomber. Studies of the last several months have been in answer to Air Force requests for such information. As these studies progressed, it became apparent that there was a definite need for an airplane of similar performance capabilities that could launch long range missiles from an advanced point to increase the effective missile range, to carry parasite aircraft for interception and high speed reconnaissance operations and to perform supply missions over long distances. From this work evolved the Model 1240 "All-Purpose" airplane, having the performance capabilities of the bomber but not being limited to normal bombing operations alone.

'As a cargo airplane, the Model 1240 can carry a normal payload of 50,000 pounds (22,680kg) with an overload capacity of 100,000 pounds (45,360kg). Sufficient cross-section (11ft width x 10ft 6in height, 3.36m x 3.05m) is available in the cargo pod to permit carrying practically all items of equipment required by Air or Ground Forces operations. This

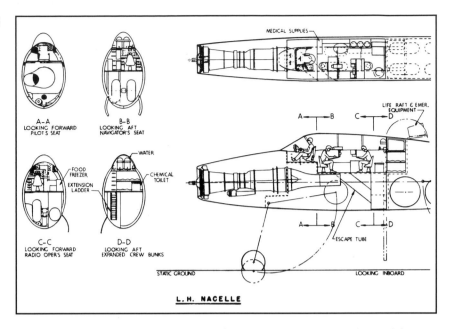

ABOVE Details of the November 1950 configuration of the early Douglas Model 1240. The propeller is not shown. *Boeing*

cargo pod may be arranged in numerous ways for specialised functions such as hospital, general purpose bombing, GCA stations, weather reconnaissance, CIC, ASW, etc, electronic operations, machine shops, aerial tanker functions, etc. The maximum overall length of the pod is limited to 100 feet (30.5m). The special purpose adaptations of the pod would be limited only by the above dimensions.'

By May 1951 the Model 1240 had seen significant design refinement with a 20% increase in wing area. The booms

were enlarged, and the crew relocated to one cabin in the port boom. Engines were changed from the 'turboprop J57' to the T34, with GE XJ53 turbojets being retained in the rear of the outboard engine nacelles.

Douglas determined that the price for the pod carrier's versatility was a 6.9% drag penalty compared to a conventional aircraft with the same cargo capabilities. In addition a conventional aircraft was likely to be lighter than the pod carrier and slightly less expensive to operate – all factors for the Air Force to evaluate.

BELOW The size of the ultimate Model 1240 is emphasised in this drawing by the crew member about to make the 15-foot climb up to the cockpit. *Boeing*

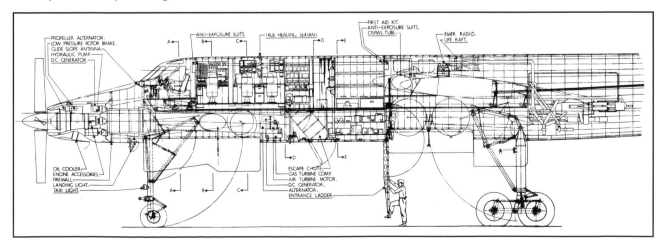

ABOVE The final version of the Douglas Model 1240 with central and auxiliary cargo pods. *John Aldaz photo*

BELOW Display models showing the Douglas Model 1240 'XC-Heavy Transport and Missile/Parasite Carrier', positioned beneath the Model 1211J Heavy Bomber proposal. *John Aldaz photo*

Douglas completed a supplemental study on 29 May 1951 evaluating the replacement of the Pratt & Whitney T34 turboprops with Wright 'TP-51C Sapphire' turboprops. This engine was a derivative of the J65, itself a licensed version of the Armstrong Siddeley Sapphire. The six-turboprop version offered improved cruise performance and greater range than the four-turboprop/twin-jet option. Eventually designated T49, the engine was much later test flown in the nose of a B-17 and also on the inboard pylons of the Boeing XB-47D test bed. However, exhibiting extremely poor propeller and gearbox reliability, the engine was soon dropped from consideration.

Douglas Model 1240 (XC-Heavy)	Model 1240 (August 1950)	Model 1240 (March 1951)
Powerplant	4 x P&W 'J57 Type' turboprops @ 8,000eshp (5,965.6kW) 2 x P&W 'J57 type' turbojets @ 14,500lb (65.5kN)	4 x P&W XT34-P-10 turboprops @ 8,300eshp (6,189.3kW) 2 x GE XJ53 turbojets @ 15,000lb (66.7kN)
Wingspan	212ft 6in (64.77m)	219ft 4in (66.85m)
Length	133ft 4in (40.64m)	155ft 11in (47.52m)
Height	44ft 6in (13.56m)	46ft 9in (14.25m)
Wing area	3,765sq ft (349.8m²)	4,250sq ft (394.8m²)
Design gross weight	337,000lb (152,860kg)	364,000lb (165,110kg)
Cargo pack (empty)	14,500lb (6,580kg)	20,000lb (9,070kg)
Payload	50,000lb (22,690kg)	80,000lb (36,290kg)
Cruise speed	324kt (600km/h)	312kt (578km/h)
Combat Speed	n/a	440kt (815km/h)
Range	4,000nmi (7,408km)	4,140nmi (7,667km)

Like the Douglas Model 1211J from the same era, the Model 1240 brought an imaginative new approach to both large aircraft configuration and to potential multiple uses of a basic airframe. The designs were only put forward after extensive examination of aerodynamic and structural feasibility. However, both were possibly too radical for the Air Force. Whatever the reason, the Model 1240 was not selected; rather it was to provide the basis for a quite different aircraft.

Lockheed L-208-7 XC-Heavy

Limited information suggests that Lockheed carried out some initial studies directed to the requirements of the XC-Heavy programme under the Temporary Designation Number (TDN) L-208. The design appears to have been based on the upper lobe of the L-89 Constitution fuselage and its empennage, combined with either straight (L-208-6) or swept (L-208-7) wings. Both designs supplemented the

Lockheed Model L-208-1 (XC-Heavy)	
Powerplant	6 x P&W T34-P-10 turboprops @ 8,300eshp (6,189.3kW) 2 x GE J53 jets (missile or parasite bomber carrier only)
Wingspan	203ft 0in (61.87m)
Length	154ft 6in (47.09m)
Wing area	4,048sq ft (376.1m²)
Max TOW	360,200lb (163,380kg)
Payload	100,000lb (45,360kg)

T34 turboprops with wingtip-mounted GE XJ53 turbojets added for the missile or parasite carrier missions.

Douglas Model 1814 (XC-132)

Air Force evaluation of the Boeing Model 497 and Douglas Model 1240 in the XC-Heavy competition resulted in neither a declared winner nor the award of a full-scale development contract. Instead, the Air Force requested that Douglas perform further evaluations of the Model 1240 variants continuing under project MX-1707.

Generally reprising the Model 1240 studies carried out a year earlier, the new Douglas designs were somewhat smaller and offered new engine options. Douglas submitted a report to the Air Force in May 1952 titled 'MX-1707

BELOW Lockheed L-208-7 general arrangement. *Lockheed*

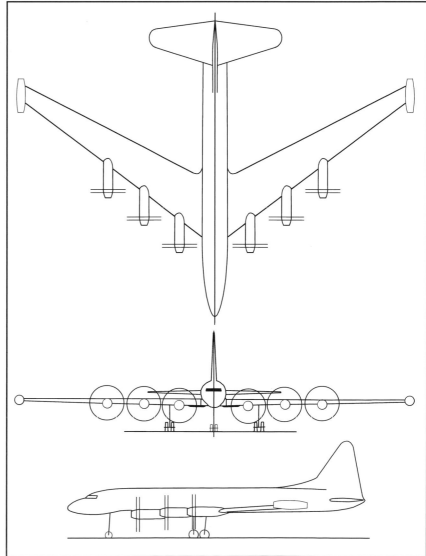

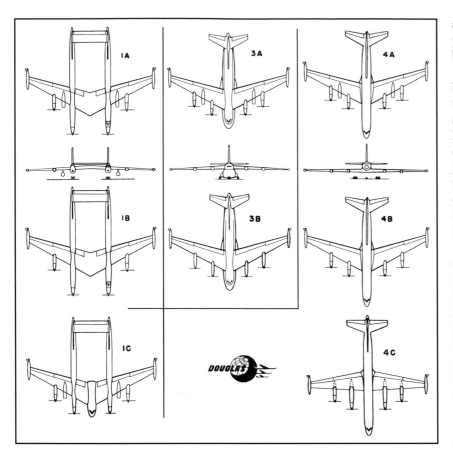

ABOVE A comparative analysis showed that for a cargo aircraft, a conventional fuselage rather than a pod was more efficient from a weight and drag viewpoint. *Boeing*

aerial refuelling had two additional podded J57 engines under the wing to boost the refuelling speed at altitude.

As a result, what started out as a twin-boom cargo pod carrier became a single-fuselage pod carrier, then morphed into a conventional configuration with a high-mounted swept wing. Further optimisation relocated the main landing gear from the inboard engine nacelles to the sides of the lower fuselage, and the earlier large cargo pod was exchanged for a fixed lower-fuselage lobe of the same size.

Contract AF33(600)-23055 was awarded to Douglas on 5 December 1952, marking the culmination of two years of study. It authorised the Phase I Mock-up and Design activities for the Model XC-132 Logistic Transport and Inflight Refueller as defined in Douglas General Specification GS-1814 dated 5 December 1952. The mock-up was defined by GS-1815, issued on 7 January 1953.

The fuselage had a 'double lobe' cross section to accommodate two decks. The upper part was pressurised forward of the wing-box for the flight crew. As a 'Logistics Transport', there was to be no provision for carrying troops; the upper aft compartment space was unused, so external doors and escape hatches and windows were not included. The lower fuselage contained an unobstructed

Study Data' exploring the variations, which included twin boom, removable pod; single boom, removable pod; high wing, single low fixed fuselage; and low wing, single high fixed fuselage. Each variation came with either Wright T47 or Pratt & Whitney T57 turboprop engines. Aircraft designs configured for

BELOW With the 'MX-1707-3A' option, the eventual form of the Douglas Model 1814 came into focus, albeit with a pair of jet engines under the wing (likely the GE XJ53) in addition to the turboprops. *Boeing*

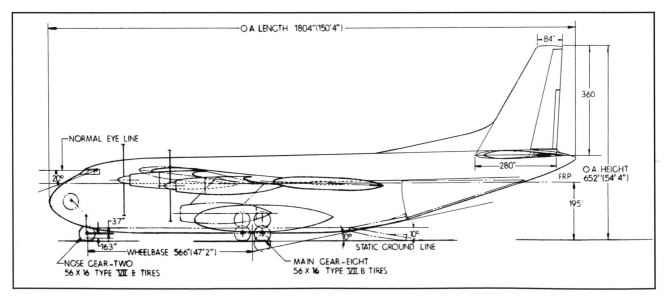

cargo bay measuring 16.5ft (5.03 m) wide by 12.5 ft (3.81m) high. This could accommodate nearly all vehicles, equipment or special weapons in use in 1953. The cargo bay was designed for forklifts to drive in and out carrying pallets of cargo. Provisions were made to anchor the cargo netting to the sidewalls of the bay.

As a Logistic Transport, the normal mission would be to carry 100,000lb (45,359kg), but cargo capacity could be traded for range:

- 100,000lb (45,359kg) of cargo carried 3,500nmi (6,479 km) or
- 140,500lb (63,730kg) of cargo carried 2,200nmi (4,074km) or
- 72,000lb (32,659kg) of cargo carried 4,500nmi (8,334 km)

As an in-flight refueller, the aircraft's empty weight would be 12,689lb (5,755 kg) heavier than the cargo version. This included the added weight of the wingtip refuelling pods with hose reels and drogues, additional fuel tanks in the cargo bay, and stronger main landing gear. The total fuel load was to be 290,000lb (131,542kg), which was to be shared between the KC-132 and the receiver aircraft. In-flight refuelling was to take place at receiver aircraft speed and at altitudes of up to 35,000ft (10,668m).

The aircraft was to be powered by four Pratt & Whitney XT57-P-1 axial-flow turboprops. This was a new engine of unprecedented size for the United States, based on the J57 turbojet, and designed to deliver 15,000shp (11,186kW).

During the early Phase I engineering period in 1953, Douglas responded to numerous Air Force requests to investigate alternative features. These resulted in the following major studies:

1. A study was made of the refuelling speed compatibility with the XB-58 supersonic bomber. It was concluded that the XC-132 had sufficient speed margin to refuel the XB-58, assuming that it could use normal thrust on the back side of the drag versus speed curve. (This also presumed that the XB-58

ABOVE The early Douglas XC-132 configuration shows the original mid-wing engine mounting and lack of weather radar radome. *Boeing*

BELOW An early study of the Douglas Model 1814 with a lower fuselage pod upper and nacelle-mounted main landing gear. Engine exhaust was to be ducted over the wing. *Boeing*

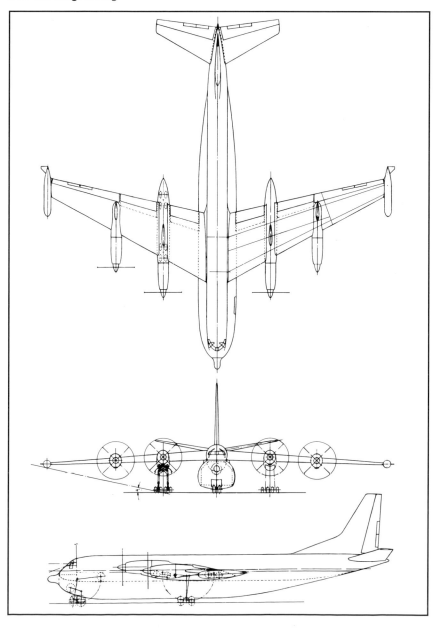

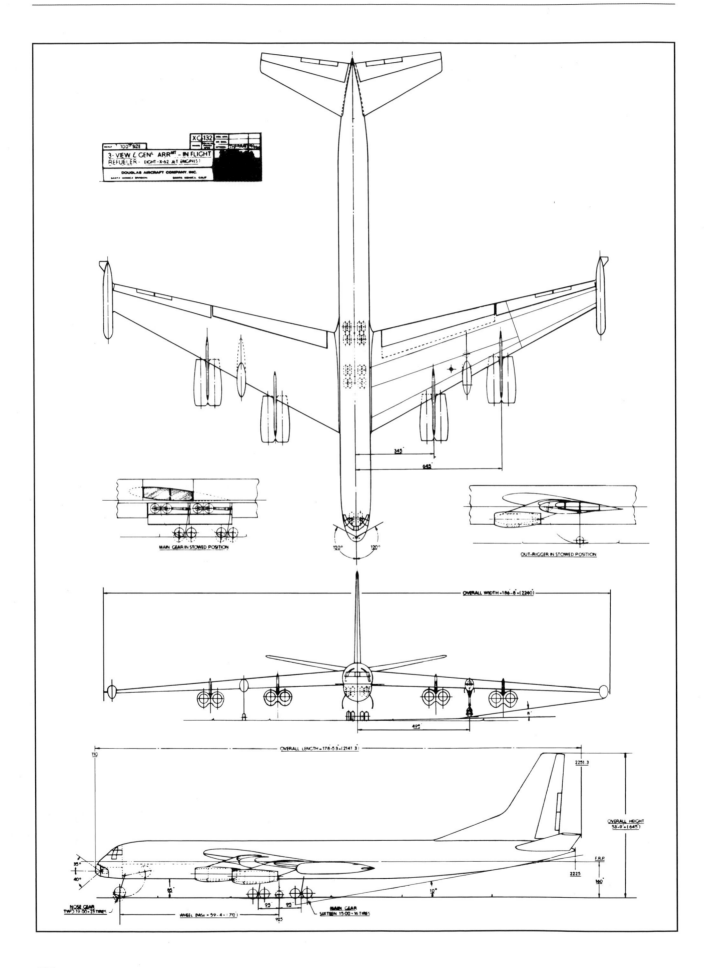

Douglas Model 1814 (XC-132) proposed variants	C-132 logistics transport	KC-132 in-flight refueller
Cruise speed	380kt (703.8km/h)	420kt (777.9km/h)*
Empty weight	161,618lb (73,309kg)	174,307lb (79,064kg)
Maximum payload	146,907lb (66,696kg)	180,700lb (82,038kg)
Max gross TOW	433,000lb (186,582kg)	469,225lb (212,307kg)
* maximum refuelling speed		

Douglas Models 1814 and 1905 comparison	Model 1814	Model 1905
Engine rating	16,000eshp (11,940kW)	20,000eshp (14,920kW)
Cruise speed	385kt (713km/h)	420kt (777.8km/h)
Maximum payload	146,907lb (66,696kg)	180,700lb (82,038kg)
Max gross TOW	433,000lb (186,580kg)	488,000lb (221,550kg)

would be equipped for probe and drogue refuelling at this early date.)

2. Studies were made of various methods of increasing the refuelling speed of the XC-132. These included reducing the size of the aeroplane for single-point refuelling, providing special small-diameter fuselages on the refueller aeroplanes to reduce parasite drag, and

installing two J57 turbojet engines in addition to the T57s. All these methods produced significant increases in refuelling speed, at the expense of cargo-carrying ability and operating costs.

3. Several studies were made of the effect of installing advanced engines with higher power. Results of these studies showed that the XC-132

configuration did indeed have the growth potential to utilise such engines as they became available.

As part of the Phase I engineering effort, a full-scale engineering mock-up was built in 1953 at the Douglas plant in Santa Monica, California. It was remarkably detailed with functioning ramps and doors, avionics racks, engine bays, instrumented flight deck, landing gear and a large amount of life-like flight equipment and systems. The Air Force Development Engineering Inspection (DEI) of the completed mock-up was conducted in January 1954. This was followed by the formal Air Force Mock-up Inspection (MI) on 15-17 February 1954. As part of the effort, Douglas demonstrated cargo loading as well as engine removal and installation.

Two prototypes were ordered under the designation YC-132, and in October 1956 Pratt & Whitney began flight testing the T57 turboprop in the nose of a Douglas C-124.

ABOVE The Douglas XC-132 mock-up undergoing loading demonstrations at Santa Monica in the hangar (Building 8) that had been built for manufacturing the [then] 'World's Largest Airplane', the B-19 bomber. The aft section of the mock-up shows the lack of windows and doors. *Boeing*

OPPOSITE A study of a high-speed refueller using the upper fuselage, wings and empennage of the XC-132. The engines were specified as the General Electric 'X-60'. *Boeing*

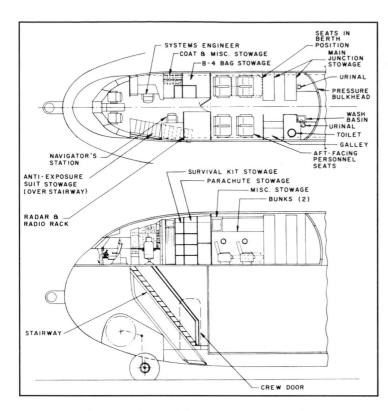

ABOVE The XC-132 mock-up's cockpit is dramatically lit to show the interior and the flight crew. *Boeing*

LEFT Arrangement of the XC-132 cockpit and crew compartment. An escape chute (under the entry ladder) allowed the crew to bail out in a trajectory away from the propellers. *Boeing*

BELOW The XC-132 cockpit and Flight Engineer's stations. *Boeing*

ABOVE The Douglas YC-132 depicted in flight with the lowered engine configuration. *Boeing*
BELOW Douglas YC-132 general arrangement. *Boeing*

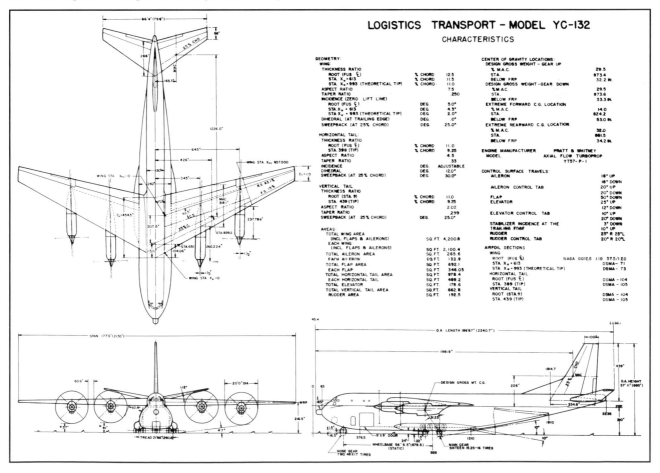

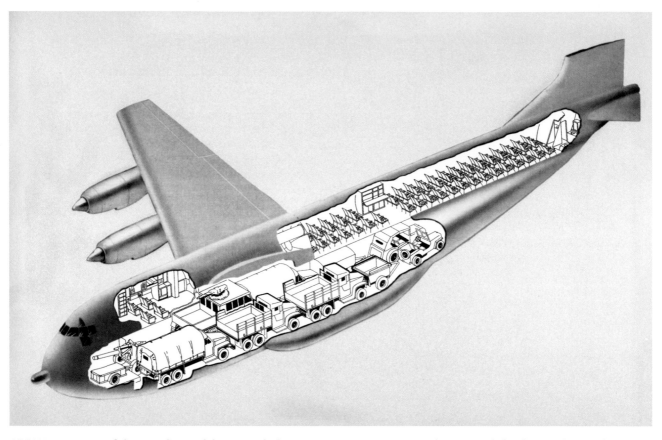

ABOVE A cutaway of the Douglas Model 1905 with the passenger compartment in the upper aft fuselage and revised engine positioning. *Boeing*

Douglas Model 1905 troop carrier

By December 1955 Douglas had developed the Model 1905, a version of the C-132 designed to take advantage of the expected growth of the T57 engine to 20,000eshp. With the 20% increase in power, the revised design offered greater payload, speed and range. The overall dimensions and external configuration were unchanged. To take advantage of the added performance, the hitherto empty upper aft compartment was to be pressurised and have permanent accommodation for up to 100 troops. A tunnel connecting the flight deck to the troop compartment would be routed between the upper fuselage skin and the wing carry-through structure.

C-132 development

After the successful mock-up review in January 1954, development continued on an extended schedule, possibly paced to match Pratt & Whitney's development of the T57 engine. With a relatively low work priority (approved by the Air Force) the number of engineers assigned ranged from a high of just below 200 in November 1953 to a low of about 40 in May 1955. As the design crystallised, a Design Specification (DS-1814) was issued on 15 April 1954 by Douglas embodying the requirements levied by the Air Force and specifying how the Model 1814 would meet them.

Design changes during this period were relatively few. To reduce adverse flow interactions with the wing and reduce drag, the engine nacelles were lowered approximately 18in (45.72cm) with respect to the wing leading edge. To deal with limited control authority in certain flight regimes, the horizontal stabiliser was changed from a fixed to a fully adjustable surface. This in turn drove changes to the aft fuselage shape that made it 'slab sided', lowering the horizontal stabiliser and increasing the

dihedral from 10° to 12° to compensate. Engine power increased from 15,000eshp to 16,000eshp (11,190kW to 11,940kW). At the request of the Air Force, Douglas also studied how to make the vertical tail foldable (as on the B-52); this was found to be possible at the cost of 350lb (159kg) for additional structure and actuators.

While all this development work was progressing, the Air Force changed its mind and cancelled one of the aircraft's missions, deleting the In-Flight Refueller requirement (leaving only space *provision* for single-point tail refuelling). This was probably a result of the selection of Lockheed as the winner of the jet tanker competition and the decision to acquire 'interim' Boeing KC-135As (as described in the following chapter). In two short years events and technology had overtaken the KC-132. Nonetheless, the YC-132 capabilities to transport 110,000lb (49,895 kg) of fuel within a radius of 2,500nmi (4,630 km) were retained.

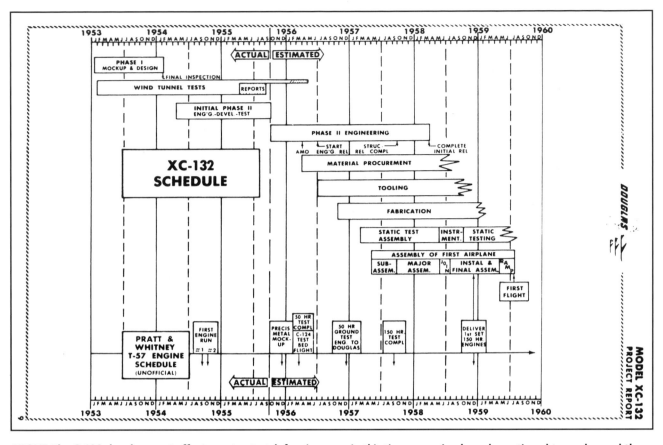

ABOVE The C-132 development effort was to stretch for six years. In this time, perceived needs continued to evolve and the project, the only user of the T57 turboprop, became less attractive, particularly after the tanker mission was cancelled. *Boeing*

In the second half of 1955 Douglas began negotiations with the Air Force to transfer the entire programme from the Santa Monica Division to the Tulsa, Oklahoma, Division of the company. There was likely never any intent to manufacture the C-132 in Santa Monica; with its small airfield and its facilities fully occupied by DC-6 and DC-7 production and by DC-8 engineering, there simply was not enough room. The same situation existed at Long Beach, where C-133 production was crowding out the smaller B-66 programme. The solution was to transfer the B-66 and C-132 programmes to the Tulsa facility, where licensed production of the B-47 was winding down.

Thus in January 1956 the entire C-132 project, including the mock-up, was relocated from Santa Monica to Tulsa as the DC-8 engineering effort ramped up at Santa Monica. This coincided with the beginning of the C-132 Phase II Engineering effort, and the Materiel

BELOW The fuselage cross section shows the relatively small C-132 aft loading door size. Atlas missile loading would have been problematic. *Boeing*

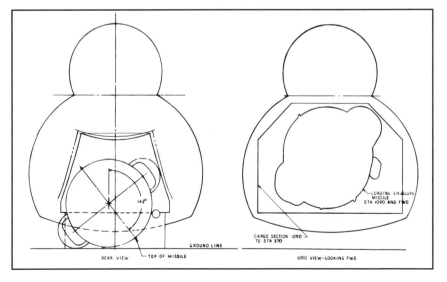

Procurement, Tooling and Fabrication efforts. The Assembly phase was due to begin in May 1957 with the construction of the first airframe subassemblies. Fuselage join was scheduled for June 1958, rollout for May 1959 and first flight for August 1959.

However, the C-132 programme was abruptly cancelled on 29 March 1957 together with the T57 powerplant, just before manufacturing of the first subassemblies was about to begin. The cancellation was part of a round of DoD budget cuts, but clearly the Air Force

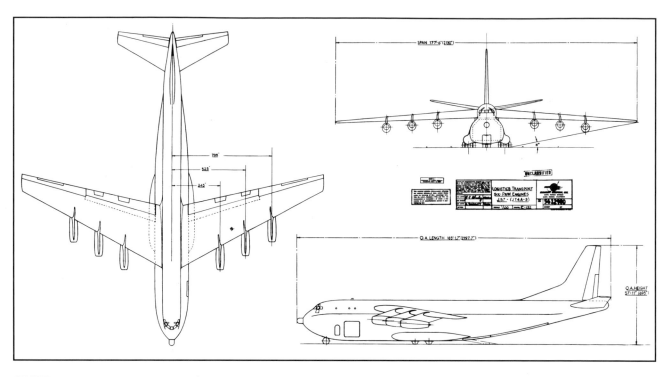

ABOVE Drawn in Santa Monica in February 1957 – less than a month before programme cancellation – this six-jet (Pratt & Whitney JT4C) 'XC-132' concept pointed the way to the future. *Boeing*

declined to fight to save the project. The most likely reasons were threefold. First, the cargo space was actually quite small relative to the overall size of the aircraft; second, the promised pressurised troop-carrying compartment was not likely to be available until 1963 with the Model 1905; and third, missile loading was expected to be difficult (the C-132 having been designed before the Atlas missile). With the missile-carriage modifications introduced in the C-133B (which used the existing C-133A airframe and engine), the need for the C-132 for this role disappeared.

Perhaps the final nail in the C-132's coffin was that it was to be wholly dependent on a new engine that was being specifically developed for the project. There was no other turboprop of similar power to the T57 in prospect, and no other aircraft planning to use the engine. The C-132 programme would therefore have had to bear all the development costs and would have been entirely dependent on its successful outcome. Whatever the reasons, the USAF ended up with a smaller, less ambitious aircraft – the C-133 – which as discussed earlier was

based initially on the C-124, a service-proven military transport with a long design ancestry.

The early 1950s in perspective

The 1950s started with the Air Force operating a fleet of piston-engine transport aircraft largely based on adaptations of earlier airliners or bombers, supplemented by two tactical military transports (the C-82 and C-119), which would provide invaluable service but proved to have limited development potential. The Korean War and the Cold War quickly established that much greater capability was needed.

Coupled with the growing maturity of the turbine engine, this pressure led to a series of initiatives that, by the end of the decade, resulted in a specialist fleet of airlifters. However, despite two industry-wide competitions and the exploration of a wide range of potential options, only two major designs from the first part of the decade (the C-130 and the C-133) resulted in production orders.

Moreover, both were fairly conventional configurations: four-

engined with high-mounted straight wings, rear-loading cargo doors, main landing gear housed in fuselage-side fairings, and conventional empennage. The designs resulted not from conservative thinking but rather from considerable studies that proved them the most effective solutions. A seemingly promising concept, the cargo pod and its carrier aeroplane, was extensively investigated but led nowhere.

Meanwhile, a parallel line of development was under way that would have important consequences. Air-to-air refuelling had established itself in the early 1950s as a vital component of the USA's strategy for nuclear deterrence. Although the new technology had proved remarkably effective, there was a performance mismatch between the tankers and the bombers. There was, therefore, a need to produce an air-refuelling tanker with a speed more closely matched to the swept-wing jet-engined bombers that it supported. The pursuit of this goal was to lead to a new generation of high-speed transport aircraft that would ultimately transform not only military airlift but also civil aviation.

Chapter Seven
Strategic Air Command's Tanker-Transport

Transforming the future of air transportation

ABOVE The Douglas Model 1274E with T34 turboprops is depicted here in Douglas 'house colours'. *Boeing*

The introduction of the jet engine for military transportation purposes did not come via its use in cargo or passenger aircraft, but rather through a different requirement: the need for a high-speed air-refuelling tanker.

As the 1950s progressed, the Strategic Air Command (SAC) increasingly needed an air-refuelling capability to extend the range of its new (and growing) fleet of jet-powered bombers.

The requirement had been foreseeable from 1948, when Boeing finalised the design of its long-range high-speed B-52 Stratofortress strategic bomber, changing the design from turboprop power to jet engines, with their higher fuel consumption.

While Boeing and the Air Force were finalising the B-52 design, Boeing was simultaneously designing advanced tankers to extend the huge bomber's range. The Model 491, with twin fuselages, was one early configuration. Originating in December 1949, it was a

very large refueller, with performance matching that of the B-52. Total fuel load was 232,650lb (105,530kg), which could be used to either fuel its own engines or be offloaded to the bomber. Its flying boom was perfected on KB-29 tanker conversions, and 'flew' in the starboard tail-supporting boom, transferring up to 6,000 gallons (22,700 litres) per hour. The crew of six was housed in the centre fuselage. But the design proved premature, since the B-52 itself was still undergoing changes in both design and capability.

Boeing Model 491 tanker transport

Powerplant	6 x Allison T40 turboprops @ 7,500shp (5,593kW)
Span	208ft (63.4m)
Length	109ft (33.2m)
Height	39ft (11.9m)
Wing area	3,000sq ft (278.7m²)
Design gross weight	375,000lb (170,100kg)
Maximum speed	490 mph (km/h)

Aerial refuelling decisions

Before evaluating and purchasing a fleet of refuellers, the Air Force had to make two overarching and interrelated decisions: exactly how to refuel the bombers and what type of aircraft to refuel them with. This decision was time-critical – the bomber manufacturers needed to know so that the chosen design could be integrated into their receiver bombers, already planned and in production.

BELOW The Boeing Model 491 from December 1949 was a six-turboprop dedicated refueller planned by Boeing for extending the range of the B-52. *Boeing*

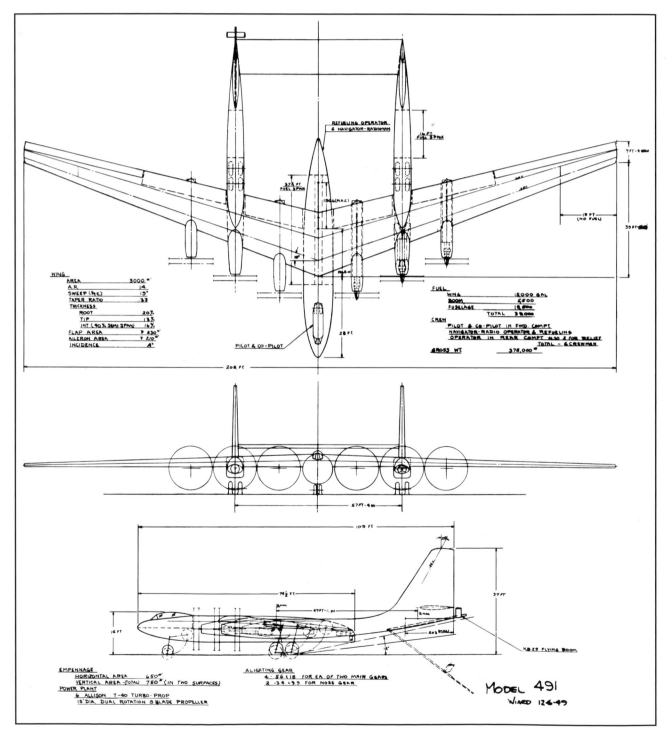

By 1949, there were four systems available:

- The hose grappling technique, requiring the receiver aircraft to 'capture the hose' and manually connect it.
- The 'probe and drogue' method pioneered by Flight Refuelling Ltd in the UK.
- The Boeing rigid flying boom system, requiring the receiver to fly behind the tanker.
- The Douglas rigid tandem coupling method where the receiver flew in front of the tanker.

The grappling technique was rejected almost immediately because it required a high degree of manual operation; it was also dangerous during night-time, inclement weather, high speed or high altitude – all conditions that would be expected during SAC combat operations.

ABOVE The hose grappling method was demonstrated in 1929 when the 'Question Mark', a Fokker C-2, was kept aloft for 150 hours 40 minutes by in-flight transfers of fuel (as well as engine oil, food and sundries). *R. G. Smith via the Mike Machat collection*

BELOW The British company Flight Refuelling Limited (FRL) devised the 'hose and drogue' refuelling method seen here on the one-off YKB-29T. This technology remains in use today, since pod installations require minimal modification to the tanker aircraft and multiple systems on one tanker can simultaneously refuel several aircraft. *Boeing*

Engineers evaluated the British 'probe and drogue' method pioneered by Flight Refuelling Ltd, which had the advantages of requiring minimum modification to the tanker aircraft, as well as the capability to refuel several (smaller) aircraft simultaneously. Nonetheless, it could not match the Boeing flying boom's ability to provide the fast fuel flow rate required for a large bomber. It also had the disadvantage that all the receiver aircraft pilots needed to become skilled in initiating contact with the tanker, whereas in the Boeing system this skill was concentrated in a limited number of specialist boom operators. Douglas, under Air Force contract, investigated a 'lance' method requiring the refueller aircraft to approach the receiver from the rear, then connect and initiate the

transfer. Eventually, however, the flying boom approach prevailed, and is still used today by all large USAF aircraft.

After the Air Force selected the refuelling mechanism, the next task was to select the refuelling aircraft. The choices were:

- Convert existing long-range aircraft.
- Create tanker versions of future bomber aircraft.
- Create a derivative cargo/tanker aircraft.
- Design a new tanker/transport aircraft.

An immediate decision was made in May 1949 to convert existing Second Word War-vintage B-29 piston-engine bombers, providing a rudimentary capability to extend the range of SAC's

B-50 bombers (a post-war growth version of the B-29). The next step was to adapt an existing cargo aircraft for the tanker role. Three C-97A Stratofreighters were modified for test purposes and, after successful evaluation, the new tanker was ordered into production as the KC-97A. This led to a number of successively improved variants, with 816 tankers being delivered to SAC between 1952 and 1956, all convertible to transports if required. Meanwhile, the Tactical Air Command, unable to procure KC-135s due to SAC taking priority in the late 1950s, acquired obsolete ex-SAC B-50 bombers and converted them to three-point 'hose and drogue' tankers.

While this resolved the immediate need, it was a temporary solution; the KC-97 simply could not match the

BELOW The Douglas tandem coupling refuelling concept is illustrated here with the passive receiver B-52 flying in front of the probe-equipped KC-124B tanker. *Boeing*

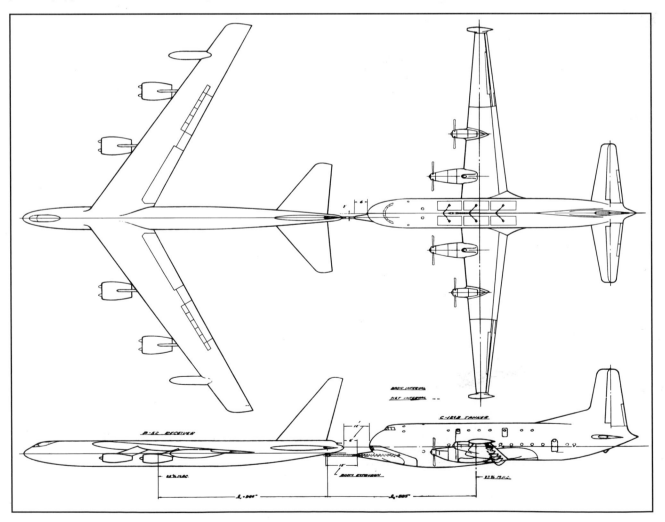

ABOVE A detailed view of the Douglas tandem coupling tanker (left) and receiver aircraft (right) during a ground test. *Boeing*
BELOW B-29 bombers flight test the Douglas tandem coupling refuelling system over Edwards Air Force Base. *USAF*

ABOVE SAC preferred the Boeing flying boom photographed here on a KB-29P, because of its controllability and high rate of fuel flow. *Mike Machat collection*

performance of the bombers it was supporting. Indeed, the Boeing B-52 had to go into a high-drag landing configuration, with its undercarriage down, to fly slow enough to match the tanker's maximum sustainable speed. Nor was it a quick process. Even using the Boeing high-transfer-rated flying boom that SAC adopted, it could take more than thirty minutes to refuel a B-52. The Air Force desperately needed a tanker aircraft that matched the bomber's performance without the latter slowing down or descending to a lower altitude for rendezvous. An alternative mission profile, where the tankers were to escort the bomber force to a refuelling point, was impossible with the piston-engine KC-97; it had neither the speed nor the altitude capability to keep up with the B-52s.

Another option was modifying bombers into tankers (a route later followed by the British with their V-bomber fleet), and the Air Force considered proposals for a KB-36, a KB-47 and a KB-52. That approach had

the advantage that the tankers would have the same performance as the bombers, and offered the bonus of operating and maintaining a common fleet. It was not pursued, however, since planners felt that the bomber-derived tankers would count against the end-strength of the fleet, reducing the number of bombers. Additionally, the bomber-tankers would lack a secondary airlift capability.

A third option was to design an uprated derivative of an existing cargo aircraft. Anticipating this, Boeing had already proposed a number of higher-speed turboprop and jet-powered Model 367 (C-97) tankers from 1949 to 1951. But none of these proved acceptable to SAC. The Douglas KC-124B (already in development) programme was also rejected, although limited development continued on the aircraft as a test bed for turboprop engines. Even the enormous KC-132 would be found wanting – possibly due to its lengthy development schedule with a projected first flight in 1959.

The final option was for the Air Force to specify and procure a jet tanker that could match the bomber fleet's performance. However, as discussed in the following pages, several factors short-circuited this path, including both Boeing's decision to build the Model 367-80 as a technology demonstrator, and SAC commander General Curtis LeMay's insistence that 'good enough' and 'soon' were far superior to 'technically perfect'.

Building on early post-war jet transport proposals

The steps that led to SAC's first high-speed tanker come into sharper focus with a review of studies undertaken for jet airliners in the immediate post-Second World War years. With the war's end, the major aircraft producers forecast that the civil market would offer the greatest opportunities. Military expenditures were severely cut, but airlines worldwide were gearing up for a new era of air travel.

The advanced designs developed during the war – the DC-6, Constellation and Boeing Stratocruiser – offered a variety of suitable aircraft to meet the market's demands, and advances in aeronautical engineering held out even greater promise. The jet engine, together with new research into high-speed aerodynamics, offered the possibility for passenger transportation at much greater speeds – albeit if only for the wealthy minority.

The earliest concepts, such as Lockheed's L-152 from 1944, began with a standard straight-wing configuration and simply replaced the traditional prop-driven engines with jets (in this case Lockheed L-1000 jet engines mounted within the wing roots).

But as early as 1947 aircraft like the F-86 and B-47 were proving the performance advantages that swept wings offered. Manufacturers quickly began to incorporate wing sweep into

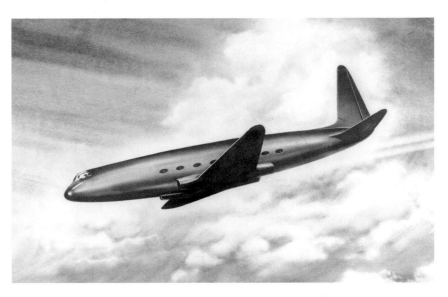

ABOVE Dating from 1944, this L-152 concept was one of the first Lockheed jet transport studies, with seating for thirty-two passengers. *Jane and Winfield Arata papers (courtesy of Martha and Allen Arata)*

their commercial proposals, including Boeing's Model 473-28 (which featured a similar wing to the B-47) and Lockheed's L-179 family of designs. Even more exotic proposals emerged, some with the then new delta wing configuration; both Boeing's Model 493-10A and the Douglas Model 1067 (derived from the Model 1064 bomber studies) were designed to exploit its potential.

BELOW Douglas Model 1042-O general arrangement, dated 5 September 1946. Powered by four Rolls-Royce Nenes, the 1042-O had an unusual nacelle design. One engine was mounted forward of the wing and fed by a nose intake, with the exhaust ducted over the wing. The second engine was mounted in the aft nacelle and fed by a side intake. Other designs in the Model 1042 exploratory family tried out different wing, nacelle and empennage configurations using a common fuselage. *Boeing*

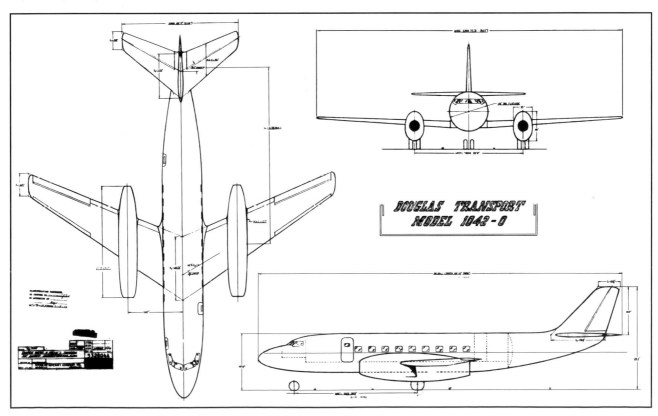

Many of these designs were ahead of their time. As the British found with their Comet airliner, there was still more to learn about the challenges of sustained high-speed, high-altitude flight. Nonetheless, the studies showed a path forward for the following decade's developments, when jet-powered transports would become the norm. Ironically, the transformation was led not by a passenger or even a cargo transport, but by a category of aircraft not even imagined in the 1940s: the air-to-air refueller.

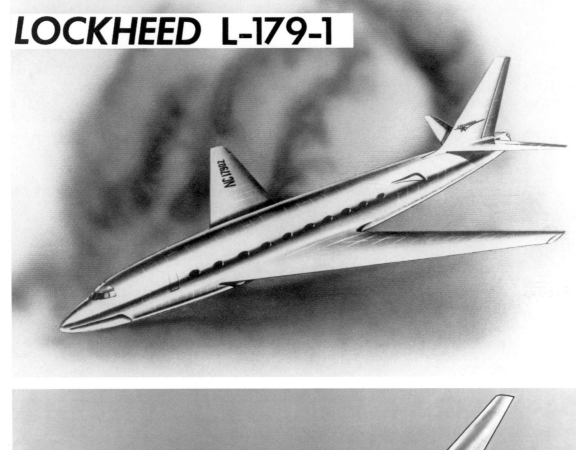

LOCKHEED L-179-1

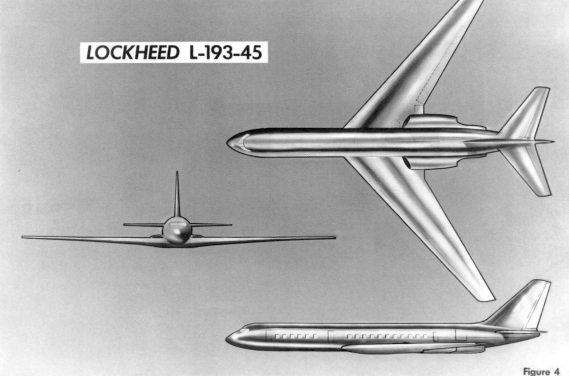

LOCKHEED L-193-45

Figure 4

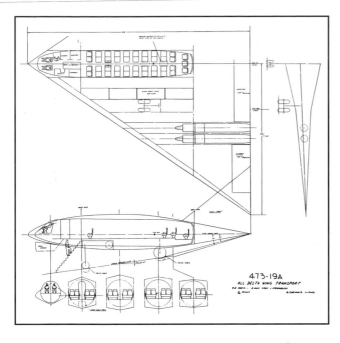

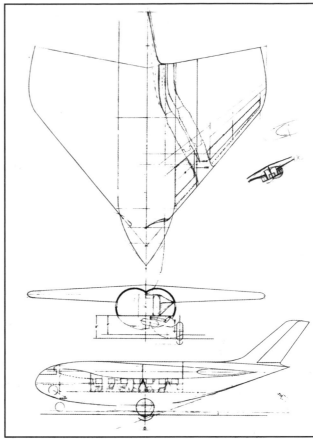

ABOVE The Boeing 473-19A delta wing transport preliminary layout from 1949. *Boeing*

RIGHT Sketch of a Douglas clipped delta high-wing airliner in the Model 1067 family from May 1947. The wing planform was drawn from the Model 1064 Strategic Bomber design study, while the dual lobe fuselage was unique. *Boeing*

Boeing's route to the KC-135 and 707

Although airlines had rejected its early jet transport studies, and the Air Force had rebuffed its initial jet tanker proposals, Boeing continued to pursue both concepts. On 22 May 1952 company directors committed to invest $15 million to develop and construct a prototype of a jet transport. It was a remarkably bold play: the amount was double the previous year's entire profit. It would, of course,

OPPOSITE TOP The Lockheed L-179-1 airliner from 1946 featured two jet engines in the wing root fed by nose intakes, and another two engines in the aft fuselage fed by NACA-type intakes. Studies in the L-179 family ran for about eighteen months and eventually relocated the engines in a 'four-pack' under the wing.
Jane and Winfield Arata papers (courtesy of Martha and Allen Arata)

OPPOSITE BOTTOM Lockheed's L-193-45 airliner design, circa 1953.
Jane and Winfield Arata papers (courtesy of Martha and Allen Arata)

pay off handsomely in the long term. It is hard to imagine today, but at that time Boeing had virtually no presence in the commercial market, rating fifth in terms of market position behind Douglas, Lockheed, Martin and Convair.

Boeing's confidence was undoubtedly boosted by the company's unique experience in designing and building large, high-performance bombers, dating back to the early post-war years and the B-47 Stratojet. When it first flew in 1947 – having taken advantage of German wartime work on high-speed aerodynamics and swept wings – the B 47 represented an astounding leap forward in performance, doubling the speed and operating altitude of its immediate predecessors. However, its significance goes beyond its increase in capability. The B-47 is described by Mike Lombardi, Boeing's Chief Historian and Archivist, as 'the most important aircraft that Boeing ever produced'. It set the pattern for large jet aircraft – swept wings, swept tail surfaces, and engine nacelles carried on pylons beneath the

wings – for generations to come. Today, virtually every large jet transport aircraft still follows that same configuration.

Boeing recognised early the potential for high-speed commercial transportation offered by the new technologies, and began investigating jet airliner concepts well before the tanker requirement became evident. Indeed, Boeing's first ideas for a swept-wing, jet-powered passenger aircraft can be traced back to 1946, and were originally based on the B-47 bomber, although the latter had yet to fly.

On 1 May 1947 Boeing's advanced design group opened a new model number – 473 – for jet airliner preliminary studies. Short-, medium- and long-range designs would be studied, all with jet and turboprop propulsion. Many succeeding iterations were variations of the B-47 formula of a high wing and bicycle landing gear, which proved to be poorly suited for the civil market (with the landing gear taking up valuable space in the fuselage).

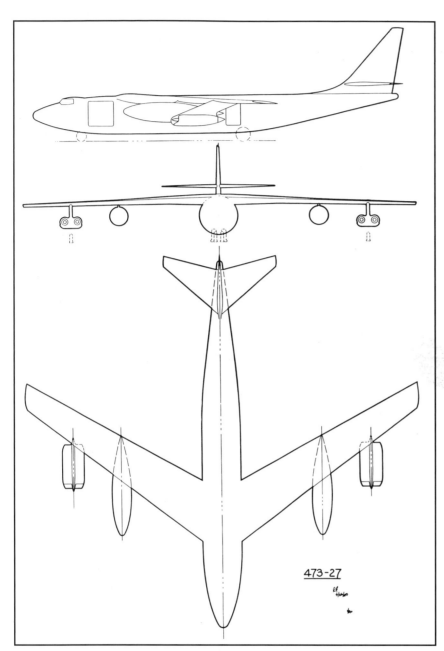

473-27

LEFT Boeing Model 473-27 troop carrier and cargo transport general arrangement. As a troop carrier, it could seat fifty-six soldiers. *Boeing*

Boeing Model 473-27 cargo/troop transport	
Powerplant	4 x Westinghouse 24C-10 turbojets @ 4,200lb thrust (16.68kN)
Span	101ft 6in (30.94m)
Length	94ft 6in (x128.80m)
Cruise altitude	40,000ft (12,192m)
Cruise speed	500mph (805km/h)

By 1949 the studies had progressed through a series of iterations to become the Model 473-28, and by the following year the large airliner design progression had reached the Model 473-60C, whose design had converged with that of the military 367-70-2. Subsequent Model 473 designs explored turboprop airliners; commercial jetliner studies (parallel to the military 367-80 series) were then conducted under the newly assigned Model 707 designation which was opened on 18 September 1951.

Finalising the 'Dash-80' design

Having swept the wings, swept the tail surfaces, and introduced new engines, the design team still grappled with fuselage issues centred on its cross section. The basic design of the 367 was based on that of the B-29, retaining the latter's fuselage as a lower lobe. While the cross section made it less than ideal for high-speed flight, this lower space was useful for cargo or for possible seating in the C-97. In its civil guise (the Model 377), the area in the lower aft fuselage was ideal as a passenger lounge.

The cross section's profile, however, produced drag. While not excessive at piston-engine speeds, it was a major issue at jet speeds. Further, the accentuated 'double bubble' exacerbated airflow problems at the junction of the wing with the fuselage, necessitating heavy, drag-

LEFT The Boeing Model 473-28 airliner version of the 473-27 was smaller and lighter than the B-47 while exhibiting common design elements. Capacity was to be thirty-six passengers.
Author's collection

ABOVE An illustration of the Boeing 473-60C passenger jetliner. *Author's collection*

BELOW An illustration of the Boeing 473-60C passenger jetliner, with an additional side view of the military 367-70-2 (lower right). The narrow wheel track of the main landing gear necessitated retractable skids mounted in the bottom of the engine nacelles. *Author's collection*

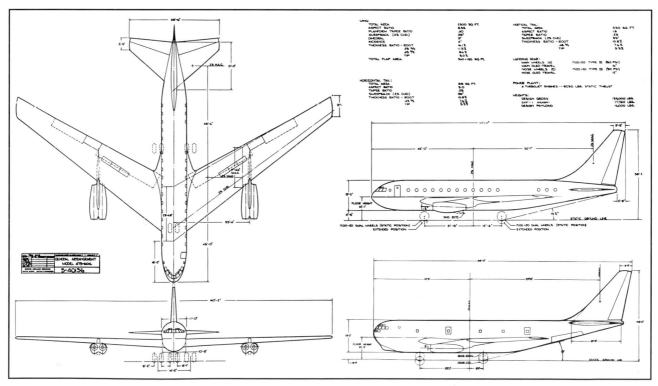

producing fillets. Both problems were addressed by 'shallowing' the lower lobe and filling in the crease between the lobes. Giving up the habitable lower deck was key to the new fuselage. On the other hand, the lower lobe could not be eliminated, since it provided room for cargo or below-deck fuel tanks in the refuelling role. The 132in (3.35m) width of the Model 367 upper lobe (sufficient for five-abreast passenger seating) was retained in the 367-80 prototype.

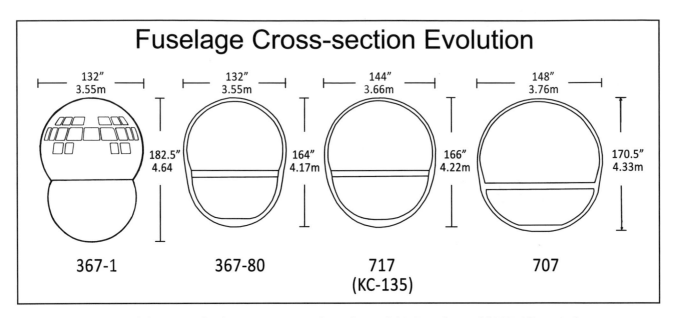

Fuselage Cross-section Evolution

| 132" | 132" | 144" | 148" |
| 3.55m | 3.55m | 3.66m | 3.76m |

182.5"
4.64

164"
4.17m

166"
4.22m

170.5"
4.33m

367-1   **367-80**   **717**   **707**

(KC-135)

ABOVE The evolution of the Boeing fuselage cross sections from the Model 367 to the Model 707 airliner. *Authors*

The upper deck had to be widened at the Air Force's insistence to 144in (3.66m) for the KC-135, and at the airline customers' demands to 148in (3.76m) outside diameter for the Model 707 – to be wider than the competing proposal, the DC-8. This severely reduced the commonality between the military and civil versions of what looked superficially to be the same aeroplane, albeit with windows. The Model 707 airliner also lowered the deck within the fuselage to provide its greatest width at passenger shoulder height.

BELOW This artwork shows the initial Boeing Model 367-80-70. The new fuselage has been married to the wings (with trailing edge modification), engines and empennage of the 367-70 series. The designs in the 367-80 series all had three small 'eyebrow' windows above the pilot and co-pilot. The vertical tail outline is reminiscent of the B-47. *Boeing*

The 'Dash 80', as it was known within the company, reached Preliminary Design project status in December 1951. It received formal engineering project status on 12 May 1952, being assigned its model number the same month. The basic design was frozen in July 1952 and the first metal was cut in October 1952. Final assembly began in October 1953, and the completed aeroplane was rolled out on 14 May 1954, with its first flight on 15 July.

The subsequent production military variants received the Model 717 designation, with the evolved

commercial models designated Boeing Model 707. Over the following years, several further developments were considered and a number produced, though most adhered closely to the original configuration.

With its new aircraft, Boeing was ready to take advantage of the Air Force's recognition that the Model 367-80 could be easily adapted into a high-speed tanker.

Boeing Model 367-80-70 transport	
Powerplant	4 x P&W J57 turbojets
Span	130ft 0in (39.62m)
Length	126ft 4in (38.51m)
Height	39ft 6in (12.04m)

BELOW A display model of the Boeing Model 367-80, as built with two left-side cargo doors. *Boeing*

Model 367-81 series alternative jet variants

Even as metal was being cut on the 'Dash-80', design studies continued, seeking improvements. One recognised shortcoming was the limited power from the first-generation Pratt & Whitney J57 engine (rated at approximately 9,500lb (45.26kN) thrust). With a maximum weight of 190,000lb (86,180kg), the thrust-to-weight ratio was 0.2 to 1, a barely adequate number at high- altitude airfields, leaving little margin for safety if an engine failed on take-off.

Alternative configurations investigated the use of the Wright 'J67-W-X' engine with take-off afterburners (Model 367-81-95) and the Pratt & Whitney J75-P-1X with water injection (Model 367-81-96). For the KC-135A (Model 717-100A), neither advanced engine was selected and the J57-P-43W engine was used. This engine had the take-off thrust boosted to 13,759lb (61.16kN) with water injection. These alternative engine versions had few, if any, visual differences from the J57-equipped designs.

Model 367-81 series turboprop variants

Boeing also investigated replacing the jet engines with turboprops. Although these would limit the speed of the proposed designs compared to pure jet engines, the gross weight could be increased, fuel efficiency was better, and their range greatly increased.

The March and April 1953 studies diverged into several families. One group was based on the basic 'Dash 80' wing of 2,400sq ft (223m²), although overall wingspan would vary due to the size of the wingtip pods. The fuselage cross section would also remain the same as the 'Dash 80', but various fuselage lengths were analysed.

Specific configurations investigated included the Model 367-81-104, the slightly longer 367-81-119, and the much extended -119B at an overall length of 161ft 2in (49.12m). The powerplant was to be the Wright T47,

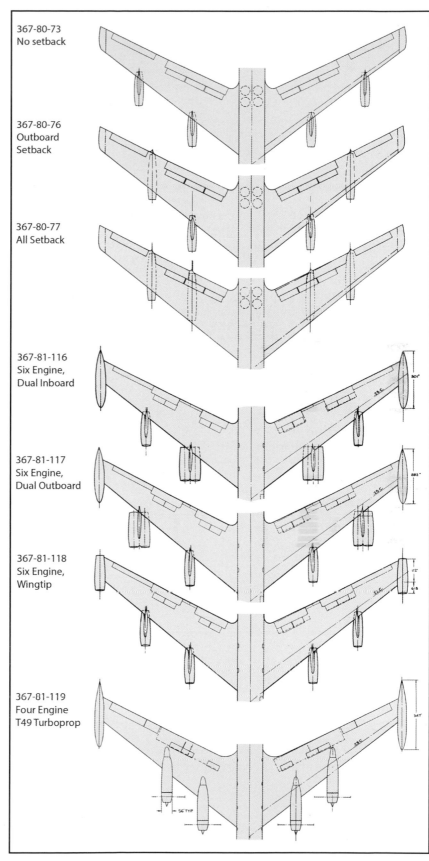

367-80-73
No setback

367-80-76
Outboard
Setback

367-80-77
All Setback

367-81-116
Six Engine,
Dual Inboard

367-81-117
Six Engine,
Dual Outboard

367-81-118
Six Engine,
Wingtip

367-81-119
Four Engine
T49 Turboprop

ABOVE Once the issue of wing and fuselage design was settled, Boeing evaluated how many engines were needed and where to place them.
Boeing, modified by authors

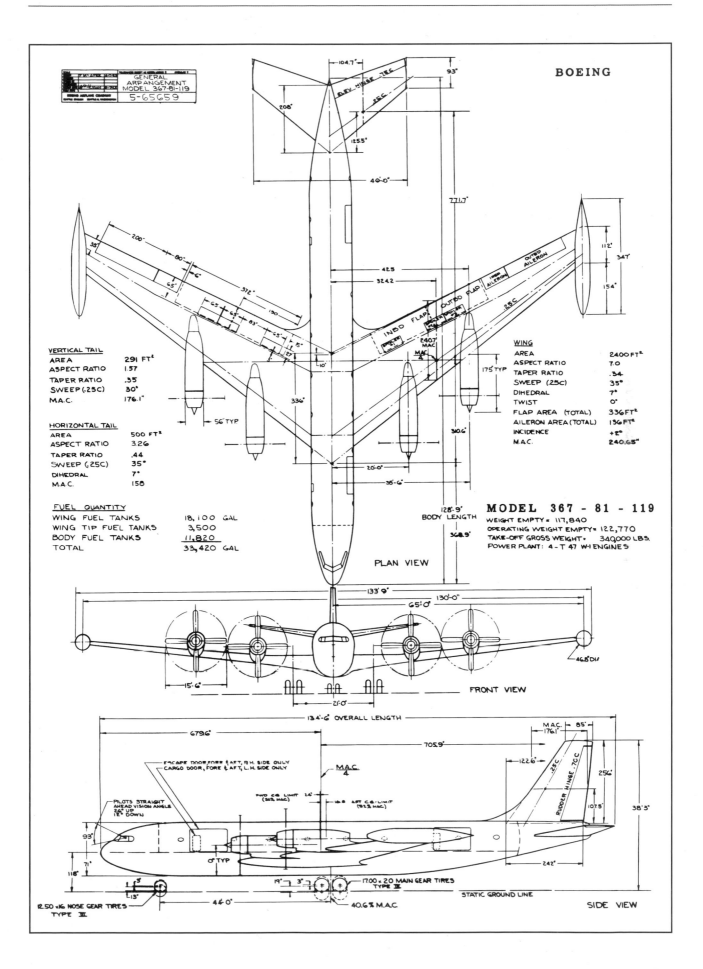

BOEING

GENERAL
ARRANGEMENT
MODEL 367-81-119
5-65659

VERTICAL TAIL

AREA	291 FT²
ASPECT RATIO	1.57
TAPER RATIO	.35
SWEEP (.25C)	30°
M.A.C.	176.1"

HORIZONTAL TAIL

AREA	500 FT²
ASPECT RATIO	3.26
TAPER RATIO	.44
SWEEP (.25C)	35°
DIHEDRAL	7°
M.A.C.	158

FUEL QUANTITY

WING FUEL TANKS	18,100 GAL
WING TIP FUEL TANKS	3,500
BODY FUEL TANKS	11,820
TOTAL	33,420 GAL

WING

AREA	2400 FT²
ASPECT RATIO	7.0
TAPER RATIO	.34
SWEEP (.25C)	35°
DIHEDRAL	7°
TWIST	0°
FLAP AREA (TOTAL)	336 FT²
AILERON AREA (TOTAL)	136 FT²
INCIDENCE	+2°
M.A.C.	240.65"

MODEL 367 - 81 - 119

WEIGHT EMPTY = 117,840
OPERATING WEIGHT EMPTY = 122,770
TAKE-OFF GROSS WEIGHT = 340,000 LBS.
POWER PLANT: 4 - T 47 W. ENGINES

PLAN VIEW

FRONT VIEW

SIDE VIEW

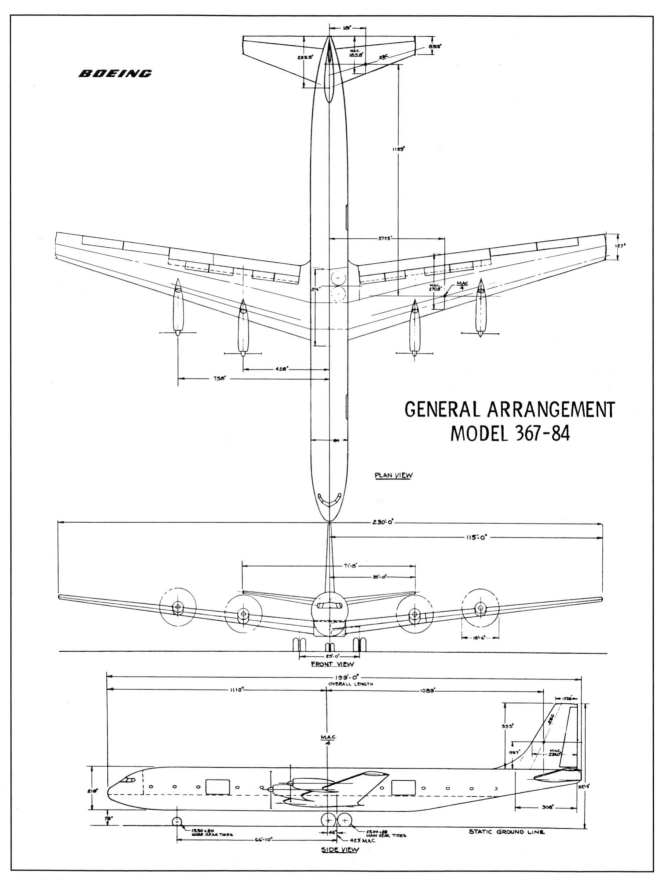

GENERAL ARRANGEMENT
MODEL 367-84

ABOVE The Boeing Model 367-84 turboprop airlifter with a wing area of 4,800sq ft (446m²). The wingspan of 230ft (42.72m) exceeded that of the later 747-8 airliner. *Boeing*

The second group of designs incorporated the Pratt & Whitney PT-5 engine (which became the XT57-P-1) and all shared a sharper 25° swept wing. The fuselage upper lobe was enlarged to a width of 190in (482.6cm) and the rear side-loading door was deleted in favour of a rear cargo ramp. Variants were the 709-3, -4, -5 and -6, again with differing fuselage lengths and gross weights.

The exact stimulus for these design efforts is unclear, but drawing dates of March and April 1953 may indicate some Boeing activity to compete with the Douglas Model 1333, which was placed in development status and under contract by the Air Force on 24 March 1953.

Boeing Model 709-5 turboprop transport	
Powerplant	4 x P&W XT57-P-1 (PT5) turboprops
Span	190ft (57.90m)
Length	186ft 6in (56.85m)
Height	55ft 3in (16.84m)
Wing area	4,000sq ft (372m²)
Design gross weight	430,000lb (195,000kg)

The formal tanker competition

On 5 May 1954 the Air Force officially announced both the requirement for a new tanker and a design competition to fill it. Boeing, Douglas, Fairchild, Lockheed and Martin were all invited to participate, with proposals due by 27 August of that year. However, the playing field was hardly level: Boeing already had a suitable aircraft flying. Indeed, in July – on only on its seventh flight – the 'Dash 80' carried out a practice air-refuelling rendezvous with a B-52.

SAC, led by its formidable commander General Curtis LeMay, was also pressing the urgent need to strengthen the Air Force's aerial refuelling capability, stressing that SAC could not wait for the outcome of the competition; any new design would require years of development. Responding to these pressures, on 30 July 1954 the ARDC recommended the purchase of seventy to a hundred

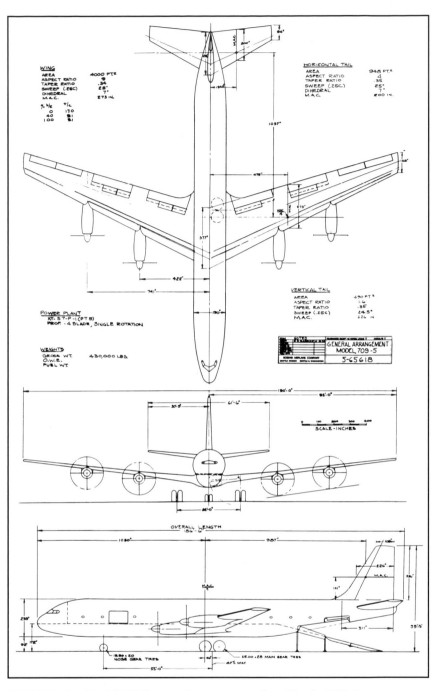

ABOVE Boeing Model-709-5 general arrangement from March 1953. *Boeing*

'interim' Boeing 367-80 tankers. These were to be acquired 'pending availability of the aircraft selected as a result of the current competition'.

On 5 August the Air Force Secretary announced the procurement of twenty-nine Boeing jet tankers; weeks later the Air Force announced its order for eighty-eight additional jets. Despite the orders, there were two weeks still left before tanker proposals were due to be

submitted, so the formal competition continued.

Boeing 367-81-139 'Big Wing' tanker-transport

Although Boeing now had a viable tanker, which had been ordered into production for the Air Force, the company continued to study options for improving performance at high gross weights.

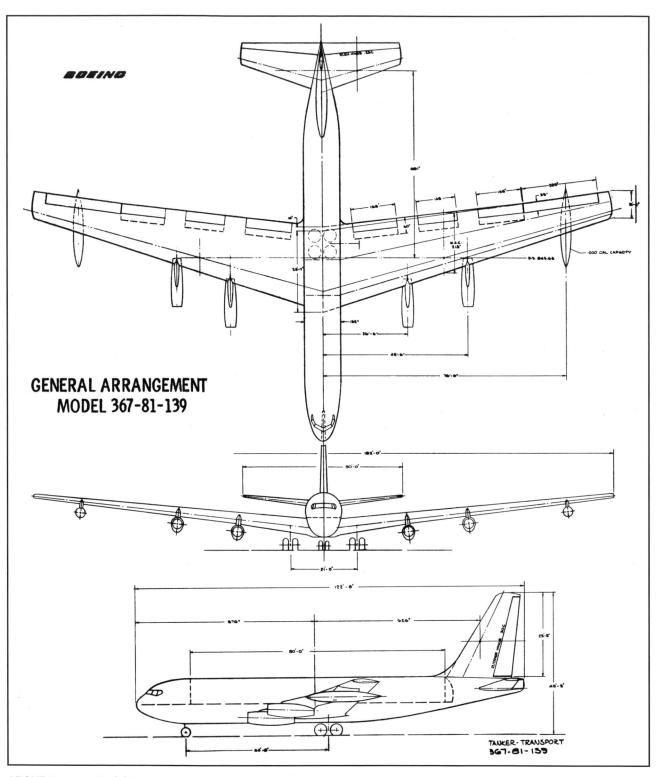

**GENERAL ARRANGEMENT
MODEL 367-81-139**

ABOVE Boeing's Model 367-81-139 tanker-transport with the reduced-sweep wing. *Boeing*

The Model 367-81-139 was optimised for the tanker transport role with a larger wing (3,000sq ft/278.7m²) and a reduced sweep of 15°. This gave better take-off, landing and high-altitude performance, but at the cost of a decreased payload resulting from the heavier wing.

Boeing refined this design into alternative proposals designated Models 718-1 and 719-1 in June and July 1954 under the respective titles of 'Study ... Redesign of Jet Tanker-Cargo Transport'. The Model 718-1 wing increased to 3,200sq ft (297m²) with a 25° sweep, while the Model 719-1 retained the identical area but increased the sweep to 35°.

Boeing Model 367-81-139 tanker-transport	
Powerplant	4 x P&W JT3C-3W (J57) turbojets
Span	182ft 0in (55.47m)
Length	122ft 8in (37.39m)
Height	43ft 3in (13.18m)
Wing area	3,000sq ft (278.7m²)

Boeing Model 367-81-140 tanker-transport	
Powerplant	4 x P&W Advanced J75 turbojets
Span	130ft 11in (39.90m)
Length	145ft 7in (44.37m)
Height	38ft 5in (11.71m)
Wing area	3,000sq ft (278.7m²)

Boeing 367-81-147 (single-purpose) tanker

The basic KC-135 was essentially a multi-purpose airframe, suitable for passenger or logistics use, and adapted for the tanker role. Boeing began looking at how to further optimise the design's air refuelling capabilities. Although the term 'tanker' implies bulk, based on images of ships and fuel trucks, an air-to-air

RIGHT The Boeing Model-367-81-140 was another improved-performance variation with a stretched fuselage, an enlarged 3,000sq ft (278.7m²) wing, advanced J75 engines and B-52-styled external underwing fuel tanks. *Boeing*

BELOW The inboard profile of the Boeing 367-81-147 details both the 'hose and drogue' (inset) and flying boom refuelling options. Only the forward fuselage and aft 'boomer' compartments were pressurised, with a tunnel connecting them. *Boeing*

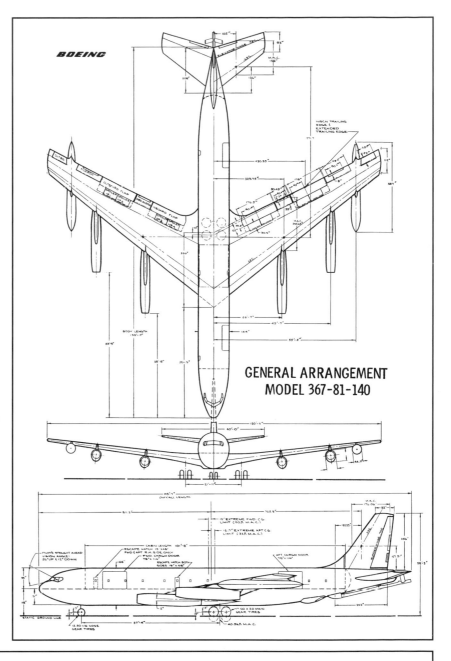

GENERAL ARRANGEMENT
MODEL 367-81-140

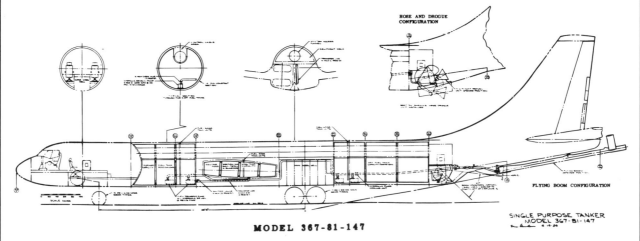

MODEL 367-81-147

HOSE AND DROGUE CONFIGURATION

FLYING BOOM CONFIGURATION

SINGLE PURPOSE TANKER
MODEL 367-81-147

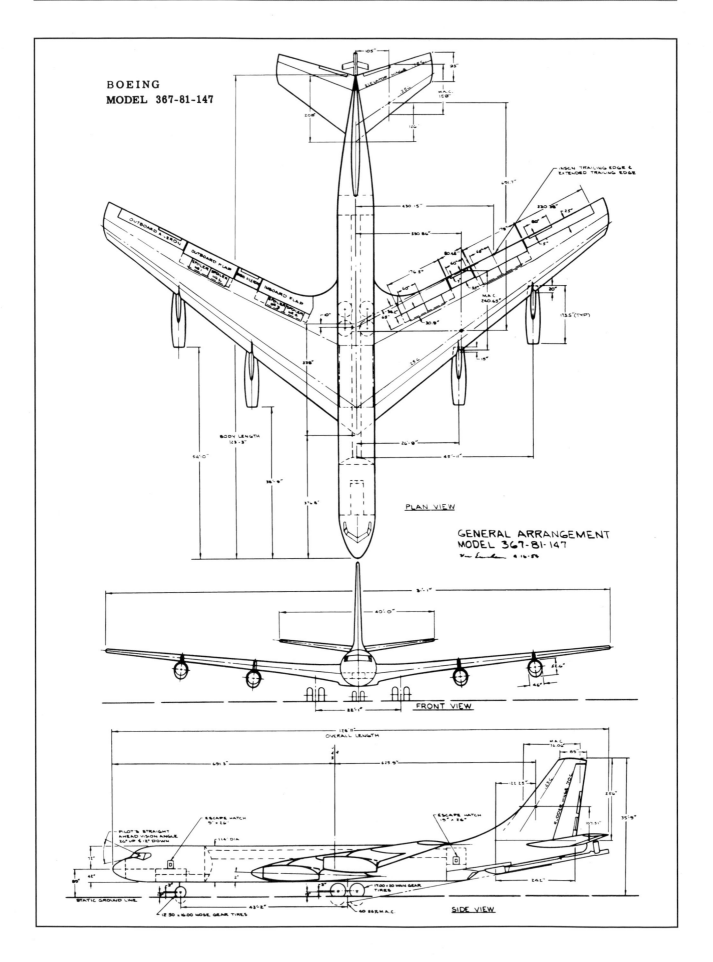

BOEING
MODEL 367-81-147

PLAN VIEW

GENERAL ARRANGEMENT
MODEL 367-81-147

FRONT VIEW

SIDE VIEW

refuelling aircraft has no need of massive internal volume. The maximum amount of fuel it can carry is limited by weight, not volume. An aircraft's maximum payload takes up far less volume carrying fuel than it does carrying passengers or cargo. Boeing therefore targeted drag and airframe weight reductions by slimming the base design's fuselage. The Model 367-81-147, drawn up in April 1954, was the result.

Boeing Model 367-81-147 tanker	
Powerplant	4 x P&W turbojets
Span	131ft 1in (39.95m)
Length	121ft 11in (37.16m)
Height	35ft 9in (12.12m)

Douglas refueller/ transport developments

Compared to its Boeing rival, Douglas was late entering the jet transport market, having concentrated on turboprop-powered versions of highly successful propeller-driven airliners like its Model 1134, derived from the DC-6/C-118/R6D. Douglas had studied tanker versions of the piston engine C-124, designated the YKC-124B (Model 1183E) turboprop, and was under contract for the YKC-132 (Model 1814). All of these were propeller-driven. At the same time, Douglas (like its rival) was well advanced with a series of jet transport aircraft studies, driven initially by the need for high-speed, high-altitude refuelling for the B-52 and the upcoming B-58.

The ultimate DC-6/C-118: the Douglas Model 1274

The traceable design path for Douglas's big jet refuellers appears to have begun with the Model 1274. Laid out in August 1951, it combined the DC-6's stretched fuselage with a new swept wing, a revised swept empennage, and jet powerplants. Curiously, the Douglas wing

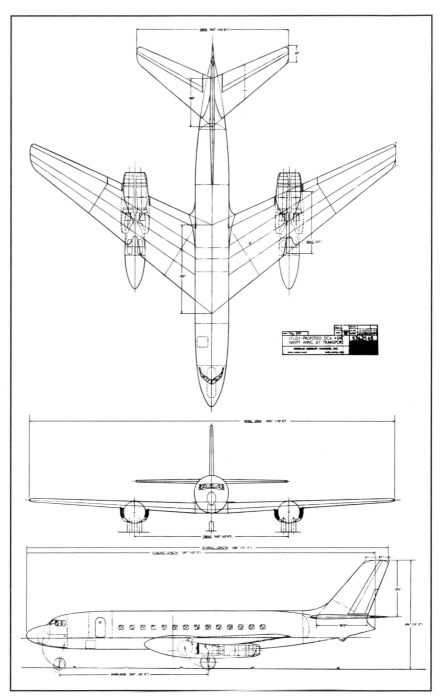

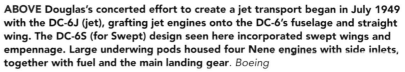

ABOVE Douglas's concerted effort to create a jet transport began in July 1949 with the DC-6J (jet), grafting jet engines onto the DC-6's fuselage and straight wing. The DC-6S (for Swept) design seen here incorporated swept wings and empennage. Large underwing pods housed four Nene engines with side inlets, together with fuel and the main landing gear. *Boeing*

development path was the reverse of that pursued by Boeing, which progressively and incrementally increased the sweep of its advanced Model 367 designs. In contrast, the initial Douglas Model 1274 featured a 40° wing sweep (at quarter chord), but subsequent iterations reduced its sweep to 35°.

OPPOSITE Boeing Model 367-81-147 general arrangement, showing the standard wing and engine placement, and the reduced-diameter fuselage for the dedicated refuelling mission. *Boeing*

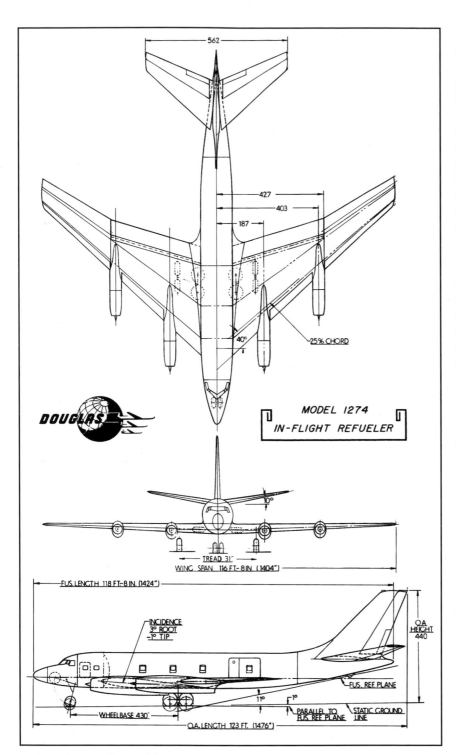

ABOVE The Douglas Model 1274 was derived from the DC-6/C-118/R6D. *Boeing*

Douglas Model 1274 jet or turboprop transport/refueller	
Short fuselage – 40° sweep	**Long fuselage – 35° sweep**
Model 1274 Turbojet refueller	**Model 1274A** Turbine-propeller transport for the US Navy
	Model 1274B Turboprop air refueller for the Air Force
	Model 1274C Turbojet airliner for domestic operations
	Model 1274D Turbojet airliner for overwater operations
	Model 1274E Turboprop airliner for overwater operations
	Model 1274A J57 turbojet-powered transport

The Model 1274 was probably the most radical proposal derived from the DC-6. Of note, reports released to prospective customers in October and November 1951 describe the Model 1274 as being based on the proven C-118 (for the Air Force), the proven R6D (for the Navy) or the proven DC-6 (for the airlines). In reality, all shared a common base design. The result (in terms of outward appearance) resembled none of these, and was arguably one of the most aesthetically pleasing transport designs ever proposed.

The initial base configuration was described as 'a refueller with a single drogue'. The fuselage added a new, more streamlined nose and a new swept empennage. That was then married to a completely new wing with a leading edge sweep of 40° at quarter chord. Powerplants would have been either four turbojets or four turboprops, initially unspecified.

By September 1951 the design had been refined, reducing the wing sweep to 35° and extending the fuselage by 160in (4.06m). Propulsion was now defined as being either Pratt & Whitney J57-P-7 jet engines or Pratt & Whitney YT34-P-12 turboprops (with options for upgrade to the future XT34-P-6 or XT34-P-10). Most of the studies were completed by October 1951. Although not identified as such in contemporary Douglas reports, this model was later described several years later as the '1274/DC-8'.

Although the Model 1274 ultimately proved to be a dead end, refinement efforts continued with the transitional Model 1274-A. It retained the wing but replaced the fuselage with a circular cross-sectional design, 130in (3.30m) in diameter. Importantly, the jet engines, previously in a 'slipper' arrangement, were suspended on short pylons and slung under the wings. Engines were upgraded from the Pratt & Whitney J57 to the more powerful Wright J67 (the planned engine based on the British Olympus). First reported in April 1952, the configuration began wind tunnel testing later that year.

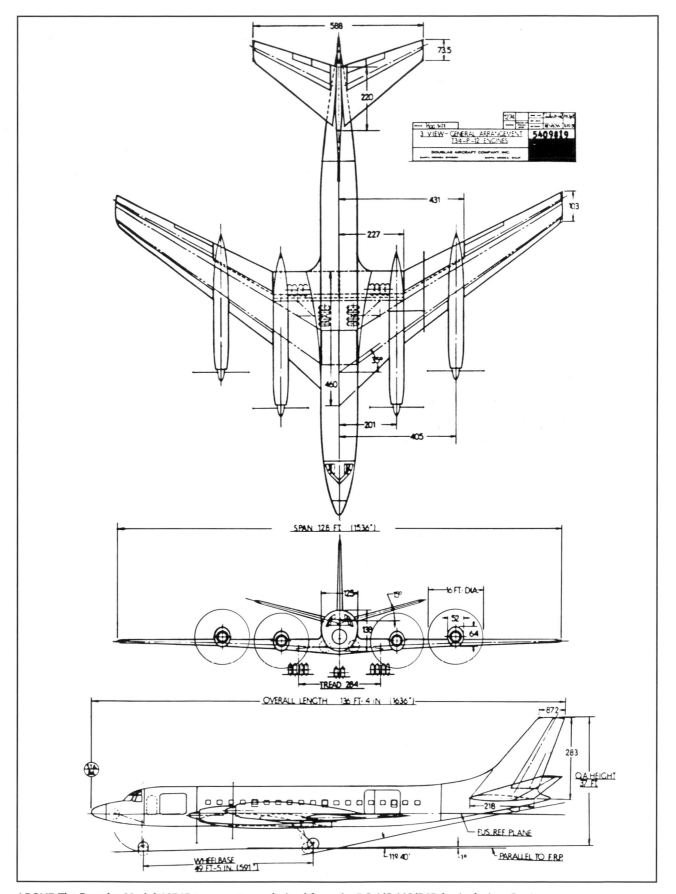

ABOVE The Douglas Model 1274B transport was derived from the DC-6/C-118/R6D basic design. *Boeing*

Douglas Model 1274 jet or turboprop transport/refueller			
	Model 1274 Jet	Model 1274B Jet	Model 1274B Turboprop
Powerplant	n/a	4 x P&W J57-P-7 turbojets	4 x P&W XT34-P-10 turboprops
14,500lb (64.5kN)	8,300eshp (6,189.3kW)	n/a	
Wingspan	116ft 8in (35.66m)	128ft 0in (39.01m)	128ft 0in (39.01m)
Length	118ft 8 in (36.17m)	136ft 4in (41.55m)	136ft 4in (41.55m)
Height	36ft 8in (11.18m)	37ft 0in (11.28m)	37ft 0in (11.28m)
Wing area	n/a	2,433sq ft (266.0m²)	2,433sq ft (266.0m²)
Wing sweep	40°	35°	35°
Design gross weight	n/a	200,500lb (90,950kg)	211,000lb (95,710kg)*
Cruise speed	n/a	454kt (841km/h)	404kt (748km/h)

* with engine nacelle saddle fuel tanks

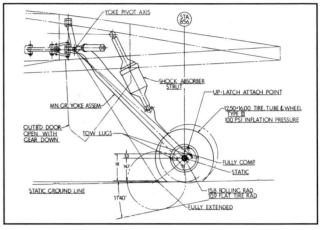

ABOVE The Model 1274's main landing gear, looking inboard. The struts retracted inwards, with the wheels rotating 90° for stowage into the lower fuselage, aft of the wing. Because this space was cramped, all four wheels were mounted on a single axle. *Boeing*

ABOVE A display model of the Douglas Model 1274B. *Author's collection*

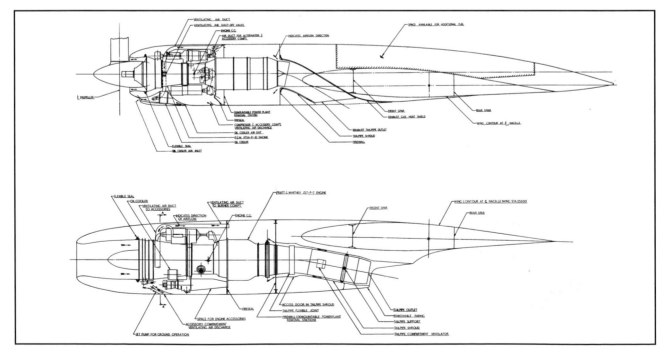

ABOVE Comparison in the same scale of the XT34-P-10 turboprop on the Model 1274B (upper) with the XJ57 in the Model 1274 (lower). Additional fuel was carried in overwing 'saddle' tanks. The J57 installation was surprisingly bulky and, after refinement, was changed to a low pod-and-pylon configuration. *Boeing*

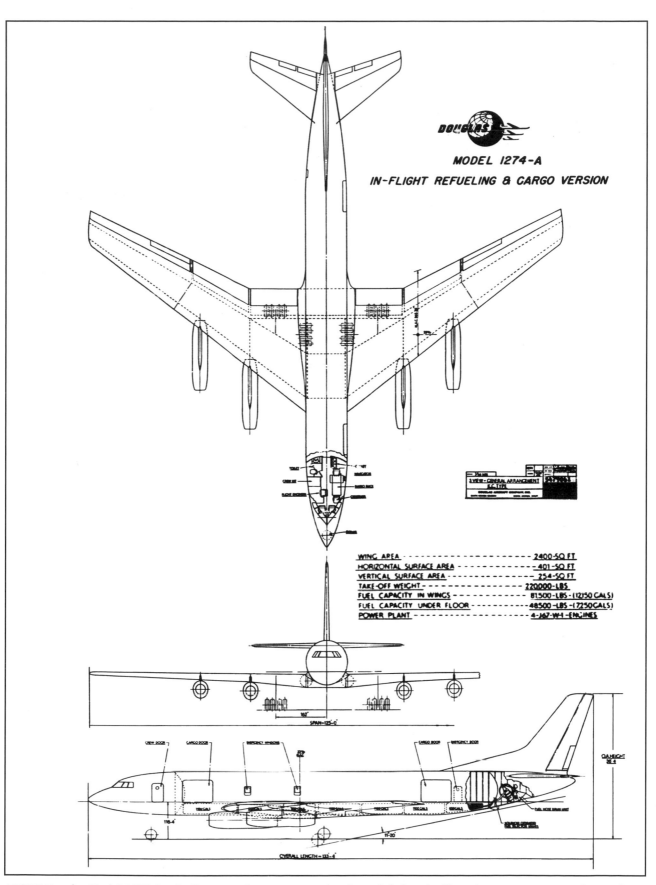

ABOVE Douglas Model 1274-A refueller general arrangement, showing subtle but significant improvements over the previous 1274 designs, including a circular fuselage cross section and main landing gear stowage in the thickened inner wing. *Boeing*

ABOVE The Model 1274-A model in the wind tunnel shows a configuration with the engine nacelles on short pylons below the wing. Leading edge flaps are in the extended position; wing fences were installed to control spanwise airflow. *Boeing*

ABOVE The positioning of the fuselage-mounted airbrakes was also tested on the Model 1274-A wind tunnel model. The largest of the airbrakes were an initial design feature on the DC-8 prototype, but proved ineffective during flight test and were later omitted. *Boeing*

Douglas Model 1274-A in-flight refueller	
Powerplant	4 x Wright J67-W-1 turbojets @ approx 11,000lb (48.93kN) thrust
Span	135ft (41.15m)
Length	125ft (38.10m)
Height	38ft 4in (11.68m)
Wing area	2,600sq ft (241.55m²)
Take-off gross weight	220,000lb (99,790kg)
Maximum transfer speed	480kt (889km/h)
Radius	1,000nmi (1,850km) (refuelling)

BELOW A Douglas mock-up of the spacious 144in (366cm) fuselage section, with employees serving as stretcher patients. *Boeing*

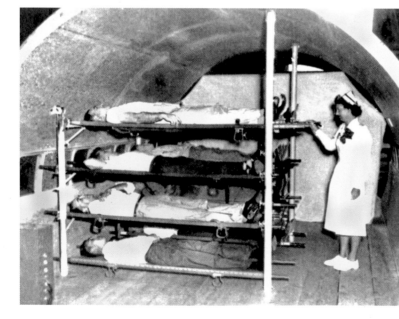

Douglas Model 1840 tanker-transport

The next incremental step was the Model 1840. Work on this design continued throughout the autumn of 1953, with the first summary engineering report issued on 12 November. The gap between Model 1274 and the 1840 development was probably caused by the award of advanced design work for the XC-132 to the Santa Monica Division. Douglas Santa Monica was also deeply involved in guided missile work for the Army and the Navy, as well as preliminary medium-range ballistic missile designs that would mature into the Air Force's Thor

programme. Added to the workload, commercial DC-7s were rolling off the production line and the DC-7C loomed on the horizon. No matter the reason, at the time that Model 1840 studies were under way, Boeing was cutting metal for the 367-80 prototype.

The Model 1840 marked a significant step towards Douglas's final tanker-transport and airliner designs. Most notably, the wing sweep was further reduced to 30° (at quarter chord), an angle that would remain for the life of the later DC-8.

Just as critically, the fuselage cross section had been revised to a two-lobe design whose interior fuselage width increased to 144in (3.66m) – 12in (0.30m) greater than that of the Boeing 367-80. The increase allowed six-abreast seating in the military transport configuration and, in the medical evacuation configuration, for transverse mounting of litters with a roomy side walkway. The lower lobe was now large enough to house the main landing gear wheels, which retained the unusual co-axial design with all four wheels mounted on a common axle.

The baseline aerial refueller (Model 1840) was a spartan aircraft, with most of the cabin unpressurised to save weight. A single large cylindrical fuel tank on the main deck supplemented the wing tanks. Refuelling would be

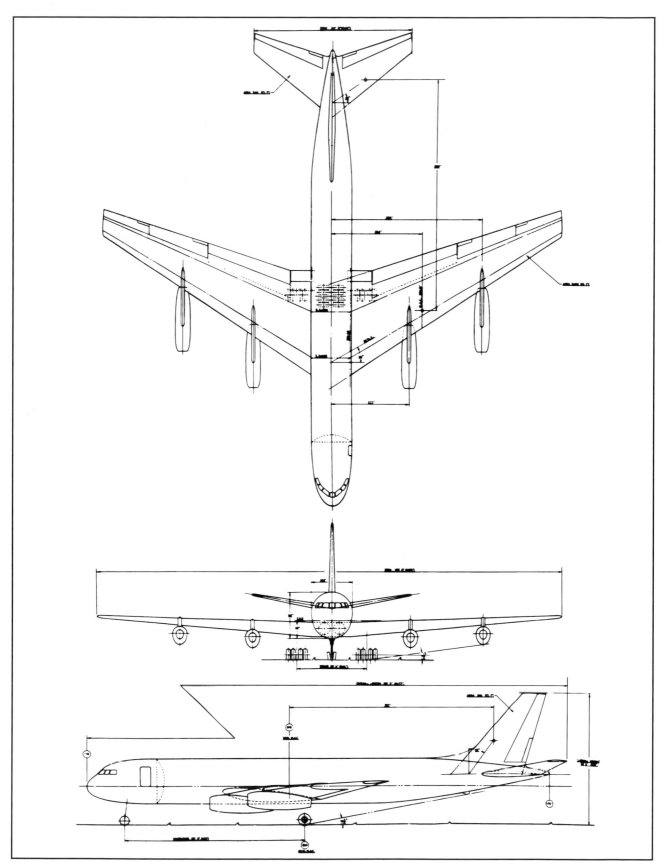

ABOVE Douglas Model 1840 aerial tanker general arrangement. It was the first design to closely resemble the DC-8 jetliner of the future. In the refueller the pressure bulkhead was just aft of the cockpit access door, leaving most of the fuselage unpressurised.
Boeing

accomplished from a single 'hose and drogue' unit in the lower aft fuselage, and be controlled from the cockpit. The aeroplane could transfer 60,000lb (27,200kg) of fuel in sixteen minutes. A small nose radome housed the Sperry APN-59 search/weather radar.

Douglas also outlined alternative versions of the basic design. The personnel version could carry 104 passengers and 4,720lb (2,141kg) of cargo 4,400nmi (8,149km). The medical evacuation version could carry sixty litters, six passengers and 3,140lb (1,424kg) a maximum distance of 4,700nmi (8,704km). The cargo/airlifter version carried a maximum load of 58,020lb (26,317kg) for 3,500nmi (6,842km) at a reduced load factor of 2.0G.

To boost take-off performance the Model 1840 'I' featured a variant of the Pratt & Whitney JT3C-1 engine fitted with a '25% afterburner' that would raise take-off thrust to 15,300lb per engine.

Douglas Model 1856 tanker-transport

With the tanker competition now formalised in 1954, the Model 1856 was a refinement of the Model 1840 and showed continued maturation of the design concept. Douglas offered it in both flying boom and 'hose and drogue' variants. Two large side cargo doors on the left side of the fuselage were now part of the basic design, 90in high by 124in wide (2.29 by 3.15m) forward, and a smaller door, 78in by 104in (1.98 by 2.64m) aft.

Engineers lengthened the fuselage, which allowed all fuel to be stored in wing and underfloor tanks (this space would eventually be occupied by luggage in the DC-8). They also modified the aft fuselage, increasing the upsweep and the maximum tilt-back angle from 10° on the Model 1840 to 13°. The new design retained the large ventral side-by-side speed brakes that sat under the fuselage, just forward of the main landing gear. The nose shape was revised and sharpened for a much larger radome enclosing an advanced AN/APS-23 search radar antenna (the same as used on the B-36, B-47 and B-52).

Douglas Model 1840 in-flight refueller	
Powerplant	4 x P&W JT3C-1W (J57) turbojets @ 12,500 lb (55.60kN) (Models 1840A-J) with water injection
	4 x P&W J57 turbojets @ 15,000 lb (66.72kN) (Models 1840T & U) with partial afterburning
	4 x Wright J67 turbojets @ approx 11,000lb (48.93kN) thrust (Model 1840K-M)
Span	135ft (41.15m)
Length	123ft 1in (37.51m)
Height	37ft 5in (11.41m)
Wing area	2,600sq ft (241.55m²)
Take-off gross weight	235,500lb (106,590kg)
Payload	60,000lb (27,220kg)
Cruise speed	470kt (871.4km/h)
Radius	1,500nmi (2,780km) (refuelling mission)
Range	4,400nmi (8,150km) (104 passengers and 4,700lb (2,130kg) of cargo)

Douglas Model 1856/1856A tanker-transport*	
Powerplant	4 x P&W JT3C-2 turbojets @ 13,750lb (61.16kN) with water injection
Span	135ft 0in (41.15m)
Length	140ft 6in (42.83m)
Height	40ft 9in (12.40m)
Wing area	2,600sq ft (241.55m²)
Design gross weight	305,000lb (138,350kg)
Payload	88,200lb (40,000kg) of fuel at 1,500nmi (2,780km)
	47,500lb (21,550kg) of fuel at 2,500nmi (4,630km)
	80 passengers and 44,942lb (20,385kg) cargo
Cruise speed	461kt (854km/h)
Maximum speed	510kt (945km/h) at 40,000ft (12,190m)

*Model 1856 had 'hose and drogue' refuelling; Model 1856A had flying boom refuelling

The formal Request For Proposal (RFP) for the tanker-transport was issued by the Air Force on 18 June 1954. Reflecting Boeing's enormous lead, the 367-80 made its first flight just four weeks later. Douglas submitted its proposal on 23 August 1954 together with Design Specification DS-1856 and General Specifications GS-1857 (Wind Tunnel Model Specification) and GS-1858 (Mock-up Specification).

BELOW A Douglas company model of the Model 1856A, displaying its flying boom configuration. *Boeing*

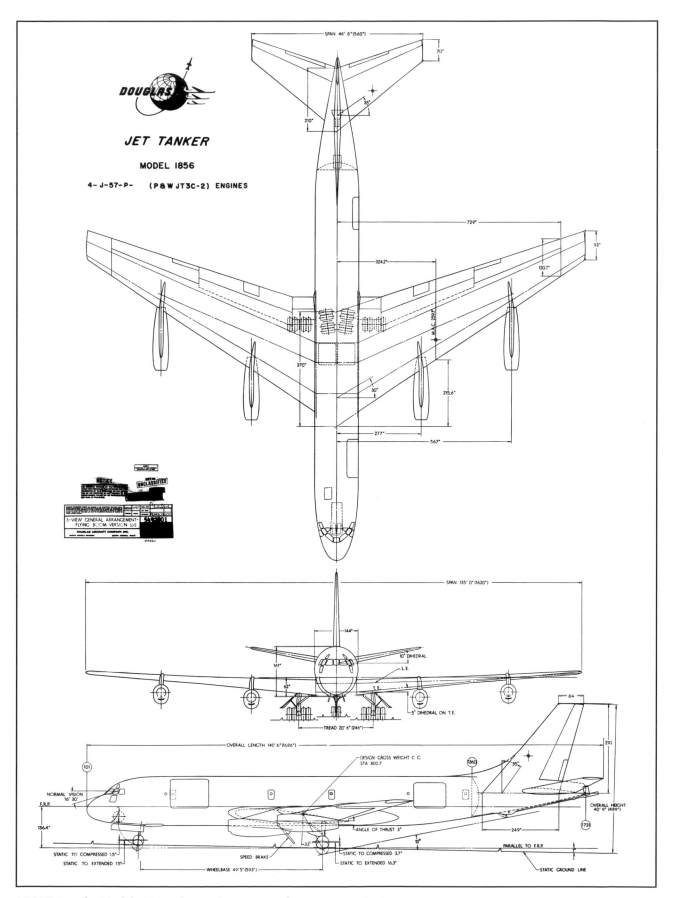

ABOVE Douglas Model 1856 tanker-transport general arrangement. *Boeing*

ABOVE Almost, but not quite, a DC-8, the Douglas Model 1856 tanker-transport sports a larger dorsal fin, a streamlined station for the refuelling operator and a large radome for the search/mapping radar. *John Aldaz collection*

BELOW After Douglas lost the tanker competition, the company concentrated on the commercial DC-8. Here the first wooden mock-up is shown under construction in November 1955 in Santa Monica; the tail of the XC-132 mock-up looms in the background. Further Douglas military transport work, including the Model 1920, would be based on the commercial DC-8 rather than the Model 1856. *Boeing*

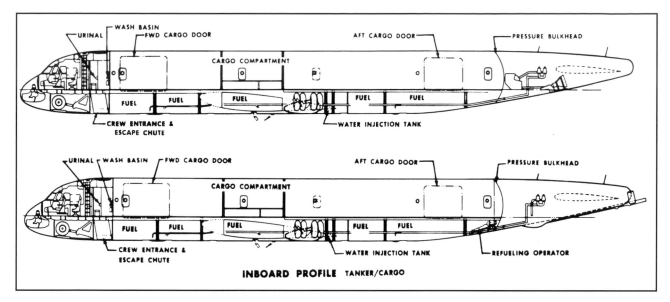

ABOVE Inboard profiles of the Douglas Model 1856 (above) with 'hose and drogue' refuelling, and the Model 1856A (below) with the flying boom. *Boeing*

BELOW An artist's concept of the Douglas Model 1856 in flight. *Boeing*

Lockheed CL-291-1

The Model CL-291 was Lockheed's entry into the tanker-transport competition. (With the establishment of the Lockheed Georgia Company, the company's preliminary design numbers had gained plant prefixes: 'CL' for a Burbank, California, design and 'GL' for aircraft from the Marietta, Georgia, design offices.)

The CL-291 was designed to meet the basic requirement of transferring 60,000lb (27,216kg) of fuel at a 2,500nmi (4,630km) radius when flying to a rendezvous with a Boeing B-52 bomber. It had a high-mounted swept wing with underslung pylon-mounted engines projecting behind the trailing edge of the wing. In fact, Lockheed's design team was quite opposed to placing pod-mounted engines forward of the wing. Chief design engineer C. L. 'Kelly' Johnson explained the reasoning:

'Summing up some very extensive studies, the rear engine mounting for jet power plants seemed to have the following advantages over pylon-mounted engines located normally on a wing:

1. Substantially greater safety, particularly in a crash landing.

2. Substantial advantage in cabin and exterior noise. (The fuselage shields some noise effects for many angles around the aircraft.)

3. Excellent drag characteristics.

4. Protection of the inlets from stones and ground objects, particularly when the inlet is kept forward of the trailing edge of the wing.

5. Improved maximum lift, due to the use of uninterrupted flap span.

6. Substantially simpler systems, in terms of control routing, length of air ducting, electrical leads, etc.

7. Favourable balance, which results in placing much of the fuselage ahead of the wing, so that more passengers obtain a good view.

8. When properly placed over the wing, the wing acts as a guide vane to direct the inlet flow. For a change of angle of attack of the airplane of approximately 19°, the change of angle of attack into the nacelle is less than 3°.

9. The high location of the inlet in a protected location provides safety to the ground crew members when walking around the airplane when engines are running.

10. The ditching characteristics are improved by not having the nacelles located where they can dig into the water.

11. A failed turbine wheel cannot go through the pressurised area of the fuselage or fuel tanks.

12. The offset thrust after losing an engine is very low, so that an improved one-engine-out climb and control are available. Holding in a traffic pattern can readily be done with one-half of the normal power plants out of operation, as all aircraft flight characteristics remain essentially unchanged.

'Proponents of pylon-mounted wing nacelles bring up the following objections to fuselage-mounted pylons:

1. The engine weight is not available for reducing wing bending moments and acting as a flutter counter-balance. They claim lighter structural weight with the wing nacelles. Any slight difference in this regard, I feel, is completely cancelled by a saving in flap complications and system weights, described above.

Lockheed CL-291-1 tanker-transport	
Powerplant	4 x P&W J75 turbojet @ 17,000lb (75.65kN) thrust
Span	155ft 8in (47.48m)
Length	152ft 3in (46.44m)
Height	48ft 8in (14.83m)
Wing area	3,123sq ft (290.5m²)
Max TOW	361,000lb (163,890kg)
Cruise speed	480kt (888km/h)
Range (full fuel load)	2,500nmi (4,630km)

2. When the double fuselage pod is used, a failure of a turbine disc in one engine might knock out another. The writer does not feel this problem to be in any manner acute, and is more than balanced by other improvements of safety, such as not having a hot disc go through a wing spar, a fuel tank, or passengers.

'Again, the problem of gear-up landings with the wing installation certainly merits a great deal of consideration… The L-193 was well worked out by 1953, when efforts were made to sell the airplane to various airlines. Many airlines, such as Pan American and Air France, were very much impressed with the L-193. Lockheed was unable to get orders, however, to carry the program forward. The huge financial risk which must be undertaken to develop a 280,000lb transport was the final deterrent factor which kept Lockheed out of the large turbojet passenger field.'

Underwing placement of the CL-291 engine might seem to violate this reasoning, but the position of the engines under the high wing was approximately the same as over the low wing of the L-193 airliner design.

Lockheed study variants for the CL-291 tanker included:

■ **CL-291-1** The -1 was Lockheed's initial design iteration and it turned out to be the basis of the definitive submission to the Air Force.

■ **CL-291-2** Based on the -1, but with six engines underwing. The extra power was negated by the additional structural, engine, and fuel weight resulting in little useful performance increase.

■ **CL-291-3** Low-wing version based on the larger L-193-55 airliner, but fuel quantity transfer was found to inferior to the -1.

■ **CL-291-5A** Smaller version of the -1, designed as a minimum-size aircraft, but it too had had fuel transfer deficiencies.

ABOVE Lockheed built a partial mock-up of the L-193-55 configuration to explore the overwing engine location and integration with the aft fuselage (the wing spar is below the intake). A modified version of this airliner was the basis of the CL-291-3 alternative tanker design. *Jane and Winfield Arata papers (courtesy of Martha and Allen Arata)*

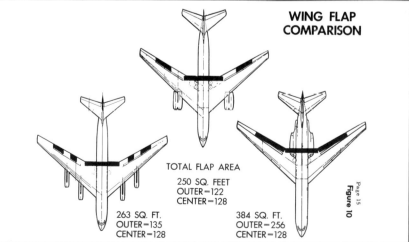

WING FLAP COMPARISON

TOTAL FLAP AREA

250 SQ. FEET
OUTER=122
CENTER=128

263 SQ. FT.
OUTER=135
CENTER=128

384 SQ. FT.
OUTER=256
CENTER=128

Page 15
Figure 10

RIGHT Lockheed's analysis of flap area for different engine locations was one factor driving their fuselage-mounted position. *Jane and Winfield Arata papers (courtesy of Martha and Allen Arata)*

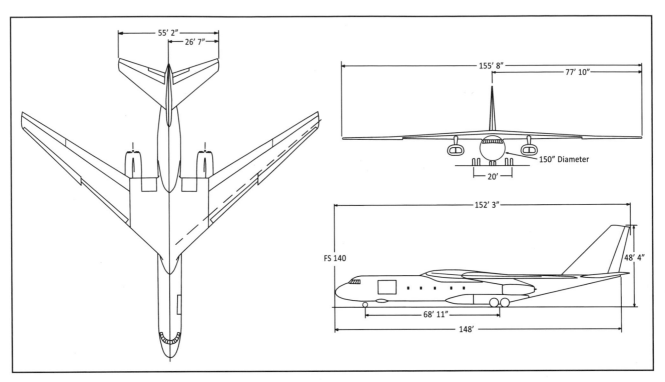

ABOVE The winner (and ultimate loser) of the tanker competition, the Lockheed CL-291. *Lockheed*

BELOW Changing of the guard: the first KC-135A (dubbed 'The City of Renton') is seen after its official rollout ceremony on 18 July 1955. To the right on the Renton ramp is the last C-97 variant built, a KC-97G. As this last airplane made its way through assembly, the C-97 tooling was disassembled behind it to make room for the KC-135s to be built. *Boeing*

ABOVE Unidentical twins: the very first KC-135A is paced by the 367-80 prototype over the West Seattle shoreline. Boeing Field is hidden by the nose of the KC-135. *Author's collection*

The outcome of the formal tanker competition

In February 1955 Air Force Secretary Harold F. Talbott announced that Lockheed's CL-291-1 had won the competition, based on its technical potential, and that at least one prototype would be purchased and built immediately. But simultaneously he announced a $700 million increase in funding for production of the Boeing KC-135A tanker, sufficient for a fleet of 286 aircraft.

In his book on the KC-135, Robert Hopkins appropriately summarised the ironic outcome: 'Paradoxically, the winner of the tanker competition was funded to build only a prototype whereas one of the losers was funded to buy a sizeable fleet of airplanes.' Unsurprisingly, the Lockheed aeroplane was never built; whatever its technical merits, there was never a realistic

prospect of SAC operating a mixed fleet of tankers with duplicate logistics systems, maintenance procedures, spares inventories and crew training.

The SAC tanker-transport in perspective

The Strategic Air Command order was the first of any kind for a Boeing jet transport. Once in production, Boeing redesignated the tanker-transport aircraft as the Model 717. Although its external appearance differed little from that of the commercial 707-120, it was designed to meet a far different operational environment. Flying only a tenth as many hours in a year as a commercial airliner, its service life, and differing design philosophies ('safe life' versus 'fail safe'), dictated the use of alternate alloys in its construction.

This was not the first time, and it would certainly not be the last, that an airframe designed as an airliner would become the basis for an aerial tanker, whether purpose-built or as an aftermarket conversion. The DC-10, Lockheed L-1011, Boeing 707, Boeing 747, Boeing 767, Vickers VC10 and Airbus A330 would all serve successfully as templates for conversion into military tankers.

The Boeing 707/717 family and its derivatives went on to transform the nature of air travel, and they defined the underlying configuration for the DC-8, Convair 880/990 and most large jet passenger aircraft for decades to come. The Air Force's search for a high-speed tanker-transport would have ramifications far beyond satisfying SAC's immediate requirement.

227

Chapter Eight
The Emergence of the Modern Airlifter

1955 to 1960: Keeping pace with ever-escalating demands

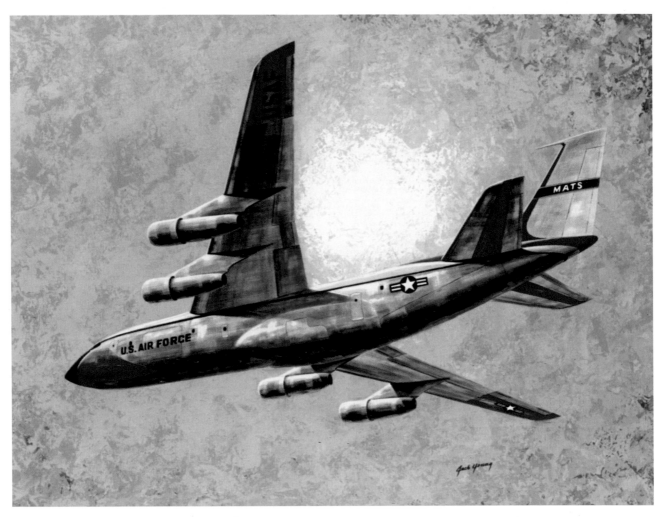

ABOVE This artist's concept of the Boeing Model 731 clearly shows its Model 707 design heritage. *Boeing*

In the last half of the 1950s, with the Strategic Air Command (SAC) having ordered the KC-135 tanker and the airlines in the process of ordering jet airliners, Air Force attention inevitably turned to the idea of jet transportation for troops and materials. General Operational Requirement 89 was established on 20 April 1955, calling for a 'quick response' aircraft type for carrying high-priority cargo and/or personnel under emergency situations. However, this GOR then languished for several years, pushed aside by the development of the Douglas XC/YC-132 and C-133 projects, described earlier.

The cancellation of the C-132 and a degree of disillusionment with the C-133, coupled with the limitations of the ageing piston-engine C-97/C-118/C-121/C-124 fleet, obliged the Air Force to revisit requirements for a high-speed airlifter. Although Boeing was building the KC-135, SAC had taken up the entire production capability for its role as a tanker (leaving no capacity even for tankers for other Air Force commands). Accordingly, when the Douglas YC-132 programme ended in March 1957, the Air Force Air Staff resuscitated the concept embodied in GOR-89.

It was the start of a long process, involving fierce competition by all the major aircraft manufacturers, which would eventually lead to the Air Force's first purpose-designed jet airlifter.

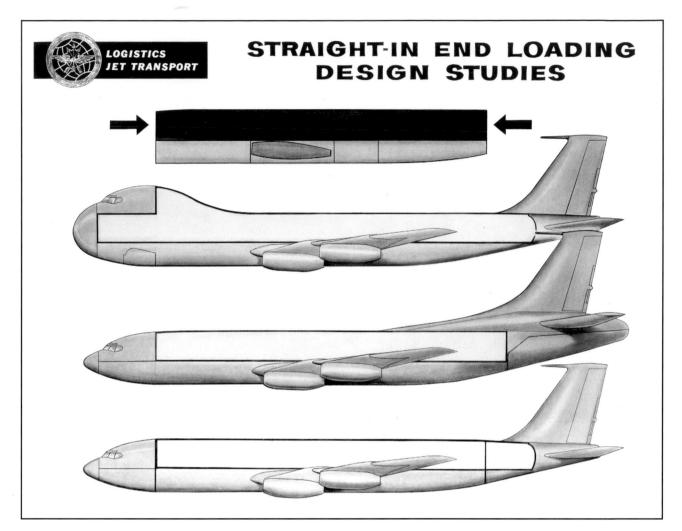

LOGISTICS JET TRANSPORT

STRAIGHT-IN END LOADING DESIGN STUDIES

ABOVE 'Minimum modification' (and cost) was Boeing's justification for the swing- and lift-tail alternatives (bottom profile). *Boeing*

'C-Jets': adapted 'Commercial Jet' transport designs (GOR-89)

By 1958 Boeing, Douglas and Convair all had high-performance commercial airliners that they were pushing the military to consider as troop transports. Adaptability as a tanker was not the same as adaptation as a logistics transport for the reasons already discussed. Logisticians were understandably unenthusiastic about narrow cargo bays, 14ft (4.27m) above the ground. Moreover, these aircraft required massive investments in long runways and ground-handling facilities – unlikely to be readily available in a war zone.

Because it represented an adaptation of airliners under development, the GOR-89 airlifter was called the 'Commercial Jet', or 'C-Jet' for short. Boeing, Convair and Douglas all proposed variations of their airliner designs: the Boeing 735 and 738 (derived in part and using elements from the 707/717); the Douglas Model 1920 (based on the DC-8); and the Convair Model 30 (based on its Model 600, later rebranded as the Convair 990).

Boeing Model 735 and 738

Boeing proposed two military transports: the Models 735 and 738. The company studied the requirements for a straight-in, rear-loading transport, as opposed to simply having side-loading doors. To save development cost and time, nose-loading concepts were discarded, due to the modifications needed in the cockpit area together with performance penalties. Likewise, a concept with an aft fuselage modified to accommodate loading doors was also discarded. The most efficient concept was judged to be a hinged aft fuselage that would swing open, either to the side or upwards. Settling on this approach, Boeing established these parameters:

1. Provide straight-in loading with cargo package size limited only by cargo compartment cross section and length, and compatible with rapid cargo handling systems.

2. Retain the aerodynamic characteristics of high-speed jet transports.

3. Minimise procurement cost by using existing KC-135 and 707 components and tooling.

LEFT Lt Gen F. H. Griswold inspects a Boeing model of the swing-tail 735 airlifter. *Boeing*

306,000lb (138,920kg), and according to its press release (dated 21 October 1959) its maximum payload was claimed to be 100,000lb (45,360kg), though there was no mention of any corresponding range.

Confusingly, Boeing later regrouped the models functionally, the side-swing designs (commercial and military) under Model 735 and the upwards-opening designs under the Model 738 family. As such, the military was offered upward-swing-tail cargo versions of the KC-135 (738-2), the 707-120 (738-1 and 738-6), and the larger 707-320 (as the 738-4).

With a maximum take-off weight of 337,000lb (153,000kg), the Boeing 738-4 had a normal maximum payload of 100,000lb (45,400kg), with an overload capacity of 120,000lb (54,480kg). It could cruise at 450 knots (833km/h) and had a range of 5,500 miles (8,850km).

Initially, swing-tail variants derived from commercial 707-120 and 707-320 variants were grouped under the Model 735 and those derived from the military Model 717 (KC-135) were grouped under the Model 738 family. This was probably because, from the engineering point of view, the commercial 707 and military 717, despite looking almost identical, were vastly different under the skin and were tailored to their respective customers' needs and certification requirements.

The Model 735-320 was a straightforward cargo-carrying adaptation of the Boeing 707-320. Despite the structural strengthening required for the swinging tail, empty weight decreased by almost 3,000lb (1,360kg). This reduction resulted from deleting the passenger cabin fittings (a net decrease of 8,394lb or 3,810kg) and the replacement of the JT4A engines with the lighter JT3D turbofans (a net decrease of 2,553lb or 1,160kg). Its maximum take-off weight was given as

Boeing Model 735	
Powerplant	4 x P&W JTD-3 turbofans @ 18,000lb (80.07kN) thrust
Span	142ft 5in (43.44m)
Length	152ft 11in (46.64m)
Height	38ft 8in (11.79m)
Max TOW	305,000lb (138,470kg)
Payload	100,000lb (45,360kg)
Max cruise speed	600mph (965km/h)

Convair Model 30 (Model 600/990)

Convair's entry into the long-range jet airliner market was late and proved troublesome and expensive. The company's initial offering, the Model 880, was designed for the short-to-medium-range markets and carried fewer passengers than the competing 707 or DC-8. Moreover, and of great significance, it was several years behind them in getting to market. Its main advantage was speed but this came at the

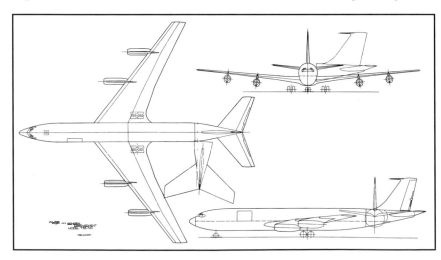

LEFT The Boeing 735 was based on the 707-320 Intercontinental. *Boeing*

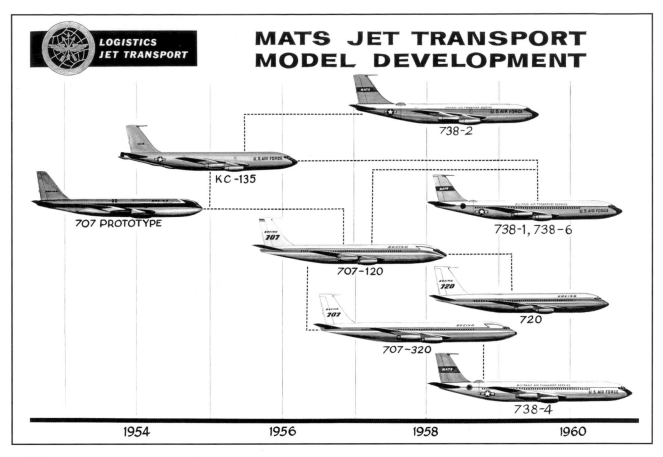

ABOVE A depiction of the Model 738 family tree. *Boeing*

BELOW Details of the lift tail and rerouting of control cables. *Boeing*

BELOW The military 'C-Jet' operational logistics concept. The airlines felt that this sort of scheduled supply network intruded into what they could and should do under contract. *Boeing*

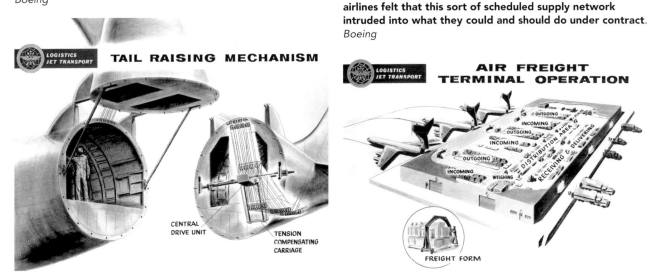

expense of higher fuel consumption. Last, its narrower cabin outside diameter of 138in (3.51m) limited seating to just five abreast.

Boeing successfully met the challenge posed by the 880 with its Model 720, a shortened and lightened version of the 707-100 series airliner. When the Pratt & Whitney JT3D turbofan engine became available, Boeing added it to the design, resulting in the 720B with lower fuel consumption.

Stung by the loss of a thirty-jet order to United Airlines in late 1957, Convair offered American Airlines a stretched version of the 880, replacing the GE CJ805-3 turbojets with GE CJ805-21 turbofan engines. This version was dubbed the 'Convair 600' for marketing purposes, but was designated the Model 30 internally. The naming confusion was

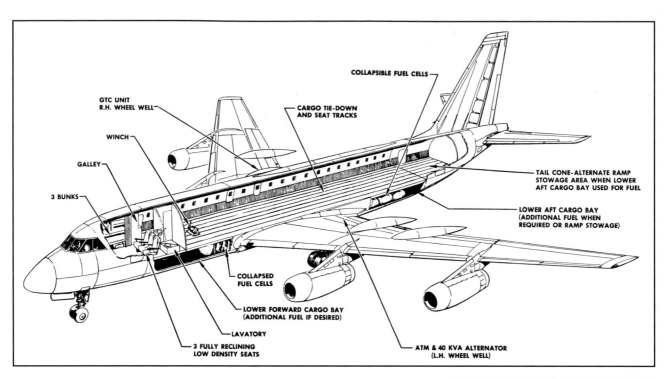

COLLAPSIBLE FUEL CELLS

GTC UNIT
R.H. WHEEL WELL

CARGO TIE-DOWN
AND SEAT TRACKS

WINCH

GALLEY

3 BUNKS

TAIL CONE-ALTERNATE RAMP
STOWAGE AREA WHEN LOWER
AFT CARGO BAY USED FOR FUEL

LOWER AFT CARGO BAY
(ADDITIONAL FUEL WHEN
REQUIRED OR RAMP STOWAGE)

COLLAPSED
FUEL CELLS

LOWER FORWARD CARGO BAY
(ADDITIONAL FUEL IF DESIRED)

LAVATORY

3 FULLY RECLINING
LOW DENSITY SEATS

ATM & 40 KVA ALTERNATOR
(L.H. WHEEL WELL)

ABOVE A cutaway drawing of the all-cargo swing-tail Convair Model 990. *San Diego Air and Space Museum*

compounded when the aeroplane was rebranded as the 'Convair 990' in the spring of 1960 (while still retaining the Model 30 designation for engineering purposes).

Technical issues during development added to the aeroplane's problems, and Convair eventually suffered one of the largest corporate losses ever recorded. Only sixty-five Model 880s and thirty-seven Model 990s were built.

Nonetheless, Convair proposed a military adaptation of the aircraft in early 1959, with the original marketing Model 600 designation, emphasising its speed advantage. The aircraft was offered with a side-hinged tail and also with an up-swinging tail as an alternative.

Convair Model 600/990 transport	
Powerplant	4 x GE CJ805-22 turbofans @ 16,050lb (714kN) thrust
Span	120ft 9in (36.58m)
Length	139ft 3in (42.59m)
Height	39ft 6in (12.04m)
Wing area	2,250sq ft (209m²)
Design gross weight	253,000lb (111,670kg)
Cruise speed	484kt (896km/h)
Maximum speed	540kt (1,000km/h)
Maximum range	3,595nmi (5,785km)

Douglas Model 1920 Jetmaster

Douglas did not commit to building the DC-8 jetliner until 7 June 1955, when Donald Douglas Sr made the formal announcement. This was more than a year after the Boeing 367-80 had rolled out. The design then moved out of the Douglas project/specification number series to the commercial marketing name of 'DC-8'. The last known prior designations for the airliner were Model 1881 for the domestic and Model 1910 for the overwater version. The design paths for the military and commercial transports appear to have run in parallel, with much cross-pollination.

LEFT A Convair 600 desk model. *Author photo*

ABOVE The Douglas Model 1920 (initial mixed cargo/passenger configuration). *Boeing*

LEFT The Convair 600 with alternative swing- and lift-tail arrangements. *San Diego Air and Space Museum*

BELOW A company model of the Douglas Model 1920. *Boeing*

The DC-8, a direct competitor to the Boeing 707, made its first flight on 30 May 1958 and entered airline service on 18 September 1959. Like its main competitor, Douglas foresaw the USAF's need to modernise its transport fleet and quickly began examining potential DC-8 military applications.

The proposed Model 1920 of 1956 was derived from the commercial Model 1910 overwater version of the DC-8 and differed substantially from the previously proposed Model 1856 military tanker/cargo aircraft. In the following two years, Douglas put forward numerous variations to the Air Force. To quote from Douglas's proposal for the Model 1920 to the Air Force: 'The philosophy of airlift to assure

intelligent anticipation of national requirements has been the subject of continuing study by the Douglas Aircraft Company for over a decade.'

The design went through many iterations, all under the designation Model 1920, which started out as described in the accompanying table.

For the 'C-Jet' proposal, the Model 1920W in its final form was powered

by Pratt & Whitney TF33 (JT3D-2) turbofans and introduced a swing-tail loading arrangement. Additional fuel was carried in fuselage tanks that extended into wing leading-edge fillets, with a capacity of about 1,380 gallons (5,224 litres). With that and the centre wing auxiliary tank, total fuel capacity was to be 23,307 gallons (87,722 litres) or 151,100lb (68,600kg).

Initial Douglas Model 1920 variants

Model	Engine	Arrangement
1920	J75	Designed for military cargo, personnel and evacuation operations
1920A	J75	Personnel transport with minimal changes from the commercial DC-8
1920B	J75	As for the Model 1920 but with a lower empty weight
1920C	J57	Identical to Model 1920 except for engines
1920D	J57	Identical to Model 1920A except for engines
1920E	J57	Identical to Model 1920B except for engines

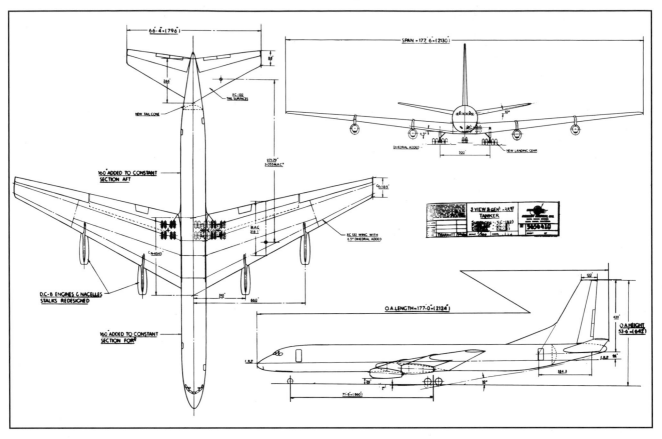

ABOVE Strangely looking like neither of its forebears, the Douglas Model 1924 was a design exercise combining a stretched Model 1920 (DC-8) fuselage with the wings and empennage of the Model 1814/XC-132. *Boeing*

BELOW The initial version of the Douglas Model 1920 with turbojet engines and dual side-opening cargo doors. *Boeing*

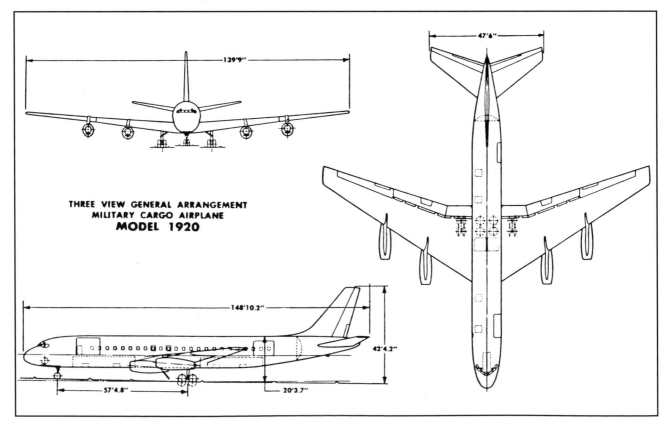

THREE VIEW GENERAL ARRANGEMENT
MILITARY CARGO AIRPLANE
MODEL 1920

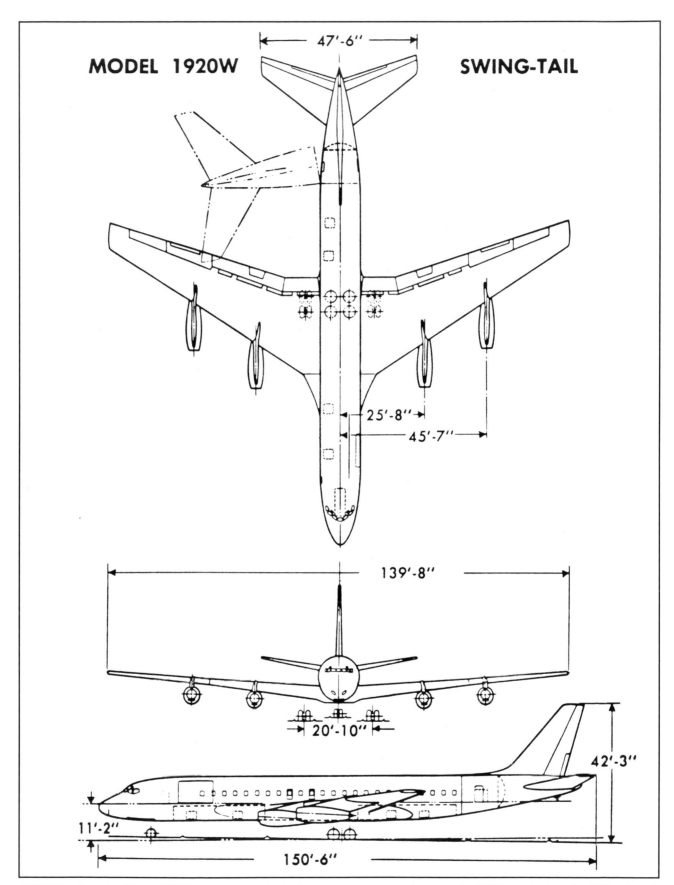

ABOVE The Douglas Model 1920W as proposed, had a forward cargo door and swing tail, JT4C (non-afterburning J75 turbojet) engines and added fuel capacity in the extended wing roots. *Boeing*

ABOVE Frank Fleming, Head of Douglas's Advanced Development, stands inside the DC-8 swing-tail engineering mock-up at Santa Monica. *Boeing*

Douglas Model 1920W swing-tail Jetmaster	
Powerplant	4 x P&W JT4A-10 turbojets @ 18,000lb (80.1kN) thrust
Span	139ft 8in (42.60m)
Length	150ft 6in (45.90m)
Height	42ft 4.2in (12.9m)
Wing area	2,758sq ft (256.49m²)
TOW	310,000lb (140,740kg)
Max payload	69,000lb (31,330kg)
Cruise speed	468kt (866km/h)
Range	5,000nmi (9,260km) with 37,000lb (19,740kg) payload, or 3,500nmi (6,480km) with 69,000lb (31,330kg)

'C-Jet' rejected by Congress

By early 1959 the 'C-Jet' programme was ready to proceed. On 25 March 1959 the 'Source Selection Evaluation – Turbo-jet Transport System' was released to the contractors, with a selection decision due by the summer. A provision of $53 million for ten aircraft was included in the proposed FY 1960 Defense budget. In May 1959 source selection recommendations were forwarded to Headquarters, USAF. However, the House Armed Services Committee abruptly terminated the process that same month. Budgets had shrunk, resulting in withdrawal of funding for the 'C-Jet', together with jet navigation trainers and jet utility aircraft. The case for the 'C-Jet' – which looked like a civilian transport – was further undermined by opposition from the airline industry, which saw it as a threat to its business of providing additional transportation to the Air Force.

Defense Secretary Neil McElroy appealed to the Senate Armed Services Committee for funding to be restored, but although the utility aircraft and navigation trainer cuts were rescinded, the withdrawal of funding for the 'C-Jet' stood. In the same budget, $85 million of the 1960 MATS budget was earmarked for the purchase of commercial air transport services. In retrospect, this seems hardly surprising given the long-standing principle in the United States that the Government should not use taxpayer's money to perform services internally that can be provided by private business. That is to say, the Government should not compete with business.

The final 'C-Jet' choice (between Boeing, Convair and Douglas) was rendered immaterial by the denial of funding and was never revealed by the Defense Department. The airline industry view had prevailed, at least for the time being.

'C-Jet' redux – a year later

By the following year, all parties had softened their positions somewhat. Budget pressures had eased, the airlines had gained their commitment to extra expenditure, and – given that it was about to launch a major new procurement programme in the shape of SOR 182 (described below) – the Air Force was prepared to accept a limited procurement of an 'interim' jet transport to help modernise the MATS fleet.

Under the new requirements, the elaborate (and costly) swing/lift tail was abandoned. Douglas proposed the Model 2212, based on the DC-8-55JT Jet Trader and featuring two left-side cargo doors. Boeing proposed minimally changed versions of the KC-135 as the Models 717-157 (turbojet) and 717-158 (turbofan).

In addition, Canadair put forward its CL-44D-5, developed from the Bristol Britannia (for which the Canadian company had a licence) with a lengthened fuselage, and powered by four Rolls-Royce Tyne 11 turboprops. It first flew in 1959, becoming the first (and so far only) large production aircraft to have a hinged rear fuselage. Its cruise speed of 402kt (647km/h), a range of 2,875nmi (4,627km) at maximum payload, and cargo capacity over 66,000lb (29,960kg) gave it superior performance, but politically it would have been very difficult for the USAF to order a foreign-built aircraft when there was no shortage of American contenders.

In May 1960 Congress approved the purchase of fifty Boeing airlifters at a cost of $169 million. Forty-eight were actually procured; fifteen were built as the C-135A (Model 717-157) – with

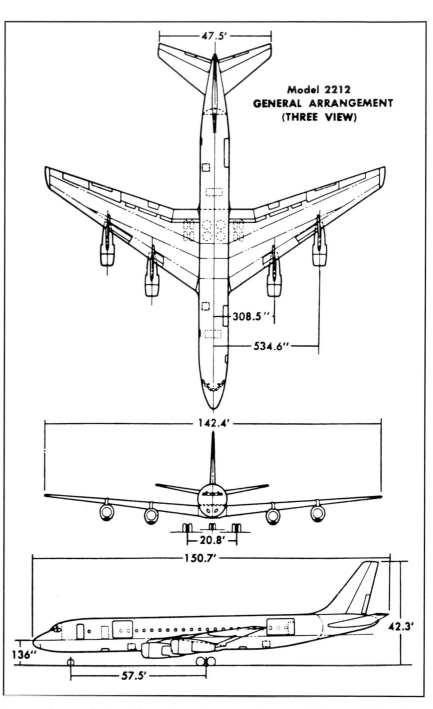

ABOVE The Douglas Model 2212, the military version of the DC-8-55JT Jet Trader. *Boeing*

Canadair CL-44D

Powerplant	4 x Rolls-Royce Tyne turboprops @ 5,730hp (4,270kW)
Span	142ft 4in (43.37m)
Length	136ft 11in (41.73m)
Wing area	2,075sq ft (192.7m²)
Max TOW	210,000lb (95,000kg)
Payload	66,048lb (29,959kg)
Max speed	417mph (670km/h)
Cruise speed	402kt (646km/h)
Range	5,588mi (8,990km)

three KC-135As converted to C-135A on the production line – and thirty as C-135B (717-158) turbofan versions. The first C-135A was delivered to the 18th ATS at McGuire AFB on 12 August 1961. However, the C-135 would serve a short life in the airlift role, being rapidly displaced by the purpose-built and more versatile C-141A (discussed later in this chapter). Ironically, some of these airframes outlived the C-141, having been converted to aerial reconnaissance platforms (OC-135, RC-135W); they are flying today with their original mission long since forgotten. Oddly, C-135s built from the ground up for reconnaissance were designated in the Model 739 family as the 739-700 (RC-135A) and 739-445B (RC-135B).

ABOVE The prototype Canadair CL-44 swing-tail cargo aircraft in flight. *Canadair Ltd*

The need for a true jet airlifter

Despite the introduction of dedicated military transport aircraft in the 1950s, the requirements of the Army had progressively outstripped the USAF's delivery capability. A major US Armed Forces exercise in March 1960, known as Operation 'Big Slam/Puerto Pine', dramatically illustrated this. Over a two-week period 21,000 men and 10,000 tons (10,160,000kg) of military equipment were transported from fourteen different bases in the United States to the island of Puerto Rico. The outcome was widely covered in the media, and alarmed Congress, exposing dramatic shortfalls in existing air transport capabilities.

MATS needed aircraft that were bigger and could fly faster and further than its ageing piston-engined fleet of C-97s, C-118s, C-121s and C-124s, and could carry far more than the interim C-135s.

Whatever the background, the Air Force clearly wanted to enlarge its own cargo-carrying fleet and avoid excessive reliance on commercial services. It eventually won the argument and succeeded in getting Congressional backing for a $2 billion modernisation programme. The campaign was led by General William H. Tunner, the MATS Commander, who earlier in his career had played a leading role in the Berlin Airlift. He summarised the immediate need for a new aircraft as follows:

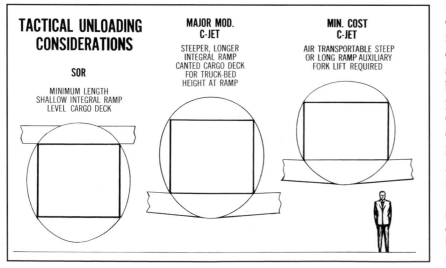

LEFT This Convair graphic neatly delineates the choices facing the Air Force and the drawbacks of the 'C-Jets'. *San Diego Air and Space Museum*

- A big plane that could carry heavy as well as bulky loads – because, as he put it, 'in both the Hump and the Berlin Airlift we had to cut up heavy equipment in order to get it on the airplane.'
- Straight-in loading from the front or the rear.
- A cargo floor at truckbed height … which meant a high-wing configuration.
- A maximum range of 7,000 miles (11,260km), with optimum range/payload trade-off.
- Powered by turboprops or turbojets.
- Low operating costs.

Overall, General Tunner saw the new aeroplane as the Military Airlift Command's (MAC) future workhorse: big, easy to load and cheap to operate. Interestingly, maximum speed was not one of the criteria. With air transport already saving weeks over surface delivery, the saving of an additional hour or two in flight length was not seen as material.

Looking back to the autumn of 1958, airlifter prospects had changed substantially from earlier plans. The cancellation of the XC-132 had left a gap in the heavy transport development effort. Further, despite advanced developments of the C-133 proposed by Douglas, the Air Force had become disenchanted with the aeroplane's engine, propeller and aerodynamic and structural difficulties. In November 1958 its disappointment led the Air Force to permanently reduce the C-133 procurement from 109 aircraft to fifty. In

twenty months, Douglas's domination of the future military airlift field had crumbled. Jet transports had become the Air Force's new direction.

With the loss of the 'C-Jet' programme in May 1959, the development of a dedicated airlifter assumed even greater importance. Desired characteristics began to evolve as Specific Operational Requirement (SOR) 182.

The Air Force Transport Panel's senior leadership decided to proceed with the SOR 182 draft publication on 24 July 1959. Rather than undertake a lengthy internal evaluation of possible technical solutions to the requirements, the Air Force went to industry for representative designs that could possibly fit the SOR requirements. This began a process whereby the requirements and contractor designs would be modified and harmonised to match; it was not a final design competition. Further complicating industry efforts, various factions in the Air Force were advocating turboprops while others were pushing for the turbofan.

At the time there was also a strong argument for developing a much larger long-range strategic airlifter. However, funding constraints would not allow the acquisition of a substantial fleet of both aircraft, so the Air Force opted for a medium-sized aeroplane, relying on the small Douglas C-133 fleet to handle outsize loads through the 1960s.

Boeing Model 731 designs

During the previous three years, Boeing Wichita had produced a number of designs for tanker/cargo aircraft under the generic designation of Model 731 – the designation subsequently used for its submission to SOR 182 in 1960. These studies were subsequently taken up by Boeing Seattle. Although largely new, they drew heavily on Boeing's experience, in particular exploiting B-52 and Model 707-320 wing technology. The accompanying table illustrates some of those studies.

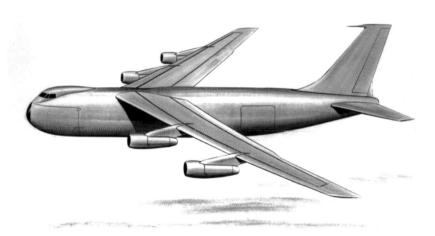

MODEL 731-8

RIGHT A Boeing Wichita study of the Model 731-8. *Boeing*

Boeing Model 731 studies

Model	Type of aircraft	Engines	Span	Weight
731-1	High-wing cargo using 707-320 wing	4 x P&W JT4D-1	147ft (44.80m)	350,000lb (158,900kg)
731-1A.1	Low-wing tanker	6 x P&W JT4C-2	188ft (57.34m)	600,000lb (272,400kg)
731-3	Low-wing cargo	6 x P&W JT4C-2W	188ft (57.34m)	600,000lb (272,400kg)
731-4	Low-wing tanker	6 x P&W JT4C-2W	188ft (57.34m)	600,000lb (272,400kg)
731-5	Low-wing cargo with hinged tail	6 x P&W JT4C-2W	188ft (57.34m)	600,000lb (272,400kg)
731-8	High-wing tanker or cargo	6 x P&W JT4C-12W	188ft (57.34m)	600,000lb (272,400kg)
731-8	Four-engine version; high-wing cargo	4 x P&W JT4D-1	188ft (57.34m)	405,000lb (183,900kg)
731-9	High-wing cargo based on B-52 wing	6 x P&W JT4D-1	188ft (57.34m)	405,000lb (183,900kg)

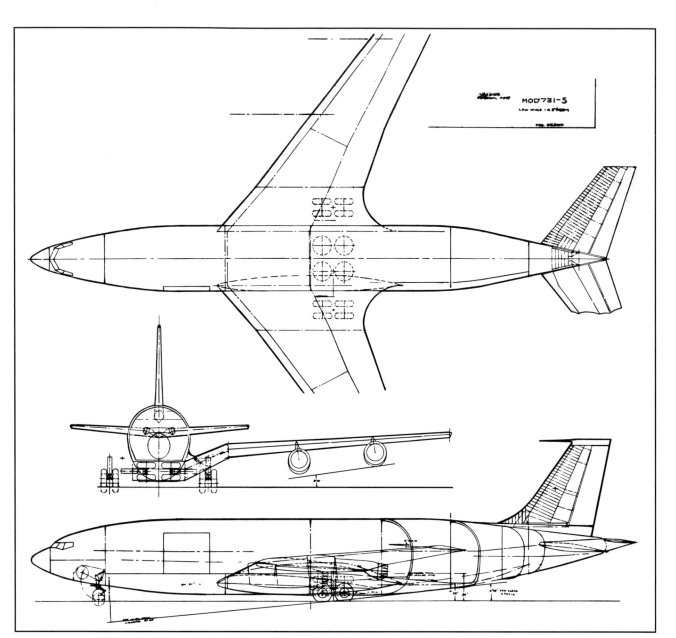

MOD731-5

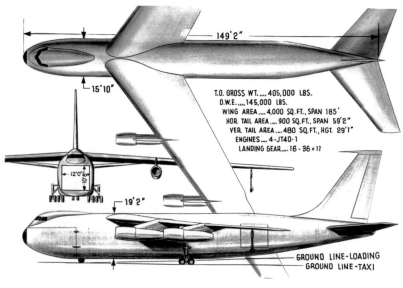

T.O. GROSS WT. .... 405,000 LBS.
O.W.E. .... 145,000 LBS.
WING AREA .... 4,000 SQ.FT., SPAN 185'
HOR. TAIL AREA .... 900 SQ.FT., SPAN 59'2"
VER. TAIL AREA .... 480 SQ.FT., HGT. 29'1"
ENGINES 4-JT4D-1
LANDING GEAR .... 16 - 36 × 17

149'2"

15'10"

12'0"

19'2"

GROUND LINE-LOADING
GROUND LINE-TAXI

ABOVE A design sketch of the Boeing Model 731-5, a gull-wing, large-cabin aircraft using 717 components. *Boeing*

LEFT Boeing Model 731-8 general arrangement. This design featured cargo loading through a set of nose doors and a side-opening cargo door in the aft fuselage. *Boeing*

OPPOSITE Boeing 731-15 preliminary general arrangement, powered by four turboprop engines. This design explored a smaller cargo box. *Boeing*

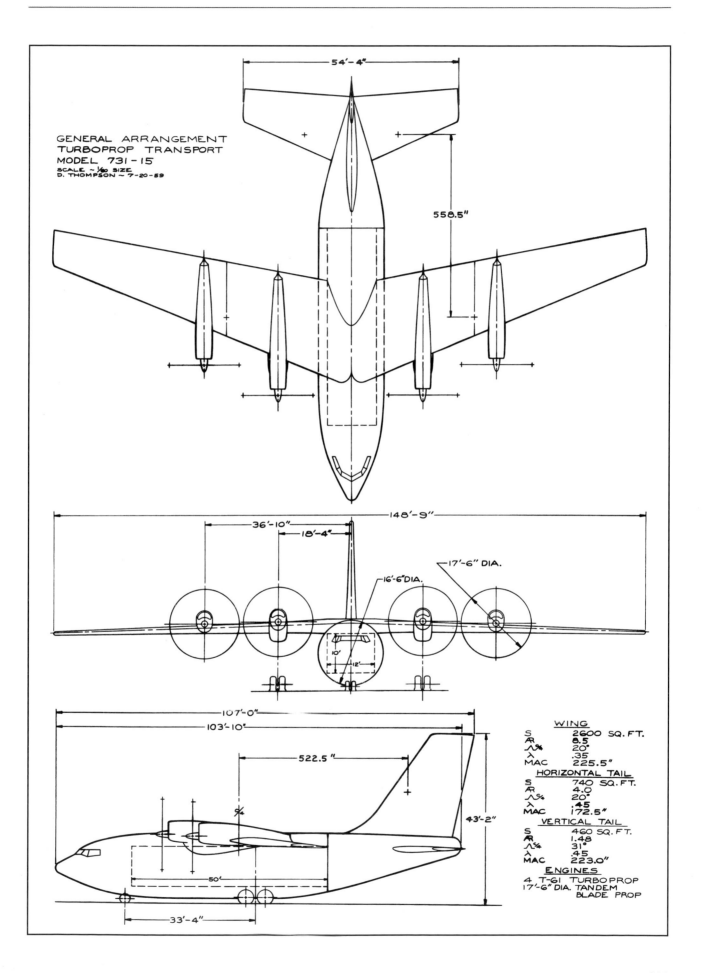

GENERAL ARRANGEMENT
TURBOPROP TRANSPORT
MODEL 731-15
SCALE ~ 1/80 SIZE
D. THOMPSON ~ 7-20-59

54'-4"

558.5"

148'-9"

36'-10"
18'-4"

17'-6" DIA.

16'-6"DIA.

10'
12'

107'-0"
103'-10"

522.5"

3/4

43'-2"

50'

33'-4"

WING
S   2600 SQ.FT.
AR   8.5
Λ¾   20°
λ   .35
MAC   225.5"
HORIZONTAL TAIL
S   740 SQ.FT.
AR   4.0
Λ¾   20°
λ   .45
MAC   172.5"
VERTICAL TAIL
S   460 SQ.FT.
AR   1.48
Λ¾   31°
λ   .45
MAC   223.0"
ENGINES
4 T-61 TURBOPROP
17'-6" DIA. TANDEM
        BLADE PROP

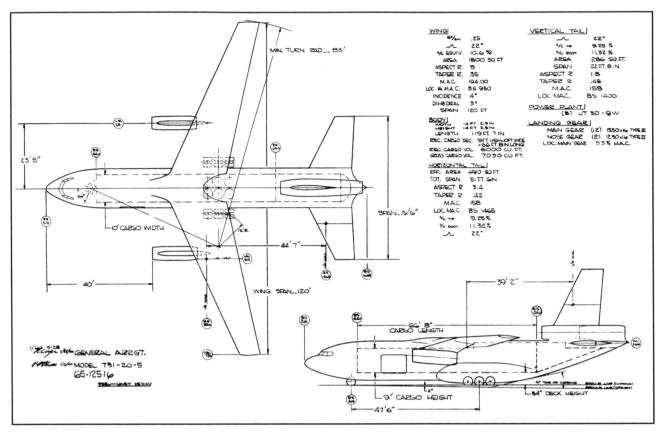

ABOVE The preliminary design layout for the Boeing Model 731-20-4, which explored a smaller design with three jet engines. *Boeing*

Boeing 731 (731-16)

The Boeing Model 731-16 featured a high wing, jacking landing gear, a truckbed-height cargo deck, and a large rectangular cargo compartment. The aft section accommodated a lowering ramp tail door,

120in wide by 108in high (3.05m by 2.74m), designed to facilitate both easy ground loading and air-dropping. The total cargo bay had an unobstructed length of 68ft 10 in (21.0m) and a total volume of 10,140cu ft (287m³).

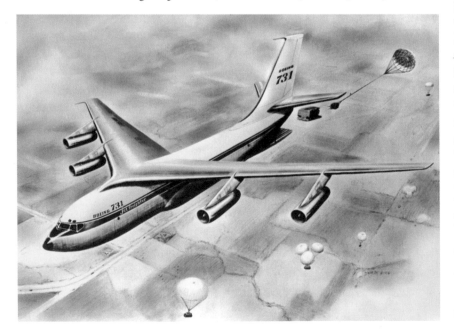

The wing was that of the 707-120B with improved trailing-edge flaps for take-off and landing, and added a leading-edge extension to reduce high-speed drag with full-span leading edge slats to improve take-off and landing performance. The horizontal stabiliser was from the larger 707-320 Intercontinental commercial airliner. The cockpit arrangement and equipment including windows were identical to those of the KC-135. The size of the vertical fin was increased, and to cope with a single-engine-out emergency a tandem (two-segment) rudder system was specified. The aft rudder was manually powered and balanced for high-speed flight while the forward rudder was to be fully power-boosted, augmenting the aft rudder for low-speed flight.

Engines were JT3D-4W turbofans with a sea level static thrust rating of 22,500lb (102.1kN) each. Boeing stated

LEFT The Boeing Model 731-16. *Boeing*

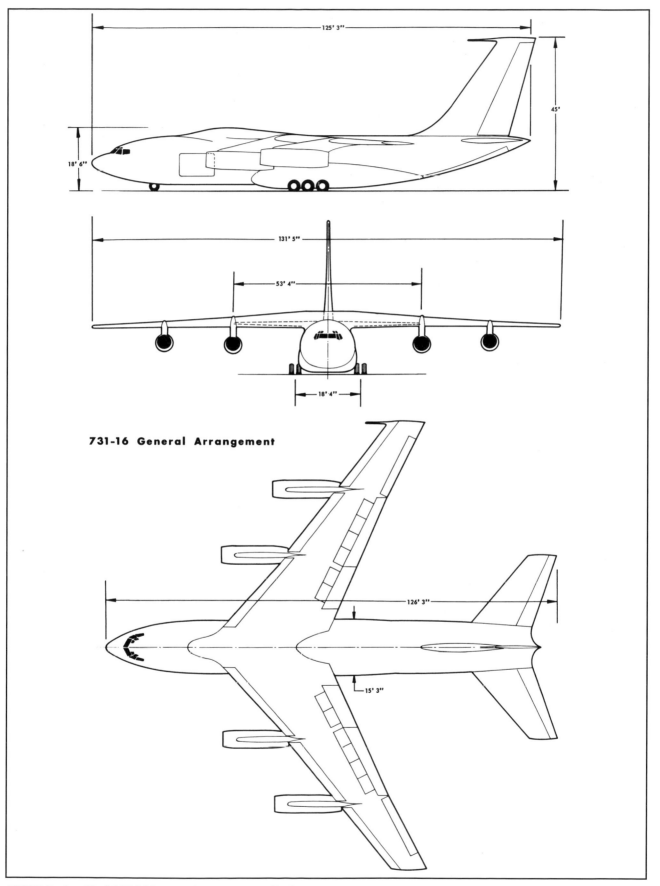

731-16 General Arrangement

ABOVE Boeing Model 731-16 general arrangement. *Boeing*

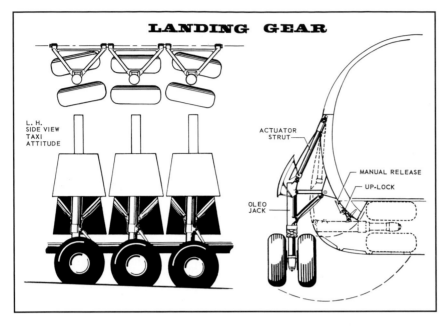

ABOVE The complex landing gear design for the Model 731-16 featured steerable front and back bogies for a tighter turn radius. *Boeing*

BELOW Model 731-16 engine accessories were mounted in the pylon, and the nose cowl tilted for better airflow during take-off. *Boeing*

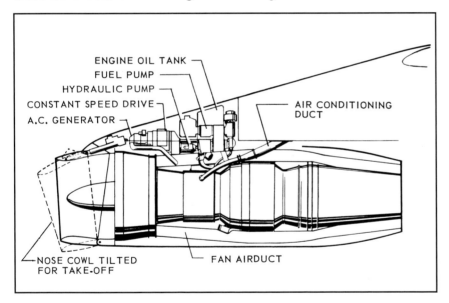

Boeing Model 731-16	
Powerplant	4 x P&W JT3D turbofans @ 22,500lb (100.1kN) thrust
Span	131ft (39.93m)
Length	125ft 3in (38.70m)
Height	45ft (13.91m)
Max payload	97,600lb (44,310kg)
Cargo volume	8,950cu ft (315m³)
Payload/range	20,000lb (9,080kg) 5,500mi (8,850km) 40,000lb (18,160kg) 4,000mi (6,440km) 60,000lb (27,240kg) 2,000mi (3,220km)

that the 'combination of high wing with improved flaps, engines with high take-off thrust ratings and modest cruise thrust ratings permit the design of a relatively small airplane with big capacity and big performance, a craft in which power plants and airframe are matched for efficient high-altitude cruise.' However, the Air Force viewed the 731-16 as being overly capable (too large and likely too expensive) compared to the preliminary GOR-182 requirements.

Convair 'Model 105'

General Dynamics in the late 1950s made a strong play to expand its position in the transport market. Produced by the San Diego-based Convair Division, the Model 220/340/440 airliners and their military T-29 and C-131 counterparts had carved a profitable niche in the post-war airline market.

By 1958 Convair was deep into development of the 880 airliner, but was determined to compete in the military jet airlifter market, and its Model 105 entry was considered to meet all the requirements of the proposed GOR. Although the Convair model number is quoted as '105' in an Air Force report, this is out of sequence for the model numbers as revised after the company's purchase by General Dynamics. In the absence of specific Convair documentation, the Air Force number is used here.

The design was marked by the use of a distinctive twin-engine pod arrangement, and main landing gear that retracted into the large fairing between and behind the

BELOW The alternative Convair 'Model 105' bowloader with 'cabover' cockpit. The very large nacelle afterbody housed the main landing gear. *Convair*

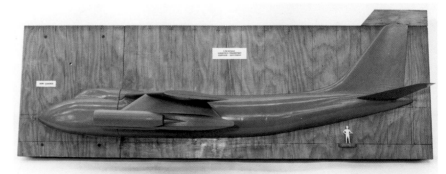

engines. This arrangement allowed the use of shorter struts, saving weight. Both tail-load and nose-load configurations were studied.

Douglas pre-SOR-182 studies

As with Boeing, Douglas conducted numerous studies, many at the Long Beach Division.

Douglas (Long Beach) Model 1467-79

The Douglas Model 1467-79 was an atypical Douglas design with the four TF75 engines (TF75 being a working name for the planned turbofan version of the J75 turbojet) installed two to a pod on either wing. The airlifter incorporated a new fuselage of circular cross section fuselage together with a landing gear that enabled the aircraft to 'kneel'. The upward-opening aft fuselage had a small swing-up door – a hallmark of Long Beach designs – in the bottom for added vertical clearance during the loading process.

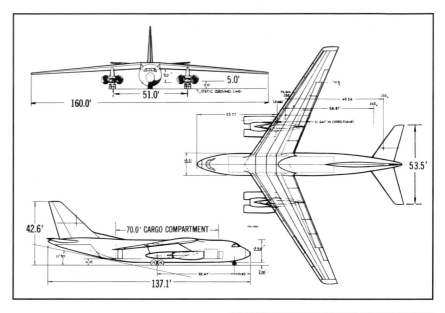

ABOVE Convair's preferred 'Model 105' design had aft fuselage loading doors.
San Diego Air and Space Museum

BELOW The Douglas Model 1467-79 was a lift-tail design using elements and concepts from the DC-8. *Boeing*

Douglas Model 1467-79 lift-tail airlifter	
Powerplant	4 x P&W 'TF-75' turbofans @ 24,000lb (106.8kN) thrust
Span	177 ft (53.95m)
Length	167 ft (50.90m)
Height	58ft 7in (17.86m)
Wing area	4,500sq ft (418.1m²)
Gross take-off weight	482,000lb (218,630kg)
Maximum cargo	100,000lb (45,360kg)

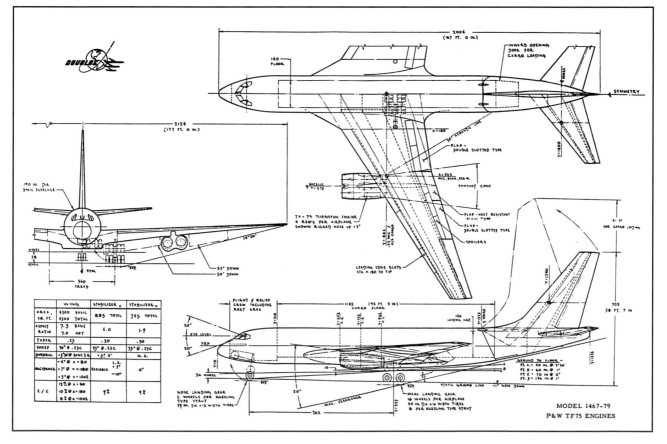

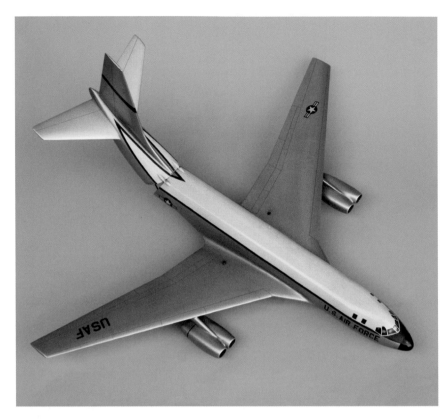

Douglas (Long Beach) Model 1467-55

Like Boeing, Douglas was pursuing a number of different designs in an effort to have a product that would fill whatever niche that the Air Force finally decided it wanted. Both the Long Beach and Santa Monica Divisions generated studies in 1959, and throughout that period Douglas persisted with low-winged designs despite the problems posed by a high cargo deck. And while 'kneeling' landing gear partially corrected the issue, its weight and complexity generated other problems.

ABOVE This model of the Douglas 1467-79 shows its unique (for Douglas) dual engine pods. *Author photo*

BELOW The Model 1467-79 also had 'kneeling' landing gear to lower the cargo deck height. *Author photo*

Douglas Model 1467-55 lift-tail airlifter	
Powerplant	4 x Allison T61-550-B4 turboprops @ 7,100eshp (5,300kW)
Span	167.5ft (51.10m)
Length	162.5ft (49.53m)
Height	49.16ft (14.98m)
Wing area	2,850sq ft (264.77m²)
Design gross weight	320,000lb (145,150kg)
Maximum cargo	100,000lb (45,360kg)
Maximum range	4,200nmi (7778km) with 100,000lb (45,360kg) payload

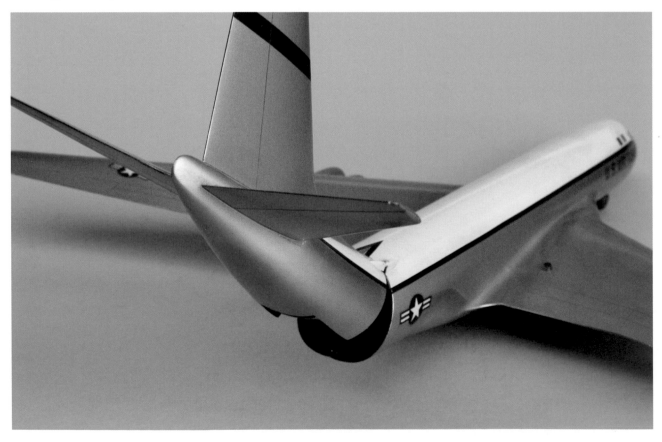

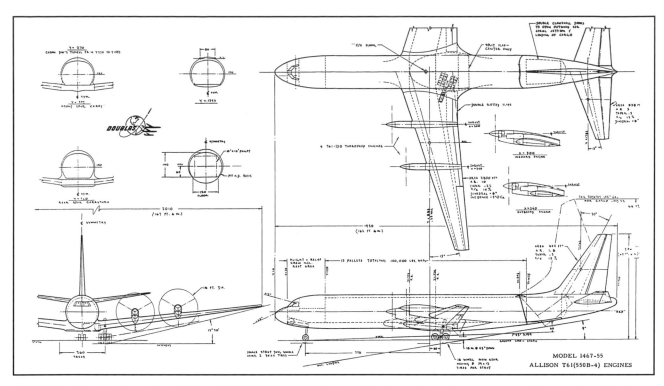

ABOVE The Douglas (Long Beach) Model 1467-55 is representative of the low-wing turboprop-powered design investigations. The fuselage diameter was to be 190in (4.83m). *Boeing*

BELOW The Douglas (Long Beach) Model 1491 was an attempt to lower the fuselage to the ground by eliminating the engine pylons and raising the engines. The latter were to be the Pratt & Whitney TF-52', a temporary designation for the turbofan version of the military J52 turbojet that would become the renowned JT8D used on the Boeing 727, 737 and Douglas DC-9 airliners. The very similar Model 1490 had Allison T61-550-B6 turboprop engines and a smaller wing. *Boeing*

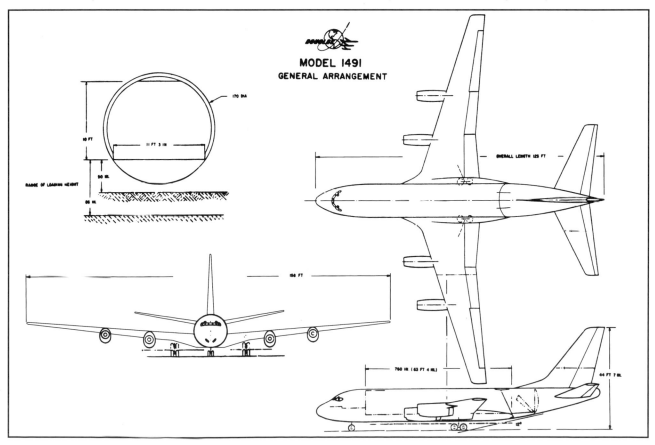

Douglas (Santa Monica) Model 2204

Inspired by the Model 1920P Atlas missile carrier study of March 1957, the Model 2204 undertook to inexpensively enlarge the upper lobe of the DC-8 fuselage, enabling it to carry larger payloads. Many of the existing fuselage skin panels were to have been used with minor modification, with new lengthwise panels inserted to increase the circumference. Additionally, the design lengthened the cargo deck by 30in (0.76m), to 100.84ft (30.74m).

Most unusually, hydraulic rams forward of the main landing gear would tip the aeroplane back to lower the deck for easier loading and unloading, rather than incorporating a jackable or 'kneeling' landing gear. This concept, first explored for the DC-6, also permitted a shorter and lighter loading ramp. An extendable overhead hoist was also proposed for cargo loading.

Douglas (Santa Monica) Model 2204 airlifter	
Powerplant	4 x P&W JT3D-8 turbofans @ 20,000lb (88.97kN) thrust
Span	142.4ft (142.84m)
Length	155.7ft (47.46m)
Height	45.2ft (12.86m)
Wing area	2,880sq ft (267.56m²)
Design gross weight	325,000lb (147,420kg)
Max payload	91,000lb (41.280kg)
Range	5,500nmi (10,180km) 20,000lb (9,080kg) payload 4,000nmi (7,400km) 40,000lb (18,160kg) payload

Fairchild Model M-270 'Jet Wing'

Fairchild started at a disadvantage compared with three of the other four competitors. Although it had produced a series of highly successful military transports, it had no experience of producing large-scale, long-range, swept-wing jets. In a competition demanding confidence in the supplier to deliver the

selected aircraft while meeting the performance criteria, on time and to budget, this was undoubtedly a handicap. This was a major contract that not only the USAF but also Washington would be watching. Nevertheless, Fairchild submitted a noteworthy design with its Model M-270.

The M-270D had emerged from a series of studies dating back to October 1958. It was actually the fourth ('D') iteration of a design that had begun as a much smaller aircraft intended to meet a TAC Study Requirement (SR 185). This first version of the aircraft had a gross weight of 150,000lb (68,100kg) and was intended to be able to operate from an unprepared airstrip with a ground roll of just 500ft (152m). Fairchild progressively scaled up this design as the USAF's requirements evolved.

Like many of the other submissions, it had a high-mounted swept wing carrying the double-podded engines on pylons. Its particular distinction lay in the use of a 'jet flap' or 'blown flap' arrangement. Under this system, the bypass flow from the engines was directed up through the pylons before flowing through the flaps to augment the lift of the moderately swept wing (23° at quarter chord). This greatly reduced the landing and take-off speeds, and hence ground roll. Bypass air also flowed through the tail fin and tailplane, increasing their effectiveness at very low speeds.

A drawback of the arrangement centred on the required ducting in the wings, which took away volume normally dedicated to carrying fuel. That fuel would thus have needed to be carried in tip tanks and in bladders above and below the passenger cabin, both practices discouraged by the Air Force for safety reasons.

The M-270 had a T-tail, projecting over a configuration with a lower door opening downwards, two angular-hinged doors opening sideways, and two upper doors folding up into the rear fuselage beneath the fin. There was no fuselage-side cargo door.

The landing gear was also unusual, consisting of two sets of main wheels, in

BEOW The Douglas Model 2204 was basically a DC-8 with an enlarged upper fuselage lobe. The white areas in the top profile indicate new structure, and the grey elements from the DC-8 that were common. Tilting the entire aircraft was a pragmatic, if unusual, approach to the loading problem and harked back to concepts first investigated a decade earlier on the DC-6. *Boeing*

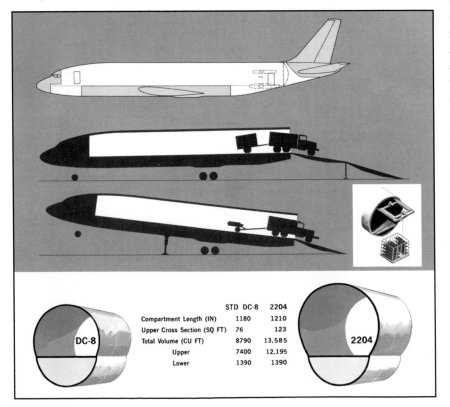

	STD DC-8	2204
Compartment Length (IN)	1180	1210
Upper Cross Section (SQ FT)	76	123
Total Volume (CU FT)	8790	13,585
Upper	7400	12,195
Lower	1390	1390

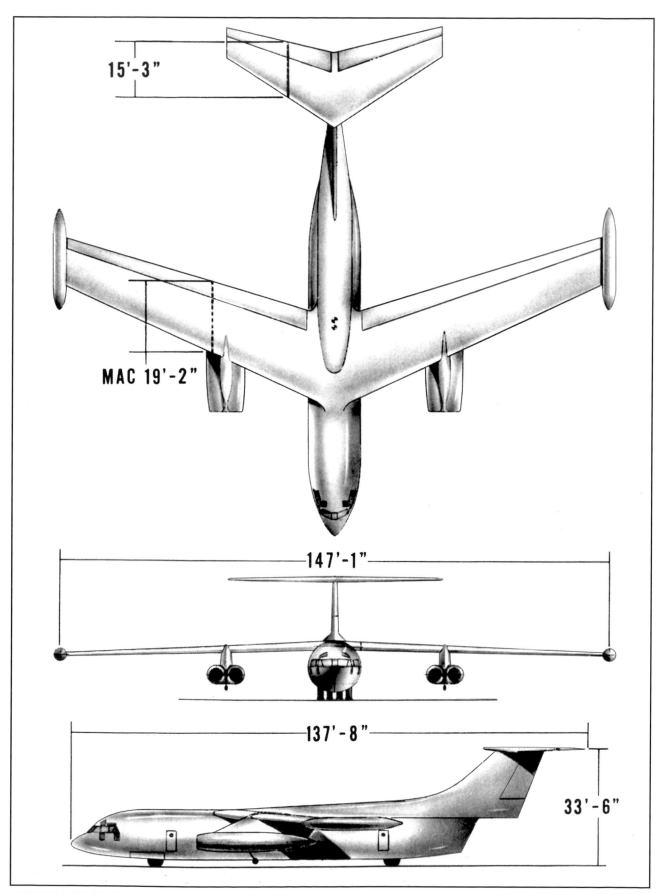

15'-3"

MAC 19'-2"

147'-1"

137'-8"

33'-6"

ABOVE Fairchild M-270 general arrangement. *NASM*

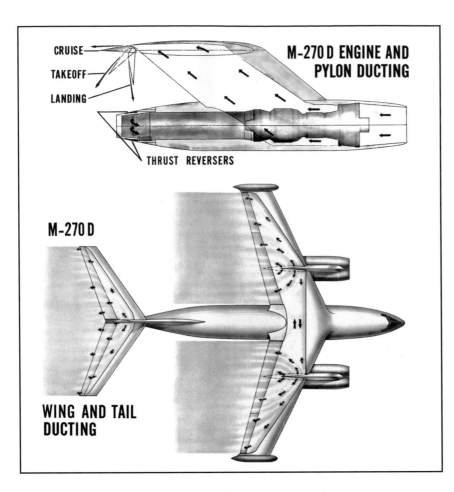

CRUISE
TAKEOFF
LANDING

M-270 D ENGINE AND PYLON DUCTING

THRUST REVERSERS

M-270 D

WING AND TAIL DUCTING

ABOVE The Fairchild Model M-270's 'jet flap' system. *NASM*

Fairchild Model M-270D 'Jet Wing' airlifter	
Powerplant	4 x P&W JT3D turbofans @ 21,000lb (93.45kN) thrust
Span	147ft 1in (44.86m)
Length	137ft 8in (41.99m)
Height	33ft 6in (10.35m)
Wing area	2,704sq ft (251.5m²)
TOW	285,000lb (129,390kg)
Max payload	70,000lb (31,780kg)
Range	5,500nmi (10,180km) 20,000lb (9,080kg) payload 4,000nmi (7,400km) 40,000lb (18,160kg) payload

a bicycle arrangement, with outrigger gear retracting into the engine nacelles. This was made possible by the jet-lift arrangement that permitted take-off and landing with very little rotation of the aircraft. The rear landing gear retracted into the fuselage, stowing aft of the loading ramp; the configuration required the aft gear to be extended so that the ramp could be lowered for air-drops.

Lockheed GL 207-23 and -25 'Super Hercules'

Unsurprisingly, in the latter part of the 1950s Lockheed also explored a number of options to further develop its C-130, which was already proving to be a highly effective operational aircraft. These proposals sought to exploit advances being made in both available and prospective engines.

In April 1959 Lockheed announced the GL-207-25 'Super Hercules', a much larger and more capable development of the C-130B, powered by four Allison 550-B7 (T61) turboprops. They were each rated at 6,500hp (4,847kW) compared with the 4,050hp (3,020kW) Allison 501-D22s installed in the C-130B. This increased the maximum take-off weight from 135,000lb (61,290kg) to 235,000lb (106,700kg), with a maximum payload of 76,240lb (34,610kg). Span was increased by 12ft 6in (3.81m), giving the wing a much higher aspect ratio and, although the fuselage retained the same cross section as the standard C-130, its length grew by 25ft (7.62m), giving the aircraft a much more elegant appearance. Additionally, Lockheed completely revised the rear fuselage. The undercarriage also had to be modified; to accommodate the much greater overall

BEOW The length of the Lockheed Model GL-207-25 and enlarged gear sponson are emphasised in this profile view. *Lockheed*

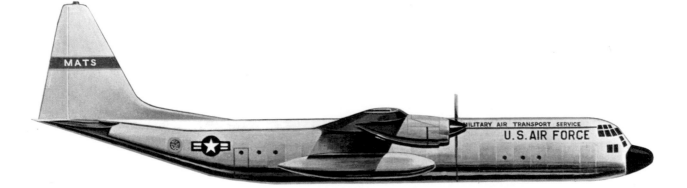

RIGHT The black sections in this illustration indicate elements identical to the C-130B, and the brown sections indicate structure that was new for the GL-207-25. *Lockheed*

weight, the main landing gear was replaced by dual eight-wheel bogies with smaller, high-pressure tyres.

A version of the aircraft, termed the 'Super Hercules Airfreighter', was also offered to the commercial market. Both Slick Airlines and Pan Am placed provisional orders; however, they were conditional on orders forthcoming from the military.

Lockheed Model GL-207-25 'Super Hercules'	
Powerplant	4 x Allison 550-B7 (T61) turboprops @ 6,500eshp (4,850kW)
Span	145ft 1in (44.25m)
Length	122ft 9in (37.40m)
Height	38ft (11.58m)
Wing area	2,041sq ft (189.6m²)
Max TOW	235,000lb (106,690kg)
Payload	76,240lb (34,610kg)
Cruise speed	333kt (617km/h)
Range (max payload)	3,564nmi (6601km)

When the Air Force cancelled development of the T61 engine, Lockheed offered an alternative version, the GL-207-39, which was to be powered by Rolls-Royce Tynes. It offered a slightly reduced maximum weight (230,000lb or 104,420kg), though with a slightly increased maximum payload (77,000lb or 34,960kg). Lockheed also claimed that it would be capable of performing STOL missions, lifting a payload of 23,000lb (10,440kg) and transporting it over 1,500nmi (2,780km), with a ground roll of just 750ft (229m).

Given the successful experience with the C-130, the GL-207 must have appealed considerably to the Air Force, and the aircraft may have come close to being produced. However, no orders were forthcoming. This was the high point of C-130 basic airframe development with respect to weight and power. Further development and increase in capabilities would require jet power; there were no other high-powered turboprop engines available.

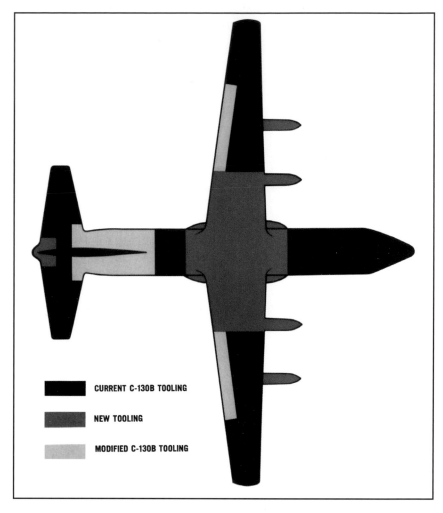

■	CURRENT C-130B TOOLING
■	NEW TOOLING
■	MODIFIED C-130B TOOLING

BELOW Loading comparisons: the DC-8 cargo deck is 12.1ft above the ground and, due to the cargo door arrangement, the C-133 opening height for straight-in loading is less than that of the 'Super Hercules'. *Lockheed*

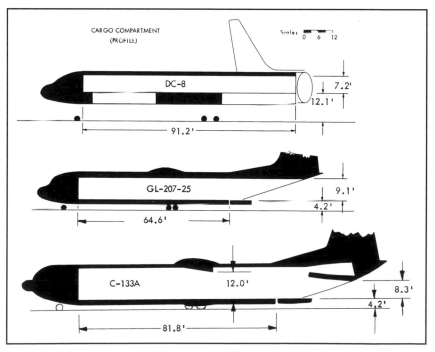

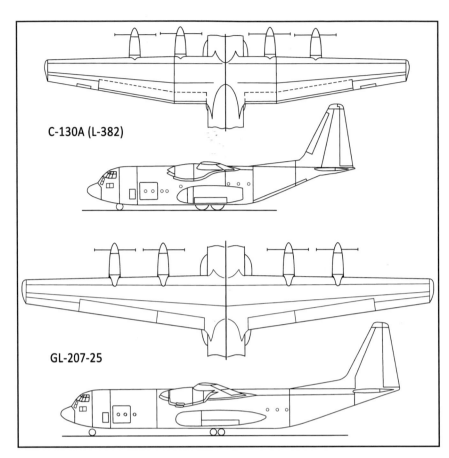

C-130A (L-382)

GL-207-25

ABOVE Comparisons between the standard-length C-130A and the GL-207-25. *Lockheed*

BELOW Lockheed Model GL-268 general arrangement. *Lockheed*

Lockheed GL268-1

One of Lockheed's most intriguing advanced design studies was the GL268-1. This was a twin-finned, tailless proposal, with a 'lambda wing'. It was designed to cruise at speeds approaching Mach 0.91 while carrying a payload of up to 50,000lb (22,700kg). That was not only faster than most other airlifter proposals of the era, but was also faster than virtually anything proposed since. This reflects parallel experience in the commercial sector, where the marginal gain in transit time gained from cruising at high subsonic Mach numbers has been judged not to be worth the associated penalties in terms of extra drag. As a result, today's jet airliners fly no faster, indeed often slower, than those designed in the 1950s.

Lockheed GL-268 airlifter	
Powerplant	4 x MF239-C GE turbofans
Span	140ft (42.70m)
Length	118ft 8in (36.19m)
Height	34ft 10in (10.62m)
Wing area	5,889.7sq ft (547.2m²)
Max take-off weight	316,500lb (143,560kg)
Payload	50,000lb (22,680kg)
Cruise speed	Mach .91
Range	4,000nmi (7,410km)

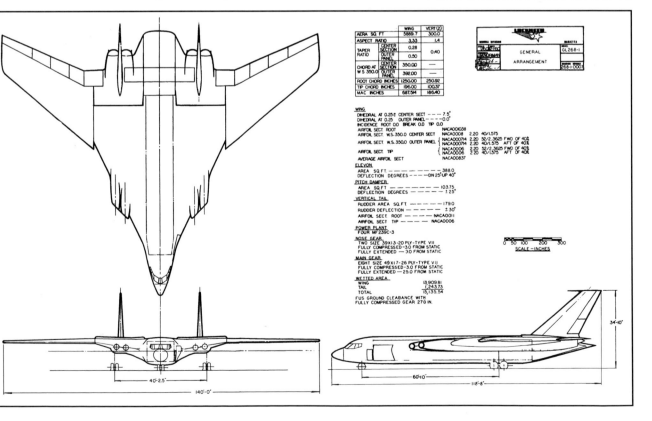

Lockheed considered submitting the GL 268 as its candidate for SOR 182, but eventually decided to propose a more conventional design.

Civil Reserve Air Fleet (CRAF) considerations

The airlines had hoped that the military's deficiency in airlift capability would result in a great opportunity to expand their operations, but they were thwarted by Air Force lobbying in Washington. The airlines may have hurt their cause when they failed to support a Bill before Congress that would have given the Civil Aeronautics Board authority to guarantee loans for acquiring cargo aircraft that met DoD and FAA specifications. The airlines were reportedly unhappy with the prevailing MATS method of awarding contracts, which was on a short-term, lowest-bid basis with the tender going to scores of carriers, many of whom had no aircraft of their own but simply relied on leased transports. They complained that this resulted in heavy financial losses and instability in the industry; whether this was true or not, it obviously provided no incentive to invest in new aircraft specifically to meet military requirements.

The SOR 182 competition

SOR 182 (to provide Support System WS-476L) was formally issued by the USAF on 4 May 1960, followed up by a short addendum, SOR 182-1, in August 1960; the addendum changed little of significance but simply clarified or restated points in the earlier document. Incredibly, by later norms the first document ran to just eight pages and the addendum to just four. The world was clearly very different in 1960.

The requirements called for a cargo aircraft support system for use in both military and commercial operations. Although briefly set out, the specification was quite demanding, stating that 'In the military role the aircraft will be employed in both inter- and intra-theatre operations. In the civil role the aircraft

will be employed in both domestic and international operations… The aircraft will be capable of worldwide, all-weather operations from established air bases.'

The reasons for specifying a dual military/commercial aircraft were twofold: one was to make it more attractive from the manufacturers' viewpoint by spreading the cost of development; the other was to enable the Air Force to call upon further resources in the event of an emergency. Indeed, the latter was specifically mentioned as a possibility in the SOR.

SOR 182 specified that the aircraft must carry a payload of up to 70,000lb (31,780kg) over a range of 4,000nmi (6,440km), with the capability to operate in the Pacific with a reduced payload over a range of 5,500nmi (8,850km).

Emphasis was also placed on the available space within the cargo area. The capacity had to be not less than 6,000cu ft (170m³) of usable space with at least 700sq ft (65.1m²) of floor space. Furthermore, to cope with bulky cargo a rectangular space was required, at least 70ft long, 10ft wide and 9ft high (21.35m by 3.03m by 2.75m), including an extra crew compartment.

SOR 182 also called for straight-in tail loading at truckbed height (approximately 48in or 1.20m above ground level), together with a secondary side-loading door, 108in (2.74m) wide by 78in (1.98m) high. The military version was additionally required to have the capability of opening the tail-loading doors in flight (albeit at reduced speed) to enable air-dropping. Take-off and landing, clearing a 3ft (0.91m) obstacle on three engines with normal maximum load, had to be achieved within 6,000ft (1,830m). Cruising speed was not specified, being regarded as a secondary to the other design aspects, other than stating that 'the highest possible cruise speed is required'.

Although the competition only allowed six months for the preparation and submission of a response, the major aircraft companies had, as discussed above, been carrying out design studies for the next generation of transport aircraft long before the official release

of SOR 182. It was clear to everyone that the Air Force's airlift capability needed to be modernised and extended, regardless of whether the USAF won its battle to keep this within MAC's fleet, or be forced to share it with the commercial airlines. Either way, there would be a requirement for a new strategic transport aircraft.

Proposals were received from four companies: Boeing (Model 731), Convair (Model 63), Douglas (Model 2085), and Lockheed (GL 207-45 'Super Hercules'). Three of these companies were already building long-range swept-wing jet aircraft and the other had been supplying military transports; all of them were engaged in design studies that sought to exploit their experience. Several of these earlier design studies were described in Chapter Five.

Boeing Model 731

Boeing's final submission was its Model 731 (no suffix), an aircraft with a high-mounted wing and powered by four turbofans mounted on pylons beneath the wings. The tailplane was mounted on the top of the fuselage, which curved up at the back to accommodate a down-swinging ramp that could accommodate both ground loading and air-dropping. The rear fuselage also incorporated a deflector door that swung outwards to protect paratroopers from the slipstream. In all, it was a tailored, refined design compared to its 731-16 predecessor.

By now Boeing had far more experience of designing and building large-scale, swept-wing jet aircraft than any other company in the world. The 731 drew heavily on that experience, which was emphasised in the proposal document. The wing design, for example, was based on recent development work done on the 707-320 and the 727. This featured a combination of the 707-120 outer wing and the -320 inner wing with extended leading and trailing edges. These changes, together with span increases at the root and at the wingtip (increasing the aspect ratio) resulted in a 13% improvement in range at economy speeds.

Boeing Model 731	
Powerplant	4 x P&W JT3D-8A turbofans @ 22,500lb (100.1kN) thrust
Span	152ft 8in (46.53m)
Length	136ft 2in (41.50m)
Height	42ft 7in (12.98m)
Wing area	3,000sq ft (279m²)
Design gross weight	296,500lb (134,500kg)

Maximum payload was tailored to Air Force requirements, decreasing to 70,000lb (31,780kg) from the 97,000lb (44,040kg) payload of the Model 731-16. This resulted in a simpler and lighter main landing gear consisting of two four-wheel bogies.

Convair (San Diego) Model 63

Convair's Model 63 was an attractive high-wing aircraft. Unusually for any high-wing aircraft, the main undercarriage was not housed in the fuselage. The company's display model shows the revised design with main wheels retracting into large fairings that extended beyond the trailing edges of the wings, a change from the previous 'Model 105' where the main undercarriage retracted into enlarged engine pylons. That design would have required much shorter gear struts, but exposed the struts and tyres to jet blast from the engines. Loading was by way of an integral ramp that retracted upwards into the rear fuselage.

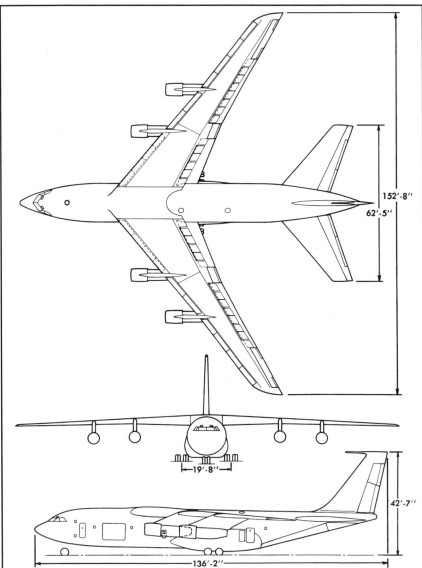

Convair Model 63 airlifter	
Powerplant	4 x P&W JT3D-4 turbofans @ 18,000lb (80.1kN) thrust
Span	165ft (50.35m)
Length	135.5ft (41.33m)
Height	46.5ft (14.18m)
Wing area	3,400sq ft (316.2m²)
Max TOW	284,800b (129,300kg)
Payload	70,000lb (31,780kg) or 100 troops
Max payload	93,500lb (42,450kg)
Range at max payload	1,890nmi (3,500km)
Max speed	506kt (937km/h)

LEFT Boeing Model 731 general arrangement. *Boeing*

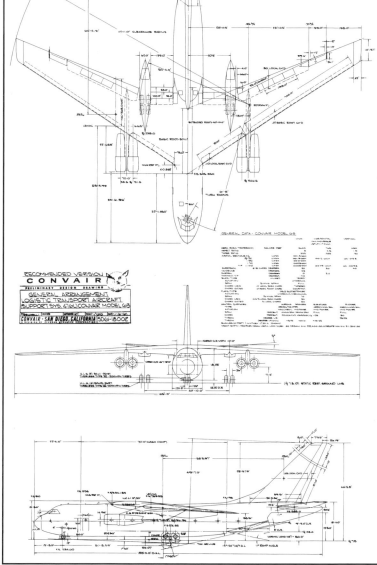

ABOVE The Convair Model 63 loading mock-up. The cabin width is filled by the 463L pallet and cargo, with a crewman to the left. The Model 63 upper aft doors were double hinged and could swing outwards, or inwards as shown.
San Diego Air and Space Museum

RIGHT Convair Model 63 general arrangement.
San Diego Air and Space Museum

BELOW RIGHT A belly view of the Model 63, detailing the landing gear arrangement.
San Diego Air and Space Museum

BELOW A Convair Model 63 display model.
San Diego Air and Space Museum

Compared to the 'Model 105', the Model 63 had grown by several feet in both fuselage length and wingspan, and was now powered by four Pratt & Whitney JT3D-4 turbofans, still mounted in pairs on under-wing pylons.

Douglas (Santa Monica) Model 2085

Although Douglas had studied designs with cylindrical fuselages in 1960, its proposal from the Santa Monica Division presented a 'double-lobe' fuselage that positioned the flight deck above the cargo compartment, reminiscent of the XC-132. Designated the Model 2085, the aircraft was to be powered by four Pratt & Whitney JT3D-8A turbofans, with the option to switch later to the projected Pratt & Whitney JT3D-12A or the General Electric MF239-C3 to accommodate growth.

Douglas's design again incorporated elements and structures from (or very similar to) the DC-8, which was already engineered and in production. These included the empennage, outer wings, engine nacelles and cockpit cab. The cargo compartment was 10.3ft wide by 9ft high (3.14 by 2.75m) and cargo was loaded through outward-opening doors in the aft fuselage, supplemented by a side-opening loading door in the forward left side of the fuselage, below and aft of the cockpit.

Douglas noted that the double-deck arrangement would allow:

■ Flight crew stations situated above the cargo compartment

■ An efficient, continuous structure for wing-to-fuselage junction and horizontal tail mounting

■ Minimised interference drag thanks to mounting the horizontal tail surface on the fuselage

■ Greater separation of aircraft system components for simplified maintenance

The Douglas proposal emphasised the company's experience in supplying previous aircraft to MATS. It also asserted that its understanding of logistics operations could lead to a high degree of confidence in the submission. It also stated, 'Furthermore, the Contractor's sound experience of commercial requirements will develop and support the commercial market for the system,' reflecting the prevailing expectation that civilian sales would help support the development of the selected aircraft.

Douglas further noted:

'The Model 2085 is designed to meet the basic mission of 50,000lb of cargo for a range of 4000 nautical miles at a take-off gross weight of 294,000lb with the cargo on pallets, or at a take-off gross weight of 191,000lb in a non-pallet mode representative of operational missions. Both cases meet the 6,000-foot take-off requirement at a 2.5 load factor.

Although it is understood that a considerable cargo will be transported on pallets, the aircraft has been designed with a complete cargo floor capable of transporting all types of general cargo, wheeled vehicles, and personnel without additional support equipment. The basic mission has been shown in this proposal at the 292,000lb gross weight because it illustrates the capability of the aircraft in the configuration that provides the maximum efficiency and flexibility for the total mission spectrum.'

In addition to the rear cargo loading ramp, a 78in by 108in (1.98 by 2.74m) cargo door was designed into the forward left side of the fuselage. Aerial refuelling was accommodated with a receptacle forward of the cockpit.

BELOW A Douglas Model 2085 desk model. *Boeing*

Douglas Model 2085	
Powerplant	4 x P&W JT3D-8A turbofans @ 18,000lb (80.1kN), with JT3D-8A or GE MF239-C3 turbofans as alternatives
Span	148ft 1.6in (45.17m)
Length	136ft 1.5in (41.50m)
Height	50ft 0in (15.24m)
Wing area	2,978sq ft (276.7m²)
Gross weight	292,000lb (132,570kg)
Max payload	70,000lb (31,780kg)
Cruise speed	463kt (857km/h)
Range	5,500nmi (10,180km) with 20,500lb (9,310kg) payload 3,100nmi (6,480km) with 70,000lb (31,780kg) payload

ABOVE The Douglas Model 2085. *Boeing*
BELOW Douglas Model 2085 general arrangement. *Boeing*

Lockheed GL-207-45 (L-300)

Lockheed submitted its proposal as the GL 207-45 'Super Hercules' on 20 December 1960. Leading up to its submission, engineers had examined many other layouts. Looking back some years later, Lockheed's Wilfred C. Garrard reflected:

'During the preliminary design phase of the C-141 aircraft a small team was given the task of comparing all configurations that could be conceived for performing the C-141 mission. The hope was that a new configuration could be developed which would be superior … either in speed or cost or some other major characteristic. One factor in our minds was that something new or different would catch the imagination of USAF and if it offered one or more advantages, we would have an overwhelming competitive advantage. Unfortunately our hopes were dashed in this endeavor…'

In the end Lockheed opted for a high-wing, T-tailed configuration with four turbofans slung on wing-mounted pylons. The wing's moderate sweep (25° at quarter chord) traded a reduction in cruise speed for an increase in payload for the same size wing. The reduced sweep also decreased approach speeds, allowing Lockheed to eliminate leading edge slats.

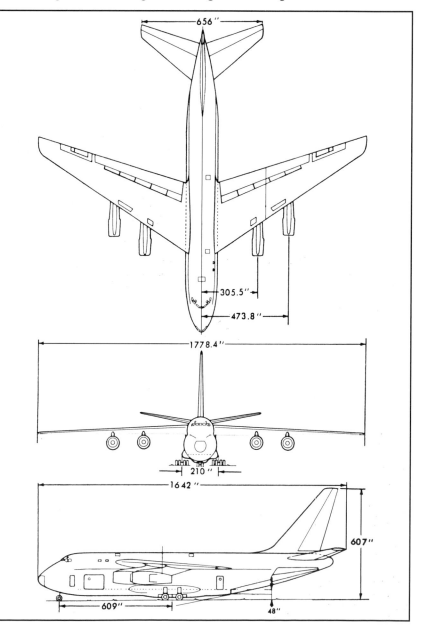

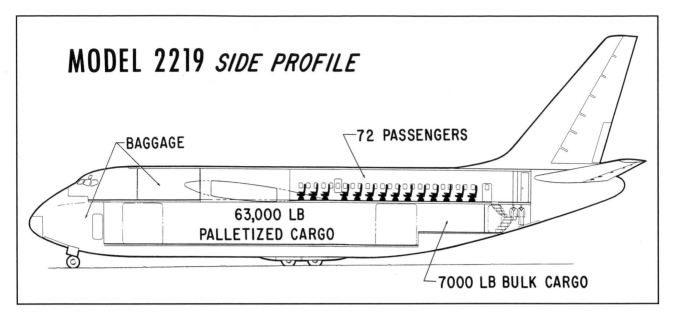

MODEL 2219 *SIDE PROFILE*

BAGGAGE

72 PASSENGERS

63,000 LB
PALLETIZED CARGO

7000 LB BULK CARGO

ABOVE The Douglas Model 2219 was a civilian mixed cargo/passenger jet version of the Model 2085. Cargo would be loaded on the main deck through two side-opening doors in the left side of the aircraft. *Boeing*

As previously noted, the name 'Super Hercules' had earlier been applied to the GL 207-25, an enlarged C-130 development. The reuse of the name was clearly intended to emphasise the line of descent from the earlier, highly successful aeroplane, as was the retention of the same GL-207 series number. The fuselage had the same cross-sectional dimensions and the proposal document stressed the link: 'In its basic design and manufacturing philosophy, it leans heavily on the C-130 … and much of the functional sub-systems are developed directly from those of the C-130 series.' The tone of the entire submission was clear: here was an aircraft that could fully meet the requirement, at the least cost, at the earliest possible date.

It was designed to be powered initially by four Pratt & Whitney JT3D-4 engines, with the option to eventually take advantage of the more powerful JT3D-8A. An alternative powerplant, the GE MF239 C-3, was offered on the understanding that it was a 'paper' engine and would not be available in time for the airframe.

LEFT The Lockheed GL207-45 'Super Hercules'. *Lockheed*

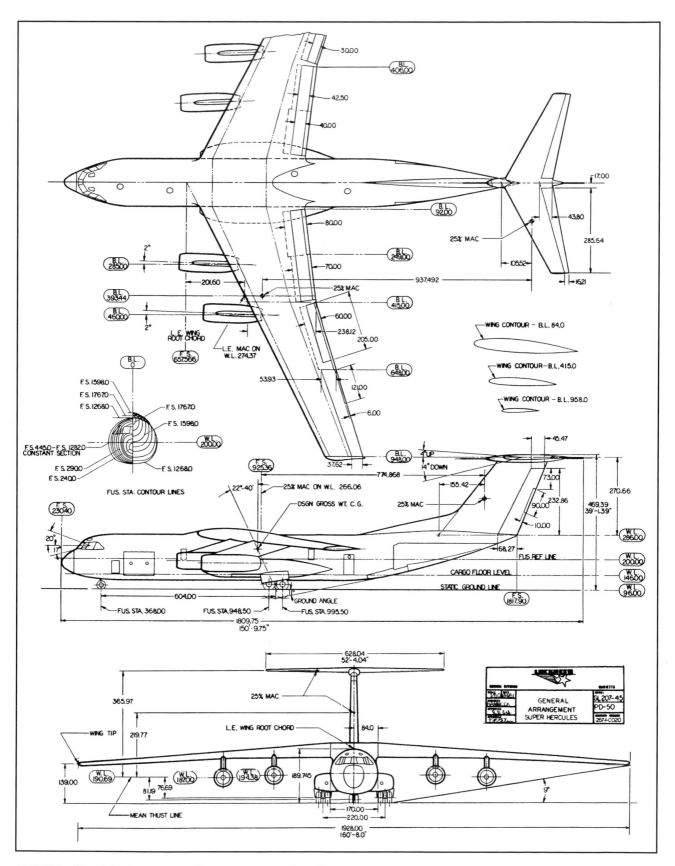

ABOVE Lockheed GL-207-45 general arrangement. *Lockheed*

Lockheed 'Super Hercules' and Starlifter			
	GL-207-45 'Super Hercules'	C-141A	C-141B/C
Powerplant	4 x P&W JT3D-4 turbofans @ 18,000lb (80.1kN) thrust	4 x P&W TF33-P-7 turbofans @ 20,250lb (90.08kN) thrust	4 x P&W TF33-P-7 turbofans @ 20,250lb (90.08kN) thrust
Span	160ft 8in (48.97m)	160ft (48.80m)	160ft (48.80m)
Length	150ft 10in (46.00m)	145ft (44.22m)	168ft 4in (51.34m)
Wing area	3,228sq ft (300.2m²)	3,228sq ft (300.2m²)	3,228sq ft (300.2m²)
Max TOW	315,000lb (143,010kg)	323,100lb (146,690kg)	342,100lb (155,310kg)
Max payload	80,000lb (36,320kg)	62,717lb (28,474kg)	88,152lb (40,000kg)
Cruise speed	440kt (814km/h)	478mph (769km/h)	478mph (769km/h)
Range	3,880nmi (7,180km) @ 70,000lb (31,780kg)	4,155mi (7,690km) 5,500nmi (10,180km) @ 20,000lb (9,080kg)	3,200mi (5,920km)

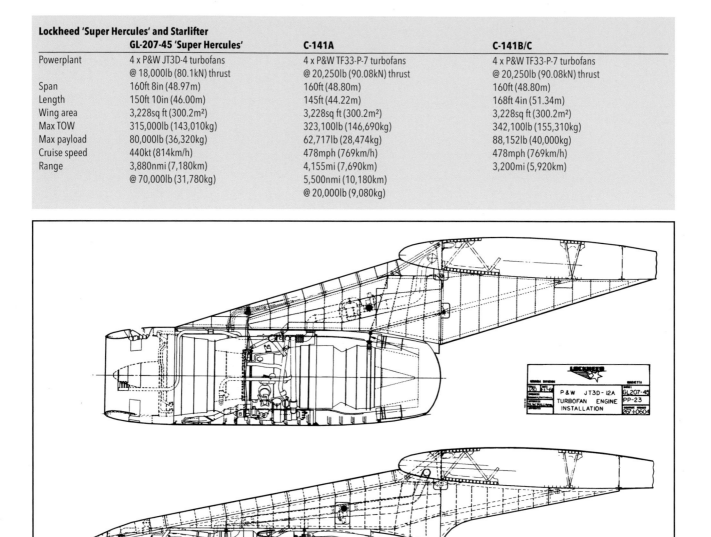

ABOVE Comparative installation diagrams of the Pratt & Whitney front-fan TF33 (top) and the alternative GE MF239 C-3 aft fan engine (bottom), which was considerably bulkier. *Lockheed*

As detailed previously, Lockheed had also explored the innovative 'lambda-wing' GL-268 airlifter design. However, after reviewing SOR 182, Lockheed decided to propose a more conservative aircraft. Nonetheless, the company included details in its formal proposal document for the GL-207-45, describing the GL-268 – remarkably candidly in the briefing package – as, 'We feel that it gives you more than you requested, later than you want it, for more than we think you

want to pay.' In retrospect, discussion of the GL-268 was probably included for two reasons. One was to show that Lockheed fully understood and endorsed what the Air Force was seeking, even though it could have submitted a more sophisticated design. The other was to provide insurance in the event that one of the other contenders offered something more advanced – making it clear that Lockheed could have done the same but chose not to do so.

After evaluating all proposals, in March 1961 the Air Force selected the Lockheed design, and ordered the building of five development aircraft under the designation C-141A. Even before the first of these had flown, a contract was placed for 132 production aircraft, which was subsequently increased to 248. Lockheed delivered the first C-141A to the Air Force in October 1964 and the final example in February 1968.

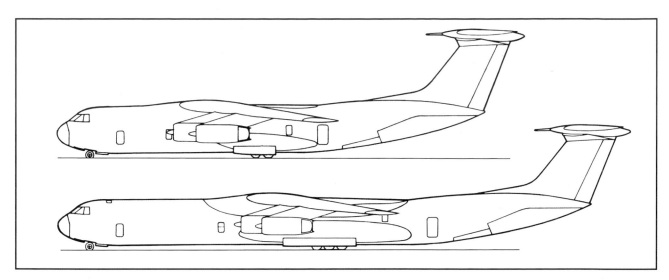

ABOVE As part of the GL-207-45 proposal, Lockheed offered a 37ft stretch of the basic design, which required a new six-wheel landing gear. *Lockheed*

Reflecting the original concept, Lockheed also designed a version aimed at the civil market, known as the L-300 Super Starlifter. The company built a demonstrator that flew in 1963, but it attracted no orders – calling the original rationale behind the dual-purpose specification into question.

The C-141 in retrospect

The C-141 was arguably the USAF's first strategic jet airlifter. It was not, however, without its limitations. A report published in January 1973 by the USAF's Office of MAC (Military Airlift Command) History, noted that it had

'…a shorter fuselage than the C-133 and DC-8F; its maximum payload of 34 tons less than that of the Boeing 707-300 series (44.9 tons) and Douglas DC-8F (38.7 tons); its economy cruise speed fell 35mph short and 64mph below the 707-320B and DC-8F respectively; while its maximum range was some 500 miles less than that of either the 707 or DC-8F. In addition … the C-141 was incapable of carrying the outsized cargo that the C-124 or C-133 could.'

Nevertheless the report makes clear that the C-141 gave MAC what it had long wanted: a fast cargo aircraft, with a troop-carrying capability. It may not have had the outsize cargo capability of the C-124, but it did cruise at twice the speed and, compared with the other fast aircraft, the 707 and DC-8, it could carry cargo that they could not. Like all designs, it was a compromise, and overall it proved a successful one. Having entered service in 1964, the last examples of the C-141 were not retired until September 2004. This very lengthy operational life was in no small part due to a substantial mid-life modification programme. The process extended the fuselage by adding two plugs, one of 13ft 4in (4.07m) ahead of the wing, the other of 10ft (3.05m) aft of it. It also added in-flight refuelling capability by inserting a boom receptacle in the top of the fuselage aft of the cockpit. These changes were tested on a prototype (designated the YC-141B) in 1977, and over the following five years 270 C-141As were converted into C-141Bs. Some of these aircraft received avionics and cockpit display upgrades, becoming C-141Cs.

The C-141 is also significant in the history of airlifter design for its configuration, which would become the norm for virtually every future large military transport: high mounted swept wings, T-tail, and fuselage-attached main undercarriage. In years to follow the Lockheed C-5, McDonnell Douglas Boeing C-17, Ilyushin IL-76, Kawasaki C-1 and C-2, Embraer KC-390, Xi'an Y-20, and Airbus A400M would all embrace the C-141's basic design features.

Other directions: heavier and faster

Going beyond the requirements foreseen by the Air Force, both Boeing and Douglas explored further directions for air transport development. Boeing looked at the potential for a much heavier type of aircraft, and the Air Force had Boeing and Douglas looking at one that was much faster.

Boeing 820 Long-Range Military Air-Logistics System (LRMALS) studies

In parallel with the increasing Air Force airlifter activity in 1958, Boeing management assigned a new task to its Seattle Division: it was to explore the potential for an air-logistics system capable of transporting large military loads at high speed over great distance. These were to be known as the Long-Range Military Air-Logistics System (LRMALS) studies, with tentative design points set at a payload of 100,000lb (45,359kg) and a range of 4,500nmi (8,330km).

Boeing developed a number of outline configurations under the generic Model 820 designation. They initially centred on relatively conventional turboprop and turbofan aircraft; subsequently the Model 820 studies included flying boat, amphibian, STOL and nuclear-powered aircraft, all using roughly the same fuselage.

Boeing Model 820 LRMALS

	Model 820-101	Model 820-103A
Powerplant	4 x P&W T57 turboprops @ 15,000shp (11,185kW)	8 x P&W JT3D-1 or GE J79-X220 turbofans
Span	200ft (60.96m)	210ft (60.01m)
Length	170ft 6in (51.97m)	170ft 6in (51.97m)
Height	55ft 8in (16.97xm)	55ft 7.8in (16.97m)
Wing area	4,475sq ft (510.97m²)	5,500sq ft (510.97m²)
Design gross weight	500,000lb (226,800kg)	550,000lb (249,480kg)
Payload	100,000lb (45,360kg)	100,000lb (45,360kg)
Cruise speed	403kt (746km/h)	454kt (841km/h)
Maximum range	4,500nmi (8,330km)	4,500nmi (8,330km)

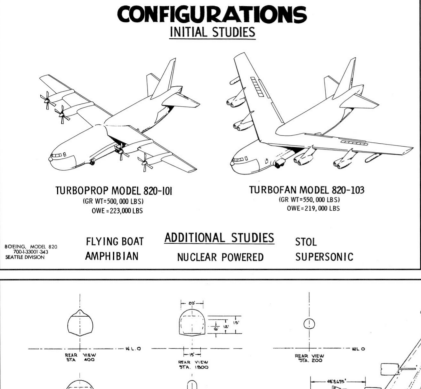

CONFIGURATIONS
INITIAL STUDIES

TURBOPROP MODEL 820-101
(GR WT=500, 000 LBS)
OWE = 223,000 LBS

TURBOFAN MODEL 820-103
(GR WT=550, 000 LBS)
OWE = 219,000 LBS

BOEING, MODEL 820
700-I-33001-343
SEATTLE DIVISION

FLYING BOAT
AMPHIBIAN

ADDITIONAL STUDIES

NUCLEAR POWERED

STOL

SUPERSONIC

The process involved consultations with various Air Force representatives, and progressive refinement of the configurations. This work did not lead to detailed work on any particular proposal, but the studies provided valuable insights into the use of a very wide (20ft or 7.32m) cargo deck and the challenges involved in handling outsize payloads. The studies also identified those approaches that looked unlikely to succeed. Engineers determined, for example, that marrying B-52 wings and empennage to a cargo-optimised fuselage would be a poor match for meeting the requirement. These were perhaps Boeing's first studies looking at aircraft with an unobstructed cargo hold that was 20ft wide by 15ft high (6.1m by 4.6m). This experience would stand the company in good stead in a few short years.

LEFT The two primary Boeing LRMALS concepts shared a nearly common fuselage. *Boeing*

BELOW The Boeing Model 820-106 point design presented an amphibious airlifter. The engine position was ahead and above the wing to avoid water spray ingestion. *Boeing*

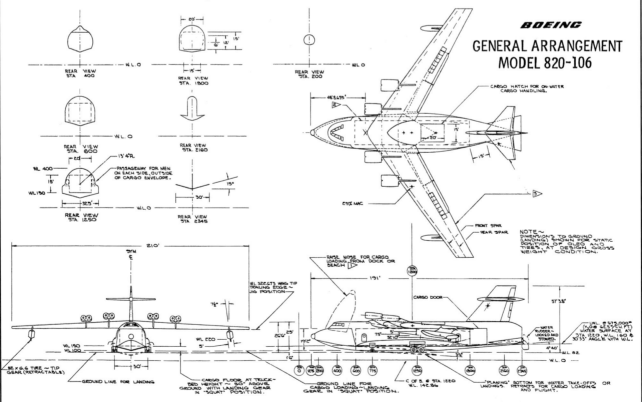

BOEING
GENERAL ARRANGEMENT
MODEL 820-106

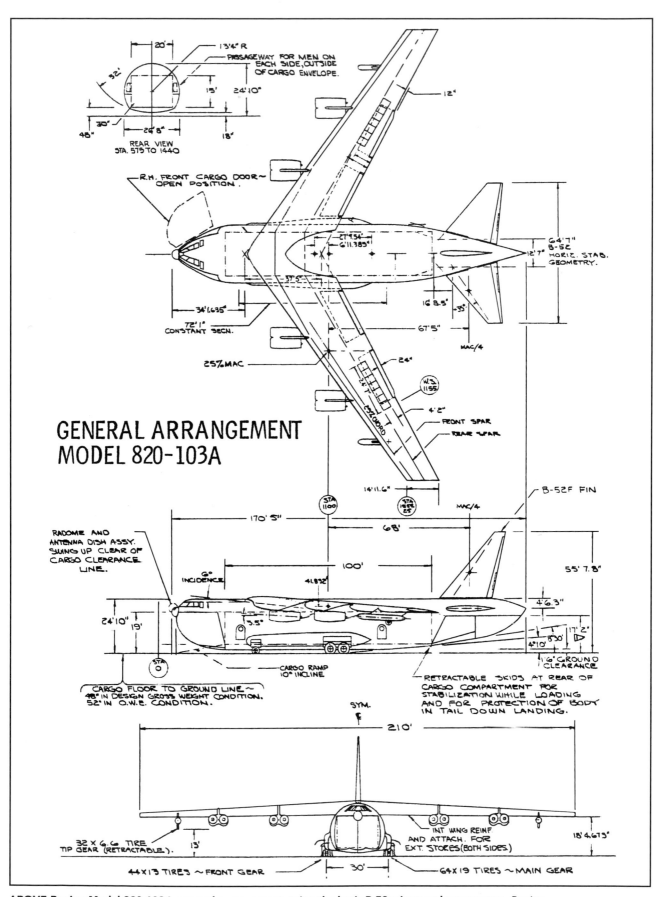

GENERAL ARRANGEMENT MODEL 820-103A

ABOVE Boeing Model 820-103A general arrangement, using the basic B-52 wings and empennage. *Boeing*

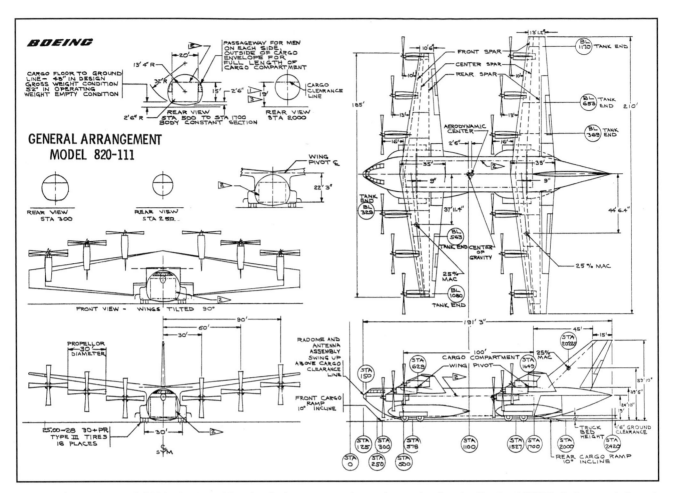

ABOVE The Boeing Model 820-111 LRMALS point design presented a twelve-engined, twin-tilt-wing V/STOL design, again based on the baseline fuselage. *Boeing*

Supersonic cargo transport studies

In early 1959 the Air Force issued a letter outlining a projected need for a supersonic cargo transport, ostensibly to support deployment of the Mach 3 B-70 bomber. Requirements included a range of 3,500 miles (5,630km) with a full payload of 100,000lb (45,360kg).

Boeing Model 820-107 supersonic cargo transport

The Boeing Model 820-107 was a LRMALS study for a supersonic cargo transport. The planform appears to have been conceptually derived and extrapolated from the much smaller Model 818-104/5 two-man V/STOL fighter project. That design had used a large number (twelve) of non-afterburning Pratt & Whitney JT12 engines, housed in four swivelling podded clusters, to give the V/STOL capability. The engine type in the supersonic transport was undefined and, while the engines would rotate, it is unclear whether designers intended a VTOL capability.

Since the airlifter was equipped with centreline bicycle landing gear, it was unable to rotate to a higher angle of attack for take-off or landing (the same limitation as Boeing's B-47 and B-52). The solution was to extend the forward landing gear and partially retract the aft landing gear to position the aircraft at the correct angle.

The design had three cargo bays: forward, between, and aft of the landing gear. The cargo floor for each would lower vertically for loading and unloading.

Boeing Model 820-107 supersonic cargo transport	
Powerplant	16 x unspecified turbojets
Span	148ft 3in (45.19m)
Length	338ft (103.02m)
Height	40ft 5in (12.32m)
Cargo holds:	
Forward	10ft x 10ft x 35ft
	(3.05m x 3.05m x 10.67m)
Middle	10ft x 10ft x 100ft
	(3.05m x 3.05m x 30.48m)
Aft	10ft x 10ft x 35ft
	(3.05m x 5.05m x 10.67m)

Douglas Model 1470 supersonic cargo transport

As well as Boeing, Douglas was also conducting studies to assess the potential uses of a supersonic cargo transport.

In an unpublished memoir, Douglas Long Beach Division design engineer

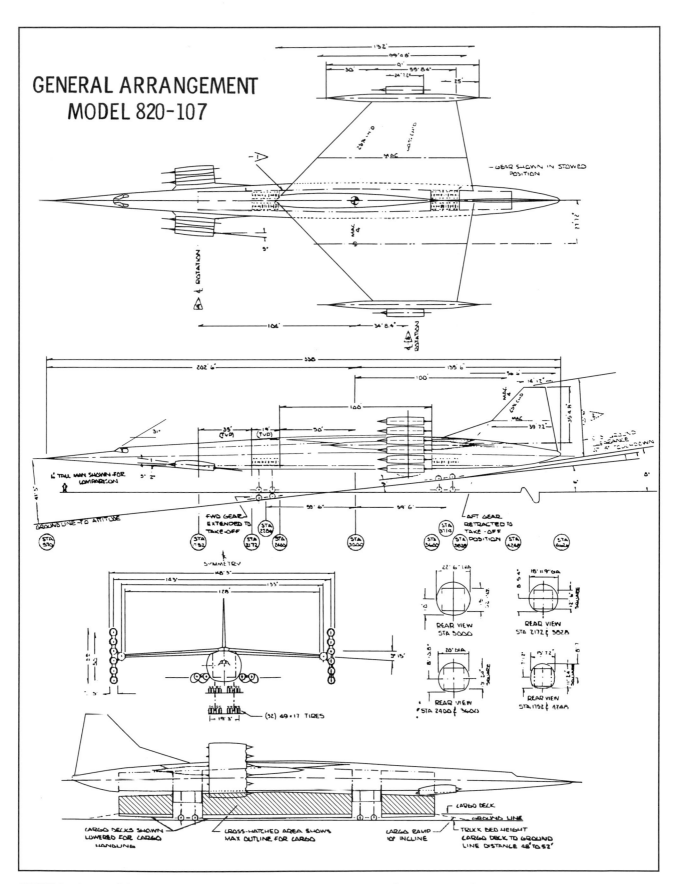

ABOVE Boeing Model 820-107 supersonic cargo transport concept general arrangement. *Boeing*

Richard T. Cathers recalled:

'I was assigned to create imaginatively all possible configurations – no holds barred. This was pure fun – high, mid, low wings; engines forward or aft; low or high horizontal tail. Many wing planforms. I can't recall how many variations I made, but there were many dozen. What I was not aware of was that the men in Santa Monica were doing the same exercise.

'We presented Mr [George] Worley [chief of Preliminary Design, Santa Monica] with the collection of concepts of the USAF Supersonic Cargo plane, consisting of several dozen arrangements. Our reception was one of contempt: "Couldn't you guys make up your mind?" We had taken a broad spectrum approach with an "open mind", whereas Worley had selected two or three concepts, mostly based on the NACA X-3 Supersonic research plane.'

Nonetheless, the preliminary design point study report in March 1959 described an aircraft with a 'cargo box' 10.3ft wide by 10ft high (3.15m by 3.05m) above a very highly swept 73° delta wing, selected for its minimal shift in aerodynamic centre of pressure between sub- and supersonic flight. Trimming was accomplished via an all-moving canard.

The aircraft was to be powered by six scaled Pratt & Whitney STJ-19A non-afterburning turbojets with an alternate Wright SE-105 'dual cycle' engine with turbine blade cooling (both being unfunded 'study' engines at the time). A 'kneeling' landing gear was used to bring the cargo deck height down to about 8.3ft (2.53m) above the ground from the normal height of 18.3ft (5.58m). With a payload of 100,000lb (45,360kg), a maximum take-off weight of 616,620lb (279,950kg) was projected.

Douglas (Long Beach) Model 1470 supersonic cargo transport	
Powerplant	6 x P&W STJ-19A non-afterburning turbojets
Span	82ft 0in (24.99m)
Length	225ft 0in (68.58m)
Height	40ft 5in (12.32m)
Wing area	5,250sq ft (487.74m²)
Take-off gross weight	616,200lb (179,500kg)
Payload	100,00lb (45,360kg)
Cruise speed	Mach 3.0
Maximum range	3500nmi (6480km)

The first purpose-designed jet airlifter in perspective

Despite the very early adoption of high-performance, long-range jet bombers, it was another ten years before the Air Force placed an order for its first purpose-designed jet airlifter, by which time the airlines were already flying long-range jet aircraft around the world. In some ways it could be argued that it was worth the wait, in that the Lockheed C-141 was an aircraft that was tailor-made for its intended mission rather than an adaptation of an aeroplane designed primarily for another purpose. Moreover, although more radical designs had been considered along the way, the configuration of the C-141 would set the pattern for most future military transport designs. It would also serve for forty years.

The process to produce this first jet airlifter had been fiercely contested by all the leading aircraft manufacturers, which resulted in a plethora of impressive

BELOW Douglas Model 1470 supersonic cargo transport general arrangement. *Boeing*

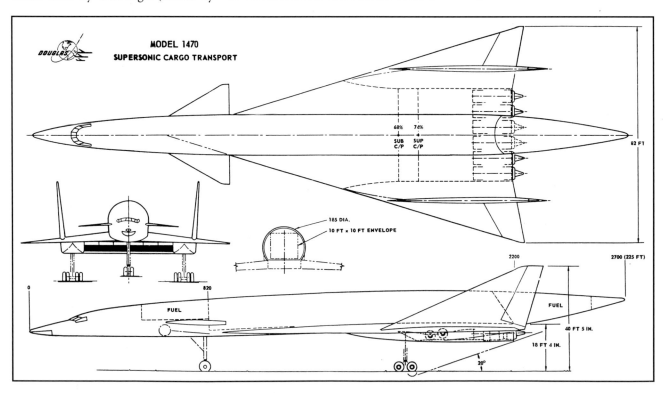

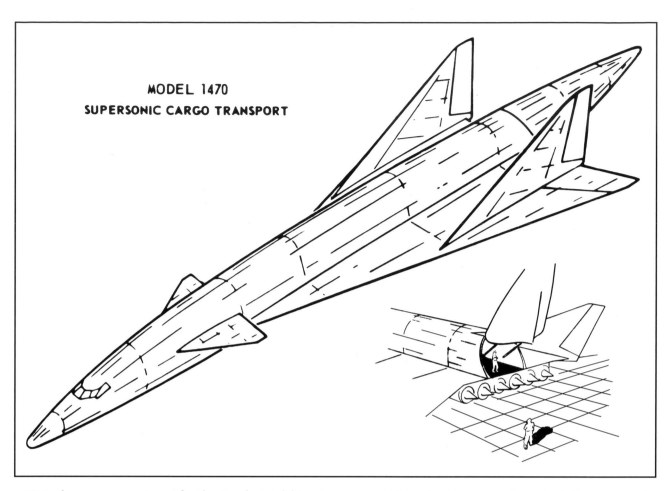

MODEL 1470
SUPERSONIC CARGO TRANSPORT

ABOVE The cargo compartment for the Douglas Model 1470 was accessed through a large upward-opening tailcone. The main landing gear was of the 'kneeling' type, which lowered the cargo deck for loading/unloading access. *Boeing*

designs. Some, like the intriguing proposals for supersonic transports, proved in retrospect to be beyond the realms of feasibility. Others were

BELOW Douglas Model 1470. *Boeing*

undoubtedly viable options for the Air Force. However, the conclusion of the competition to provide the C-141 was far from the end of the road for US airlifter development. New demands and new technology would ensure that there

would be many more competitions over the following decades and many more, imaginative proposals. These are described in the accompanying volume *American Secret Projects 3: Airlifters from 1962 to the present day*.

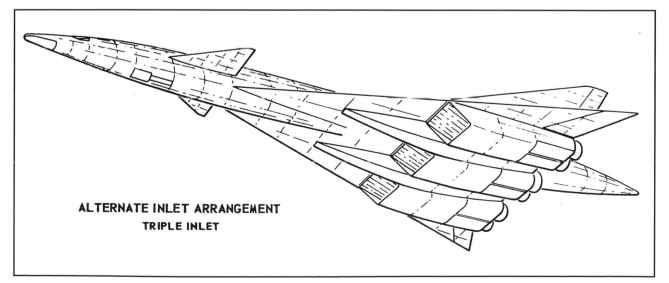

ALTERNATE INLET ARRANGEMENT
TRIPLE INLET

Chapter Nine
New Light Airlifters

1956 to 1961: Attempting to reinvent a concept

ABOVE **The full-size mock-up of the Boeing Model 815 at Wichita.** *Boeing*

Although much of the airlifter effort in the second part of the 1950s had concentrated on large aircraft, there was also a need for an improved small assault transport to deliver soldiers and materiel to unprepared airstrips as close as possible to the front line. Either in response to, or anticipating, this need, several contractors came forward with proposals.

Boeing (Wichita)
Model 815

Boeing Wichita began to explore market opportunities for an Army airlifter in 1956 with what it termed its 'Utility Market Study'. This was followed in 1957 by a 'STOL Utility Study'. Both studies forecast a need for a utility transport in the 3-5-ton payload class (just over 5,000kg) for both military (namely Army) and possibly commercial application. STOL capability, all-weather operation, maximum permissible cargo compartment size, and reliability at low operating cost were all required qualities. Subsequent design studies began in February 1958, focusing primarily on twin-turboprop-powered designs, and Boeing's Model 815 was the outcome.

Its main competition was the de Havilland Canada DHC-4 Caribou, which at this time was already in initial production for the US Army. However, studies had shown that a transport aircraft in this class needed to be able carry the majority of the Army's heavy equipment, and Boeing felt that this capability was beyond that of the Caribou. The Army's 'Military Characteristics' specified a cargo compartment 90in wide, 78in high and 30ft long (2.29m by 1.98m by 9.15m), which was what Boeing used throughout the Model 815 design study.

By July 1958 it was clear that, to interest the military, more was needed than the usual 'paper' engineering studies. Boeing management considered, then authorised a full-scale mock-up in mid-July, and construction began one week later.

It duplicated the look and feel of the actual aeroplane. Propellers were powered and the outer wing panels and vertical tail folded. The only structure left out was the starboard wing. Boeing made *815 Appointment*, a colour movie with sound, and from mid-November 1958 to February 1959 gave demonstrations to the Air Force, Army, Navy, Department of the Interior, and even the Forestry Service.

However, by March 1959 the prime customer's stated position clearly indicated an inability to fund the Model 815's development. Company management also felt that the potential market was insufficiently firm to warrant the investment required. It subsequently terminated the programme, and the mock-up was dismantled in July 1959.

The Model 815 was revisited from March to May 1960 for a study of a 'Super' V/STOL transport, capable of carrying a payload greater than 6,000lb (2,722kg). The Army Study Requirements (ASR) Review Board later issued a report on ASR 3-60 indicating that the service would pursue development of an aeroplane in this size range. However, the Model 815 was destined to go no further.

Boeing (Wichita) Model 815	
Powerplant	4 x Lycoming T55-L-11 @ 2,150shp (kW)
Span	75ft (22.86m)
Length	68.84ft (20.93m)
Height	32.07ft (9.77m)
Wing area	804sq ft (74.69m²)
Normal gross weight	32,000lb (14,510kg)
STOL gross weight	27,700lb (12,570kg)
Normal payload	12,700lb (5,760kg) for 200nmi (370km)
STOL payload	8,150lb (3,700kg) for 200nmi (370km)
Best cruise speed	218kt (404km/h)
Maximum speed	280kt (519km/h)
Maximum range	2,500nmi (4,630km) (with ferry kit)

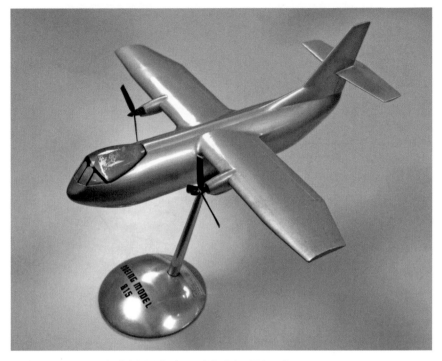

ABOVE A Boeing Model 815 desk model. *John Aldaz photo*
BELOW Boeing Model 815 general arrangement. *Boeing*

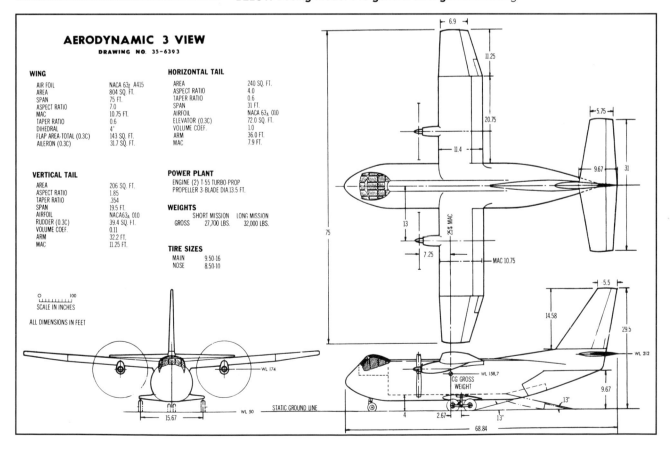

269

ABOVE The Boeing Model 815 is depicted here in many roles, including as a Navy COD with folding wings and tail. *Boeing*

de Havilland (Canada) DHC-4 Caribou

Unfortunately for Boeing, de Havilland Canada had already established itself with the US Army as a supplier of rugged STOL aircraft with single-engine aeroplanes like the U-6 Beaver and U-1 Otter. In 1955 the company decided to develop a much larger, twin-engine STOL design that could function as a tactical transport in forward battle areas. The company designated it the DHC-4, and such was its appeal that the Army ordered five pre-production examples – despite USAF objections – even before the prototype had flown. Named the Caribou, it first flew on 30 July 1958, and the Army received its first example, designated the YAC-1, in October 1959. Despite protests from the USAF that it was more than three times the empty weight limit imposed on Army-operated aircraft under the inter-service Memorandum of Understanding of 1952, a substantial order followed. This left no opportunity for designs like Boeing's Model 815.

Fairchild M-253 and M-253A

Fairchild also explored options for four-engine turboprop versions of the C-123. Studies successively compared engining it with the Rolls-Royce Dart (M-253), Lycoming LTC-4A (M-253A) and General Electric T64 (M-253C). Although these studies spanned six years, none resulted in a production aircraft.

Fairchild first discussed the four-engine option in an internal Operations Analysis report dated 6 March 1957. In

LEFT The prototype de Havilland DHC-4 Caribou has a Canadian civil test registration. *de Havilland Canada*

order to provide an aeroplane with an early delivery date as well as appeal to a wider market, it was to be initially powered by four Rolls-Royce R.Da.6/Mk 511 Darts, as flown on the Fokker F-27 (using the F-27 'Quick Engine Change' [QEC] hardware from the firewall forward). This approach would create a turboprop cargo transport at less cost and earlier availability than any other route. Fairchild predicted that the change would also result in improved short-field performance and better engine-out flight characteristics.

The initial (first-stage) prototype was to be the C-123B with the following changes:

- Wider-tread landing gear (then being flight tested on the YC-123H).
- Horizontal empennage end plates, added for improved directional stability and control.
- Four Rolls-Royce Dart turboprops, replacing the two R-2800 engines.

The follow-up (second-stage) design incorporated the following improvements:

- Elimination of the pylon tank and the nacelle tank by adding internal wing fuel tanks (a wet wing).
- A pressurised cockpit to permit better cruise altitude.
- Introduction of the R.Da.6/Mk 525 engine with higher ratings when available.

By deleting the nacelle and eliminating external fuel tanks, Fairchild expected that the lower drag would improve performance in this second-stage aeroplane. A third-stage version was also suggested, using Lycoming's T55

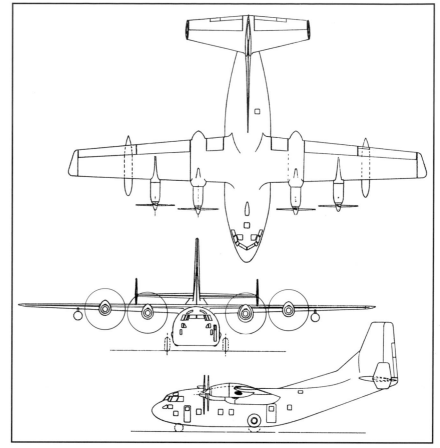

ABOVE The first Fairchild M-253 design used Rolls-Royce Dart engines from the Fairchild/Fokker F-27 light airliner. *Jane and Winfield Arata papers*

power plant when it became available.

Fairchild's Advanced Design group responded on 17 April 1957 with a more detailed report proposing a different prototype approach. Phase I would install four Lycoming T55 (LTC4A-1) engines with minimum airframe changes, and the maximum gross take-off weight would remain at 59,000lb (26,762kg). Phase II would add boundary layer control (BLC) to permit STOL operation; a Bristol BE-49 air compressor mounted in the aft fuselage would supply BLC air

to the flaps. The structure and landing gear would be strengthened to raise the maximum take-off weight to 75,000lb (34,019kg).

Fairchild's President, Richard Boutelle, announced corporate approval on 23 April 1957 for a prototype development programme for the aircraft; he called it the 'Turboboxcar', which would fly in 'mid-1958'. With BLC, the Turboboxcar could operate from both short fields and aircraft carriers.

By 7 June 1957 the project had become more ambitious, resulting in the M-253A. It retained the Lycoming T55 engines but introduced an enlarged (stretched by 30in, or 76.2cm) and pressurised cockpit accommodating a flight engineer and optional navigator.

In a final attempt to solve the aircraft's directional stability issues, Fairchild modified the aft fuselage to more of a 'pod and boom' configuration, moving the tail aft by 30in (76.2cm). Since its first

Fairchild Model M-253	Fairchild M-253	Fairchild M-253A
Powerplant	4 x RR Dart R.Da6 Mk.511 turboprops @ 1,670hp (1,245kW)	4 x Lycoming T55 (LTC4A) turboprops @ 1,600shp (1,193.1kW)
Wingspan	110ft 0in (33.53m)	110ft 0in (33.53m)
Length	76ft 3in (23.24m)	81ft 3in (24.77m)
Height	34ft 1in (10.4m)	35ft 9in (10.9m)
Wing area	1,223.22sq ft (113.6m²)	1,223.22sq ft (113.6m²)
Max TOW	64,000lb (29,030kg)	65,000lb (29,483.5kg)
Payload	16,150lb (7,300kg)	n/a
Cruise speed	239kt (443km/h)	n/a
Range	1,200nmi (2,222km)	1,500nmi (2,778.0km)

ABOVE This illustration, based on a retouched photo of a C-123, depicts the Fairchild M-253A with the Lycoming T55 engines, modified aft fuselage and wide-track main landing gear. *Fairchild*

BELOW Fairchild M-253A general arrangement. *Fairchild*

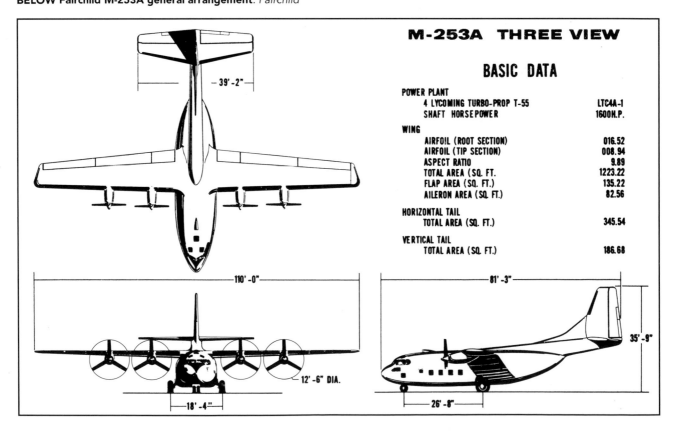

M-253A THREE VIEW

BASIC DATA

POWER PLANT

4 LYCOMING TURBO-PROP T-55	LTC4A-1
SHAFT HORSEPOWER	1600H.P.

WING

AIRFOIL (ROOT SECTION)	016.52
AIRFOIL (TIP SECTION)	008.94
ASPECT RATIO	9.89
TOTAL AREA (SQ. FT.)	1223.22
FLAP AREA (SQ. FT.)	135.22
AILERON AREA (SQ. FT.)	82.56

HORIZONTAL TAIL

TOTAL AREA (SQ. FT.)	345.54

VERTICAL TAIL

TOTAL AREA (SQ. FT.)	186.68

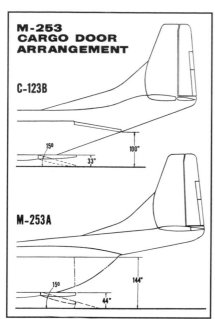

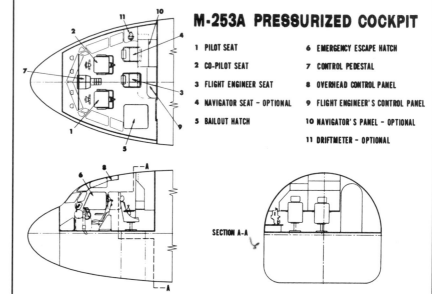

ABOVE Cargo door and aft fuselage differences between the production Fairchild C-123B and the M-253A. *Fairchild*

ABOVE The Fairchild M-253A borrowed the enlarged, pressurised cockpit first designed for the M-231. The original Chase XCG-20 glider had no need for a flight engineer or navigator, and there was no room added for them in the C-123 cockpit. *Fairchild*

flight, the C-123 had encountered issues caused by the broad aft fuselage blanking the airflow to the vertical tail at high angles of attack. Adding a very large dorsal strake significantly improved handling. However, additional stability requirements created by the outboard engines had to be countered by adding greater aft vertical surfaces.

This could be done by introducing a 'Pi Tail' to increase the size of the vertical stabiliser, or by adding endplates to the horizontal stabilisers (as in the initial first-stage prototype described above). Reconfiguring the aft fuselage offered the additional benefit of incorporating a revised rear cargo door that allowed better access for truck-height loading as well as a significant drag reduction.

In retrospect, Fairchild was clearly working to position the Turboboxcar as a credible competitor to the Douglas Models 1906 and 1940, then being aggressively promoted to the Air Force, Marine Corps and Navy. None of these projects came to fruition and the Turboboxcar faded away, only to be resurrected in 1962 with another change of engines as the M-253C. No data for the (presumed) M-253B is available.

Fairchild Military F-27 (Models M-258G, J and K)

Fairchild submitted an unsolicited proposal to the Army via two letters dated 29 April and 10 May 1960, in which the company presented the 'F-27 Military Transport Configuration'. This offering outlined four different versions of the basic aircraft, designated as the M-258G, M-258H, M-258J and M-258K.

The original F-27 aircraft had been designed by Fokker in the Netherlands and produced as a medium-range commercial transport. It was licensed for production to Fairchild for sales in the US. Construction had supplanted that of the C-123 in the Hagerstown factory and the F-27 was successfully marketed to several feeder airlines. The fundamental concept of the basic aircraft, for which there would be four versions, was a twin-turboprop, high-wing, medium transport layout with

limited STOL capabilities.

At the time the Army had only one aircraft relatively comparable to the M-258, the de Havilland Caribou. It evaluated both aeroplanes and concluded that the basic M-258 was not a true STOL aircraft. However, the Rolls-Royce RDa7 Dart-powered M-258G and H had slightly better STOL characteristics than the Caribou, with the General Electric T64-powered M-258K being the absolute best. The Models M-258J and K additionally incorporated a revised aft fuselage with side-opening clamshell doors and a powered ramp under a raised tail.

However, the Caribou was in full production for the Army and the Fairchild proposal was rejected. Eventually 159 Caribous were purchased and saw service into the 1980s.

Fairchild Military F-27	Model 258G	Model 258K
Powerplant	2 x RR Dart RDa.7 Mk 528 turboprops @ 2,015eshp (1,503kW)	2 x GE T64-GE-4 turboprops @ 2,850shp (2,130kW)
Span	95ft 2in (29.01m)	95ft 2in (29.01m)
Length	77ft 2in (23.52m)	77ft 2in (23.52m)
Height	27ft 6in (8.38m)	29ft 2in (8.89m)

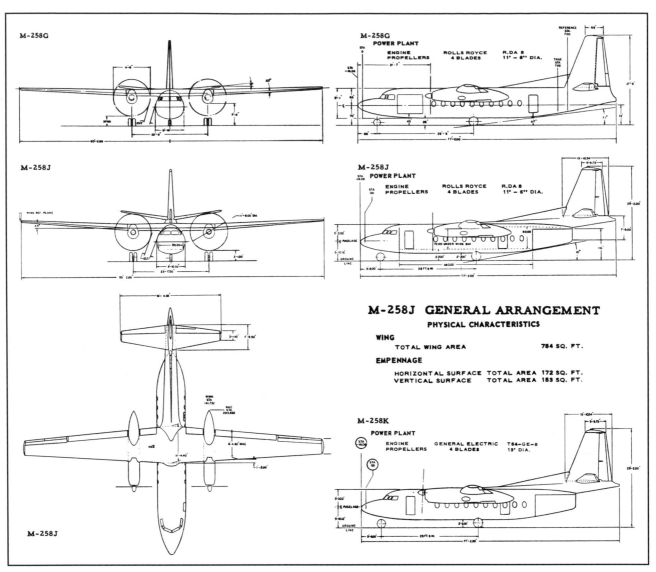

M-258J GENERAL ARRANGEMENT

PHYSICAL CHARACTERISTICS

WING

TOTAL WING AREA	784 SQ. FT.

EMPENNAGE

HORIZONTAL SURFACE TOTAL AREA	172 SQ. FT.
VERTICAL SURFACE TOTAL AREA	153 SQ. FT.

ABOVE Fairchild M-258J general arrangement, with side views of the M-258G (top right) and M-258K (bottom right). *NASM*

LEFT A model of the Fairchild M-258G displays the revised aft fuselage with loading ramp and new double-slotted flaps. *Fairchild*

Two other designs of this period (but not part of this competition) were the Fairchild M-268C and the Martin Model 371 airlifters, both presumably aimed at the Army.

The M-268C was a STOL transport with a wing of limited tilt capability. It had two other unique features, the pitch control system and the high-floatation (Hi-Flo) tyres. The M-268C had used two Allison YT63 turboshaft engines driving pitch fans buried in the

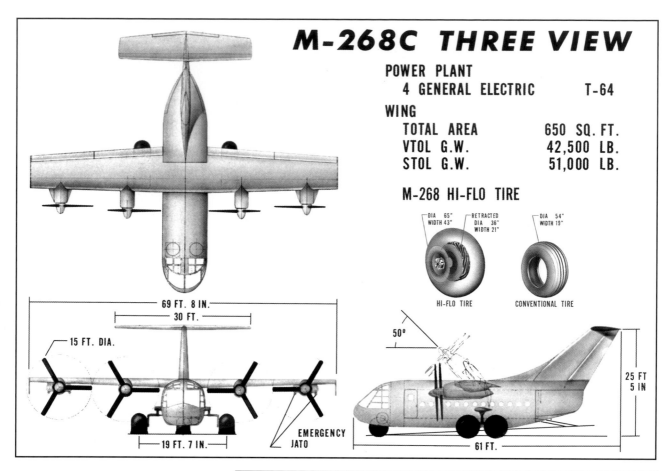

M-268C THREE VIEW

POWER PLANT
4 GENERAL ELECTRIC   T-64

WING
TOTAL AREA	650 SQ. FT.
VTOL G.W.	42,500 LB.
STOL G.W.	51,000 LB.

M-268 HI-FLO TIRE

DIA 65" WIDTH 43"   RETRACTED DIA 36" WIDTH 21"

HI-FLO TIRE

DIA 54" WIDTH 19"

CONVENTIONAL TIRE

69 FT. 8 IN.

30 FT.

15 FT. DIA.

19 FT. 7 IN.

EMERGENCY JATO

50°

25 FT 5 IN

61 FT.

ABOVE Fairchild M-268C general arrangement. *Fairchild*

RIGHT Fairchild Model M-268C inboard profile. *Fairchild*

Fairchild Model M-268C	
Powerplant	4 x GE T64 turboshafts @ 2,810shp (2,095kW) 2 x Allison YT63-A-3 turboshafts @ 250shp (186kW)
Span	69ft 8in (21.23m)
Length	61ft (18.59m)
Height	25ft (7.62m)
Wing area	650sq ft (60.39m²)
VTOL gross weight	42,500lb (19,280kg)
STOL gross weight	51,000lb (23,130kg)

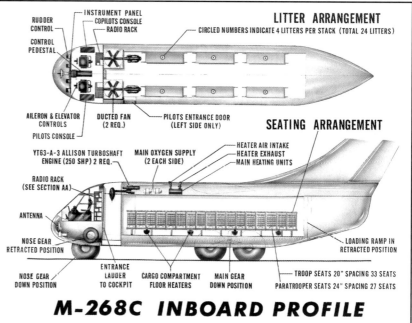

LITTER ARRANGEMENT
CIRCLED NUMBERS INDICATE 4 LITTERS PER STACK (TOTAL 24 LITTERS)

RUDDER CONTROL
INSTRUMENT PANEL
COPILOTS CONSOLE
RADIO RACK
CONTROL PEDESTAL
AILERON & ELEVATOR CONTROLS
DUCTED FAN (2 REQ.)
PILOTS CONSOLE
PILOTS ENTRANCE DOOR (LEFT SIDE ONLY)

SEATING ARRANGEMENT

YT63-A-3 ALLISON TURBOSHAFT ENGINE (250 SHP) 2 REQ.
MAIN OXYGEN SUPPLY (2 EACH SIDE)
HEATER AIR INTAKE
HEATER EXHAUST
MAIN HEATING UNITS
RADIO RACK (SEE SECTION AA)
ANTENNA
NOSE GEAR RETRACTED POSITION
LOADING RAMP IN RETRACTED POSITION
NOSE GEAR DOWN POSITION
ENTRANCE LADDER TO COCKPIT
CARGO COMPARTMENT FLOOR HEATERS
MAIN GEAR DOWN POSITION
TROOP SEATS 20" SPACING 33 SEATS
PARATROOPER SEATS 24" SPACING 27 SEATS

M-268C INBOARD PROFILE

forward fuselage. Because they were positioned forward of the CG, the fans provided positive lift that counteracted the nose-down pitch caused when the wing tilted. Unfortunately, the drawbacks of this approach included taking up valuable cargo space as well as lengthening the fuselage, which increased weight.

The Hi-Flo tyres were another unique feature. Almost comically oversized when inflated, they enabled operation on ground surfaces that otherwise afforded very poor load-bearing capability. When deflated in flight, the tyres would collapse to a small percentage of their former volume.

Less is known about the proposed Martin Model 371 light airlifter, designed for the Army in the late

ABOVE This model of the Martin Model 371 displays the clamshell opening in the aft fuselage and the swing-open cockpit module. *John Aldaz photo*

BELOW A model of the Martin M-371. *John Aldaz photo*

ABOVE The prototype de Havilland DHC-5 Buffalo STOL airlifter in US Army markings. *de Havilland Canada*

1950s. It featured a highly accessible drive-through fuselage, with front and rear loading facilitated by means of a swing-aside cockpit and aft clamshell doors respectively. The two turbine powerplants could possibly have been General Electric T64s.

Army STOL airlifters: Round Two

With the AC-1 Caribou in production, de Havilland (with Army support) investigated improvements. The first priority was an engine upgrade, replacing the piston powerplants with General Electric T64 turboshaft engines in 1961. The successor aircraft continued to evolve and was later designated the DHC-5 by the manufacturer.

However, DoD thwarted the Army's initial plan to award a sole-source (non-competitive) contract for the DHC-5 (as it had for the DHC 4). Acting in response to protests by the US industry and Congress, the Army then announced a design competition, with the RFQ being issued in the third week of April 1962. With responses due in thirty days, there was no time for the contractors to create a completely new design. Those responding were Alfred E. Bloomquist & Associates, de Havilland Canada, Fairchild, McDonnell/Breguet, and Vought/Ryan/Hiller.

de Havilland DHC-5 Buffalo

Not surprisingly, the Army selected the DHC-5 'Caribou 2' as the winner of the competition (initially designated the AC-2, later redesignated the C-8A Buffalo) and awarded de Havilland a $7 million development contract for four initial aircraft. Total development cost was estimated at $21 million; the Canadian Government shared the cost as it was interested in the design (and would eventually order fifteen aircraft). However, the US never purchased additional Buffalos. The Air Force had successfully challenged the legitimacy of the Army purchase based on a 'roles and missions' argument. This argument continued into 1967, when the Army was forced to transfer its Caribou fleet to the Air Force in accordance with the Johnson-McConnell agreement of 1966.

Fairchild M-258/F-27 and M-253C/C-123 proposals

Fairchild (now renamed Fairchild Stratos) initially planned to respond to the Army's design competition by resubmitting the M-258 version of the F-27. But after examining the Army's requirements in detail, the company realised that the M-258's compartment size would disqualify it. Since a redesign of the fuselage was impossible in the time remaining (and in any case, would significantly increase the cost), Fairchild turned to the M-253C, which was derived from the four-turboprop C-123/M-258 family dating back to 1957.

The modified C-123 was to have four of the Army-favoured T64-GE-8 engines, auxiliary outboard vertical tail surfaces, a trimmable stabiliser, revised fuel system, and dual-wheel landing gear with larger wheels and tyres better suited to soft-field operations (similar to those of the YC-134). However, it not have the resculpted aft fuselage of the original M-253A.

Other losing competitors included Albert E. Bloomquist & Associates of New Jersey, offering a Burnelli design

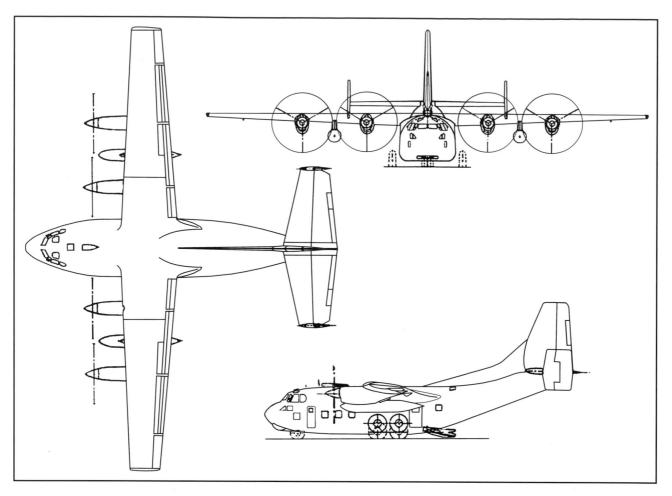

ABOVE The Fairchild M-253C for the Army. *Fairchild*

described as an 'all wing STOL aircraft'. McDonnell teamed with Breguet to offer Breguet's Model 941 STOL transport, while the Vought/Ryan/Hiller team submitted an XC-142A design variant that limited the tilt-wing travel to eliminate VTOL capability but still provided STOL performance.

One of the four Buffalo airframes built for the Army had the unique distinction of being owned and operated by three services (Army, Air Force and Navy) in turn before being retired in the late 1980s. Two other airframes went to NASA for modification into STOL technology test beds. One had two Rolls-Royce Spey low-bypass turbofan engines as the Augmenter Wing test bed, and the other incorporated four Lycoming ALF-502 high-bypass turbofans to become the Quiet Short-haul Research Aircraft (QSRA).

Douglas assault transport proposals of the late 1950s

While the various companies were preparing these Army assault transport proposals, Douglas was developing a range of somewhat more capable assault transports, which would become Models 1906, 1940 and 2042.

In October 1955 the Santa Monica Division of Douglas began a series of conceptual studies for a light assault transport, powered by a new generation of small turboshaft engines then in early development. The high-wing transports aimed at the dual roles of Carrier On-Board Delivery (COD) and land-based assaults, and the Air Force, Army, Marines and Navy were all potential customers.

The initial study version of the Model 1906 was a high-wing nose-loader. An STOL version with a tilt wing (limited to about 40° of travel) followed, powered by two sets of coupled turboshaft engines. The third variation, featuring a tail ramp, was selected for further development.

Engineering studies proceeded through the spring of 1956, and Douglas initiated a marketing campaign for the airlifter. The Model 1096A was offered as a Navy COD and Marine assault version, and the 1906C as an Airborne Early Warning variant.

Although less emphasis was placed on the Air Force, which had just begun receiving brand-new C-123s from Fairchild, Douglas did propose the Model 1906B to the USAF Far East Air Force (FEAF) in February 1957. The company suggested that, 'The minimal airport requirements of the Model 1906 enable the integration of air transport into the Air Force logistic system to a degree not previously

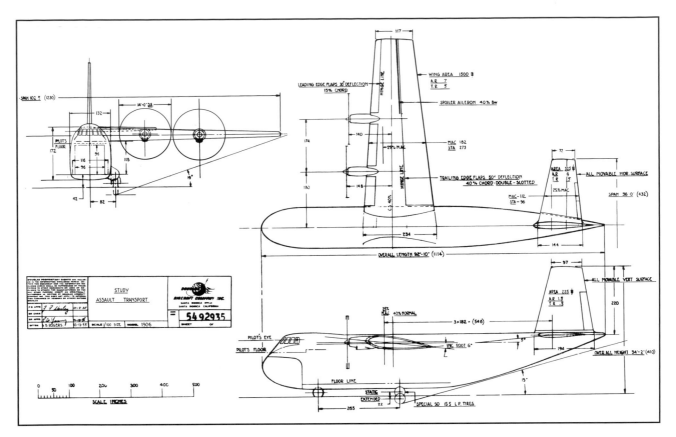

ABOVE This October 1955 study is for the Douglas Model 1906 as a nose-loading assault transport. *Boeing*

BELOW Drawn on 18 January 1956, this Model 1906 study depicts a relatively conventional tail-loader. *Boeing*

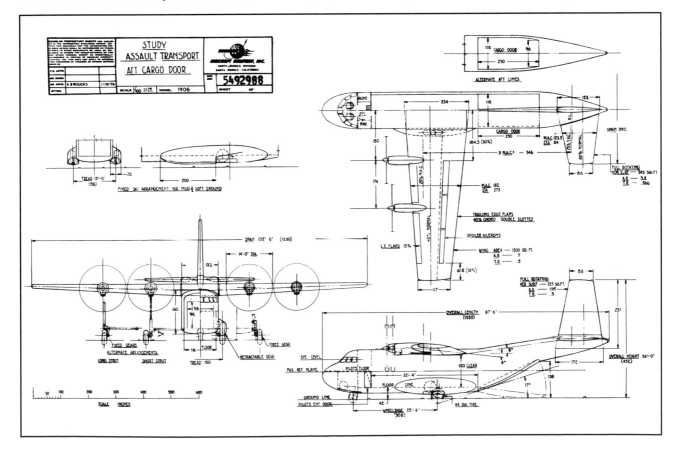

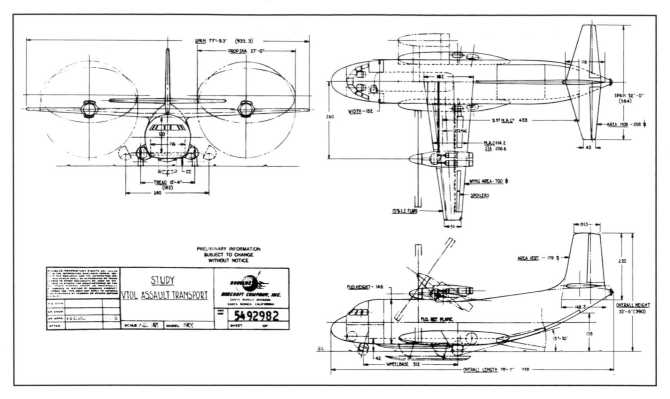

ABOVE This Douglas study drawing shows the Model 1906 as a tilt-wing transport. It was equipped with a large centreline ski and dual stabilising floats that would slide out from the fuselage. *Boeing*

possible. Now a true "door-to-door" aerial delivery system is possible, suggesting decentralised supply areas with numerous small airstrips to reduce vulnerability in atomic warfare.'

The first submission for any of the aircraft was the Model 1906B, and by May 1958 the family had been expanded and comprised the variants listed in the accompanying table..

All the assault versions were able to operate from grass airstrips, and all the COD variants were carrier-compatible. Of note, other than the Allison T56 all

the specified powerplants remained under development with no production engine yet available. However, Douglas stressed the low-risk approach of the basic design of the aircraft, stating that it was 'well within the state of the art and makes maximum use of components which are either in use or under development.'

The family of aircraft featured a common wing design utilising a full-span double-slotted trailing edge flap supplemented by a full-span leading edge flap. Roll control was accomplished via spoilers on the wing rather than ailerons.

The 1906A was also pitched to the Marine Corps as a carrier-compatible assault transport, as described in *American Secret Projects 3*. Douglas further proposed an AEW (Airborne Early Warning) variant for the Navy, designated as the Model 1906C-1. The company had certainly maximised all sales opportunities offered by the design's flexibility.

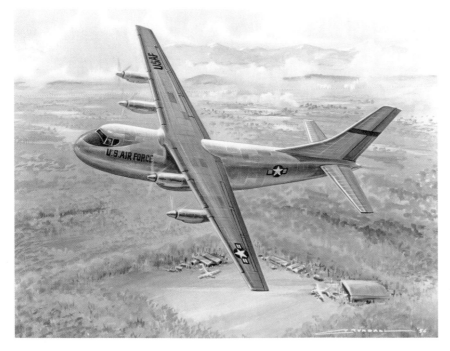

LEFT The Douglas Model 1906B as proposed to the Air Force. *Boeing*

Douglas light transports, 1956-59

Model No	Mission	Powerplant
1906		
1906A	Navy COD, ASW	4 x Lycoming T55
1906B-1	Assault	4 x Lycoming T55
1906B-2	Assault, COD	4 x Lycoming T53
1906B-3	Assault, COD	2 x Allison T56
1906C	AEW/CIC	4 x Lycoming T55
1940		
1940	Civil airline	4 x Lycoming LTC-4A
1940A	Short/Medium Range Utility Transport	4 x Lycoming LTC-4A
2007		
2007-1A	Assault, COD	4 x Lycoming T53
2007-2A	Assault, COD	2 x GE T64
2042		
2042	Assault	4 x Lycoming T53
2042A	COD	4 x Lycoming T55 or 4 x GE T64

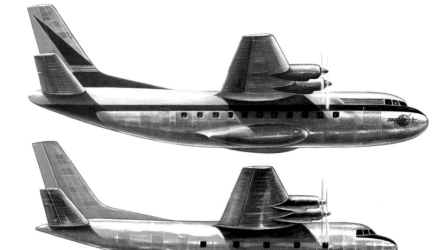

While Douglas was defining the Model 1906, it was also developing the stretched Model 1940 as a sixty-passenger commercial DC-3 replacement. The base model was stretched by 80in (2.03m), while the Model 1940A retained the 1906's length (without radome) and was positioned as a commercial/military cargo transport. Douglas was unsuccessful in selling the Model 1940 family, possibly having been beaten to the market by Fairchild, with its production licence for the Fokker F-27.

The last variation was the Model 2042/2042A, which appeared to have been a rebranded twin-engine Model 1906B-3; Douglas introduced it in October 1958, with promotions aimed at the Army, Navy and Marine Corps. The campaign was again unsuccessful, as was Fairchild's effort to sell additional, improved C-123s.

LEFT The Douglas Model 1940 derivative was marketed as a civil feederliner (above), and the shortened 1940A (below) as a civil/military cargo transport. *Boeing*

BELOW As seen in this Douglas cutaway model of the Model 1906B, the ramp was placed unusually far forward in the cargo deck. *John Aldaz collection*

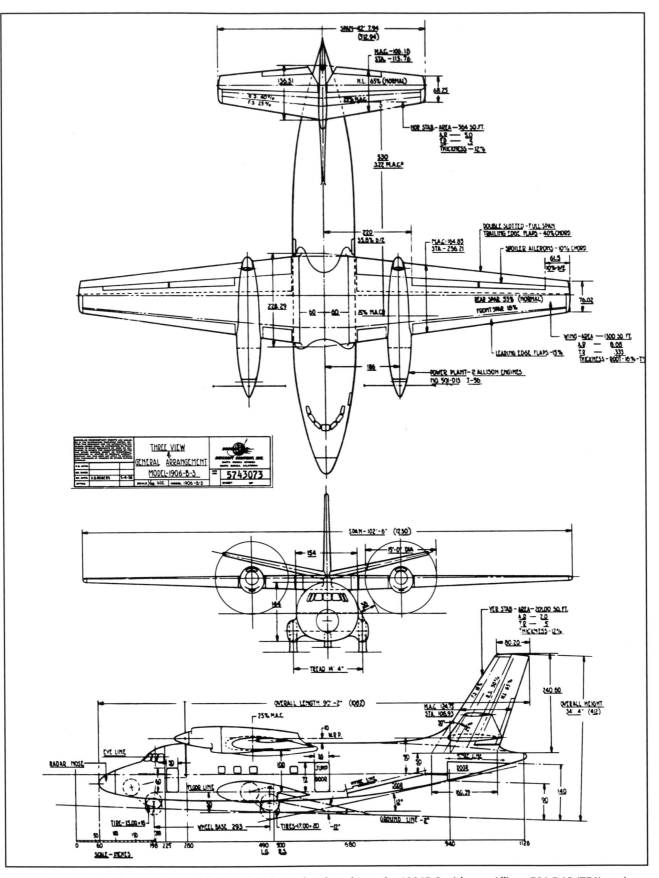

ABOVE By May 1958 the Douglas Model 1906B had been developed into the 1906B-3 with two Allison 501-D13 (T56) engines.
Boeing

Douglas light transports, 1956-59

Douglas Model 2042 and 2042A	Model 2042	Model 2042A
Powerplant	4 x Lycoming T53 turboprops @ 960hp (715kW)	4 x Lycoming T55 or GE T64 turboprops
Span	79ft 4in (24.18m)	n/a
Length	86ft 2in (26.28m)	86ft 2in (26.28m)
Height	30ft 8in (9.35m)	30ft 8in (9.35m)
Wing area	1,050sq ft (97.55m²)	1,300sq ft (120.77m²)
Max TOW	48,200lb (21,860kg)	55,560lb (25,200kg)
Payload	6,000lb (2,720kg)	8,000lb (3,630kg)
(unprepared strip)	(unprepared strip)	
10,000lb (4,540kg)	18,000lb (8,170kg)	
(hard surface)	(hard surface)	
Average cruise speed	234kt (433km/h)	291kt (539km/h)
Assault radius	250nmi (463km)	250nmi (463km)
COD range	1,500nmi (2,780km)	2,200nmi (4,070km)

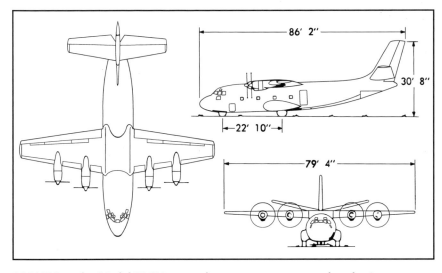

ABOVE Douglas Model 2042A general arrangement, proposed to the Army as an assault transport in 1958 and to the Navy as a COD. *Boeing*

BELOW A comparison of Models 1906 and 2042 for size and cargo loading/capacity. *Boeing*

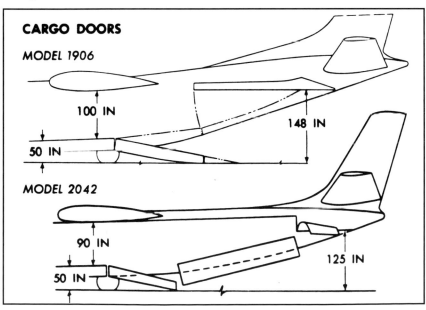

Douglas STOL proposals

In the late 1950s/early 1960s Douglas extensively researched STOL airlifters and submitted a number of proposals, although none of them made it to prototype stage. However, they would prove to be steps that led eventually to the C-17 some thirty years later, as fully detailed in *American Secret Projects 3*.

Douglas Model 2217

In October 1962 Douglas initiated a company-funded study of an airlifter with a 10-ton (10,160kg) payload, initially called 'Studies for a C-123 Replacement'. Six months later, after consulting the Army and Air Force for their likely requirements, the company began to design an aircraft that could meet those needs. The outcome was the Model 2217. After discussing the design with the Air Force, Douglas refined it into the Model 2217A.

Douglas opted for two turbofans, judging that the increased fuel penalty was more than offset by the arrangement's simplicity. It chose a configuration that was becoming the accepted norm for airlifters: high-mounted wings with underslung podded engines, an upswept rear fuselage, and a T-tail. The only unusual feature of its design was the low aspect ratio of its high-lift wings. Both engines employed thrust deflection, with paired exhaust nozzles that could rotate through 120°. The nozzles were kept in the horizontal position at the start of the take-off roll, then deflected partially downwards at the point of lift-off. They could also be deflected by 45° for paratroop dropping at the very slow airspeed of 80kt (148km/h). Power-on stall was a remarkably low 53.5kt (99km/h).

During this period, companies worldwide were studying lightweight lift engines to add V/STOL performance to their aircraft, and Douglas did likewise for the Model 2217. The company ran comparative studies using banks of Rolls-Royce RB-162 lift engines, both inboard and outboard of the propulsion engines. Engineers concluded that the additional

ABOVE The Douglas Model 2217, powered by two Pratt & Whitney TF33 (JT3D-8B) engines. *Boeing*

RIGHT A detailed view of the bifurcated deflected thrust arrangement. *Boeing*

BELOW Douglas Model 2217 general arrangement. *Boeing*

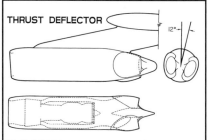

THRUST DEFLECTOR

12°

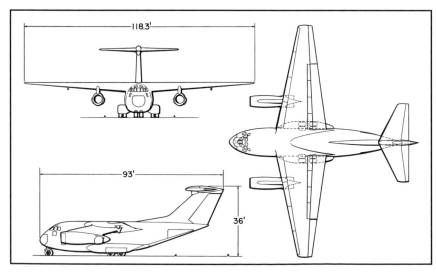

Douglas Model 2217	
Powerplant	2 x P&W TF33-P-7 turbofans @ 21,000lb (93.41kN) thrust
Span	118.3ft (36.06m)
Length	93ft (25.35m)
Height	36ft (10.98m)
Wing area	2,000sq ft (185.81m²)
Combat weight	96,000lb (43,550kg)
Design gross weight	130,000lb (58,970kg)
Payload	20,000lb (9,070kg)
Cruise speed	375kt (695km/h)
Maximum speed	400kt (741km/h)
Maximum range	2,300nmi (4,260km)

ABOVE A wind tunnel model of the Douglas Model 2217. *Boeing*
BELOW The VTOL version of the Douglas Model 2217. *Boeing*

cost and complexity, together with the negative impact on performance in areas such as initial climb rate, compared unfavourably with the proposed deflected thrust STOL arrangement.

Douglas Model 2252

Despite the earlier rejection of using turboprops to power the Model 2217, Douglas proceeded to develop a new aircraft, designated the Model 2252, based on the earlier design and powered by four General Electric T64 turboprop engines. In doing so, it did not carry out a comparative evaluation of the two, but just simply offered the new design as a further option.

Douglas Model 2252	
Powerplant	4 x GE T64-GE-6 turboprops @ 2,850shp (2,125kW)
Span	118.3ft (30.06m)
Length	93.4 ft (28.47m)
Height	35.8ft (10.91m)
Wing area	2,000sq ft (185.81m²)
Combat weight	86,000lb (39,000kg)
Design gross weight	119,000lb (53,980kg)
Payload	25,000lb (11,340kg)
Cruise speed	250kt (463km/h)
Maximum speed	260kt (782km/h)
Maximum range	2,900nmi (5,370km)

The Model 2252 was designed for the same basic mission as the Model 2217 and had a similar configuration. The wing had a slightly different planform, but still had a low aspect ratio. The cargo bay incorporated the same 9ft by 10ft (2.74m by 3.05m) cross section, allowing it to carry cargo of the same size as the C-130 and C-141.

The Model 2252 would use the same General Electric T64-GE-6 engines, gearbox, propellers and cross-shafting

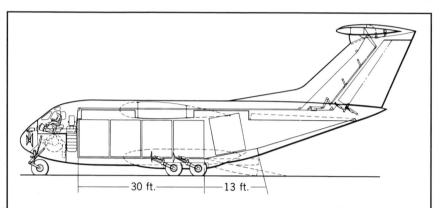

FUSELAGE COMPARTMENT COMPARISON

AIRPLANE	MAIN COMPARTMENT					RAMP				
	HEIGHT (FT.)	WIDTH (FT.)	LENGTH (FT.)	VOLUME (CU.FT.)	FLOOR AREA (SQ.FT.)	LENGTH (FT.)	VOLUME (CU.FT.)	FLOOR AREA (SQ.FT.)	TOTAL VOLUME (CU.FT.)	TOTAL FLOOR AREA (SQ.FT.)
C-123	–	–	–	–	–	8.3	–	–	3570	450
C-130	9	10	41	3690	410	11	420	110	4160	520
C-141	9	10	70	6300	700	12.5	800	150	7100	850
Model 2252	9	10	30	2700	300	13	550	100	3250	400

ABOVE Douglas Model 2252 inboard profile and cargo compartment comparison. *Boeing*

BELOW Douglas Model 2252 general arrangement. *Boeing*

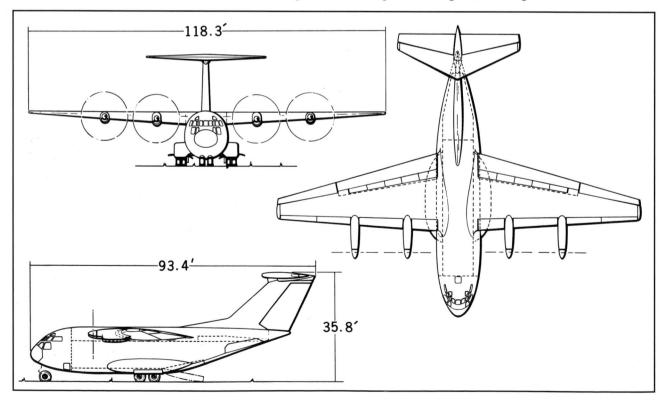

ABOVE This 'tail-off' model of the Douglas Model 2252 in the United Aircraft Research Laboratories wind tunnel shows the deployed leading edge slats and double slotted flaps. *Boeing*

BELOW The 'Super STOL' version of the Douglas Model 2252 with lift-jet engines in the wingtip pods. *Boeing*

used in the C-142. This enabled the same propulsion system to be used on both the 8,000lb (1,810kg)-payload (V/STOL) aircraft and the 20,000-24,000lb (9,070-10,890kg) STOL aircraft, clearly reflecting an expectation that the C-142 was likely to succeed and enter service.

Capitalising on the earlier work with the Model 2217, Douglas also looked at boosting performance by adding banks of lift engines to the wings.

Douglas R-VTOL

The last known Douglas V/STOL project of the early 1960s was documented in a proposal for a Douglas/Army/NASA research programme for the R (rocket) VTOL. The proposal outlined a test bed based on the Beech L-23 Twin Bonanza.

The company further sketched out the design of an Army transport application with a payload of 10,000lb (4,540kg), together with a proposed feasibility test programme utilising a throttleable Rocketdyne LR105 liquid fuel rocket engine (the Atlas sustainer engine), rated at 57,000lb (253.55kN) thrust. This engine used liquid oxygen and JP-1 kerosene, but Douglas stated that the ultimate goal was to develop an 'Air Turbo Rocket' having a specific impulse of approximately 2,500, which was much higher that the LR105's sea-level value of 220. Because air would replace liquid oxygen as the oxidiser in such an engine, the design would also reduce propellant requirements.

ABOVE An artist's impression of a notional Douglas R-VTOL transport in the 30,000lb (13,608kg) weight class. The fully developed 'Air Turbo Rocket' R-VTOL offered a 50% payload increase over current V/STOL aircraft designs by radically decreasing the powerplant weight. *Boeing*

While the concept found no favour at the time, it resurfaced in 1980 with solid fuel rocket motors grafted onto a C-130 for SSTOL (Super-STOL) performance.

The C-123 replacement – a market window that never opened

The opportunity for the type of assault aircraft described above seemed clear. C-123 production was ending in

1957-58, and Fairchild doggedly tried to upgrade the aircraft from its humble beginnings. The C-123's detractors pointed out that its antiquated design was more than ten years old and it was underpowered, with significant flaws including poor directional stability. Nonetheless, the C-123s were proving perfectly serviceable (and would remain so for decades).

Douglas (and others) worked hard to fill the impending void, only to discover that the void did not exist. Perhaps this was because the military expected the next generation of assault transports to have VTOL capability, but that technology was not yet ready. The Douglas light airlifters probably would have been good, solid STOL performers, had that been what the customer was seeking. However, the work was not entirely wasted. The experience can be seen carried through in the early Douglas/MDC ATT (1968) studies and the subsequent MST and AMST proposals of the 1970s.

BELOW The proposed R-VTOL test bed is depicted in STOL mode. Rocket nozzles would swivel aft for acceleration and forward for deceleration. *Boeing*

Conclusion

1941 to 1961: American airlifter development in perspective

Unlike many other aspects of aviation, military air transport is not something that progressively evolved from the First World War onwards. While interceptors, bombers, attack and reconnaissance aircraft were continuously developed in the period between the two World Wars, little attention was paid to the potential of the aeroplane for flying troops and their equipment. Nor was there perceived to be any pressing need to do so; the railroad, the truck and the troopship could amply meet every known requirement. Aeroplanes were limited in what they could carry; they were expensive; and they needed specially-prepared airfields. The only advantage they offered was speed, and there appeared to be no real need this. Civil aviation had certainly progressed but this was primarily aimed at flying small numbers of passengers in a high degree of comfort or transporting high-value items, such as mail. The Army Air Force had a number of small aircraft scattered around its bases for similar purposes, but there was no over-arching transport command. Accordingly at the time of the outbreak of the Second World War, there were no aircraft available which had been designed for the task of military transportation.

Time did not allow for the design, development and production of specialised aircraft, although as described in this book several innovative proposals were put forward. Fortunately, the immediate requirement could be met by adapting aircraft which had been designed for the civil market. While not intended for military use, they were aircraft which represented the peak of aeronautical engineering for their time. They were impressed into service, produced in huge members, and did an outstanding job. Their capability was further extended by taking advantage of new engines and of parallel advances in bomber structures and aerodynamics.

Meantime, two distinctive categories of military transport emerged. One was for the strategic supply of bases around the world; the other was at the tactical level, supporting assault forces. These two complementary requirements would provide the framework for the scores of competing designs over the following years.

The immediate period following the Second World War, saw an understandable cut-back in military expenditure. Moreover, the funds available for developing new aircraft went largely to interceptors and bombers as the jet engine rendered their wartime equivalents obsolete. However, the continued development of the Douglas line of four-engine transports led to the C-124, the first aircraft designed for large loads, and to the first purpose-designed military transport, the Fairchild C-82 which was developed into the more capable C-119. The newly-formed USAF was thus starting to build-up a specially-equipped transport capability. This was to prove crucial as the end of the war had given only a temporary respite in the need for such a capability. The relationship between the West and its former ally, the Soviet Union, rapidly deteriorated, progressing towards a long-term military stand-off.

As the 1950s opened with an uneasy peace, Fairchild (with the C-119) and Douglas (with the C-124) dominated the future order books. The advent of the Korean War, and the subsequent detonation of the first Soviet hydrogen bomb caused vast sums of money to be injected into the US Defence budget. One effect was the XC-Medium airlifter competition, which was won by Lockheed with the C-130, whose importance was not fully appreciated at the time (with an expected production run of only 300 aircraft, the same as the C-123).

Douglas's dominance of the airlifter field was extended in the mid-1950s with the C-133 and XC-132 airlifters under development. However, the company's fortunes changed over the next several years with the C-133 proving a disappointment and the XC-132 cancelled outright. At the end of the decade Douglas had no airlifter in production for the military – a drought that would continue into the 1970s despite many imaginative designs. Only in 1972 would the company build another airlifter – the YC-15 AMST prototype (notwithstanding the limited sales of converted DC-9s as C-9s) – and that would be under the McDonnell Douglas nameplate.

Falling even harder was the Fairchild Aircraft & Engine Company. Although it was in a strong position at the beginning of the decade with C-119 production, the company chose not to enter the XC-Medium competition, apparently believing that the C-119H was slated for production instead of cancellation. The C-123 came after the C-119 but was not extended beyond the original production order. Fairchild then switched to licence production of the Fokker F-27 for the commercial market, which was curtailed by an economic recession. The company then retrenched with subcontracting efforts and acquiring other companies, becoming Fairchild Stratos, Fairchild Hiller and Fairchild Republic in turn. Fairchild never again produced an aircraft of its own design after the C-119 despite the many innovative and creative designs proposed in the 1950s.

Boeing fared better, entering the 1950s with the Model 367, which was a solid design, followed by the ground-breaking 367-80/707/717 family. It is rather remarkable that the vast majority of these aircraft were bought by one customer – the Strategic Air Command. Between the tanker-transport and bomber product lines Boeing enjoyed a hard-earned near monopoly in these fields. However, the company well recognised the dangers of relying on one customer and strove to diversify as the decade closed. For the first - but not the last - time, the development of a military transport would have a profound influence on the future of civil aviation.

Lockheed began the decade with the Second World War-vintage Constellation as its only production transport, but won the XC-Medium competition with what became the C-130. By the late 1950s the C-130 became the underpinning product for the Lockheed Georgia Company and the Marietta facility. With the GOR-182/C-141 competition at the end of the decade, and the award of the contract, Lockheed's star was on the rise.

As the major competitions described in this book were being played out, a number of other aeronautical technologies were evolving. In many ways the 1950s represented the golden age of aviation progress. As turbine technology matured and the understanding of high-speed aerodynamics spread, new designs – for all types of military and commercial aircraft – proliferated. Every aspect of performance progressed. By the end of the decade, passengers were routinely flying the Atlantic at speeds that would have been close to the world airspeed record at the decade's start.

However, in one area the promise would take decades more before the expected capability materialised. As take-off and landing speeds increased and aircraft weights grew, the requirement for longer and better-prepared runways became a major constraint. From a commercial aviation viewpoint, this demanded ever-larger airports, far out from city centres. From a military standpoint, it limited the ability to deliver men and materials to the front line.

Surely, with the advance in power-to-weight ratio of the new engines, the time would soon come when aircraft would not need to accelerate for anything up to a mile before leaving the ground? In every 1950s article predicting the future of aviation, the concept of vertical take-off figured large. In practice, it proved far harder to achieve than anyone imagined, but the challenge resulted in no end of imaginative designs, as will be seen in *American Secret Projects 3*.

The 1950s concluded with the United States still needing to vastly improve its military transport capability. Despite all the airlifter designs developed and proposed, only three basic types had entered service, and all of them (C-123, C-130 and C-133) were propeller-driven. Amazingly, a total of only three individual dedicated-transport jets were in service, all three being VC-135s – airliners converted to carry the President. The other operational jet aircraft, the KC-135, was generally restricted to SAC use and unsuited to assault cargo operations.

However, the true airlifter had been born and the following decade would see its capability finally realised. It would herald the arrival of giant airlifters over ten times the weight of the largest transports used in World War Two. The story of these projects, the fierce competition behind them and the further highly-innovative proposals to which they were to lead, are described in *American Secret Projects 3 - Airlifters 1962 to the Present Day*.

BELOW The Douglas Model D-902 was one of the first 'clean sheet' designs that led to the C-5 Galaxy – described in American Secret Projects 3. *Boeing*

Glossary

Abbreviations

ACFC	Air Corps Ferrying Command
AEDC	Arnold Engineering and Development Center
AEW	Airborne Early Warning
AEW&C	Airborne Early Warning and Control
AFB	Air Force Base
AFRL	Air Force Research Laboratory
AMC	Air Materiel Command
APU	Auxiliary Power Unit
ARDC	Air Research and Development Command
ASD	Aeronautical Systems Division
ASW	Anti-Submarine Warfare
ATC	Air Transport Command
bhp	brake horsepower
BLC	Boundary Later Control
BuAer	Bureau of Aeronautics
CIC	Combat Information Center (or Communication & Information Center)
CL	California Lockheed (Lockheed California Company design prefix)
CNO	Chief of Naval Operations
CRAF	Civil Reserve Air Fleet
CTA	Cold Thrust Augmentation
CTC	Contractor's Technical Compliance [Inspection]
CTOL	Conventional Take-Off and Landing
CX-HLS	Cargo Experimental – Heavy Logistics System
DARPA	Defense Advanced Projects Research Agency
DDR&E	Director of Defense Research and Engineering
DEI	Development Engineering Inspection
DEW	Distant Early Warning
DoD	Department of Defense
DS	Design Specification (Douglas Aircraft Company usage)
DTS	Detailed Type Specification (Douglas Aircraft Company usage)
EBF	Externally blown flap
ECP	Engineering Change Proposal
eshp	equivalent shaft horsepower
EW	Electronic Warfare
FAA	Federal Aviation Administration
FOD	Foreign Object Damage
fpm	feet per minute
fps	feet per second
FY	Fiscal year
GE	General Electric
GL	Georgia Lockheed (Lockheed Georgia Company design prefix)
GOR	General Operational Requirement
GS	General Specification (Douglas Aircraft Company usage)
GTOW	Gross take-off weight
ICBM	Intercontinental Ballistic Missile
IOC	Initial Operating Capability
IR	Infrared
IRBM	Intermediate Range Ballistic Missile
JATO	Jet Assisted Take-off
kN	kiloNewton
kW	kilowatt
LG	Lockheed Georgia (Lockheed Georgia Company design prefix)
MATS	Military Air Transport Service
MI	Mock-up Inspection
mph	miles per hour
MSN	Manufacturers Serial Number
N	Newton
NAA	North American Aviation
NACA	National Advisory Committee for Aeronautics
NARA II	US National Archives and Records Administration site at College Park, Maryland
NAS	Naval Air Station
NASA	National Aeronautics and Space Administration
NASM	[US] National Air and Space Museum
NATO	North Atlantic Treaty Organisation
NATS	Naval Air Transport Service
nmi	nautical mile
NMUSAF	National Museum of the United States Air Force
ONR	Office of Naval Research
OWE	Operating Weight Empty
OSD	Office of the Secretary of Defense
P&W	Pratt & Whitney
PDP	Project Definition Phase
psi	pounds per square inch
QEC	Quick Engine Change
RFI	Request For Information

RFP	Request for Proposal
RFQ	Request For Quote
rpm	revolutions per minute
SAC	Strategic Air Command
SL	Sea Level
SOR	Specific Operational Requirement
STOL	Short Take-Off and Landing
TAC	Tactical Air Command
TDN	Temporary Design Number (Lockheed)
TOW	Take-off weight
TS	Type Specification (Navy usage)
UHF	Ultra High Frequency
USA	United States Army
USAAC	United States Army Air Corps
USAAF	United States Army Air Force
USAF	United States Air Force
USCG	United States Coast Guard
USMC	United States Marine Corps
USN	United States Navy
USPTO	United States Patent and Trademark Office
VHF	Very High Frequency
VLF	Very Low Frequency
VTOL	Vertical Take-Off and Landing
V/STOL	Vertical/Short Take-Off and Landing
WADC	Wright Air Development Center (USAF)
X	Experimental

Terms

Ailerons	Hinged surfaces on the outer trailing sections of the wing, used to control the aircraft in roll.
Airfoil or aerofoil	The cross-sectional shape of a wing or other flying surface.
Aspect ratio	The ratio between the span of the wings and their average chord. A high aspect ratio aircraft will have long slender wings; a low aspect ratio will have shorter stubbier ones.
Boundary Layer	The thin layer of air next to the surface of the aircraft.
Boundary Layer Control	A system of forcing high-pressure air over the wing to keep the airflow following the contour of the airfoil, rather than breaking away to cause drag.
Canard	An aircraft configuration in which the horizontal stabiliser is placed ahead of the wings rather than in the normal aft position.

Catapult	A launching mechanism employed on aircraft carriers, whereby the aircraft's take-off acceleration is greatly boosted by means a high-pressure steam-driven piston or electromagnetic shuttle, located immediately beneath the forward deck.
Chord	The distance between the leading and training edges of the wing.
Elevator	A hinged surface on the rear of the horizontal stabiliser (tailplane), used to control the pitch of the aircraft.
Empennage	The aft end of the aircraft, consisting of the vertical stabiliser (fin), horizontal stabiliser (tailplane) and their supporting structure.
Fairing	An aerodynamically shaped non-load-bearing addition to the aircraft's structure, covering protuberances or linking parts of the airframe to maintain the intended lines of airflow and reduce drag.
Flap	A hinged surface on the rear edge of the wing, lowered to increase lift at slow speeds, normally used during take-off and landing.
Fowler Flap	An advanced flap arrangement whereby the flap extends (sliding out from within the wing structure) as well as hinging downwards.
Fin	Vertical stabiliser.
Fuselage	The body of the aircraft, excluding wings and tail surfaces.
Gross weight	The designed maximum weight of the aircraft including fuel, crew and cargo.
Horizontal stabiliser	The horizontal surfaces at the rear of the aircraft designed to provide stability in pitch, to which the elevators are normally attached.
Nacelle	A non-load-bearing part of the aircraft structure designed to accommodate the engines and their support equipment in a streamlined housing.
Payload	The weight of useful load – cargo or passengers – that can be carried; it excludes crew and fuel.
Pitch	Rotation of the aircraft about a horizontal axis between the wingtips (i.e. with the nose either rising or falling). It is normally controlled by deflection of the elevator.
Pylon	A streamlined part of the structure carrying or supporting an engine nacelle.

Radial engine	A piston engine in which the cylinders are arranged around the crankshaft, like the spokes of a wheel.
Roll	Rotation of the aircraft about a horizontal axis between its nose and the tail. It is normally controlled by differential movement of the ailerons.
Rudder	A hinged surface at the rear of the vertical stabiliser, used to control yaw.
Turbofan	A jet (gas turbine) engine in which all of the air goes through a fan at the front of the engine but part of the flow then bypasses the compressor, fuel injection/ignition and turbine. Thrust is a combination of both the exhaust from the latter and the fan.
Turbojet	A jet (gas turbine) engine in which all of the air passes the compressor, fuel injection/ignition system and turbine, with the thrust being created by the exhaust gases.
Turboprop	A gas turbine engine in which the turbine is linked by a driveshaft to a propeller, with only a small amount of residual thrust being provided by the exhaust gases.
Undercarriage	Landing gear.
Wind over deck	The combination of wind speed and ship speed when an aircraft carrier is heading into wind.
Vertical stabiliser	The vertical surface at the rear of the aircraft designed to provide lateral (weathercock) stability, of which the rudder normally forms part.
Yaw	Lateral rotation of the aircraft about a vertical axis through its centre of gravity (i.e. with the nose swinging left or right), normally controlled by the rudder.

Units

The units used throughout this book are given in the form in which they originally appeared in the source material. The metric equivalent is also given in each case.

1 inch (in)	= 2.54cm
1 foot (ft)	= 0.305cm
1 square foot (sq ft)	= 0.093m²
1 cubic foot (cu ft)	= 0.0284m³
1 mile	= 1.609km
1 nautical mile (nmi)	= 1.851km
1 mile per hour (mph)	= 1.609km/h
1 knot (kt)	= 1.851km/h
1 pound (weight: lb)	= 0.454kg
1 pound per square foot (lb/sq ft)	= 4.84kg/m²
1 pound thrust	= 4.45N
1 horsepower (hp)	=0.746kW

Military Engine Designations

Engine designations used by the US military have been presented in this book in the form prescribed by Air Force/Navy Aeronautical (ANA) Bulletin 306 dating from 1947 (ANA-306) and later by MIL-STD-879; and currently defined by the current MIL-HDBK-1812 standard. Piston engine designations were initially governed by ANA-395.

Under these regulations, piston engine designations are hyphenated:

R-2800

Jet, turboprop and turbofan designations are not hyphenated:

J57

T56

TF33

Throughout the time period covered, this presentation appears to have been almost universally more respected in the breach than in the observance; perhaps in confusion with aircraft designations which are hyphenated:

C-141

Some designations such as 'TF-52' or 'TF-75', while appearing to be military designations, were actually industry placeholder designations to be used until a military designation could be allocated (which were not, in these two cases).

A more common 'temporary usage' was in the case where a military designation was established, but a version number had not been yet assigned. In this case, the hybrid form 'military designation'-'manufacturer designation' was used such as:

T61-550B3 (later YT61-A-1) or

XJ53-X10 (later XJ-53-GE-1)

Reference sources and Bibliography

Archives

Air Force Materiel Command History Office, Wright Patterson AFB, Ohio

Air Force Historical Research Agency, Maxwell AFB, AL

American Aviation Historical Society (AAHS), Huntington Beach, CA

Avro Heritage Centre, Manchester, UK

Boeing Company Archives (Boeing content), Bellevue, WA

Boeing Company Archives (Douglas content), Huntington Beach, CA

Glenn L. Martin Maryland Aviation Museum, Middle River, MD

Greater St Louis Air and Space Museum, St Louis MO

Grumman History Center, Bethpage, NY

Jane and Winfield Arata papers (now accessioned into The Huntington Library, San Marino, CA), courtesy of Martha and Allen Arata

Northrop Grumman Aerospace Systems Sector Archives, Redondo Beach, CA

National Air and Space Museum (NASM), Washington DC

National Archives and Records Administration, College Park, MD (NARA II)

San Diego Air and Space Museum, San Diego, CA

Wright State University Libraries, Special Collections and Archives, Dayton, OH

Bibliography

Abel, Alan *Fairchild's Golden Age* (Wind Canyon Books)

Adcock, Al *C-123 Provider in Action (Aircraft Number 124)* (Squadron/Signal Publications)

Andrade, John M. *US Military Aircraft Designations and Serials – 1909 to 1979* (Midland Counties Publications)

Beck, Simon D. *Fairchild C-82 Packet – The Military and Civil History* (McFarland)

Berlin, Earl *Douglas C-124 (Air Force Legends Number 206)* (Ginter Publishing, 2000)

Bowers, Peter M. *Boeing Aircraft since 1916: Volume 1* (Putnam)

Bradley, Robert E. *Convair Advanced Designs, Secret Projects from San Diego 1923-1962* (Specialty Press)

Breihan, John R., Piet, Stan and Mason, Roger S. *Martin Aircraft 1909-1960* (Narkiewicz//Thompson)

Brown, David A. *The Bell Helicopter Textron Story* (Aerofax)

Buttler, Tony *American Secret Projects – Bombers, Attack and Anti-Submarine Aircraft 1945 to 1974* (Midland)

Caiden, Martin *The Long Arm of America* (E. P. Dutton & Co)

Cenker Jr, August *Aerospace Technologies of Bell Aircraft Company: A Pictorial History 1935-1985* (AuthorHouse)

Chambers, Joseph R. and Chambers, Mark A. *Radical Wings & Wind Tunnels – Advanced Concepts Tested at NASA Langley* (Specialty Press)

Chong, Tony *Flying Wings & Radical Things: Northrop's Secret Aerospace Projects & Concepts 1939-1994* (Specialty Press)

Converse III, Elliott V. *Rearming for the Cold War 1945-1960 (History of Acquisition in the Department of Defense, Vol I)* (Office of the Secretary of Defense, Historical Office)

Cook, William H. *The Road to the 707: The Inside Story of Designing the 707* (TYC Publishing)

Dabney, Joseph E. *Herk, Hero of the Skies (Revised Edition)* (Larlen)

Francillon, René J' *Boeing 707 Pioneer Jetliner* (MBI Publishing)

Grumman Aircraft since 1929 (Putnam)

McDonnell Douglas Aircraft since 1920: Volume 1 (Putnam)

McDonnell Douglas Aircraft since 1920: Volume 2 (Putnam)

Lockheed Aircraft since 1913 (Putnam)

Futrell, Robert Frank *Ideas, Concept, Doctrine Volume I – Basic Thinking in the United States Air Force 1907-1960* (Air University Press)

Volume II – Basic Thinking in the United States Air Force 1907-1960 (Air University Press)

Galvin, John R. *Air Assault: the Development of Airmobile Warfare* (Hawthorn Books)

Gann, Harry *Douglas DC-6 and DC-7 (Airliner Tech Series Vol 4)* (Specialty Press)

Gavin, Major General James M. *Airborne Warfare* (Infantry Journal Press; reprint; print on demand)

General Electric Company *Eight Decades of Progress – A Heritage of Aircraft Turbine Technology* (GE Aircraft Engines)

Gibson, Chris *On Atlas' Shoulders – RAF Transport Projects since 1945* (Hikoki Publications)

Gunston, Bill *World Encyclopedia of Aero Engines* (Patrick Stephens Limited)

The Development of Jet Turbine Aero Engines, 4th edition (Haynes North America)

Habermehl, C. Mike and Hopkins III, Robert S. *The B-47 Stratojet – Strategic Air Command's Transitional Bomber* (Crécy)

Harding, Stephen *US Army Aircraft since 1947* (Specialty Press)

Holder, Bill and Vadnais, Scott *The 'C' Planes* (Schiffer)

Holley Jr, Irving Benton *Buying Aircraft: Materiel Procurement for the Army Air Forces* (Office of the Chief of Military History, Department of the Army)

Hopkins III, Robert S. *Boeing KC-135 Stratotanker – More than just a Tanker* (Midland Publishing)

Hurturk, Kivane *Individual Aircraft History of the 707* (BUCHair (USA), 1998)

Johnsen, Frederick A. *Lockheed C-141 Starlifter (Warbird Tech Series Vol 39)* (Specialty Press)

Johnson, E. R. *American Military Transport Aircraft Since 1925* (McFarland & Company)

Keeshen, Jim *Secret US Proposals of the Cold War – Tactical Concepts in Military Aircraft* (Crécy)

Leonard, John M. *The Allison Engine Catalog 1915-2007* (Rolls-Royce Heritage Trust – Allison Branch)

Lloyd, Alwyn T. *Fairchild C-82 Packet and C-119 Flying Boxcar* (Midland Publishing)

Miller, Jay *Lockheed Martin's Skunkworks, The Official History (updated edition)* (Midland Publishing)

Mitchell, Kent A. *Fairchild Aircraft 1926-1987* (Narkiewicz//Thompson)

Mrazek, James E. *Airborne Combat, The Glider War/Fighting Gliders of WWII* (Stackpole Books)

Newhouse, John *The Sporty Game – The High-Risk Competitive Business of Making and Selling Commercial Airliners* (Alfred A. Knoff)

Norton, Bill *American Aircraft Development of WWII, Special Types 1939-1945* (Crécy Publishing)

American Military Gliders of World War II (Schiffer)

Paszek, Lawrence J. *A Guide to Documentary Sources* (Office of Air Force History)

Proctor, Jon *Convair 880 & 990 (Great Airliners Series, Vol 1)* (World Transport Press Inc)

Pyeatt, Don and Jenkins, Dennis R. *Cold War Peacemaker – The Story of Cowtown and the Convair B-36* (Specialty Press)

St Peter, James *The History of Gas Turbine Engine Development in the United States: A Tradition of Excellence* (The International Gas Turbine Institute of the American Society of Mechanical Engineers)

Staszak, Richard and Staehr, Nancy *Military Transports In Detail, Volume 1* (Air Transport Publications)

Sterling, Robert *Boeing: Legend & Legacy* (St Martins)

Taylor, Cal *Remembering an Unsung Giant – The C-133 Cargomaster and Its People* (Firstfleet)

Thum, Marcell and Thum, Gladys *Airlift: The Story of the Military Airlift Command* (Dodd, Mead & Company)

Veronico, Nicolas A. *Boeing Stratocruiser (Airliner Tech Series Vol 9)* (Specialty Press)

Waddington, Terry *Douglas DC-8 (Great Airliners Series, Vol 2)* (World Transport Press Inc)

White, Graham *R-4360 – Pratt & Whitney's Major Miracle* (Specialty Press)

Williams, Nicholas M. *Aircraft of the United States Military Air Transport Service* (Midland)

Yenne, Bill *The 377 Stratocruiser & KC-97 Stratofreighter* (Crécy)

Zichek, Jared A. *The B-52 Competition of 1946 … and Dark Horses from Douglas 1947-1950 (American Aerospace Archive 3)* (MagCloud [www.jared.zichekmagcloud.com; print on demand])

Motherships, Parasites & More: Selected USAF Strategic Bomber, XC-Heavy Transport and FICON Studies, 1945-1954 (American Aerospace Archive 5) (MagCloud [www.jaredzichek.magcloud.com; print on demand])

- *The Jet Engine* (Rolls-Royce, Wiley)

Reports and papers (in chronological order)

Preliminary Performance of the Douglas Combat Transport Airplane Model 415, Douglas Aircraft Company, Report SM-3485, 20 January 1942

Detail Specification Fairchild Model M-78, Fairchild Aircraft, Report 78-001, 9 March 1942

Flight Investigation of the Effect of the Mockup T-9 Tanks and Tank Fairing on Performances – Model C-54 Ship No AAF 41-20139, Douglas Aircraft Company, Report SM-3936, 15 December 1942

Calculated Performance Kaiser Flying Wing, Pillsbury, E. R., Kaiser, 16 October 1943

C-47 Glider Modification, Douglas Aircraft Company, Report SM-5150, 11 December 1943

Estimated Weight and Balance – Model C-74 Spec DS-415A Rev 1 April 1945, Douglas Aircraft Company, Report SM-3545, 1 April 1945

Preliminary Aerodynamic Report on Glenn L. Martin Model 229 Military Transport Landplane, Hook, G. R., The Glenn L. Martin Company, Engineering Report 2177, 10 September 1945

Model Specification – Glider and Troop Transport, Powered – Chase Model MS-5, Chase Airplane Company Inc, Report 200, 12 November 1945

Model Specification for Four Engine Cargo Transport, Four Pratt & Whitney Engines (Side-by-side Arrangement) Model M99-06, Young, F. C., Fairchild Aircraft, R99-003, 11 March 1946

Proposed Model Specification for Radical Low Wing Type Cargo Aircraft – Four Curtiss Turbine Engines (Side-by-side Arrangement) Model M99-07, Young, F. C., Fairchild Aircraft, R99-0004, 12 March 1946

Preliminary Investigation Airborne Operations Model M99-05 and M99-06, Davis, R. W., Fairchild Aircraft, R99-013, 14 March 1946

Development of Transport Airplanes and Air Transport Equipment, Brown, Dr Genevieve, Historical Division, Intelligence T2, Air Technical Service Command, USAAF, Historical Study 277, 1 April 1946

Development of Transport Airplanes and Air Transport Equipment, Air Technical Service Command, 1 April 1946

Aerodynamics Report on the Glider, Cargo Type Model 1028, Douglas Aircraft Company, Report LB-10208, 8 April 1946

Brochure of New and Novel Features 8,000 Pound Useful Load Cargo Glider, Bell Aircraft Corporation, D44-945-003, 10 April 1946

Glide – Assault, Light Hughes Model No 31, Brooks, J. G., Hughes Aircraft Company, Report No 31-1, 18 April 1946

Aerodynamics Report on Heavy Assault Glider Model 1029, Douglas Aircraft Company, Report LB-10213, 6 May 1946

Glider – Assault, Heavy Hughes Model No 32, Dieter, W. L., Hughes Aircraft Company, Report No 32-1, 15 May 1946

Glider – Assault – Heavy 16,000, Report Lbs (Useful load) Proposal Specifications, Bell Aircraft Corporation, D45-947-001, 20 May 1946

Model Specification – Glider, Cargo and Troop Transport, Towed, Chase Model MS-3, Chase Aircraft Company Inc, Report 150, 24 May 1946

MD54 – New Special Aircraft – Transport, Gliders and Liaison Airplanes, Guest Lecture of the New Development Division Command and Staff Course, AAF School, Maxwell Field, Alabama, 25 June 1946

General Data Douglas Transport DS-1072, Douglas Aircraft Company, Report LB-10249, 6 January 1947

Aerodynamic Report on Light Assault Transport Airplane Models 1044-E and 1072, Douglas Aircraft Company, Report LB-10248, 11 February 1947

Model Specification, Glider, Cargo and Troop Transport, Towed – Army Air Forces Model XCG-20, Chase Model MS-3A, Chase Aircraft Company Inc, Report 3001, 1 March 1947

Summary of Fairchild C-119A Aircraft, Fairchild Aircraft, 1 August 1947

Preliminary Stress Analysis of 50,000 Pound Payload Cargo Airplane – Model 1128 & 1129, Report LB-10307, 2 December 1947

Detail Specification for Douglas Heavy Cargo Transport Model C-124A, Douglas Aircraft Company, DS-1129A, 20 January 1948

Investigation of a 1/7-Scale Powered Model Twin Boom Airplane and a Comparison of Its Stability, Control, and Performance with those of a Similar All-Wing Airplane, Brewer, Gerald W., and Mary, Ralph W. Jr, Langley Aeronautical Laboratory, NACA, TN-1649, 1 October 1948

Models C-124A and C-74 Range and Performance, Douglas Aircraft Company, Report LB-10430, 14 June 1949

Model Specification, Model M-107B, Smith, C. E., and Burch, R. L., Fairchild Aircraft, R107-0001, 29 July 1949

Model C-124B Performance Summary (As Defined by DS-1197 Dated June 15, 1949), Douglas Aircraft Company, Report LB-10444, 10 August 1949

Model C-124A Performance Summary (As Defined by DS-1129A Dated July 20, 1949), Douglas Aircraft Company, Report LB-10446, 10 August 1949

Final Report of Development, Procurement, Inspection, Testing, & Acceptance of Consolidated XC-99 Cargo & Troop Transport Airplane, Carlson, R. M., USAF Air Materiel Command, AFHRA Reel 30703, TR 5950, 1 September 1949

Model Specification, Model M-142, Ireland, R. H., Fairchild Aircraft, R142-000, 1 November 1949

History of the USAF Five Year Aircraft Procurement Program (1 January 1948-1 July 1949), Self, Mary R., Air Materiel Command, US Air Force, Historical Study 247, 1 December 1949

All-Wing Cargo Pack, Northrop Aircraft Inc, NB-21, January 1950

Model C-124 In-Flight Refueler Airplane Equipped With Jet Engine Pod, Douglas Aircraft Company, Report LB-16208, 11 April 1950

Proposal for Floating Wing Tip Development, Douglas Aircraft Company, Report SM-13756, 24 April 1950

Flying Wing Progress, Northrop Aircraft Inc, NB-24, May 1950

Model 1183E Turbo-prop In-flight Refueler, Douglas Aircraft Company, Report LB-16219, 29 May 1950

Model 1182F Turbo-prop In-flight Refueler, Douglas Aircraft Company, Report LB-16222, 29 May 1950

Proposed Carrier Airplane Model 1240, Douglas Aircraft Company, Report SM-13856, 11 November 1950

Lockheed Constitution Development Story, Hawkins, W. M. Jr and Thoren, R. L., Lockheed, December 1950

Preliminary Specification for XC-Medium Cargo Airplane, Ruszaj, H. F., Boeing Airplane Company, D-11707, 30 March 1951

Medium Cargo Model-495, Boeing Airplane Company, D-11765, 1 April 1951

Model 1134C R6D-1 Turboprop Program Planning Report, Douglas Aircraft Company, Report SM-14006, 4 April 1951

General Discussion Model 1252 Medium Cargo Transport, Douglas Aircraft Company, Report SM-14000, 12 April 1951

Model 1309 Medium Cargo Transport Aerodynamics Report – Performance, Douglas Aircraft Company, Report LB-16377, 12 April 1951

Model 1316 Medium Cargo Transport Aerodynamics Report, Douglas Aircraft Company, Report LB-16379, 12 April 1951

Douglas Model YKC-124B Turbo Prop In-Flight Refueler, Douglas Aircraft Company, Report LB-16406, 22 May 1951

Preliminary Study Wright 'Sapphire' Engine Performance Model 1240, Douglas Aircraft Company, Report SM-14043, 29 May 1951

Proposal Turbo-Jet Powered Transport Model 1274A-J57, Douglas Aircraft Company, Report SM-14169, 1 October 1951

Proposed Turbo-jet Transport for Domestic Operations Model 1274C, Douglas Aircraft Company, Report SM-14179, 1 October 1951

Proposal Turbine-Propeller Powered Transport Model 1274A, Douglas Aircraft Company, Report SM-14160, 1 October 1951

Study In-Flight Refueler Model 1274-B, Douglas Aircraft Company, Report SM-14161, 1 October 1951

Proposed Turbo-jet Transport for Overwater Operations Model 1274D, Douglas Aircraft Company, Report SM-14176, 5 October 1951

Proposed Turbo-Prop Transport for Overwater Operations Model 1274E, Douglas Aircraft Company, Report SM-14178, 12 October 1951

Main Cabin Pressurization Study of the C-124 Type Aircraft, Douglas Aircraft Company, Report LB-16465, 30 November 1951

Adaptability of the C-124 Airplane to High Output Propeller Turbine Engines, Douglas Aircraft Company, Report LB-16466, 30 November 1951

Model 1324 Technical Data, Douglas Aircraft Company, Report LB-16473, 18 January 1952

Case History of the C-123 Airplane (26 April 1945-7 September 1951), Bagwell, Margaret C., Historical Office, Air Materiel Command, AFHRA Reel K2037, 1 March 1952

Performance Data for the Douglas Heavy Cargo Transport Airplane Model 1324P, Douglas Aircraft Company, Report LB-16477, 10 April 1952

In-flight Refueler-Cargo Transport Model 1274A, Douglas Aircraft Company, Report SM-14379, 25 April 1952

MX-1707 Study Data, Douglas Aircraft Company, Report SM-14375, 1 May 1952

Model 1324P Equipped with In-flight Refueling Equipment, Douglas Aircraft Company, Report LB-16503, 2 May 1952

Review of C-124X Configuration, Douglas Aircraft Company, Report LB-16594, 8 November 1952

Model 1183B Equipped for Inflight Refueling, Douglas Aircraft Company, Report LB-16202, 20 March 1953

Specification for Douglas Heavy Cargo Transport Model C-124X, Douglas Aircraft Company, DS-1333, AFHRA Reel 34184, 20 March 1953

Douglas Model 1333 Heavy Cargo Transport, Douglas Aircraft Company, Report LB-16772, 6 April 1953

Study – C-119 Advance Base Version, Fairchild Aircraft, R-194-001, 8 May 1953

Preliminary Mock-Up Report Model XC-132 Logistics Transport and In-Flight Refueler, Douglas Aircraft Company, Report SM-14797, 19 May 1953

Model 1333 Airplane Study – Logistics (Cargo) Configuration, Douglas Aircraft Company, Report LB-16871, 11 June 1953

Case History of the C-119 Airplane – September 1946 – June 1953, Frey, Royal D., Historical Branch, Air Force Materiel Command, AFHRA Reel 23715, 1 September 1953

Preliminary Model Specification TA-13, de Bettencourt, F. G., Thieblot Aircraft Company Inc, TP 13-R-001, 18 September 1953

Combined Radius Performance of the Model 1840 In-Flight Refueler and Heavy Jet Bomber, Douglas Aircraft Company, Report SM-14998, 13 November 1953

Model 1840 In-Flight Refueler, Douglas Aircraft Company, Report SM-14997, 13 November 1953

Model YC-133 Personnel Transport, Douglas Aircraft Company, Report LB-21703, 30 November 1953

Model 1840 Series In-Flight Refueler and Military Transport, Douglas Aircraft Company, Report SM-15160, 11 December 1953

Model 1840 In-Flight Refueler and Military Transport Configurations, Douglas Aircraft Company, Report SM-15160, 11 December 1953

Model XC-132 Design and Mock-Up Data, Douglas Aircraft Company, Report SM-18220, 12 February 1954

Performance Data for the DS-1182E dated May 15, 1954 YC-124B Airplane, Douglas Aircraft Company, Report LB-16509, 15 May 1954

C-123 T-56 Powerplant, Fairchild Aircraft, R206-001, 1 August 1954

Estimated Stability and Control Model 1856 Jet Tanker, Douglas Aircraft Company, Report SM-18050, 23 August 1954

Douglas Design and Service Background Model 1856 Series Jet Tanker, Douglas Aircraft Company, Report SM-18515, 23 August 1954

Model 1856M Military Jet Transport, Douglas Aircraft Company, Report SM-18637, 23 September 1954

Model C-133A Performance Summary, Douglas Aircraft Company, Report LB-21732C, 1 October 1954

Fairchild Aircraft M-214 Proposed Jet Assist Installation for C-123 Airplane, Fairchild Aircraft, R214-001, 1 March 1955

Model 1371 Logistics Heavy Cargo Transport, Douglas Aircraft Company, Report LB-22070, 15 July 1955

Model 1371A Tactical Heavy Transport, Douglas Aircraft Company, Report LB-22071, 15 July 1955

C-133A CTC Inspection, Douglas Aircraft Company, Report LB-22236, 29 November 1955

Model XC-132 Project Report, Douglas Aircraft Company, Report SM-19481, 1 December 1955

Proposed Configuration for Tactical Version of the Model C-133A, Douglas Aircraft Company, Report LB-22324, 9 December 1955

Model 1371A Proposed Configuration for Tactical Heavy Transport Airplane, Douglas Aircraft Company, Report LB-22325, 9 December 1955

Douglas Transports for Strategic Air Mobility, Douglas Aircraft Company, Report LB-22279, 10 January 1956

Some Considerations of the STOL Airplanes, Tydon, Walter, Fairchild Aircraft Division, 23 January 1956

Fairchild M-219 Military Transport, Fairchild Aircraft Division, OER-19, 1 February 1956

The Fairchild M-216 Flying Lighter for Adequate Carrier-On-Board Delivery, Fairchild Aircraft Division, MSR-1, 1 March 1956

Project History (C-133 Symposium), Douglas Aircraft Company, Report LB-25141, 25 September 1956

Douglas Model 1906 Series Aircraft, Douglas Aircraft Company, Report SM-22647, 8 November 1956

Model C-133A Feasibility as a Marine Assault Transport Aircraft, Douglas Aircraft Company, Report LB-25231, 16 November 1956

Carrier On Board Utility Assault Aircraft Operations Analysis, Douglas Aircraft Company, Report SM-22652, 19 November 1956

Carrier-On-Board Utility Assault Aircraft Technical Data and Summary Report, Douglas Aircraft Company, Report SM-22646, 19 November 1956

The Fairchild 'Provider' in Fleet Supply, Fairchild Aircraft Division, OER-1102, 1 December 1956

Model C-133A Summary Report of Flow Studies over the Tail Cone of a 1.5 Percent Scale Wind Tunnel Model (Wind Tunnel Model No LB-14D), Douglas Aircraft Company, Report LB-25234, 7 December 1956

Model 1940 Short and Medium Range Transport Airplane, Douglas Aircraft Company, Report SM-22672, 1 February 1957

Model 1940-A Short and Medium Range Utility Transport, Douglas Aircraft Company, Report SM-22673, 1 February 1957

The Model 1906 for the F.E.A.F. Combat Cargo Command 315th Air Division, Douglas Aircraft Company, Report SM-22722, 12 February 1957

C-123B Variant, Arata, Winfield H. Jr, Fairchild Aircraft Division, OER-161, 6 March 1957

Air Force Developmental Aircraft, Air Research and Development Command, AFHRA Reel K2914, 1 April 1957

C-123 with Four 'T-55' Turboprop Engines, Fairchild Aircraft Division, R253-008, 18 April 1957

M-253 Turboboxcar, Copeland, J., Fairchild Aircraft Division, R253-001, 7 June 1957

Proposal – Model 1906C-1 AEW Aircraft, Douglas Aircraft Company, Report SM-22760, 26 July 1957

Model 1382 Airborne Early Warning Equipment Test Bed Proposal, Douglas Aircraft Company, Report LB-25559, 30 August 1957

Model 2007 Carrier On-Board Delivery Aircraft, Douglas Aircraft Company, Report SM-22927, 20 September 1957

Study, Model 1906A ASW Application, Douglas Aircraft Company, Report SM-22761, 15 November 1957

Boeing 815 STOL Multi-Purpose Transport, Boeing Airplane Company, 1958

Douglas Model 1906 Series Aircraft, Model 1906B Utility Transport, Douglas Aircraft Company, Report SM-23106, 15 March 1958

Cargo Aircraft Standard Aircraft Characteristics (SAC) Charts 1949-58, USAF, AFHRA Reel KK2999, 11 May 1958

Turboprop Conversions DC-6B, DC-7, DC-7B, and DC-7C Series Aircraft, Douglas Aircraft Company, Report SM-23040, 22 May 1958

Model 820 Long Range Military Air-Logistics Systems Progress Report from April 1 to July 1 1958, Boeing Aircraft Company, D2-2895, 1 July 1958

Boeing Cargo Jets – 735 – Cargo Version of the 707, Boeing Aircraft Company Transport Division, D6-1863, July 1958

Model 2042 Army Assault Aircraft and Carrier On-Board Delivery, Douglas Aircraft Company, Report SM-23249, 14 August 1958

Development Program for a Long-Range Military Air-Logistics System, Boeing Aircraft Company, D2-3022, 22 August 1958

Estimated Weight Data Douglas Model 1920W-6 and 1920W-7 Series Military Jet Transport for the United States Air Force, Douglas Aircraft Company, Report SM-23296, 12 September 1958

Convair Military Jet Transport, Cargo Version Part 1, Convair Division, General Dynamics, ZP-58-010004, 12 September 1958

Presentation Results of Aircraft for the Supply, Assault and Support Mission, Douglas Aircraft Company, Report SM-23313, 1 October 1958

Model C-133B Modified as a Commercial Cargo Carrier Powered with Rolls-Royce Tyne 12 Engines, Douglas Aircraft Company, Report LB-30006, 2 January 1959

Conversion of the C-118A Aircraft to Turboprop Configuration, Douglas Aircraft Company, Report SM-23420, 22 January 1959

Model 1467 and 1471 Data on Advanced Cargo Transports, Douglas Aircraft Company, Report LB-30072, 25 February 1959

Model 1470 Preliminary Design of a Supersonic Cargo Transport, Douglas Aircraft Company, Report LB-30061, 11 March 1959

Jetmaster Transport Support System, Volume I, Model Specification DTS-1920, Douglas Aircraft Company, Report SM-23493, 10 April 1959

Convair Turbojet Transport System – Alternative B, Convair Division, General Dynamics Corporation, ZP-59-01003-1, 13 April 1959

Model C-133 with Swing Tail and Allison T61 Engines, Douglas Aircraft Company, Report ADR-29, 14 May 1959

Discussion of C-133 Improvement Program with Air Force, Douglas Aircraft Company, Report ADR-34, 30 July 1959

Air Cargo and Airplanes, Douglas Aircraft Company, Report SM-23588, 1 August 1959

Improved C-133 Type Aircraft Allison T61-500-B6 Engines New Production and Retrofit, Douglas Aircraft Company, ADR-36, 6 August 1959

Medium-Sized Logistics Transport Models 1486, 1487, 1490 and 1491, Douglas Aircraft Company, ADR-37, 11 September 1959

Boeing 731 Jet Freighter, Boeing Transport Division, Report D6-5044, 1 December 1959

Boeing Transport and Wichita Divisions Joint Presentation – VSTOL Summary, Boeing Airplane Company, D3-2768, 9 December 1959

M-270D Jet Wing Logistic Transport Engineering Summary Report, Fairchild Aircraft Division, R270-002, 29 January 1960

M-258 Military Transport Configuration, US Army Transportation Command, 1 July 1960

Preliminary Feasibility Study of the Transportation of the Saturn S-IV Stage by C-133 Airplane, Douglas Aircraft Company, Report SM-30380, 26 August 1960

Summary Briefing – Super Hercules GL207-45, Lockheed Aircraft Corporation, ETP-251, 26 January 1961

Vol I – Basic Proposal – Super Hercules GL207-45, Lockheed Aircraft Corporation, ETP-250, 26 January 1961

Vol II – Substantiating and Trade-off Data – Super Hercules GL207-45, Lockheed Aircraft Corporation, ETP-250, 26 January 1961

Cargo Transport Support System 476L – Basic Proposal, Boeing Transport Division, Report D6-7310, 27 January 1961

Cargo Transport Support System 476L – Detail Specification, Boeing Transport Division, Report D6-7312, 27 January 1961

Standard Aircraft Characteristics Model D-829 VTOL Transport, Douglas Aircraft Company, 31 March 1961

Studies of a C-123 Replacement Aircraft, Douglas Aircraft Company, Report LB-30579, 28 April 1961

Advanced STOL Assault & Logistics Transport Model 2217, Douglas Aircraft Company, Report LB-30684, 12 October 1961

STOL Turboprop Assault Transport Model 2252, Douglas Aircraft Company, Report LB-30959, 20 July 1962

Boeing Model Numbers (abridged), Boeing Airplane Company, D-337, Undated

Boeing Model Records Models 365-370, Boeing, D-4500 Book 8, Undated

Boeing Model Records Model 367-80, Boeing, D-4500 Book 8a, Undated

Boeing Model Records Models 485-700, Boeing, D-4500 Book 18, Undated

Lockheed C-141 Versatility, Lockheed Georgia Company, Undated

Journals (as referenced in the text)

Air & Space/Smithsonian Magazine
Aviation Week and Space Technology
Flight and *Flight International*
Journal of the American Aviation Historical Society
Naval Institute Proceedings

Websites (addresses current at time of writing)

Aerospace Projects Review: http://www.aerospaceprojectsreview.com/
Aerospace Projects Review Patreon: https://www.patreon.com/user?u=197906
Designation Systems: http://www.designation-systems.net
The Secret Projects Forum: https://www.secretprojects.co.uk

Index

General index

Aircraft and design proposals index

Amercan Secret Projects Volume 3
U S Airlifters since 1962

American Secret Projects 3 details the story of the US airlifter from the early 1960s to today's transport giants and tomorrow's stealth assault aircraft. This new book reveals numerous designs which never saw the light of day, examines the thinking behind them and gives insights into why they did, or did not, succeed. This untold story of aviation history also has a major bearing on the development of civil aviation.

Along with its companion volume, *American Secret Projects 2*, this book has been made possible by the unprecedented access the authors have been given to major aerospace company archives, here they have uncovered scores of design proposals which have never previously been revealed. As well as describing how airlifters were progressively developed to meet ever-more demanding military transport requirements, *American Secret Projects 3* looks at their other roles, from nuclear test-beds to Space-Shuttle carriers.

The book has over 500 illustrations, the majority of which have never previously been published, detailing some of the largest and most incredible aircraft ever conceived, making it an indispensable work for the historian and modeller alike.

George Cox and Craig Kaston
Hardback, 304 pages
ISBN 9781910809334
£27.50   US $44.95

Illustrated throughout with rare photographs, drawings, 3-view illustrations and colour profiles, and form an essential reference for any serious aviation and military enthusiast, modeller or historian.

Available in the UK from Crécy Publishing Ltd,
1a Ringway Trading Est, Shadowmoss Rd,
Manchester M22 5LH
Tel 0161 499 0024
www.crecy.co.uk

Distributed in the USA by Specialty Press,
838 Lake Street S.
Forest Lake, MN 55025
Tel (651) 277-1400 / (800), 895-4585
www.specialtypress.com

derived from the dual-spool YJ67 turbojet, a licensed version of the Bristol Olympus.

The 367-81-121 went to an intermediate fuselage length of 140ft 2in (42.72m). This variant was to be powered by the Wright YT49-W-1, a turboprop version of the Wright J65 (a licensed version of the Armstrong Siddeley Sapphire). Ultimately, the T47 never flew and the YT49 was test flown only on two XB-47D test beds (Model 450-162-28). The 1955 and 1956 flights totalled only 51 hours and occurred far too late for the tanker/transport programme. The YT49 engine was plagued by gearbox and propeller malfunctions, and development of the Wright turboprops went no further.

Boeing Models 367-83/84

The Model 367-81 series turboprop studies were supplanted in March 1953 by larger aircraft with new wing planforms and fuselages, designated Model 367-83 and Model 367-84. The -83 had a 3,000sq ft (278m²) wing spanning 199ft (60.66m), with a reduced sweep of 15°. Design gross weight was 450,000lb (204,117kg). The fuselage upper lobe was to be 160in (406.4cm) wide.

The 367-84 was even larger, with a scaled-up wing of 4,800sq ft (446m²) spanning 230ft (42.72m) and with a 15° sweep. Maximum gross weight was 547,000lb (248,115kg). The fuselage upper lobe was also increased, to 184in

(467.3cm). Although not stated, it appears that both versions were destined for the Wright T47 turboprop.

Boeing Model 709 'cargo-tanker transport'

The 367-83 and -84 lines of development were then spun off into the Model 709 family, comprising eight variants with different engines, wing sweeps and cargo-loading provisions. The four Wright T47-W-1-powered versions had a 15° swept wing (similar to the 367-83/84). Fuselage cargo loading was limited to dual side-loading doors. Variants were the 709-1, -2, -7 and -8 with differing fuselage lengths, gross weights and widths ranging from 160in (406.4cm) to 186in (472.4cm).

Boeing Model 367-81 turboprop tanker-transports				
	Model 367-81-104	Model 367-81-119	Model 367-81-119B	Model 367-81-121
Powerplant	4 x Wright T47-W-1 turboprops	4 x Wright T47-W-1 turboprops	4 x Wright T47-W-1 turboprops	4 x Wright T49-W-1 turboprops
Span	134ft 2in (40.89m)	133ft 9in (40.77m)	133ft 7in (40.72m)	134ft 2in (40.89m)
Length	126ft 8in (38.61m)	134ft 6in (41.00m)	161ft 2in (49.12m)	140ft 6in (42.82m)
Height	38ft 3in (11.66m)	38ft 3in (11.66m)	38ft 3in (11.66m)	38ft 3in (11.66m)
Wing area	2,400sq ft (223.0m²)	2,400sq ft (223.0m²)	2,400sq ft (223.0m²)	2,400sq ft (223.0m²)
Design gross weight	325,000lb (147,418kg)	340,000lb (154,000kg)	n/a	330,000lb (149,685kg)

OPPOSITE Boeing Model 367-81-119 general arrangement, showing a stretched fuselage married to the 2,400sq ft baseline wing, with Wright T49 turboprops positioned above the wing leading edge. Tip tanks carried an additional 3,500 gallons (13,249 litres) of fuel. A similar design was developed under the 707-7-27 number for the civil market. *Boeing*

BELOW This Boeing artwork depicts the Boeing Model 367-81-119. *Boeing*